KV-545-632

90 0898858 8

WITHDRAWN
FROM
UNIVERSITY OF PLYMOUTH
LIBRARY SERVICES

Regional and Multilateral Trade in Developing Countries

Regional and Multilateral Trade in Developing Countries

Editors
Shahid Ahmed
Shahid Ashraf

Routledge
Taylor & Francis Group
LONDON NEW YORK NEW DELHI

First published 2011 in India
by Routledge
912 Tolstoy House, 15–17 Tolstoy Marg, Connaught Place,
New Delhi 110 001

Simultaneously published in the UK
by Routledge
2 Park Square, Milton Park, Abingdon, OX14 4RN

Routledge is an imprint of the Taylor & Francis Group, an informa business

© 2011 Shahid Ahmed and Shahid Ashraf

Typeset by
Star Compugraphics Private Limited
D–156, Second Floor
Sector 7, Noida 201 301

UNIVERSITY OF PLYMOUTH

9008988588

Printed and bound in India by
Avantika Printers Private Limited
194/2, Ramesh Market, Garhi, East of Kailash,
New Delhi 110 065

All rights reserved. No part of this book may be reproduced or utilised in any
form or by any electronic, mechanical or other means, now known or hereafter
invented, including photocopying and recording, or in any information storage
and retrieval system without permission in writing from the publishers.

British Library Cataloguing-in-Publication Data
A catalogue record of this book is available from the British Library

ISBN: 978-0-415-67786-8

This book is printed on ECF environment-friendly paper manufactured from
unconventional and other raw materials sourced from sustainable and identified
sources.

Contents

Part 1: Macro and CGE Modelling of International Trade

Part 2: Regional Integration in South Asia

Part 3: Trade Integration in Africa and Arab States

Part 4: Sectoral Dimensions of International Trade

Part 5: Some Legal and Other Economic Issues of the WTO Process

List of Tables

List of Figures

List of Boxes

Acknowledgements

This book is a collection of revised version of the selected papers presented in a two-day International Conference on 'Dynamics of Regional Trade Agreements and WTO: Developing Countries' Perspectives' organised by the Department of Economics, Jamia Millia Islamia, Delhi in December 2009. Many people and organisations generously rendered their assistance and cooperation in making arrangements for the conference and also in processing the selected papers in the form of a book. We would like to place on record our gratitude to all these people and institutions. In particular, the following deserve special thanks:

Mr Najeeb Jung, Vice Chancellor, Jamia Millia Islamia, for his keen interest, encouragement and excellent leadership at various stages of the conference and publication of this book.

All our colleagues in the Department of Economics for their support and cooperation — Professor Khan Masood Ahmad, Professor Naushad Ali Azad and Dr Mirza Alim Baig, in particular, deserve special mention.

We wish to express our gratitude to all participants in this conference, particularly the contributors to the present volume, who put a lot of effort to revise their papers as per our requirements.

We also wish to express our sincere thanks to ICSSR, Delhi, for their financial support and EXIM bank, Mumbai, for their co-sponsorship of this conference.

And last but not the least, we also wish to thank the Editorial Team, Routledge, Delhi, for their hard work to bring out this book.

Shahid Ahmed
Shahid Ashraf

Introduction

The establishment of the World Trade Organisation (WTO) in 1995 has provided the institutional support to the Multilateral Trading System (MTS). Since 1995, international trade is expected to be governed by WTO rule-based regime. Doha Development Round (DDR) of WTO was initiated for removing distortions in international trade for the development oriented trade integration in the world. It is expected that the outcome of DDR of negotiations will lead to the reduction in inequities and eradication of poverty in developing countries. So far, WTO member countries could not find common ground due to strict positions of developed countries. Also, more informed and articulated positions (compared to earlier rounds) of developing countries on tariffs, subsidies and Non-Tariff Barriers (NTBs) are also leading to the tough negotiations.

In July 2008, the Doha round of talks collapsed because of a dispute between Washington and emerging economies spearheaded by India. While farm subsidy was cited as the major cause for this failure, there are many other issues that need to be addressed to conclude the Doha round in near future. The range of these issues include safeguards, non-Agricultural market access, trade related intellectual property rights, trade related investment measures, government procurement, and General Agreement on Trade in Services (GATS) that put developing economies like India at loggerheads with the developed world.

As a result, regionalism in the form of Regional Trade Agreements (RTAs) have gained prominence which is the manifestation of many factors such as repeated failures of multilateral negotiations, increased globalisation of markets and the fear of losing out to other inefficient producers. Since its inception, the rule book of WTO has allowed member countries to conclude customs unions and free-trade areas, as an exception to the fundamental principle of non-discrimination set in the Most-Favoured-Nation (MFN) clause of Article I. General Agreement on Tariffs and Trade (GATT) Article 24 allows regional trading arrangements to be set up as a special exception.

In such arrangements, duties and other trade barriers should be reduced substantially in all sectors of trade in the group. Non-member countries should not find trade with the group any more restrictive than before the group was set up. Regional integration should complement the Multilateral Trading System (MTS) and not threaten it. Article 5 of the GATS provides economic integration agreement in services. Preferential trade arrangements on goods between developing-country members are regulated by an 'Enabling Clause' of 1979. The main purpose of a RTA is to facilitate trade between the constituent countries and not to raise trade barriers to other WTO members (non-parties to the RTA).

The proliferations of RTAs or Free Trade Agreements (FTAs) have raised a number of critical issues and questions in global trade policy debate. The supporters of RTAs think it could pave the way for its members to participate more effectively in the multilateral process of economic change by providing them with opportunities to experiment with the economic change at a smaller scale and magnitude within the region. RTAs can also spur investment flows in terms of efficiency-seeking regional restructuring.

Despite recognising gains, the proliferation of RTAs has raised concerns over the prospects of MTS. Opponents view RTAs as inward-looking, discriminatory and protectionist trading entities competing for spheres of influence and becoming self-contained fortresses. It mainly pertains to the following two broad issues: (i) relative welfare effects of non-preferential across-the-board (MFN) liberalisation versus preferential liberalisation; and (ii) the long-term implications of RTAs for the MTS in general and multilateral trade negotiations in particular.

In economic literature, the proponents of regionalism consider RTAs as 'building blocks' while the opponents recognise them as 'stumbling blocks' to multilateralism. The path-breaking contributions by Bhagwati, Ethier, Findlay, Helpman, Kahler, Krishna, Krugman, Lazer, Levy, Mansfield, Meade, Oye, Panagariya, Reinhardt, Richardson, Summers, Viner and Winters (to name a few) in areas of regionalism and multilateralism have influenced new strategies in global trade policy space.

Trade theory suggests that the larger block is the most desirable trading bloc. Such a bloc comprises countries with the most diverse range of comparative advantage which affords the greatest scope for trade creation and the least scope for trade diversion. Trade theory does not provide a good guide for the existence of sub-global trading blocs. It is therefore an empirical issue to settle the debate. A large member of authors have tried to empirically test some of the propositions that have emerged in the theoretical literature, namely Aitken, Balassa, Cernat, Chang, Coulibali, Kandogan, Winters, Winters and Yeats among others.

At present, some 462 RTAs have been notified to the GATT/WTO up to February 2010. Of these, 345 RTAs were notified under Article XXIV of the GATT 1947 or GATT 1994; 31 under the Enabling Clause; and 86 under Article V of the GATS. At that same date, 230 agreements were in force. Of these RTAs, FTAs and partial scope agreements account for over 90 per cent, while customs unions account for less than 10 per cent. Large portion of world merchandise trade now occurs under the umbrella of FTAs and hence play an important role in promoting the liberalisation and expansion of trade.

A notable feature in the recent rise of regionalism is that of countries that have traditionally favoured the multilateral approach to trade liberalisation. The interactions have ranged from bilateralism to subregionalism to regionalism. Europe took the initiative in RTAs with the formation of European Economic Community which culminated into the Economic Union. Developing countries are no exception to the process of expansion and reinvigoration of the RTAs. They have actively participated in regional trade agreements among themselves (South–South) and with developed countries (South–North).

In Africa, there are a number of RTAs in force such as Arab Maghreb Union (AMU), West African Economic and Monetary Union (WAEMU), Monetary and Economic Community of Central Africa (CEMAC), Common Market for Eastern and Southern Africa (COMESA), East African Community (EAC), Indian Ocean Community (IOC), Economic Community of Central African States (ECCAS), Economic Community of West African States (ECOWAS), West African Economic and Monetary Union (UEMOA), Southern Africa Custom Union (SAUC) and Southern African Development Community (SADC).

In the Asia-Pacific region, some RTAs are currently in force, including Association of Southeast Asian Nations (ASEAN), South Asian Association for Regional Cooperation (SAARC), Economic Cooperation Organisation (ECO) in continental Asia and Melanesian Spearhead Group (MSG), Pacific Island Countries Trade Agreement/Pacific Agreement on Closer Economic Relations (PICTA/PACER) in the Pacific. Association of Southeast Asian Nation (ASEAN) is the precursor to the RTA in the region and has established the ASEAN

Free Trade Area (AFTA) with the internal liberalisation objective set for achievement in 2020.

In the Americas, there is Mercado Comun del Sur (MERCOSUR), the Andean Community, Carribean Community (CARICOM) and Central American Common Market (CACM). In the Middle East, negotiations for the Greater Arab Free Trade Area (GAFTA) were launched to reach full exemption by the end of 2010. Four Mediterranean Basin countries (Egypt, Jordan, Morocco and Tunisia) have signed the Agadir Agreement as a stepping stone towards a Euro-Mediterranean FTA to be established by 2010. In addition to these sub-regional agreements, various bilateral Preferential Trade Agreements (PTAs) have been launched among, or involving, developing countries, often on an interregional basis such as the India-Brazil-South Africa (IBSA) Dialogue Forum, the Bay of Bengal Initiative for Multi-sectoral Technical and Economic Cooperation among Bangladesh, Bhutan, Myanmar, India, Nepal, Sri Lanka and Thailand (BIMSTEC) Free Trade Agreement, Singapore-New Zealand, Chile-Mexico, Mexico-Nicaragua, Bolivia-Mexico and CARICOM-Costa Rica.

Despite regional and bilateral efforts among developing countries in terms of RTAs/FTAs, the existing trade barriers to South–South trade are higher than those governing trade to North–North trade. The continuing high average tariffs, tariff peaks and services trade barriers that tend to be maintained by developing countries act as a brake on their growth and development. Moreover, the trade profiles of developing countries are such that they tend to face average tariffs in other developing countries that are higher than those faced by developed countries.

The Weighted Applied Tariffs (WAT) of Least Developed Countries (LDCs), South Asian Free Trade Agreement (SAFTA), Sub-Saharan Africa (SSA) countries and ASEAN on imports from various developed and developing country groups are shown in Figures 1 to 4. These figures broadly indicate that there is a substantial tariff reduction in developing countries as a result of domestic reforms, WTO commitments and regional initiatives in recent years. During 2000–2009, WAT has declined for LDCs from 15.14 per cent to 8.69 per cent, for SAFTA countries from 13.46 per cent to 7.57 per cent, for SSA countries from 16.25 per cent to 7.02 per cent and for ASEAN from 6.97 per cent to 2.89 per cent. However, market access within developing countries is more restricted compared to developed coun-tries. For instance, the SSA's imports from ASEAN and SAFTA

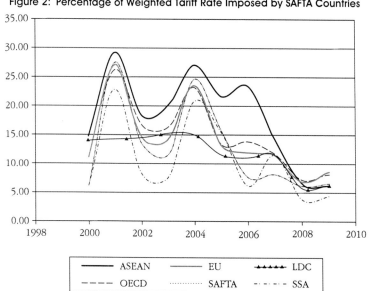

Figure 1: Percentage of Weighted Tariff Rate Imposed by LDCs

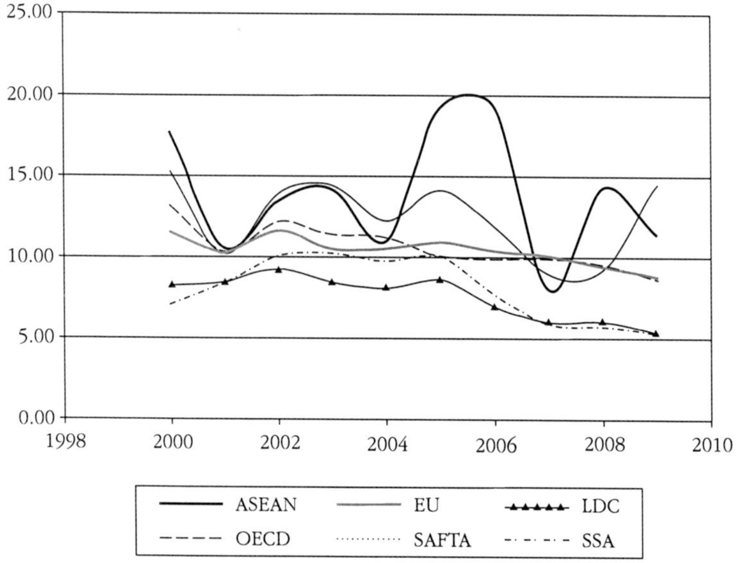

Source: COMTRADE Database (UN 2009).

Figure 2: Percentage of Weighted Tariff Rate Imposed by SAFTA Countries

Source: Same as for Figure 1.

Figure 3: Percentage of Weighted Tariff Rate Imposed by SSA Countries

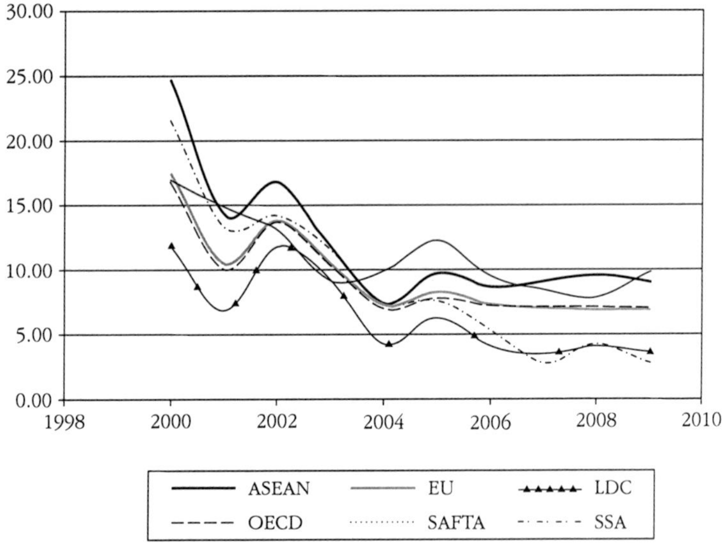

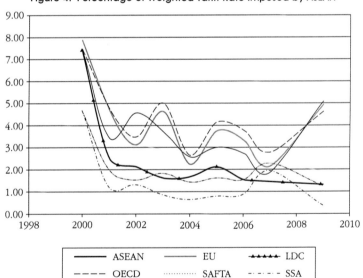

Source: Same as for Figure 1.

Figure 4: Percentage of Weighted Tariff Rate Imposed by ASEAN

Source: Same as for Figure 1.

(other developing countries) faces higher tariff compared to European Union (EU) and Organisation for economic Cooperation (OECD) countries which indicate towards untapped potential. Broadly, the data indicate substantial reduction in WAT of LDC, SAFTA, ASEAN and SSA countries, irrespective of import origin.

Trading pattern also reveals increased trade intensity among developing countries as result of lesser trade barriers in recent years. Figures 5 to 8 present the export trends of different groups of developing countries to various country groups in last nine years. Broadly, export of LDCs to developed countries, OECD and EU has shown downward trend while exports of LDCs to developing country groups — LDC, SAFTA, ASEAN and SSA — remain unchanged or increased during 2000–2008. These are the broad trends of exports of SAFTA, SSA and ASEAN countries. From these figures, there are indications of increasing South–South co-operation and also of emerging strength of these economies in the global order.

Despite trend of positive trade co-operation among developing countries to capture untapped potential, there are a number of issues for empirical verification. For instance: a) large RTAs — those whose membership covers a large share of global trade — can potentially have harmful effects for non-members leading to net trade diversion rather than net trade creation; b) the proliferation of RTAs could create competing and possibly antagonistic blocs that would erode the viability of the MTS; c) the overlapping membership would also pose tremendous administrative burden and increase transaction cost for small countries with limited negotiating and institutional capacities; d) the nature of multilateral agreements negotiation is drastically different from those of RTA negotiations as these are mostly held behind closed doors and there is lack of transparency compared to the multilateral negotiations; e) the increase in RTAs raises the potential for diverse and overlapping agreements with various types of preferential Rules of Origin; f) The issue of revenue loss as result of RTAs/FTAs which needs to be considered while evaluating gains and losses of an RTA as it is more important for developing countries due to their pressing development needs; and finally, g) there is also a danger that RTAs can act as negotiating forums virtually substituting for the WTO, thereby leading to 'forum shopping', and posing a systemic risk to the viability of the MTS.

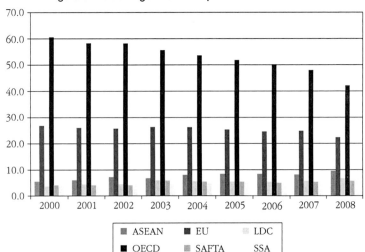

Figure 5: Percentage Share of Exports of LDCs

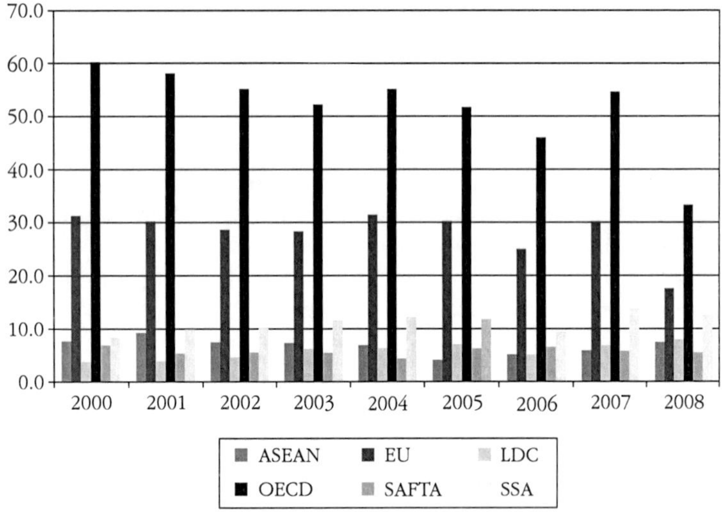

Source: Same as for Figure 1.
Note: LDCs group as classified by World Bank.

Figure 6: Percentage Share of Exports of SAFTA Countries

Source: Same as for Figure 1.

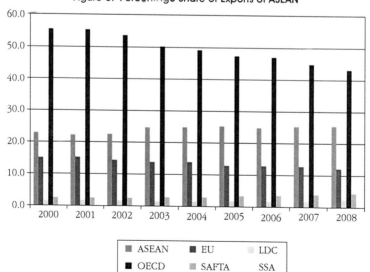

Figure 7: Percentage Share of Exports of SSA Countries

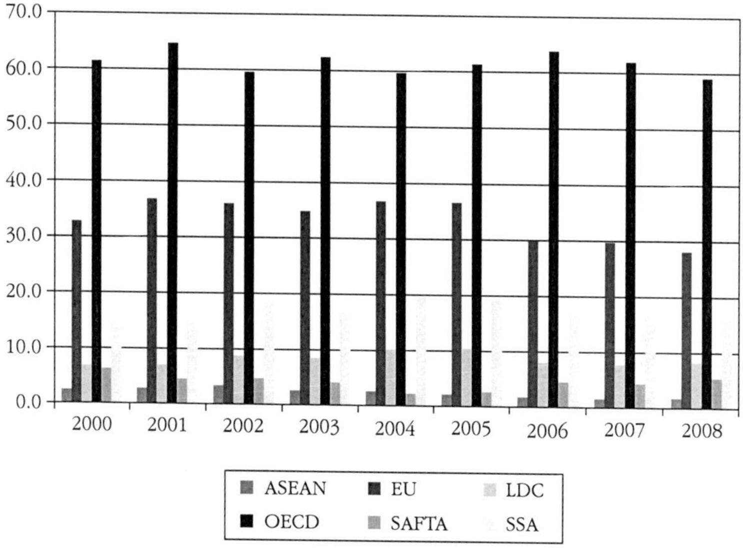

Source: Same as for Figure 1.

Figure 8: Percentage Share of Exports of ASEAN

Source: Same as for Figure 1.

It is also important to recognise that developing countries are not a homogeneous group. There are significant differences between countries on many levels, including population and labour force, size of economy, industrial and trade structure, levels of economic and social development, and income distribution. At one end of the spectrum are China and India, the world's most populous countries, with rapidly expanding industrial sectors based on labour intensive manufacturing. At the other end of the spectrum are countries of the Pacific, Caribbean and least developed small/island economies and resource-based African economies, most of which rely extensively on primary commodities and tourism. Their ability to absorb the impacts of trade liberalisation typically is weaker than larger developing countries and therefore requires different policy responses to address these issues. With such a diverse group, there is clearly not a single strategy that developing countries can adopt when it comes to policies to promote growth and reduce poverty. Hence, it is not possible to generalise the effects of RTAs because they differ greatly in form, content and extent of liberalisation.

In view of the above, there is need for informed debate on trade issues, awareness and new policy inputs to concerned parties to harmonise trade policy-making at the regional and multilateral level. Given the wide implication of RTAs and WTO negotiations on economic development, it is essential to examine the macro and micro effects of international trade flows on welfare, revenue, poverty, environment, etc., particularly in the light of diversities, heterogeneities, limited institutional and financial capacity of developing countries. Most of the RTAs/WTO processes are gender blind and hence it will also be important to explore the gender dimension of international trade, particularly in the context of developing countries where vast gender gap does exist on various development parameters. It is pertinent to analyse and predict outcome of RTA engagements and identify constraints for trade-led development.

It is against this backdrop that the Department of Economics, Jamia Millia Islamia, organised a two-day international conference on 'Dynamics of Regional Trade Agreements and WTO: Developing Countries' Perspectives'. How far we have succeeded is reflected through the pages of the present volume, which is a collection of the selected revised papers presented in the conference. We are conscious that many crucial theoretical, empirical and policy issues could not find place in this volume. With all humility, we do accept the primacy of these issues. Whatever we have presented is expected to prove itself as a useful addition to the literature on dynamics of international trade, WTO and RTAs, particularly from developing countries' perspective. It is hoped that it will serve, in some way, as a fruitful guide to formulation of trade and economic policies for the benefit of developing countries. It is also expected that research methodologies and databases used in the various chapters of this book will be useful reference to the future trade research.

This book has been organised in five sections. Section I predicts the trade outcome using macro econometric and computable general equilibrium modeling approach. This section contains three chapters and broadly deals with the issue of the macro effects of global economic crisis on trade, economic growth and poverty in India; gender-wise implications of trade liberalisation of textile sector in Pakistan; and predicting economic effects of prospective India–EU FTA. It highlights the spiral effect of external shocks and derives the lessons for long-term stability. In this section, the proposed India–EU FTA has been evaluated in terms of welfare, output, employment and trade flows. It argues that both India and EU gain in terms of welfare from the prospective India–EU FTA, but warns against hurriedly opted tariff liberalisation. It recommends partial and selected tariff liberalisation as the best strategy in the interest of India. Further, CGE results for Pakistan reveal that Pakistan benefits from quota elimination against its exports in terms of higher textile production and exports. The section indicates that global liberalisation has positive, though small, aggregate impact on welfare of both rural and urban households in Pakistan. Energy shortages negatively affect textile production as well as trade; therefore, investment in energy sector is necessary to reap the benefits of liberalisation of textile trade.

Section II focuses paper on regional integration in South Asia and has three chapters covering wide issues. The potential of South Asia region in global world order has been highlighted. This section reveals that the trade potential of SAFTA broadly remains untapped due to lack of political will. The increasing tendency of South Asian countries towards signing bilateral trading agreements is unintentionally going against the SAFTA goals. The region can promote trade by formulating devices which will enhance intra-industry trade on the basis of the competitive advantages of each country in areas such as wages, technological structure, transportation cost, human and natural resources. Further, this section examines the feasibility and benefits of optimum currency area in South Asia. With cooperation already in place and progress being made in terms of trade, investment, WTO issues, tourism and others, the prospects for greater economic integration through co-ordination of macro economic policies seems to be brighter.

Section III of the book discusses trade integration in Africa and Arab states and contains three chapters. There has been a divergence of opinion as to what extent the regional trade agreements have been able to minimise the trade barriers on Africa's exports. It is inferred that products of relevance to African countries are confronted with higher trade restrictions, mostly in the South countries than in the developed countries, due to the fact that these South countries have not granted appropriate trade preference to African countries to gain access to these markets. It also reports that integration of small and landlocked African economies need emphasis on more regional cooperation on public good provisions such as better institutional cooperation, infrastructure and communication, etc., rather than on trade which increases the provision of private goods. This section further highlights the economic integration among states in the Arab region and its consequent application to growth. The effect of extra-regional and intra-regional trade on growth was tested using econometric techniques. It reveals that the impact of extra-regional trade on output growth is higher compared to intra-regional trade.

Section IV of this book deals with sectoral implications of international trade and contains five chapters. This section looks into the trade structure of India and ASEAN countries to identify complementary sectors and product groups for enhanced trade cooperation. It tries to identify the likely impact of the India–ASEAN pact on plantation, textiles and clothing sectors of India. This section also reveals the impact of FDI on overall performance and competitiveness of an economy and analyses FDI flows into the Indian auto industry.

Section V deals with legal and other economic issues arising from WTO process and contains four chapters. This section highlights different exceptions to the GATT which give WTO members the right to intervene in the working mechanism of international trade rules and limits the full adherence to such rules under certain circumstance and conditions. Interventions may take the form of measures to protect national industries from injury related to the unusual flow of imported goods or unfair trade practices of exporting countries; financial support measures to improve national productivities through national programmes of subsidies; and/or modification to the globalised application of international trade rules by developing small trading blocks between countries with shared economic interests. It also elaborates on use of exception clauses in the GATT as NTBs against developing countries. A detailed argument has been presented to rationalise current dispute settlement practice. Finally, this section emphasises the need of quantification for the degree of multilateral orientation and suggests a symmetry measure of the trade flows based on the concept of entropy for this purpose. It has been discussed that WTO issues such as subsidies, safeguards, Non-Agricultural Market Access (NAMA), Trade Related Intellectual Property Rights (TRIPS), Trade Related Investment Measures (TRIMS) and GATS provide more gaining opportunities rather than any RTAs.

Part 1

Macro and CGE Modelling of International Trade

1

Macro Effects of Global Economic Crisis on Trade, Economic Growth and Poverty in India

K. N. Murty

A large number of studies for modelling macro dimensions of Indian economy has been undertaken by number of scholars whose detailed review can be read in Jadhav (1990), Klein and Palanivel (1999), Krishnamurty (2001), Pandit and Krishnamurty (2004) and Bhattacharya and Kar (2005). However, modelling the external sector was not a major concern in the earlier models because of restrictions on trade. But in the recent years, several models emerged with detailed emphasis on the external sector and its interlinks with the monetary and fiscal sectors. Krishnamurty and Pandit (1996) modelled the merchandise trade flows in supply–demand framework and included disaggregated output, prices and investment behaviour. Rangarajan and Mohanty (1997) postulated that fiscal deficit increases the absorption in the economy relative to output and the output effect of deficit follows with a lag using macro model. While Sastry et al. (2003) has analysed the sectoral linkages between agriculture, industry and services in the Indian economy.

Since the beginning of 2008, there has been a lot of public debate about (a) the global economic crisis, trade liberalisation, their recessionary effects on the Indian economy; (b) measures to overcome further sliding down of the economy; (c) the role and potential of infrastructure sector in accelerating the GDP growth; and (d) the ways and means of raising resources for public investment in infrastructure sector. Economy-wide macro econometric models can help in understanding the main macro-economic problems of a country and attempt to obtain quantitative answers for fiscal, monetary, trade and other policy initiatives.

This chapter attempts to address these issues and seeks quantitative answers in a macroeconomic theoretical framework for India. The tool of counter factual policy simulation is used for this purpose.

Theoretical Framework

This chapter tries to extend the work by Murty and Soumya (2007) wherein they attempted to build a small macroeconometric model for India using the absorption approach of Pollak. The model emphasises the interrelationships between internal and external balances and also the relation between money, output, prices and balance of payments.

The model strives for a balance between the two polarised approaches of the classicals and the Keynesians. While classicals contend that changes in money supply ultimately results in changes in the price level, the Keynesians on the other hand postulate that the changes in money supply eventually leads to changes in output, under conditions of less than full employment. Viewing reality lying somewhere in between these two extremes, one can postulate that changes in money supply affect both the output and the price level. Thus, the model tries to capture the effects of changes in money supply on both output and price level. The model mainly focuses on the level of economic activity measured by production and also determination of money supply and its links with fiscal operations. Capital formation, price behaviour are also modelled in detail. The economy is divided into four sectors namely (i) Agriculture including allied activities; (ii) manufacturing including mining and quarrying; (iii) infrastructure including electricity, gas, water supply, construction, transport, storage and communication; and (iv) services including trade, financing, insurance and public administration. Besides modelling output, capital formation and price behaviour, the model also includes separate sub-models on fiscal and monetary sectors and external sector. The level of economic activity is supply driven in agriculture, infrastructure and services sectors. In the manufacturing sector, it is a mixture of both supply and demand factors. Besides net capital stock, infrastructure output, rainfall and gross cropped area affects output in agriculture sector. In the case of manufacturing sector, besides net capital stock, aggregate demand for domestically produced goods or in other words, real private absorption, and imports have a significant impact on total output.

In the proposed model, private investment is assumed to be explained by (a) public investment in that specific sector, (b) real interest rate, (c) public sector resource gap and (d) relative price or sectoral terms of trade. The variable public sector resource-gap, defined as the difference between gross public sector savings and investment, is common to all the four sub-sectors and is expected to have a negative correlation with private investment. Based on the net effect of the above four explanatory variables of private investment, we classify whether there exists 'crowding-in' or 'crowding-out' between public and private investments. If the net effect is positive (negative), we say that there exists crowding-in (crowding-out) respectively.

It also has an interest rate equation, which is an inverse demand function for money. The interest rate determinants are real output, money supply and rate of inflation. Price behaviour is explained through sectoral wholesale price indices. Money supply per unit of GDP, intended to measure overall liquidity in the economy, is a common determinant of price level in all sectors. Wholesale prices in manufacturing sector are also influenced by unit value index of imports and wholesale price index of minerals, fuel and power, light and lubricants. The sub-model on fiscal and monetary sectors includes the set of government activities and its links with monetary operations. External sector is modelled through supply of exports, demand for imports and unit value (price) of exports specified as an inverse demand function for Indian exports. The export supply depends on lagged relative export price adjusted for India–US bilateral exchange rate and lagged real domestic income. The import demand function depends on the domestic absorption and the relative import price adjusted for effective India–US bilateral exchange rate, using per unit average tariff rate of imports. The bilateral India–US nominal exchange rate is kept exogenous, in view of substantial intervention by the RBI in foreign exchange market.

In order to link poverty reduction with economic growth, the model postulates a simple relationship between head count ratio and the per capita real income separately for rural and urban areas in India. Due to space constraint, the detailed model specification is omitted from here. The description of all variables used in the model is given in Appendix I.

Data

The data were taken from the *National Accounts Statistics* (NAS), published by CSO, and the *Handbook of Statistics on Indian Economy*, published by the RBI. The poverty estimates are based on the National Sample Survey (NSS) data.

The study period is 1978–1979 to 2005–2006. For any macro-econometric model, the choice of sectoral break-up is very important and it determines the overall size of the model. Here, we chose a 4-sector disaggregation for the investment and outputs of the real sector from the NAS. These four sub-sectors are: (i) agriculture including forestry and fishing (Industry group 1), (ii) manufacturing including mining (Industry groups 2 and 3), (iii) infrastructure, which includes electricity, gas, water supply, construction, and transport, storage and communication (Industry groups 4, 5 and 7) and (iv) services sector, covering all other activities (Industry groups 6, 8 and 9). For simplicity of reference, these four sub-sectors are called: (i) agriculture, (ii) manufacturing, (iii) infrastructure and (iv) services respectively, in the rest of the chapter. Most of the variables for the real and external sectors used in the econometric analysis are in real form (1993–1994 prices) to avoid inflationary effects. The monetary and fiscal variables are in current prices. All price variables are indices with 1993–1994 as unity.

Empirical Results

The proposed macroeconometric model consists of 4 blocks — real, fiscal, monetary and external sectors. It has 74 endogenous variables (35 equations and 39 identities) and 40 exogenous variables, including eight dummy variables. The explanatory variables given in each equation are those actually found to be empirically suitable after careful search process during estimation. It is therefore more appropriate to call the given model as 'selected model' instead of 'proposed model'.

While estimating the model, a TREND variable is included in some equations to capture the autonomous time-related changes in the endogenous variables. Dummy variables are included in the model to separate the pre- and post-liberalisation (1991–1992 onwards) effects and also to capture the abnormal fluctuations in the data for certain variables. The choice of the equations was guided by expected sign as well as statistical significance for the coefficients and high goodness-of-fit, including absence of serial correlation for residuals. It may be mentioned that the choice of lag length for various determinants was also guided by expected sign and near significance. It involved careful search process. The finally selected model is given in Appendix II.

A perusal at the estimated model indicates that the model is estimated quite well. Almost all the regression coefficients are significant at 5 per cent or less level of significance. The signs of the coefficients also look appropriate, a priori. However, despite our best efforts, some of the equations still seem to suffer from the problem of serial correlation. In order to understand the direction and relative magnitude of response of each determinant on the dependent variable, the estimated mean partial elasticities are also given in each equation. It is important to note however that the direction and size of response implied by these mean partial elasticities is only indicative and the net impacts measured through policy simulations are likely to be different from these mean partial elasticities.

Thus, from the signs, magnitudes, t-ratios of the coefficients and goodness-of-fit measures of all the equations in the model, we infer that there is considerable simultaneity in the macroeconomic relationships and the model is indeed a simultaneous system. Further, due to several endogenous lags, the model is truly dynamic in nature and impacts of any exogenous change will be spread over time. There will be both short- and long-run responses, which will enable us to analyse counter factual policy simulations. The estimated model thus indicated significant crowding-in effect between private and public sector investment in agriculture, manufacturing and services sectors. Importantly, the infrastructure sector shows crowding-out between public and private sector investments. Also, there are significant complementarities between public sector investments in infrastructure and all other sectors.

Simulation Methodology

To assess the empirical adequacy of the full model in describing the historical data, EViews package was used to solve the 74 relations together iteratively and dynamically with deterministic and stochastic simulation options separately for the entire sample period, 1978–1979 to 2005–2006. Standard stochastic simulation options are used.

The allocative and dynamic effects due to the below mentioned exogenous/policy change are quantified as percentage changes (policy simulation vs. base simulation in the same year), also known as impacts/multipliers. They are reported only at four points of time, namely response in the same year of exogenous change (immediate or instantaneous or impact), response after one year (short term), response between 1–5 years (medium term) and response between 1–12 years (long term). Since the responses change each year rather slowly, the short-term, medium-term and long-term responses are simple (cumulative) averages of the respective time periods. In the case of head count ratio, rate of inflation, rate of interest and trade balance, the impacts are changes in level, not rates of change. It may be mentioned that these percentage responses are contemporaneous in nature and should not be treated as usual percentage rate of change over time.

Counter Factual Policy Simulations

Using this model, hypothetical counter factual stochastic policy simulations relating to global economic crisis and trade liberalisation are undertaken to quantify their macro effects on external trade, economic growth and poverty in India. It goes without saying that the model can analyse the impact of changes in several other policy variables on Indian macroeconomy[1]. The policy simulation can be done for any sample period or even post-sample period. Here, the period 1991–1992 to 2002–2003 is chosen to have long enough time for the stabilisation of impacts. The period also coincides with the post-reform era.

Three Per Cent Decrease in World Real Income in 1991–1992 Due to Global Economic Crisis

Since the global economic crisis is a most recent event and the actual quantification of its effect on macro variables of both world and Indian economies will take some more time, we hypothesise a 3 per cent decrease in world real income in 1991–1992 alone as a one period/temporary shock change.[2] Given the long time series nature of the data and the largeness of the model, it would be too naive to assume that the impacts being measured here are totally invariant to the timing of exogenous policy change. To have an idea of the extent of variation due to timing of the exogenous change, similar hypothetical change is postulated during 1981–1982 also. Though the impacts varied for specific years between the two alternative time horizons, the cumulative short- to medium-term responses are found to be similar in both the cases. The hypothetical change(s), envisaged as above, has both short- and long-run effects on all the sectors of the Indian economy. The impacts and the dynamic multipliers of the proposed exogenous change (one aspect of global economic crisis) are given in Table 1.1. The graphs containing actual and policy simulated series for important variables are given in Chart 1.1.

Impacts

The exogenous variables world real income, world export price, unit value of imports, import tariff rate and India–US bilateral nominal exchange rate, all appear in the external trade block of the macro model. The dependent variables are export supply, export price and import demand of India, modelled in equations 31–33. Any hypothetical change in one or more of the exogenous/policy variables in these equations like world real income will start affecting other macro variables through this trade block. We, therefore, try to trace the chain of effects from equations 31–33.

When world real income is reduced by 3 per cent in 1991–1992, since India is a price taker (small country assumption vis-a-vis rest of the world) in world exports market, the demand for Indian exports will fall due to equilibrium between export demand and export supply of Indian exports, pushing down the export price received by Indian exporters. Accordingly, UVEXP has declined by 0.5 per cent (column 3, Table 1.1), which is the percentage change of policy path over the base path for this variable. Specifically, UVEXP, an index with 1993–1994 value as unity, has fallen from 0.707 to 0.703. However, since export supply is determined by lagged UVEXP, export supply should not have been affected in the normal case. But since the simulation is stochastic and not a deterministic simulation, real export supply seems to increase initially by 0.3 per cent. This will lead to ceteris paribus, fall in India's export earnings. The response in other component of the trade block namely, demand for real imports, depends on aggregate absorption and price level, which in turn will depend on several other macroeconomic interactions in the model. Over and above, unknown stochastic errors will also affect the net effect. For the trade block, these effects are linked through changes in India's real income and wholesale price index. The net impact from the trade block is decline in trade balance to the tune of ₹ 555 crores (55.5 million).

Table1.1: Impacts of 3 Per Cent Decrease in World Real Income in 1991–1992 Due to Global Economic Crisis

Variable Name	Symbol	Immediate (1991–1992)			Short run (1991–1993)			Medium term (1991–1995)			Long-run (1991–2002)		
		BS*	PS*	% Dev†	BS*	PS*	% Dev†	BS*	PS*	% Dev†	BS*	PS*	% Dev†
Nominal Income	Y	622.8	620.7	-0.3	784.0	780.2	-0.5	954.7	948.7	-0.6	1478.0	1467.0	-0.7
GDP Deflator	PGDP	0.9	0.9	-0.3	1.0	1.0	-0.4	1.1	1.1	-0.4	1.3	1.3	-0.3
Real Income	YR	716.6	716.4	-0.0	760.9	760.1	-0.1	825.5	823.8	-0.2	1078.3	1073.2	-0.5
Agriculture	YAR	223.0	222.8	-0.1	229.4	229.4	-0.0	237.0	236.9	-0.0	262.2	262.0	-0.1
Manufacturing	YMNR	141.2	141.3	0.1	155.3	155.4	0.1	172.8	172.7	-0.1	234.0	232.8	-0.5
Infrastructure	YINFR	101.1	101.0	-0.1	104.7	104.5	-0.2	113.3	112.9	-0.3	156.9	155.9	-0.6
Services	YSRR	251.4	251.2	-0.1	271.4	270.8	-0.2	302.4	301.3	-0.3	425.3	422.5	-0.7
Real Private Investment	PITOTR	153.4	151.3	-1.3	188.0	186.5	-0.8	213.2	211.1	-1.0	205.6	203.1	-1.2
Agriculture	PIAGR	9.3	9.3	0.4	9.7	9.7	0.6	9.6	9.6	0.5	12.5	12.5	0.3
Manufacturing	PIMNR	73.5	73.1	-0.6	95.1	94.8	-0.3	107.2	106.7	-0.5	112.6	111.6	-0.9
Infrastructure	PIINFR	13.5	13.1	-2.9	16.2	15.9	-1.7	20.4	20.0	-2.1	20.7	20.4	-1.7
Services	PISRR	57.1	55.9	-2.1	67.1	66.1	-1.6	76.1	74.8	-1.6	59.8	58.5	-2.1
Real Public Investment	PCFTOTR	66.4	66.4	0.0	68.3	68.3	0.0	72.2	72.2	0.0	76.0	76.0	0.0
Public Sector Saving (N)	GDSPUB	14.2	14.0	-1.2	21.2	20.9	-1.3	27.5	27.1	-1.5	5.9	5.1	-13.0
Public Resource Gap (N)	RGPUB	42.8	42.8	0.2	46.6	46.8	0.3	51.8	52.1	0.5	97.2	97.8	0.6
Gross Domestic Saving (N)	GDS	208.8	208.0	-0.4	240.7	240.7	0.0	294.2	294.3	0.1	487.2	485.6	-0.3
Gross Capital Formation (N)	GCFADJ	183.2	183.0	-0.1	236.5	237.2	0.3	299.3	300.1	0.3	478.6	477.5	-0.2
Real Private Consumption	PCR	528.7	528.7	0.0	559.0	558.4	-0.1	594.7	593.6	-0.2	745.0	742.2	-0.4
Government Consumption (N)	GFCE	65.1	64.9	-0.3	82.3	81.9	-0.5	98.4	97.8	-0.6	166.1	165.0	-0.6
Government Current Expenditure (N)	GCE	131.0	130.8	-0.2	155.1	154.8	-0.2	185.2	184.7	-0.3	320.4	319.3	-0.3

		BS	PS	†	BS	PS	†	BS	PS	†	BS	PS	†
Government Revenue (N)	TR	120.7	120.3	-0.3	149.3	148.6	-0.4	178.0	177.0	-0.6	267.6	265.8	-0.7
Direct Taxes (N)	DT	20.8	20.7	-0.7	26.9	26.7	-0.7	33.9	33.6	-0.9	55.6	55.1	-1.0
Indirect Taxes (N)	IDT	87.9	87.6	-0.3	106.7	106.3	-0.4	126.8	126.2	-0.5	188.3	187.2	-0.6
Non-tax Revenue (N)	NTX	12.0	12.0	-0.2	15.7	15.7	-0.4	17.3	17.1	-0.7	23.7	23.5	-0.9
Fiscal Deficit (N)	GFD	59.5	59.5	0.1	65.2	65.3	0.2	71.5	71.7	0.3	115.9	116.2	0.3
Money Supply (N)	M3	399.4	396.8	-0.6	521.1	516.8	-0.8	651.3	645.2	-0.9	982.8	973.3	-1.0
Interest Rate (%) #	PLR	15.1	15.1	0.0	15.7	15.7	0.0	14.8	14.9	0.1	14.1	14.2	0.1
Wholesale Price Index	P	0.9	0.8	-0.1	1.0	1.0	-0.1	1.1	1.1	-0.1	1.3	1.3	-0.1
Inflation Rate (%) #	INFL	15.3	15.2	-0.1	13.7	13.6	-0.1	11.8	11.8	0.0	7.2	7.2	0.0
Real Exports	EXPTR	70.0	70.2	0.3	76.0	75.9	-0.0	84.9	84.7	-0.2	126.8	126.2	-0.5
Real Imports	IMPTR	55.5	55.9	0.7	65.5	65.9	0.6	80.3	80.5	0.3	129.4	128.7	-0.5
Unit Value of Exports	UVEXP	0.7	0.7	-0.5	0.8	0.8	-0.3	0.8	0.8	-0.3	1.2	1.2	-0.4
Trade Balance (N) #	TB	-2.6	-3.1	-0.6	-3.3	-3.9	-0.6	-7.6	-8.2	-0.6	-8.5	-9.2	-0.6
Head Count Ratio-Rural (%) #	HCRRUR	40.7	40.6	-0.1	39.4	39.4	-0.1	37.8	37.9	0.0	31.7	31.8	0.1
Head Count Ratio-Urban (%) #	HCRURB	38.0	38.2	0.2	36.7	36.8	0.1	35.0	35.1	0.1	28.3	28.5	0.2

Source: Author's estimates.

Note: * — ₹ '000 crore, except for GDP deflator, wholesale price index, rate of inflation, interest rate, unit value of exports, trade balance and head count ratio;

N: — Nominal, i.e., current prices; #: — Changes in level, BS: — Base simulation; PS: — Policy simulation; †: — % Deviation and equal to (BS-PS)100/BS.

To list a few of the immediate impacts, decline in trade balance will lead to decline in reserve bank foreign assets (RBFA), which will reduce reserve money and thereby money supply (0.6 per cent). Decline in money supply will cause fall in sectoral wholesale prices of agriculture (0.2 per cent) and minerals, fuel, power, light and lubricants (0.6 per cent). As a consequence, the respective sectoral price deflators and wholesale price index of all commodities (P) will decline by varying extents ranging from 0.1 per cent to 0.6 per cent, the higher values being for infrastructure (0.6 per cent) and services (0.5 per cent). Decline in price deflators will reduce nominal income (0.3 per cent). Fall in wholesale price index (0.1 per cent) will increase relative price of imports and thereby causing negative price effect. However, this negative price effect is more than offset by the increase in aggregate absorption (AD), i.e., positive income effect and thereby increasing real imports (0.7 per cent) into the country.

The real output in manufacturing is positively affected (0.1 per cent) by increase in real imports, more than offsetting the negative effect of decline in aggregate demand for domestically produced goods (ADD). The real output in infrastructure and thereby that of agriculture and services are all negatively affected (0.1 per cent) possibly due to stochastic errors. The aggregate real income falls very negligibly. Further, due to fall in nominal GDP (0.3 per cent), GDP deflator will fall (0.3 per cent). Per capita real income in India fell negligibly and the poverty ratios seem to respond differently in rural and urban India — urban poverty increases (0.2 per cent), as expected, but rural poverty declines (0.1 per cent) in 1991–1992. This may be partly due to the relative slowness in the decline of rural poverty in India.

Due to decline in sectoral price deflators and GDP deflator, the relative prices of sectoral outputs seem to decline forcing a fall in real private investment in all the sectors, except agriculture. The rise in nominal public sector resource gap (0.2 per cent), coupled with fall in aggregate investment deflator, will complement the decline in real private investment in these sectors. In agriculture, real private investment seems to go up by 0.4 per cent over base simulation whereas it fell by 0.6 per cent, 2.9 per cent, and 2.1 per cent in the other three sectors. The aggregate real private investment has thus declined by 1.3 per cent. As a consequence, the aggregate real income (output) fell negligibly.

Due to decline in nominal income, all fiscal variables decline by varying magnitudes — government consumption (0.3 per cent), government expenditure (0.2 per cent), and government revenue (0.3 per cent). Public sector savings decline faster (1.2 per cent) due to fall in revenue. Gross domestic savings declined (0.4 per cent) due to decline in private capital formation and current account balance. Thus, due to a one time 3 per cent fall in world real income caused by global economic crisis, there will be an immediate all-round decline in macroeconomic variables in the Indian economy. Poverty ratio in urban areas will go up slightly.

Dynamic Effects

The nature and magnitude of dynamic effects depends upon the extent of exogenous change that is being postulated. If the global economic crisis continues, the dynamic effects can get magnified over time. Due to one-time decline in world real income, as expected and argued above, the dynamic effects tend to weaken over time for some variables. It must be mentioned that the dampening of the dynamic effects is much slower and varied across variables in this stochastic simulation compared to the deterministic simulations observed earlier. These effects are shown in column 6 of Table 1.1. It can be seen that due to dynamic lags in the model, certain effects, which were absent in 1991–1992, show up in 1992–1993 and also continue into the future. To illustrate the point, the decline in real output in infrastructure and services has accelerated (0.2 per cent) in 1992–1993 compared to 1991–1992, whereas real output in two other sectors, namely agriculture and manufacturing, show deceleration in 1992–1993. The slower increase of real output in manufacturing could be mainly attributed to slower increase of real imports into the country.

Agriculture sector seems relatively unaffected. The external sector, which is the prime mover of all the above changes, continues its role in 1992–1993 and beyond. Unlike in deterministic simulation, even by 2002–2003, 12 years after the exogenous change, we see that most of the effects are not reduced to zero. Thus, if we take into account the stochastic nature of all the behavioural variables, the macroeconomic effects of global economic crisis may last much longer on the Indian economy. Perhaps, the hypothesised exogenous change is too large in magnitude and hence its effects may last longer than a decade as in the present case.

Conclusion

This study uses a structural macroeconometric model that has been under development by the author and his associates in recent years using annual time series data for the period 1978–2006 for India. The said model is of medium size with 74 simultaneous relations (35 equations and 39 identities) estimated using 3SLS with simultaneously iterative weights and coefficients. The model uses a mix of Classical and Keynesian frameworks in the sense that changes in money supply will affect both prices and output. It attempts a comprehensive treatment of all sectors and specifies linkages within and between them. Economic activity is measured by production functions. Capital formation and price behaviour play a major role in determining economic activity. It also incorporates the determinants of private consumption and links rural—urban poverty with real per capita income.

Using this model, hypothetical counter factual stochastic policy simulations are attempted to quantify their macro effects on external trade, economic growth and poverty in India. The policy simulations relate to decline in real world income. The post-liberalisation period 1991–1992 to 2002–2003 is used for policy analysis. Since the model is dynamic, the effects of any exogenous change will spread over time and the impacts may persist in a declining magnitude for over a decade after the initial policy change. The recovery period depends on the extent of the policy change postulated. The adverse effects of global economic crisis can be overcome through public investment in infrastructure sector (not discussed here due to space constraint), which seems to have substantial complementary effects on private investment in all other sectors and can thereby lead to non-inflationary growth and poverty reduction in India.

Appendix I

Description of Variables

Endogenous variables (₹ '000 crore)

1.	ABSP:	Real Private Absorption (NAS)
2.	AD:	Real Aggregate Absorption (NAS and RBI)
3.	ADD:	Real Aggregate Demand for Domestically Produced Goods (NAS and RBI)
4.	BCP:	Bank Credit to Commercial Sector (Nominal) (RBI)
5.	CAB:	Current Account Balance (Nominal) (RBI)
6.	DEPAG:	Real Depreciation in Agriculture (NAS)
7.	DEPINF:	Real Depreciation in Infrastructure (NAS)
8.	DEPMN:	Real Depreciation in Manufacturing (NAS)
9.	DEPSR:	Real Depreciation in Services (NAS)
10.	DT:	Direct Tax Revenues (Nominal) (NAS)
11.	EXPT:	Exports (DGCI&S) (Nominal) (RBI)
12.	EXPTBOP:	Exports (Merchandise) (Nominal) (RBI)
13.	EXPTR:	Real Exports (DGCI&S) (RBI)
14.	GCE:	Government Current Expenditure (ADORC) (Nominal) (NAS)
15.	GCFADJ:	Gross Domestic Capital Formation by Type of Assets (adj) (Nominal NAS)
16.	GDS:	Gross Domestic Savings (Nominal) (NAS)
17.	GDSADORC:	Gross Domestic Savings of ADORC (Nominal) (NAS)
18.	GDSPUB:	Gross Domestic Savings of Public Sector (Nominal) (NAS)
19.	GFCE:	Government Final Consumption Expenditure (doesn't include consumption of fixed capital) (ADORC) (Nominal) (NAS)
20.	GFD:	Gross Fiscal Deficit of both Central and State government (Nominal) (RBI)
21.	GXP:	Government Total Expenditure (including current and capital) (ADORC) (Nominal) (NAS)
22.	HCRRUR:	Head Count Ratio in Rural Areas (per cent)
23.	HCRURB:	Head Count Ratio in Urban Areas (per cent)
24.	IDT:	Indirect Tax Revenues (Nominal) (NAS)
25.	IMPT:	Imports (DGCI&S) (Nominal) (RBI)
26.	IMPTBOP:	Imports (Merchandise) (Nominal) (RBI)
27.	IMPTR:	Real Imports (DGCI&S) (RBI)
28.	KAGR:	Real Net Capital Stock in Agriculture (NAS)
29.	KINFR:	Real Net Capital Stock in Infrastructure (NAS)

30.	KMNR:	Real Net Capital Stock in Manufacturing (NAS)
31.	KSRR:	Real Net Capital Stock in Services (NAS)
32.	M3:	Money Supply (Nominal) (RBI)
33.	NTX:	Non-tax Revenues (including income from entrepreneurship and property and miscellaneous current receipts (Nominal) (NAS)
34.	P:	Wholesale Price Index (1993–1994=1.0) (RBI)
35.	INFL:	Rate of Inflation
36.	PCFTOTR:	Real Aggregate Public Investment (NAS)
37.	PCFTOT:	Aggregate Public Investment (Nominal) (NAS)
38.	PCR:	Real Private Consumption (NAS)
39.	PGDP:	GDP Deflator (1993–1994=1.0) (NAS)
40.	PGKE:	Implicit Price Deflator for Public Sector Investment (1993–1994=1.0) (NAS)
41.	PIADJR:	Real Aggregate Private Investment Adjusted to Errors and Omissions (NAS)
42.	PIAGR:	Real Gross Private Investment in Agriculture (NAS)
43.	PIINFR:	Real Gross Private Investment in Infrastructure (NAS)
44.	PIMNR:	Real Gross Private Investment in Manufacturing (NAS)
45.	PISRR:	Real Gross Private Investment in Services (NAS)
46.	PITOTR:	Real Aggregate Private Investment (NAS)
47.	PLR:	Prime Lending Ratio (RBI)
48.	PNA:	Price of Non-agriculture Sector (NAS)
49.	PPIE:	Implicit Price Deflator for Public Sector Investment (1993–1994=1.0) (NAS)
50.	PRAG:	Price Deflator for Agriculture, Forestry and Fishing (Industry group 1 of NAS) (NAS)
51.	PRINF:	Price Deflator for Infrastructure including Electricity, Gas, Water Supply; Construction; Transport, Storage and Communication (Industry groups 4, 5 and 7 of NAS) (NAS)
52.	PRMN:	Price Deflator for Manufacturing including Mining and Quarrying (Industry groups 2 and 3 of NAS) (NAS)
53.	PRSR:	Price Deflator for Services inclusive All Others (Industry groups 6, 8 and 9 of NAS) (NAS)
54.	PYD:	Personal Disposable Income (Nominal) (NAS)
55.	PYDR:	Real Personal Disposable Income (NAS)
56.	RBFA:	Net Foreign Exchange Assets of RBI (Nominal) (RBI)
57.	RCG:	Reserve Bank Credit to the Government (Nominal) (RBI)
58.	RGPUB:	Public Sector Resource Gap (Nominal) (NAS)
59.	RM:	Reserve Money (Nominal) (RBI)
60.	TB:	Trade Balance (DGCI & S) (Nominal) (RBI)

61.	TBBOP:	Trade Balance (Merchandise) (Nominal) (RBI)
62.	TR:	Government Current Revenues (ADORC) (Nominal) (NAS)
63.	UVEXP:	Unit Value of Exports (1993–1994=1.0) (RBI)
64.	WPAG:	Wholesale Price Index for Agricultural Commodities (1993–1994=1.0) (RBI)
65.	WPFPLL:	Wholesale Price Index for Minerals, Fuels Power, Light and Lubricants (1993–1994=1.0) (RBI)
66.	WPMN:	Wholesale Price Index for Manufactured Products (1993–1994=1.0) (RBI)
67.	Y:	Output at Factor Cost (Nominal) (NAS)
68.	YAR:	Real Output in Agriculture, Forestry and Fishing (Industry group 1 of NAS) (NAS)
69.	YINFR:	Real Output in Infrastructure including Electricity, Gas, Water supply; construction; transport, storage & communication (Industry groups 4, 5 and 7 of NAS) (NAS)
70.	YM:	Gross Domestic Product at Market Prices (Nominal) (NAS)
71.	YMNR:	Real Output in Manufacturing including Mining and Quarrying (Industry groups 2 and 3 of NAS) (NAS)
72.	YNAR:	Real Output in Non-agriculture Sector (=YMNR+ YINFR + YSRR) (NAS)
73.	YSRR:	Real Output in Services including all Others (Industry groups 6, 8 and 9 of NAS) (NAS)
74.	YR:	Real Output at Factor Cost (NAS)

Exogenous Variables (₹ '000 Crore)

1.	AREA:	Index of Gross Cropped Area (1993–1994=1.0) (RBI)
2.	BCG:	Commercial Bank Credit to Government (Nominal) (RBI)
3.	CRR:	Cash Reserve Ratio (RBI)
4.	DNB:	Non-Market Borrowings of both Central and State Governments (Nominal) (RBI)
5.	D81t92:	Dummy for Pre-reform Period (1981–1992)
6.	D81t94:	Dummy Variable for Unexpected Fluctuations in WPMN, NTX
7.	D81t96:	Dummy Variable for Unexpected Fluctuations in PRSR
8.	D81t97:	Dummy Variable for Unexpected Fluctuations in GFCE
9.	D81t99:	Dummy Variable for Unexpected Fluctuations in PRINF
10.	D81:	Dummy Variable for Unexpected Fluctuations in PIINFR

11.	D01:	Dummy Variable for Unexpected Fall in WPFPLL
12.	D2:	Dummy Variable for Unexpected Fall in PIAGR
13.	EXR:	Exchange Rate against US $ (Nominal, Rs/$) (RBI)
14.	EB:	External Borrowings by the Government (Nominal) (RBI)
15.	EM1:	Errors in Wholesale Price Index Identity
16.	EM2:	Errors and Omissions in Gross Capital Formation between Adjusted and Un-adjusted by Using Sectors (NAS)
17.	EM3:	Errors and Omissions in Gross Domestic Savings (NAS)
18.	GCL:	Government's Currency Liabilities to Public (Nominal) (RBI)
19.	GDSRCNDQG:	Gross Domestic Savings of Railways, Communications, Non-departmental Enterprises and Quasi Government Bodies (Nominal) (NAS)
20.	INVSB:	Invisibles in Current Account Balance (Nominal) (RBI)
21.	MISCR:	Other Capital Receipts of the Government (Nominal) (RBI)
22.	MISCRD:	Miscellaneous Bank Credit Available to Commercial Sector
23.	MISRM:	Miscellaneous Components of Reserve Money Including RBI Non-monetary Liabilities (Nominal) (RBI)
24.	NCIF:	Net Capital Inflows Including Net Capital Account in the Balance of Payments and Errors and Omissions (Nominal) (RBI)
25.	NTOT:	Aggregate Population (millions) (NAS)
26.	OGCE:	Other Government Current Expenditures (including IPD, CTS, IGAA) (Nominal) (NAS)
27.	OTP:	Other Transfer Payments (including IPD, CTS, etc.) (Nominal) (NAS)
28.	PCFAGR:	Real Gross Public Investment in Agriculture (NAS)
29.	PCFINFR:	Real Gross Public Investment in Infrastructure (NAS)
30.	PCFMNR:	Real Gross Public Investment in Manufacturing (NAS)
31.	PCFSRR:	Real Gross Public Investment in Services (NAS)
32.	RAIN:	Annual Rainfall (mm) (NAS)
33.	RBCS:	RBI Credit to the Commercial Sector (Nominal) (RBI)
34.	SUB:	Subsidies (Nominal) (NAS)
35.	UVIMP:	Unit Value of Imports (1993–1994=1.0) (RBI)
36.	UVIMP4:	Unit Value of Imports of Fuel (1993–1994=1.0) (RBI)
37.	WPEXP:	World Price Index (1993–1994=1.0) (IFS)
38.	WPRW:	Index of Procurement Prices of Rice and Wheat (1993–1994=1.0) (RBI)
39.	WYR:	Real World Income (IFS)
40.	TARRT:	Unit Tariff Rate

Appendix II

Estimated Model: Period: 1981–1982 to 2002–2003   Method: 3SLS

Real Sector

Production

Real GDP in Agriculture

1. $YAR = -210.203 + 63.861\ RAIN + 121.113\ AREA + 0.750\ KAGR_{-1} + 0.278\ YINFR$
   $\qquad\quad (-9.60)\quad\ (8.04)\qquad\quad (3.95)\qquad\qquad (14.17)\qquad\quad (6.56)$
   $\quad EL:\qquad\qquad\quad 0.25\qquad\quad\ 0.52\qquad\qquad\quad 1.00\qquad\qquad\ 0.14$
   $\qquad\qquad\qquad\qquad\qquad\qquad\qquad\qquad\qquad\qquad\qquad\qquad - 0.390\ AR\ (1)$
   $\qquad\qquad\qquad\qquad\qquad\qquad\qquad\qquad\qquad\qquad\qquad\qquad\ \ (-2.33)$

$$\bar{R}^2 = 0.99 \qquad DW = 2.00$$

Real GDP in Manufacturing

2. $YMNR = 0.085\ ADD + 0.083\ KMNR + 0.252\ IMPTR + 0.703\ AR\ (1)$
   $\qquad\qquad (3.84)\qquad\ (2.32)\qquad\quad (2.10)\qquad\quad (6.96)$
   $\quad EL:\quad 0.49\qquad\quad 0.36\qquad\quad 0.14$
   $$\bar{R}^2 = 0.99 \qquad\qquad DW = 1.38$$

Real GDP in Infrastructure

3. $YINFR = -114.670 + 0.527\ KINFR_{-1} - 0.266\ (KINFR_{-1}{}^*D81t92) + 113.409\ D81t92$
   $\qquad\qquad\ (-5.97)\quad\ (5.55)\qquad\qquad\quad (-5.44)\qquad\qquad\qquad\qquad (5.64)$
   $\quad SR\ EL:\qquad\qquad 1.72\qquad\qquad\quad -0.65$
   $\quad LR\ EL:\qquad\qquad 1.89\qquad\qquad\quad -0.71$
   $\qquad\qquad\qquad\qquad\qquad\qquad\qquad\qquad\qquad\qquad\qquad + 0.091\ YINFR_{-1}$
   $\qquad\qquad\qquad\qquad\qquad\qquad\qquad\qquad\qquad\qquad\qquad\ \ (0.47)$

$$\bar{R}^2 = 0.99 \qquad DW = 0.88$$

Real GDP in Services

4. $YSRR = -66.177 + 0.175\ KSRR_{-1} + 1.924\ YINFR - 8.095\ D81t92$
   $\qquad\qquad (2.33)\ \ (2.42)\qquad\quad (7.16)\qquad\qquad (-1.94)$
   $\quad EL:\qquad\qquad 0.48\qquad\quad 0.77$

$$\bar{R}^2 = 0.99 \qquad DW = 0.90$$

Capital Formation

Real Gross Investment in Agriculture: Private

5. PIAGR = −41.515 + 0.070 YAR + 0.915 PCFAGR$_{-1}$+ 0.116 PCFINFR
      (−4.74)   (6.49)   (3.02)   (1.83)
   EL: 1.48   0.47   0.31

    − 0.087 (PLR$_{-1}$− INFL$_{-1}$) + 27.266 (PRAG/PGDP) + 2.641 D2 − 0.196 AR(1)
    (−1.55)   (3.17)   (4.83)   (−1.00)
    −0.05   2.46
                     $\bar{R}^2 = 0.91$ DW = 2.30

Real Gross Investment in Manufacturing: Private

6. PIMNR = 0.515 YMNR + 0.489 PCFMNR + 1.523 (PIINFR+PCFINFR)
      (4.58)   (1.13)   (3.36)
   EL: 1.24   0.12   1.08

    − 1.222 (RGPUB/PGKE) − 1.838 (PLR$_{-1}$− INFL$_{-1}$) + 0.431 AR (1)
    (−5.61)   (−2.40)   (2.50)
    −1.23   −0.20
                $\bar{R}^2 = 0.80$ DW = 1.63

Real Gross Investment in Infrastructure: Private

7. PIINFR = −75.641 + 0.090 YINFR − 0.777 PCFINFR + 105.724 (PRINF/PGDP)
      (−7.44) (3.78)   (−3.15)   (7.00)
   EL: 0.70   −1.54   6.79
                                 + 8.345 D81
                                  (11.72)
                 $\bar{R}^2 = 0.80$ DW = 1.82

Real Gross Investment in Services: Private

8. PISRR = −277.653 + 0.073 YSRR + 2.033 PCFSRR + 1.208 (PIINFR + PCFINFR)
      (−5.74) (5.18)   (5.32)   (9.55)
   EL: 0.64   1.14   1.63

    − 0.721 (RGPUB/PGKE) − 1.439 (PLR − INFL)
      (−5.47)   (−3.83)
      −1.37   −0.31

         + 247.533 (PRSR/PGDP) − 0.625 AR (1)
           (5.60)   (−4.46)
           7.69
           $\bar{R}^2 = 0.88$ DW = 2.00

Adjusted Total Investment: Private

9. $\text{PIADJR} = -8.133 + 0.247\ \text{PITOTR} + 0.923\ \text{PIADJR}_{-1} - 0.260\ \text{AR}\ (1)$
   $\qquad\quad (-1.03)\quad (2.11)\qquad\qquad (11.74)\qquad\qquad (-1.38)$

SR EL:	0.21
LR EL:	2.70

$\qquad\qquad\qquad\quad \bar{R}^2 = 0.94 \qquad \text{DW} = 2.19$

Real Consumption: Private

10. $\text{PCR} = 128.804 + 0.624\ \text{PYDR} + 0.379\ \text{INFL}_{-1}$
    $\qquad\quad (23.68)\quad (99.39)\qquad (1.76)$

EL: $\qquad\qquad\ \ 0.77\qquad\qquad 0.005$

$\qquad\qquad\qquad\quad \bar{R}^2 = 0.99 \qquad\qquad \text{DW} = 0.89$

Depreciation Equations

Real Depreciation in Agriculture

11. $\text{DEPAG} = -7.645 + 0.058\ \text{KAGR}_{-1}$
    $\qquad\quad\ (-2.65)\quad (6.29)$

EL: $\qquad\qquad\qquad 1.73$

$\qquad\qquad\qquad\quad \bar{R}^2 = 0.61 \qquad \text{DW} = 1.59$

Real Depreciation in Manufacturing

12. $\text{DEPMN} = 15.188 + 0.037\ \text{KMNR}_{-1} + 0.122\ \text{AR}\ (1)$
    $\qquad\quad\ (4.39)\quad (7.25)\qquad\qquad (1.94)$

EL: $\qquad\qquad\qquad 0.60$

$\qquad\qquad\qquad\quad \bar{R}^2 = 0.74 \qquad \text{DW} = 1.88$

Real Depreciation in Infrastructure

13. $\text{DEPINF} = -4.135 + 0.079\ \text{KINFR}_{-1}$
    $\qquad\quad\ (-3.03)\ (23.03)$

EL: $\qquad\qquad\qquad 1.16$

$\qquad\qquad\qquad\quad \bar{R}^2 = 0.96 \qquad \text{DW} = 2.24$

Real Depreciation in Services

14. $\text{DEPSR} = -5.287 + 0.033\ \text{KSRR}_{-1}$
    $\qquad\quad\ (-1.72)\quad (15.64)$

EL: $\qquad\qquad\qquad 1.26$

$\qquad\qquad\qquad\quad \bar{R}^2 = 0.91 \qquad \text{DW} = 1.24$

Price Behavior

Wholesale Prices: Agriculture

15. $\text{WPAG} = 0.118 + 0.543\ (\text{M3/YR}) + 0.587\ \text{WPRW} - 0.545\ \text{AR}\ (1)$
    $\qquad\quad (6.25)\quad (11.61)\qquad\quad (19.69)\qquad\quad (-8.10)$

EL: $\qquad\qquad\quad 0.31\qquad\qquad 0.57$

$\qquad\qquad\qquad\quad \bar{R}^2 = 0.97 \qquad\qquad \text{DW} = 0.47$

Wholesale Prices: Manufacturing

16. WPMN = 0.345 + 0.195 (M3/YR) + 0.649 UVIMP$_{-1}$ – 0.138 D81t94
        (11.32)   (2.07)   (8.84)   (–8.87)
   EL: 0.12   0.60
                    $\bar{R}^2 = 0.97$ DW = 0.47

Wholesale Prices: Minerals, Fuels Power, Light and Lubricants

17. WPFPLL = 0.010 +1.267(M3/YR) + 0.006UVIMP4 + 0.136D01 + 0.211 WPFPLL$_{-1}$
          (4.56)   (21.56)   (0.52)   (12.31)   (5.959)
   SR EL: 0.69   0.01
   LR EL: 0.88   0.01
                   $\bar{R}^2 = 0.99$ DW = 0.60

Implicit Price Deflators

Implicit Price Deflator for Gross Investment: Public

18. PGKE = –0.061 + 1.097 P + 0.697 AR (1)
          (–1.84)   (39.16)   (7.28)
   EL: 1.07
                    $\bar{R}^2 = 0.99$ DW = 1.42

Implicit Price Deflator for Gross Investment: Private

19. PPIE = 0.940 P
          (62.51)
   EL: 0.99
                    $\bar{R}^2 = 0.96$ DW = 2.16

Sectoral Price Deflators

Implicit Price Deflator: Agriculture

20. PRAG = –0.051 + 1.035 WPAG – 0.449 AR (1)
          (–6.30)   (134.30)   (–3.13)
   EL: 1.05
                    $\bar{R}^2 = 0.99$ DW = 1.76

Implicit Price Deflator: Manufacturing

21. PRMN = –0.006 + 0.667 WPMN + 0.374 PRMN$_{-1}$
          (0.72)   (13.48)   (7.17)
   SR EL: 0.65
   LR EL: 1.05
                   $\bar{R}^2 = 0.99$ DW = 0.70

Implicit Price Deflator: Infrastructure

22. $PRINF = -0.171 + 0.895\ WPFPLL + 0.001\ INFL_{-1} + 0.197\ D81t99$
$\qquad$ (-2.04) $\quad$ (16.44) $\qquad$ (0.64) $\qquad$ (6.85)
$\quad$ EL: $\qquad$ 0.99 $\qquad$ 0.01
$\qquad$ $\bar{R}^2 = 0.90$ $\qquad$ $DW = 0.23$

Implicit Price Deflator: Services

23. $PRSR = 0.219 + 1.294\ (M3/YR) + 0.063\ (M3/YR)^*D81t96)$
$\qquad$ (10.76) $\quad$ (43.05) $\qquad$ (5.15)
$\quad$ EL: $\qquad$ 0.75 $\qquad$ 0.02
$\qquad$ $\bar{R}^2 = 0.98$ $\qquad$ $DW = 0.35$

Fiscal Sector

Revenues from Total Direct Taxes of (ADORC) (Nominal)

24. $DT = -2.276 + 0.052\ (YNAR^*\ PNA)$
$\qquad$ (-2.85) $\quad$ (52.52)
$\quad$ EL: $\qquad$ $\bar{R}^2 = 0.99$ $\qquad$ $DW = 2.34$

Revenues from Total Indirect Taxes (ADORC) (Nominal)

25. $IDT = 9.18 + 0.110\ YM + 0.658\ AR\ (1)$
$\qquad$ (2.57) $\quad$ (39.89) $\quad$ (5.23)
$\quad$ EL: $\qquad$ 0.93
$\qquad$ $\bar{R}^2 = 0.99$ $\qquad$ $DW = 2.09$

Total Non-tax Revenues (ADORC) (Nominal)

26. $NTX = -14.951 + 0.023\ Y + 12.298\ D81t94$
$\qquad$ (-12.94) $\quad$ (29.98) $\qquad$ (15.38)
$\quad$ EL: $\qquad$ 1.52
$\qquad$ $\bar{R}^2 = 0.96$ $\qquad$ $DW = 1.45$

Government Final Consumption Expenditure (ADORC) (Nominal)

27. $GFCE = 43.469 + 0.551\ TR - 43.594\ D81t97 - 0.847\ AR\ (1)$
$\qquad$ (25.18) $\quad$ (97.94) $\qquad$ (-36.40) $\qquad$ (-3.23)
$\quad$ EL: $\qquad$ 0.90
$\qquad$ $\bar{R}^2 = 0.99$ $\qquad$ $DW = 0.92$

Gross Fiscal Deficit (Nominal)

28. $GFD = 0.335\ RGPUB + 0.800\ GFD_{-1} + 0.438\ AR\ (1)$
$\qquad$ (4.20) $\qquad$ (10.93) $\qquad$ (2.50)
$\quad$ EL: $\quad$ 0.29
$\qquad$ $\bar{R}^2 = 0.99$ $\qquad$ $DW = 2.01$

Monetary Sector
Money Supply (Nominal)

29. $M_3 = 4.216$ RM $- 4.760$ CRR
        (47.52)   (−4.88)
    EL: 1.13   −0.09
                $\bar{R}^2 = 0.98$ DW = 0.23

Prime Lending Rate

30. PLR $= 0.012$ YR $- 0.007$ M3 $+ 0.210$ INFL$_{-1}$ $+ 0.529$ PLR$_{-1}$
        (2.50)   (−2.73)   (2.77)   (3.21)
    EL: 0.66   −0.26   0.11

                $\bar{R}^2 = 0.64$ DW = 2.05

External Sector
Real Exports

31. EXPTR $= -46.034 + 0.431$ ((UVEXP$_{-1}$*EXR$_{-1}$)/P$_{-1}$) $+ 0.155$ YR$_{-1}$
        (−8.79)   (2.14)   (16.37)
    EL: 0.11   1.50
                $\bar{R}^2 = 0.95$ DW = 0.71

Unit Value of Exports

32. UVEXP $= 0.307 - 2.019$ (WPEXP/EXR) $+ 0.00004$ WYR $+ 0.007$ EXPTR
            (2.90)   (−1.85)   (7.04)   (17.28)
    EL: −0.12   2.78   0.68
                                                $- 0.296$ UVEXP$_{-1}$
                                                    (−3.30)
                $\bar{R}^2 = 0.84$ DW = 0.41

Real Imports

33. IMPTR $= -96.322 + 0.218$AD-1.883((UVIMP*(EXR$_{-1}$ + TARRT$_{-1}$)/P) $+ 0.909$AR (1)
        (−2.91)   (10.43)   (−4.08)   (10.35)
    EL: 2.48   −0.51
                        $\bar{R}^2 = 0.99$ DW = 1.58

Poverty Ratios
Head Count Ratio: Rural

34. HCRRUR $= 64.197 - 32.825$ (PYDR/NTOT)
            (23.33)   (−9.87)
    EL: −0.70
                $\bar{R}^2 = 0.80$ DW = 0.91

Head Count Ratio: Urban

35. HCRURB $= 62.928 -35.445$ (PYDR/NTOT)
            (39.84)   (−18.58)
    EL: −0.83
                $\bar{R}^2 = 0.93$ DW = 1.35

Identities

36. ABSP = PCR + PIADJR
37. ADD = ABSP + (GFCE/P) + PCFTOTR + EXPTR − IMPTR
38. AD = ADD + IMPTR
39. PYD = YM − TR + SUB + OTP
40. PYDR = PYD/PGDP
41. P = 0.215 * WPAG + 0.147 * WPFPLL + 0.638 * WPMN + EM1
42. INFL = (P − P(−1))*100/P(−1)
43. YNAR = YMNR + YINFR + YSRR
44. YR = YAR + YNAR
45. Y = PRAG * YAR + PRMN * YMNR + PRINF * YINFR + PRSR * YSRR
46. PGDP = Y/YR
47. YM = Y + IDT − SUB
48. PNA = (PRMN * YMNR + PRINF * YINFR + PRSR * YSRR)/YNAR
49. KAGR = KAGR(−1) + PIAGR + PCFAGR − DEPAG
50. KMNR = KMNR(−1) + PIMNR + PCFMNR − DEPMN
51. KINFR = KINFR(−1) + PIINFR + PCFINFR − DEPINF
52. KSRR = KSRR(−1) + PISRR + PCFSRR − DEPSR
53. PITOTR = PIAGR + PIMNR + PIINFR + PISRR
54. PCFTOTR = PCFAGR + PCFMNR + PCFINFR + PCFSRR
55. PCFTOT = PCFTOTR * PGKE
56. GCFADJ = (PIADJR * PPIE) + PCFTOT + EM2
57. GDS = GCFADJ + CAB + EM3
58. GCE = GFCE + SUB + OGCE
59. GXP = GCE + PCFTOT
60. TR = DT + IDT + NTX
61. GDSADORC = TR − GCE
62. GDSPUB = GDSADORC + GDSRCNDQG
63. RGPUB = PCFTOT − GDSPUB
64. RM = RCG + RBCS + RBFA + GCL + MISRM
65. D(RCG) = GFD − D(BCG) − DNB − EB − MISCR
66. BCP = M3 − RCG − BCG − RBFA − GCL + MISCRD
67. EXPT = EXPTR * UVEXP
68. IMPT = IMPTR * UVIMP
69. TB = EXPT − IMPT
70. EXPTBOP = K1T * EXPT
71. IMPTBOP = K2T * IMPT
72. TBBOP = EXPTBOP − IMPTBOP
73. CAB = TBBOP + INVSB
74. RBFA = RBFA(−1) + CAB + NCIF

Note: The t-ratios are given in parenthesis. For important variables, the short- and long-run mean partial elasticity is also given below the t-ratios.

A1.1: Impacts of 3 Per Cent Decrease in World Real Income in 1991 due to Global Crisis on Selected Macro Variables

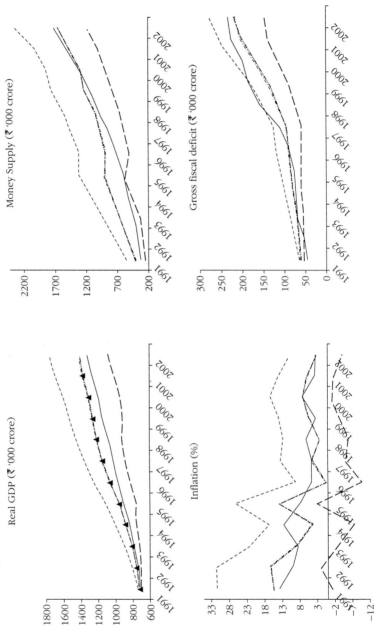

Real GDP (₹ '000 crore)

Money Supply (₹ '000 crore)

Inflation (%)

Gross fiscal deficit (₹ '000 crore)

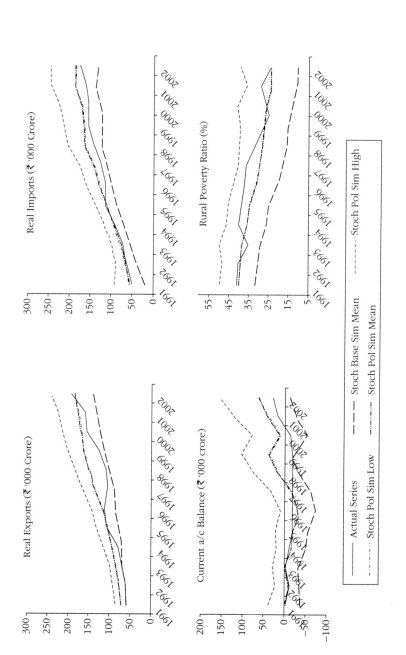

Real Exports (₹ '000 Crore)

Real Imports (₹ '000 Crore)

Current a/c Balance (₹ '000 crore)

Rural Poverty Ratio (%)

——— Actual Series

——— Stoch Pol Sim Low

— — — Stoch Base Sim Mean

-------- Stoch Pol Sim Mean

-------- Stoch Pol Sim High

✳

Notes

1. In order to ensure the symmetry of impacts for each exogenous variable, both an increase and a decrease in that variable have been attempted separately. We found that the impacts are numerically identical except for the sign change. Further, the simulation impacts due to different exogenous variables are also fully additive.
2. We experimented three different patterns of such an exogenous change, namely (a) one period decrease of 3 per cent in 1991–1992, (b) two period decrease of 2 per cent and 1 per cent in 1991–1992 and 1992–1993 respectively and (c) 1 per cent decrease in each of 1991–1992, 1992–1993, and 1993–1994, in world real income due to global economic crisis. This also provides a way of assessing the differential impact of the duration of global economic crisis, which is still anybody's guess. The short- to medium-term impacts of all the three different patterns of policy change are found to be quite similar.

References

Bhattacharya, B. B. and S. Kar. 2005. *Shocks and Long Run Growth in Agriculture: Macroeconomic Analysis*. Delhi: Development Planning Center, Institute of Economic Growth.

Jadhav, N. 1990. 'Monetary Modeling of the Indian Economy: A Survey', *Reserve Bank of India, Occasional Papers*, 11 (2): 83–152.

Klein, L. R. and T. Palanivel. 1999. 'An Econometric Model for India with Special Emphasis on Monetary Sector', *The Developing Economies*, 37 (3): 275–336.

Krishnamurty, K. 2001. 'Macro econometric Models for India: Past, Present and Prospects', *Economic and Political Weekly*, 37 (42): 4295–4308.

Krishnamurty, K. and V. Pandit. 1996. 'Exchange Rate, Tariffs and Trade Flows: Alternative Policy Scenarios for India', *Indian Economic Review*, 31 (1): 57–89.

Murty, K. N. and A. Soumya. 2007. 'Effects of Public Investment on Growth and Poverty', *Economic and Political Weekly*, 42 (1): 47–59.

Pandit, V. N. and K. Krishnamurty. eds. 2004. *Economic Policy Modeling for India*. Delhi: Oxford University Press.

Rangarajan, C. and M. S. Mohanty. 1997. 'Fiscal Deficit, External balance and Monetary Growth — A Study of Indian Economy', *Reserve bank of India Occasional Papers*, 18 (4): 583–653.

Sastry, D. V. S., Balwant Singh, Kaushik Bhattacharya and N. K. Unnikrishnan. 2003. 'Sectoral Linkages and Growth Prospects: Reflections on the Indian Economy', *Economic and Political Weekly*, 38 (24): 2390–97.

2

Changing Rules of the Game of Textile Trade: Gender Implications for Pakistan from a CGE Analysis

Rizwana Siddiqui

During 1974 to 2005, Multi-Fiber Agreements (MFA) has governed the trade of textile goods under quota restrictions. In 1994, an agreement on textile and clothing (ATC) was introduced to integrate textile items and clothing into general GATT framework — reducing quota on some textile items and extending it on the rest. January 2005 has changed the scenario by the complete abolition of all quantitative restrictions on the exports of textile and clothing and has created a new and more competitive world market for textile commodities.

Elimination of MFA quotas has not only increased market access of quota restricted countries, but also has increased competition among them. It is expected to benefit those countries only, which remain competitive after abolition of MFA quota. Pakistan is one of those countries which have comparative advantage in textile products, i.e., 60 to 65 per cent of total exports are textile-based commodities. Given the economic importance of the textile sector in Pakistan, the change in the governing rule of textile trade is expected to bring structural changes in various dimensions of Pakistani economy such as production, trade, employment, wages, welfare and poverty, etc.

Earlier studies on the textile sector of Pakistan have focused on the impact of productivity improvement (Cororaton et al. 2008), the impact of quota abolition on the structure of trade and welfare of European Union (EU) countries (SPDC 2005), the effects of quota elimination against Pakistan's exports of textile only and its effects against all countries exports of textile items on Pakistan economy. However, the focus of these studies is not gender, whereas liber-alisation of this sector may affect men and women in different ways for many reasons: (1) Textile is a sector where women are largely employed, while men are engaged in production of import competing goods. Increase in demand for female originating from this expanding export-oriented sector is expected to impinge on women's leisure; (2) women are primarily responsible for households work that includes cooking, washing, cleaning, taking care of children, the elderly and the sick, which have constrained their participation not only in market work but also their capability development, while men remain a major player in market economy and as a breadwinner have priority in skill development; (3) women and men have different education and skill levels; (4) generally women are engaged in traditional tasks and men in more mechanized tasks; and (5) women earn less than their men counterpart due to discrimination (Siddiqui 2009). In presence of these inequalities, the opening up of global markets for textile trade is expected to have a disproportionate impact on women.

Some studies have explored gendered impact. For instance Siddiqui et al. (2006) using survey data have analysed gender dimension in partial equilibrium setting, which is not enough to reveal multi-dimension impact that differs by gender such as market employment, household work, leisure and wages. These aspects have been focused on by Fontana and Wood (2000); Fontana (2001); Fofana et al. (2005); Siddiqui (2005, 2007, 2009). However, the focus of the studies for Pakistan has not been on textile and MFA quota. This study fills this gap. I use gender aware Computable General Equilibrium (CGE) model developed in Siddiqui (2009) to analyse the impact of MFA quota abolition using the most recently available Social Accounting Matrix (SAM) for the year 2002 (Dorosh et al. 2006).

The objective of the study is two-fold. First, it measures the impact of quota abolition in developed countries in two exercises: (1) abolition of quota against Pakistan's exports of textile items (AQT_P); (2) abolition of quota against all countries' exports of textile items (AQT_AC). Second, it measures the impact of change in policy in the domestic economy on the gains and losses of first two exercises: (3) AQT_AC combined with liberalisation of imports of textile items in Pakistan (AQT_AC_ml); (4) measure the constraint on expansion of textile trade due to increase in energy prices in response to energy shortage.

The plan of the study is as follows. Section 2 briefly reviews textile sector of Pakistan. Section 3 presents theoretical structure of the model. In section 4, I discuss database — SAM 2002. In section 5, I present and interpret the results of four simulations. The final section 6 discusses major findings, policies and future work.

2. Textile Sector of Pakistan

From feeble beginnings, the Pakistani textile industry has grown into the largest premier industry, i.e., from 1 mill in 1947, the number has increased to 512 mills in 2008–2009 (Government of Pakistan 2009). It produces about 46 per cent of manufacturing output and employs 38 per cent of manufacturing labour force (SPDC 2005). After fulfilling domestic demand of 163.7 million, it has 60 to 65 per cent share in total exports from Pakistan, which provide a considerable amount of foreign exchange — 10 billion of US dollars in 2007–2008. During the last several years, volume of exports exceeded all previous records and showed an increasing trend till 2007 and declined sharply thereafter (Figure 2.1). Majority of textile items exported from developing countries goes to the developed countries where MFA holds 42.5 per cent in 1990. Despite declining in 2003, these countries hold substantial shares of total trade — 33 per cent. In the post-MFA period, some of the countries have captured substantial share, while others have been wiped out.

Figure 2.1: Trend in Textile Exports Volume

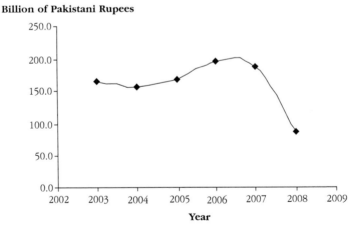

Source: Author's construction using data from Economic Survey (Government of Pakistan 2009).

Pakistan, being the 8th largest exporter of textile products, had 6.5 per cent share in world trade during 2004–2005 to 2005–2006 (SPDC 2005). Pakistan's position relative to its competitors has improved in European market[1] by just one percentage point between 2004 and 2005 (ibid.). But it remains an issue to look at in depth and investigate how MFA has affected various dimension of Pakistani economy in general and women in particular.

Textile production has strong linkages with other sectors of the economy, in particular with cotton that is a major input in textile products. Pakistan is the world's 4th largest producer and the 3rd largest consumer of cotton. Liberalisation of textile trade is expected to increase demand for cotton. In the coming years, textile sectors may face problem of availability of raw material because the area under cotton crop has substantially declined in 2008–2009, not only in Pakistan but also in the world market (Government of Pakistan 2009).

3. Methodology

CGE model is a powerful tool to analyse gender impact of trade liberalisation which allow integration of market and non-market sectors of the economy. It also has advantage over the other tools of analysis as trade restrictions involve direct and indirect impact on income via labour market effects. CGE models develop linkages with other sectors of the economy through intermediate inputs. Therefore, I use CGE model developed in Siddiqui (2005, 2009).

The model is neoclassical and static in nature and has six blocks of equations: income and saving, production, demand, prices, trade and equilibrium. The model has 13 market sectors and two representative households with four non-market sectors (two social reproduction[2] and two leisure sectors) employing four types of labour (for detail see Table 2.1 in Appendix). Non-market sectors behave like market sectors.[3] They produce goods that are consumed by the households themselves. Other factors of production in market economy are land and capital. Institutions other than households are enterprises, government and rest of the world.

Assuming men and women labour for each education level are imperfect substitutes, they are combined with a Constant Elasticity of Substitution (CES) technology in both — market and non-market sectors. Demand for labour is derived with first order condition. The price of non-marketed goods (Ph) is the weighted average of wages of the labour used in the production of household goods. Total income of a household (Y_T) is defined as the sum of receipts from the market and the non-market economies.

Maximizing Stone-Geary utility function of market goods (C_i), home produced goods (C_H), and leisure (C_L) subject to total income and time constraints, I derive household demand for goods and services. Supply of all factors of production is fixed. Labour can move between the market and non-market sectors. Capital is sector-specific. Land is specific to agriculture sectors only. Domestically produced goods and imported goods are imperfect substitutes (Armignton assumption). Exports and domestically consumed goods are of different quality. Export market equilibrium is determined by equilibrium between export demand and export supply. Households' receipts — remittances and public transfers — are fixed. I subtracted quota rent from urban household income. All exogenous variables are indexed to country price level.

The nominal exchange rate acts as the numeraire and the real exchange rate varies in order to keep the current account balance (CAB) fixed. The wage rates of men and women are determined by the supply and demand for their labour. Tax rates adjust to eliminate the impact of a reduction in tariff rates on government revenue. The household savings rate varies in order to equilibrate the investment-saving condition. To allow welfare and poverty analysis, government consumption and investment are fixed in real terms. National savings finance the fiscal deficit and domestic investment. Walras law holds.

Equivalent variation (EV) is used to measure welfare as a percentage of base year consumption. Time poverty is measured in relative terms. By taking the base year leisure as a threshold level, the change in leisure time of women or men relative to the base level measures time poverty. Using poverty line of Pakistani Rupee (PKR) 849 per adult per month for urban area, PKR 705 per adult per month for rural area and PKR 745 for Pakistan for the year 2002[4], Foster-Greer-Thorbecke (FGT) indices are calculated (Foster et al. 1984). For a detailed discussion on methodology on poverty analysis in CGE framework, see Decaluwé et al. (1999), Siddiqui and Kemal (2006) and Siddiqui (2009).

Model is calibrated to the Social Accounting Matrix (SAM) data of the economy of Pakistan for the year 2001–2002. The shift and share parameters, tariff rates, tax rates and savings rates are calculated from SAM data. Elasticities are taken from Siddiqui and Kemal (2006) and Siddiqui (2008, 2009). Gender rigidities are introduced by keeping low elasticities of substitution between the labour of men and women (Siddiqui 2009).

4. Social Accounting Matrix (SAM) — 2002 as Database

The model is built around aggregate version of the 2002 SAM for Pakistan. It has 13 production sectors and four types of labour identified by skill level using labour force survey (LFS) data and Pakistan integrated household survey (PIHS) data for the year 2001–2002 (Pakistan 2002, 2002a). All farms sizes are aggregated into one — land. Formal and informal capital is aggregated into one. It has two representative households — rural and urban.

Households receive income in the form of wages, rent from land and capital in exchange of supplying factor services. They receive transfers from government, remittances from rest of the world and dividends share from enterprises. The shares of rural households (70 per cent of the total population) in total income and consumption are 45 and 52 per cent respectively, while shares for urban households (30 per cent of total households) are about 55 per cent and 48 per cent in their respective totals. The expenditure of urban households on textile goods is significantly higher than that of the rural households — PKR 106 billion and PKR 74 billion, respectively.

Textile[5] production had 30 per cent share in manufacturing output in 2002. The share of intermediate inputs in production is 76.1 per cent. Energy share is 4.1 per cent. The textile contributes 1.2 per cent of its production to government revenue equal to 4.4 per cent of total government revenue. It has strong linkages with other sectors of the economy as 44 per cent of production is used as intermediate input in other industries (Figure 2.2). The export share is about 34 per cent and rest of 22 per cent is for final consumption of households, i.e., 13 per cent by urban households and 9 per cent by rural households.

Nine per cent of total women skilled labour contributes to cotton and textile sectors (Figure 2.3). Although unskilled labour is concentrated in textile sectors, they receive very low wages and therefore their share is less compared to that of skilled women labour.

Figure 2.2: Uses of Textile

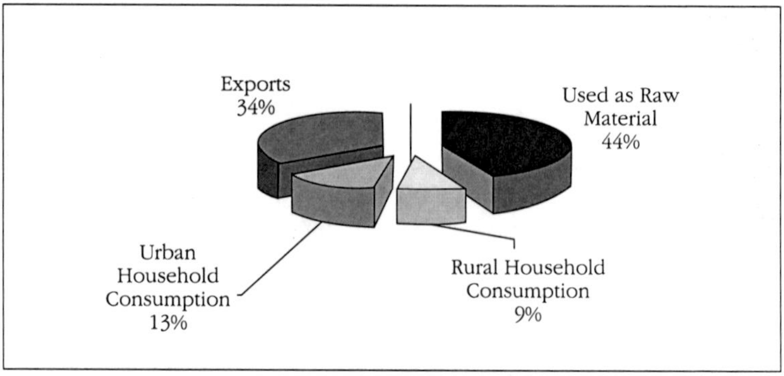

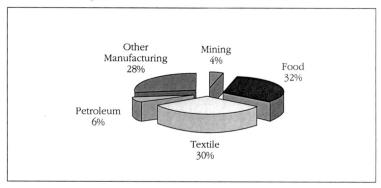

Source: Author's Construction using SAM - 2002 data.

Figure 2.3: Structure of Industrial Value Added

Source: Same as Figure 2.2.

Gender Features

Gender features are introduced in SAM 2002 on the similar lines of GSAM 1990 prepared for Siddiqui (2009). A distinct feature of this gender-aware SAM is that it incorporates data from nationally representative time use survey (Government of Pakistan 2009a). The survey contains information from a sample of 19,600 households. It is conducted in all regions of Pakistan and collects detailed information on time use in activities-defined based on SNA, ESNA and non-SNA.[6] This survey records all activities conducted in 24 hours a day that include night sleep also. Labour used is measured in hours of the individuals involved in market, household and leisure activities.

A matrix of time allocation among market, household (social reproduction) and leisure activities is constructed after subtracting time used for self-care and night sleep (Fontana and Wood 2001; Siddiqui 2009). The ratios are calculated for three types of activities for four types of labour in rural and urban households and applied to SAM data to incorporate time use module in SAM. The data confirms the findings of Siddiqui (2007, 2009) that women spend more time on household social reproductive services than men, while men spend more time in market activities. Women's total working hours (market and households) are higher than men. Time allocation to different activities varies by skill, gender and region.

5. Simulation Results

Elimination of restriction on trade promotes competition through linkages between domestic prices and world prices. Pakistan's exports to quota restricted market are about 50 per cent of the total textile exports of Pakistan. In theory, quota is equivalent to tariff and it increases local prices of the quota restricted commodity in importing country and reduces local demand for it. MFA quota abolition reduce world export price of textile and increase export demand. Consequently, exports and output expand in quota restricted exporting countries due to reallocation of resources and efficiency gain. While price received by the exporting countries declines which eliminates quota rent of exporting country. However, whether the exporting country will lose or gain from abolition of quota depends on its price changes, export supply response, export demand and their export share in quota restricted markets.

The exports of textile goods from Pakistan face average export tax equivalents of 10 per cent in the market of United States of America (USA) and 9 per cent in European Union Countries (Martin et al. 2004). Martin et al. (ibid.) shows that elimination of quota against Pakistani textile exports and elimination of quota against all countries exports of textile increases export demand of textile items from Pakistan by 31 per cent and 3.3 per cent respectively.[7] Four simulation experiments are conducted here. The first two experiments measure the impact of change of policy in global market, while the last two exercises measure the difference in impact due to change in policy in the domestic economy. The four CGE experiments are:

1. AQT_P— Abolition of MFA quota against Pakistan's export of textile items.
2. AQT_AC — Abolition of MFA quota against all countries' exports of textile items.
3. AQT_AC_ml — Abolition of MFA quota against all countries' exports of textiles combined with tariff elimination on of textile imports in domestic economy.
4. AQT_ P_Tenrg — Abolition of MFA quota against Pakistan's export of textile items and increase taxes on energy in domestic economy.

5.1. Simulation 1

Elimination of quota has two direct effects. First, it brings price of quota restricted commodity down for both countries — importing and exporting. Second, it increase demand for that commodity in importing country, while immediate response of export supply depends on the capacity of exporting country. I calculated weighted average of export tax equivalent and weighted export demand for total export of textile commodities from Pakistan[8] based on ETE and the change in export demand from the study by Martin et al. (2004).[9] In this exercise, policy analysis is conducted with lower world price of quota restricted textile items by 4.8 per cent and higher export demand of textile items from Pakistan by 16 per cent.

Price Effects

First round effects triggered from elimination of quota against Pakistan on textile exports travel into the economy through the change in world export prices to domestic prices. Export price of textile in domestic economy increases by 5.6 per cent due to substantial increase in its demand in the world market. The export prices of all other commodities increase less than the price of textile commodity (Table 2.1). With no change in import prices, consumer prices of all commodities increase with increase in domestic prices (Table 2.1).

Demand and Supply Effects

Imports become cheaper relative to domestic good. Consumers switch from locally produced commodities towards their counterparts — imported commodities. The volume of imports of all importable commodities increases except mining, which marginally decline by 0.11 per cent due to substitution effects as consumers shift towards

Table 2.1: Price Effects (Percentage Variation over Base Year Values)

Sectors	Abolition of quotas against Pakistan's export of textile (AQT_P)					Abolition of quotas against developing countries' exports of textiles (AQT_AC)					Abolition of quotas against developing countries exports of textiles and tariff elimination on textile imports in domestic economy (AQT_AC_ml)					
	Pe_fob	PD	PC	R	PVA	Pe_fob	PD	PC	R	PVA	Pe_fob	PM	PD	PC	R	PVA
Agriculture	2.5	4.97	4.84	4.81	4.84	-1.06	-2.06	-2	-2.25	-2.28	-1.31	0	-2.53	-2.47	-2.72	-2.76
Cotton	0	0	4.04	6.19	4.98	0	0	-1.83	-2.9	-2.37	0	0	0	-2.25	-3.48	-2.86
Forestry	3.41	5.32	3.94	0	4.88	-1.5	-2.4	-1.8	0	-2.31	-1.84	0	-2.92	-2.19	0	-2.79
Mining	1.68	1.6	0.31	-0.86	0.8	-0.8	-0.8	-0.16	0.14	-0.62	-0.97	0	-0.97	-0.19	0.22	-0.72
Food	2.47	4.53	4.1	1.27	1.95	-0.97	-1.74	-1.58	-0.9	-1.19	-1.22	0	-2.19	-1.98	-1.02	-1.38
Textile	5.62	4.16	3.94	7.14	6.52	-2.28	-1.6	-1.52	-3.41	-3.14	-2.73	-8.71	-2.74	-3.05	-4.07	-3.75
Petroleum	1.67	2.68	1.06	1.34	2.14	-0.61	-1.05	-0.42	-1.37	-1.6	-0.77	0	-1.31	-0.52	-1.57	-1.87
Other manufacturing	1.9	2.43	0.97	-0.85	0.47	-0.74	-0.98	-0.4	-0.36	-0.84	-0.93	0	-1.22	-0.5	-0.29	-0.91
Construction	0	0	2.59	4.35	4.68	0	0	-1.2	-2.08	-2.28	0	0	0	-1.46	-2.52	-2.75
Housing	0	0	48.09	58.08	58.08	0	0	7.39	9.31	9.31	0	0	0	5.08	6.55	6.55
Wholesale and retail trade	3.63	6.6	6.58	4.4	4.69	-0.99	-1.82	-1.82	-2.32	-2.35	-1.31	0	-2.38	-2.38	-2.77	-2.83
Energy	0	0	4.32	5.28	5.19	0	0	-1.91	-2.78	-2.7	0	0	0	-2.32	-3.31	-3.22
Other services	2.93	5.24	5.1	4.6	4.72	-0.89	-1.7	-1.65	-2.51	-2.43	-1.15	0	-2.16	-2.11	-3	-2.92

Source: Author's estimates.

Note: Pe_fob = Export price (free on board), PM = Domestic Import Price, PD = Price of locally produced Good, PC = Composite Price, R = Returns to Capital, PVA = Value Added Price.

petroleum, which becomes relatively cheaper. Domestic production of textile increases by 1.6 per cent (Table 2.2). Increase in domestic demand of 0.8 per cent of textile commodities is less than the increase in its supply — local production plus imports. The surplus is directed to world economy and volume of exports increases by 2.9 per cent equal to US$ 1 billion. Increase in textile production sends an impulse to other sectors. Cotton and energy sectors expand by 1.4 and 0.1 per cent, respectively (Table 2.2). Therefore, increase in exports can only be achieved if the government solves the problem energy.

Effects on Time Use

The structural changes in production reallocate mobile factors of production. Labour moves towards expanding sectors of textile and cotton from contracting sectors. Wage rate adjusts to bring equilibrium in labour market. On average, wage rate of unskilled labour (generally owned by poor) increase more than that of skilled labour (owned by rich). Wage of unskilled women worker increases more than that of men, whereas wage of skilled men workers increase more than that of women (Table 2.3). This indicates that elimination of quota is pro poor. Returns to capital increases in all sectors of the economy. Within industry, the largest increase can be observed in textile by 7.1 per cent (Table 2.1).

The effect on time allocation to non-market activities varies by gender and by region. The demand for labour in rural and urban households' social reproduction sector change by 2.6 and –0.6 per cent, respectively, while leisure of rural household increase by 4 per cent and leisure of urban household reduces by 0.7 per cent (Table 2.3). In urban households, relatively larger decline can be observed in the demand for unskilled women labour compared to all other types of labour in both social reproduction and leisure, who are intensively employed in textile. The results show that income effects dominate in non-market goods. Income of rural household increases the demand for non-marketed goods, while income and demand for non-marketed goods of urban household reduce. With a decline in leisure, urban women unskilled labour becomes relatively more time poor than that of unskilled men labour, while the reverse is true for urban skilled labour.

In rural area, leisure of unskilled men labour increases more than that of unskilled women and leisure of skilled women increase

Table 2.2: Trade and Output Effects (Percentage Variation over Base Year Values)

Sectors	Abolition of quotas against Pakistan's export of textile (AQT_P)					Abolition of quotas against developing countries exports of textiles (AQT_AC)					Abolition of quotas against developing countries' exports of textiles and tariff elimination on imports of textile in domestic economy (AQT_AC_ml)				
	Exports	Imports	Domestic Good	Production	Demand for Composite Good	Exports	Imports	Domestic Good	Production	Demand for Composite Good	Exports	Imports	Domestic Good	Production	Demand for Composite Good
Agriculture	-2.8	5.04	0.02	-0.03	0.15	1.24	-2.06	0.02	0.04	-0.03	1.53	-2.54	0.02	0.05	-0.05
Cotton	0	0	0	1.38	0	0	0	0	-0.65	0	0	0	0	-0.77	0
Forestry	-3.78	3.9	-2.36	-2.81	-0.81	1.76	-1.88	1.02	1.25	0.28	2.16	-2.27	1.26	1.55	0.36
Mining	-1.89	-0.11	-2	-1.98	-0.48	0.93	-0.05	0.92	0.92	0.13	1.13	-0.05	1.13	1.13	0.18
Food	-2.77	5.49	-0.42	-0.8	0.12	1.13	-2.07	0.19	0.35	-0.02	1.43	-2.6	0.24	0.44	-0.02
Textile	2.94	6.29	0.81	1.58	1.08	-1.41	-2.44	-0.38	-0.75	-0.48	-0.88	7.64	-0.88	-0.88	-0.46
Petroleum	-1.88	1.84	-0.88	-0.94	0.75	0.71	-0.82	0.26	0.29	-0.39	0.89	-1	0.34	0.37	-0.47
Other Manufacturing	-2.14	1.74	-1.39	-1.57	0.46	0.86	-0.78	0.5	0.59	-0.26	1.08	-0.95	0.64	0.75	-0.31
Construction	0	0	0	-0.47	0	1.15	-2.14	0.05	0.31	0.04	0	0	0	0.36	0
Housing	0	0	0	0	0	1.03	-2.23	-0.2	0	-0.25	0	0	0	0	0
Wholesale and retail trade	-4.01	7.53	-0.41	-0.42	-0.39	0	0	0	0.05	0	1.52	-2.77	0.08	0.08	0.07
Energy	0	0	0	0.13	0	0	0	0	-0.13	0	0	0	0	-0.14	0
Other services	-3.26	6.33	0.01	-0.18	0.17	1.15	-0.66	-0.03	-0.13	-0.03	1.34	-2.8	-0.22	-0.13	-0.28

Source: Same as for Table 2.1.

Table 2.3: Effects on Time Allocation to Market and Non-market Sectors (Percentage Variation over Base Value)

Market Activities	Abolition of quotas against Pakistan's export of textile (AQT_P)					Abolition of quotas against developing countries exports of textiles (AQT_AC)					Abolition of quotas against all developing countries exports of textiles and tariff elimination on textile imports in domestic economy (AQT_AC_ml)				
	Women Unskilled	Men Unskilled	Women Skilled	Men Skilled	Total	Women Unskilled	Men Unskilled	Women Skilled	Men Skilled	Total	Women Unskilled	Men Unskilled	Women Skilled	Men Skilled	Total
Agriculture	-0.8	-0.5	1.39	0.22	-0.01	0.14	-0.02	1.08	0.21	0.15	0.22	0.01	1.14	0.21	0.16
Cotton	0.76	1.07	2.99	1.81	1.57	-0.66	-0.82	0.27	-0.6	-0.66	-0.72	-0.92	0.19	-0.73	-0.78
Forestry	0	-3.41	0	-2.67	-2.75	0	1.09	0	1.34	1.31	0	1.41	0	1.64	1.61
Mining	-6.89	-6.61	-5.3	-5.94	-6.47	3.17	3.01	3.8	3.28	3.09	3.93	3.72	4.53	3.97	3.8
Food	-4.58	-4.29	-2.94	-3.59	-4.05	1.88	1.72	2.47	1.95	1.81	2.4	2.19	2.94	2.39	2.27
Textile	5.47	5.79	7.22	6.5	6.09	-2.81	-2.96	-2.27	-2.76	-2.85	-3.25	-3.45	-2.75	-3.27	-3.34
Petroleum	-4.35	-4.05	0	-3.32	-3.97	1.36	1.2	0	1.45	1.23	1.77	1.56	0	1.8	1.59
Other Manufacturing	-7	-6.71	-5.43	-6.07	-6.45	2.54	2.37	3.1	2.58	2.47	3.29	3.07	3.81	3.26	3.17
Construction	0	-1.03	0.31	-0.27	-0.66	0	0.32	1.01	0.57	0.44	0	0.4	1.1	0.63	0.52
Housing	0	0	0	0	0	0	0	0	0	0	0	0	0	0	0
Whole sale and retail trade	-1.14	-0.84	0.49	-0.09	-0.59	0.14	-0.02	0.67	0.23	0.07	0.25	0.04	0.73	0.26	0.12

Energy	0	0.03	1.39	0.8	0.66	0	−0.84	−0.16	−0.59	−0.64	0	−0.88	−0.2	−0.66	−0.7
Other services	−0.76	−0.46	0.79	0.21	−0.32	−0.14	−0.3	0.35	−0.08	−0.23	−0.1	−0.3	0.36	−0.11	−0.23
Non-market activities															
Rural social reproduction	2.57	2.7	3.01	2.71	2.65	0.76	0.69	0.9	0.68	0.77	0.67	0.58	0.8	0.56	0.68
Urban Social Reproduction	−0.84	−0.71	−0.35	−0.64	−0.63	−0.24	−0.3	−0.08	−0.29	−0.2	−0.21	−0.3	−0.06	−0.29	−0.18
Rural leisure	3.8	3.94	4.57	4.27	4	0.91	0.84	1.14	0.92	0.86	0.74	0.66	0.95	0.72	0.68
Urban leisure	−1.04	−0.91	−0.41	−0.7	−0.73	−0.38	−0.45	−0.19	−0.4	−0.36	−0.36	−0.45	−0.18	−0.41	−0.36
Wage rate	5.7	5.24	2.99	3.99	4.82	−2.44	−2.21	−3.3	−2.6	−2.37	−3.0	−2.71	−3.8	−3.06	−2.85

Source: Same as for Table 2.1.

more than that of skilled men labour. However, the increase in leisure may contain forced leisure because of contraction of domestic market sectors (Siddiqui 2009). Overall results show that reallocation of resources due to quota abolition increases relative time poverty among relatively poor women as leisure declines more and increases less among relatively poor households.

The Effects on Income, Consumption, Welfare, and Poverty

The increase in returns to factors of production positively affects income of both representative households — urban and rural, while elimination of quota rent reduces income of urban households. In result, nominal income of rural and urban household increases by 7 and 4.7 per cent, respectively. The Consumer Price Index (CPI) for urban households increases more than their income and real income of urban household declines, while CPI for rural household increases less than their income that lead to increase in their real income. In result, urban households' demand for goods and services reduce in real term, while that of rural households increase. In result, welfare of rural household increases by 2 per cent and welfare of urban households declines by 1.7 per cent over the base year. At the national level, positive effect of rural households dominates. However, welfare of both households deteriorates when consumption of non-marketed commodities are included (Table 2.4).

Poverty is expected to reduce if income increases more than the amount to compensate the rise in cost of living. The calculation of poverty with micro household data for more than 11,000 households show that population below poverty line increases over the base level in urban households by 0.5 per cent and reduces in rural household by 2.7 per cent over the base year. The other two measures of poverty — poverty gap and severity — also indicate decline in poverty in rural areas and increase in urban area (Table 2.4). At the national level, poverty decreases by all measures by 1.6, 2 and 2.1 per cent, respectively.

5.2. Simulation 2

In this exercise, elimination of quota on textile export from developing countries increase demand for textile exports from Pakistan by 3 per cent. The weighted averages of the change in world export price and export demand are 4.8 and 1.6 per cent, respectively, which are injected into the model.

Table 2.4: Socioeconomic Effects (Percentage Variation over the Base Year)

	Abolition of quotas against Pakistan's export of textile (AQT_P)			Abolition of quotas against developing countries exports of textiles (AQT_AC)			Abolition of quotas against all developing countries' exports of textiles and tariff elimination on textile imports in domestic economy (AQT_AC_ml)		
	Rural HH	Urban HH	Pakistan	Rural HH	Urban HH	Pakistan	Rural HH	Urban HH	Pakistan
Household income	6.99	4.66	6.29	-1.42	-2.04	-1.61	-1.95	-2.48	-2.11
Household consumption	7.15	4.87	6.47	-1.46	-2.09	-1.65	-2.06	-2.63	-2.23
CPI	5.15	6.70	5.62	-1.45	-1.09	-1.34	-1.97	-1.67	-1.88
Consumption of non-marketed goods	2.65	-0.63	1.67	0.77	-0.2	0.48	0.68	-0.18	0.42
Leisure	4	-0.73	2.58	0.86	-0.36	0.49	0.68	-0.36	0.37
EV	1.97	-1.74	0.86	0	-1.08	-0.32	-0.11	-1.07	-0.40
EVH	-0.36	-0.38	-0.37	-0.37	-0.35	-0.36	-0.37	-0.35	-0.36
Head count ratio	-2.708	0.490	-1.60	0.00	1.4	0.40	0.13	1.34	0.55
Poverty gap	-3.204	0.612	-2.04	0.02	1.5	0.46	0.16	1.55	0.58
Severity	-3.207	0.464	-2.09	0.018	1.141	0.35	0.16	1.18	0.47

Source: Same as for Table 2.1.

Price Effects

In this exercise, the shock to the economy is one-tenth of the increase in export demand in the previous exercise. The net impact of decline in world export price and loss of quota rent is negative on the domestic price of textile which reduces by 1.6 per cent, while domestic export price of textile declines by 2.3 per cent. The change in price of all other commodities is less than the change in prices of textile (Table 2.1). These changes in prices penetrate into the economy and relative domestic prices of all commodities reduce except housing — a non-trading sector. With a decline in domestic prices and no change in import prices, consumer prices also decrease (Table 2.1).

Demand and Supply Effects

With a decline in domestic prices, domestically produced good becomes relatively cheaper compared to imported counterparts. Consumers switch from imported commodities to locally produced commodities and the volume of imports of all importable commodities decreases. Despite decline in consumer price of textile goods, domestic demand for locally produced textile goods marginally decrease by 0.4 per cent as consumers switch towards relatively cheaper goods (Table 2.2). Domestic production of textile declines by 0.75 per cent. Decline in production is higher than decline in domestic demand. The exports of textile items decline in this exercise by 1.4 per cent. This indicates that elimination of quota restriction against all developing countries reduces price as export demand from Pakistan increases marginally while domestic demand reduces due to decline in real income of urban households. Reduction in textile production negatively affects cotton and energy sectors also, which contracts by 0.65 and 0.13 per cent, respectively.

Effects on Time Use

Labour demand increases in the expanding sectors and reduces in the contracting sectors. In aggregate, labour demand increases less than labour supply and therefore, wage rate adjusts downward. On average, wage rates of unskilled and skilled women workers — who are intensively employed in textile — decline more than the wage rate of men unskilled and skilled labour (Table 2.3). Returns to capital decline in majority of the sectors of the economy (Table 2.1). Within industry, the largest decline can be observed in textile by 3.4 per cent (Table 2.1).

Income-effect dominates in consumption of non-marketed goods. Demand for composite labour in non-traded and non-market sectors in rural area — social reproduction and leisure — increases by 0.8 and 0.9 per cent and decreases in urban area by 0.2 and 0.4 per cent, respectively (Table 2.4). This pattern can be observed in all types of labour used in production of non-market goods in rural and urban areas. In urban area where time poverty increases in absolute term, relative time poverty declines among women as their leisure decline less than that of men labour — skilled and unskilled. In rural area, leisure of women increases more than that of men.

The Effects on Income, Consumption, Welfare and Poverty

The real income of rural household increases as CPI decline more than their nominal income, while real income of urban household decline as CPI decline less than their real income (Table 2.4). In aggregate, expenditure of urban and rural households declines in nominal term (Table 2.4). Welfare of rural household does not change as equal change in their nominal expenditure and prices can be observed from Table 2.4. Contrarily, urban household's expenditure decline more than CPI. Welfare of urban household deteriorates by 1.1 per cent over the base year.

Population below poverty line increases over the base level in urban area by 1.4 per cent and remains at the base level in rural area. The poverty gap and severity index declines for rural households and increase for urban households (Table 2.4). At the national level, poverty increases by all measures. The results show that quota abolition against all countries does not benefit Pakistan.

5.3. Simulation 3

Since 1988, government's restructuring of tariff has reduced tariff rates as well as number of slabs. In 2002, import of textile faced tariff of 9 per cent. In this exercise, I combined abolition of quota restriction against all developing countries with elimination of tariff on imports of textile in Pakistan.

Price Effects

Elimination of tariff on imports of textile reduces import price of textile items by 8.7 per cent. This exerts downward pressure on prices in the domestic economy. In result, prices of all commodities decrease more in this exercise than in the previous exercise (Table 2.4). With the decline in import prices, consumer prices decline more than in the previous exercise. The results indicate that quota abolition combined with domestic liberalisation of textile imports has reduced demand for labour in the economy more than in the previous exercise. Returns to labour and capital decline over the base year as well as over the previous exercise (Table 2.1 and Table 2.2).

Demand and Supply Effects

The lower import price of textile items exerts upward pressure on demand for imported textile items due to substitution effect. Demand for imported textile items increases by 7.6 per cent and demand for domestic good reduces by 0.4 per cent. The production of textile items decline by 0.9 per cent over the base year and is larger than in the previous exercise. With fix import prices of other items, import response of all other sectors is negative because locally produced goods are relatively cheap. The export of textile items reduces by 0.9 per cent less than the decline in the previous exercise.

Effects on Time Use

Labour demand in textile sector declines by 3.3 per cent, which is higher than in the previous exercise. The impact quantitatively differs by type of labour. Aggregate demand for labour is lower than base year that is reflected in wage rate, which decline by 2.8 per cent. On average, wage rate of unskilled and skilled female labour declines more than wage rate of men unskilled and skilled labour (Table 2.3). A comparison across the type of labour shows that leisure of unskilled and skilled men labour decreases more than the leisure of women labour — skilled and unskilled (Table 2.3). Time poverty increases in urban households. Reduction in textile production reduces time poverty as women employment in market sectors reduces more than men employment (Table 2.3).

The Effects on Income, Consumption, Welfare and Poverty

In this exercise, income, consumption, and CPIs decline more than in previous exercise as returns to factors of production declines more in this exercise. Income effect increases in absolute term from −1.42 to −1.95 per cent for rural households and −2.04 to −2.48 per cent for urban households. CPI declines more than income for rural households and less than income for urban households that increases real income of rural households and decreases real income of urban households. Households' total expenditure declines more than prices for both representative households (Table 2.4). Therefore, domestic liberalisation deteriorates welfare of both representative households — rural and urban. Poverty increases in both households by all measures. Therefore, removal of domestic support measure to export-oriented sectors increases poverty at the national level.

5.4. Simulation 4

Currently, Pakistan is facing severe energy shortage. To curb the energy demand, the government has revised tariffs on electricity and gas several times in recent years, which has negatively affected industrial production. Textile being the largest industrial sector of Pakistan is expected to bear the largest impact. Energy has more than 4 per cent cost share in the production of textile. In this experiment, I increase tax rate on energy 3 times over the base year in presence of quota elimination against Pakistan's exports from which Pakistan benefits by all measure (see results of simulation 1). The results reveal the constraints on the output and trade due to energy deficiency.

Increase in tax on energy reduces the gains of quota elimination against Pakistan's exports. The volume of production in the most competitive and the largest supplier of exports — textile — by 0.36 per cent equal to PKR 2.8 billion. The reduction in output negatively affects employment in textile which declines by 1.4 per cent. Employment of unskilled men workers declines more than employment of skilled men workers by 1.4 and 1.3 per cent, respectively. Contrarily, it hurts more the skilled women worker than unskilled women worker, which decline by 1.8 and 1.6 per cent, respectively. However in the absolute term, loss of women employment of unskilled labour is higher. The volume of exports of textile reduces by 0.48 per cent over the base year equal to PKR 1.3 billion. There is an urgent need to increase energy supply to bridge the gap between demand and supply. However, this is one aspect which can help to achieve the government target of $ 25 billion of textile exports by the year 2014. There is a need to explore other factors that will help to make the textile sector more competitive in the world market.

5.5. Sensitivity Analysis

Except elasticities, all parameters of the model are calculated from social accounting matrix data. Therefore, sensitivity analysis is conducted with the elasticities of substitution. I rerun the experiment of

AQT_P with higher elasticity of substitution by one percentage point in all production sectors of the economy. The results show limited sensitivity to change in elasticity of substitution. The higher elasticity of substitution means a little higher gain in terms of economic variables — output, exports and wages. However, outcome variables remain the same as income and prices increase proportionately.

6. Conclusion

Pakistan benefits from quota elimination against its exports in terms of higher textile production and exports. However, energy crisis significantly reduces these benefits. Elimination of quota against all countries marginally increases export demand of textile items in presence of increased competition from other low-cost suppliers. The slight increase in export demand combined with elimination of quota rent negatively affects production and exports of textile items. Elimination of domestic support to textile enhances the negative impact of the experiment of quota elimination against all countries on output, but reduces the negative effect on exports of textile items.

Labour market effects reveal gender differentiated effects by type of households — rich and poor. Wage of unskilled labour (owned by poor) increases more than that of skilled labour (owned by rich). Wage of unskilled women workers increases more than that of unskilled men workers, while wage of skilled men workers increase more than that of women. Also, quota abolition against all countries reduces wages of women workers — skilled and unskilled — more than wages of men workers as the textile sector contracts. Elimination of domestic support to textile enhances these effects. Contraction of female intensive sector reduces women employment that results in loss of women income but reduces workload on women. Decline in leisure and increase in employment of women in the first exercise confirm the findings of Siddiqui (2009) that increase in employment of women increases workload on women as leisure reduces more than social reproduction activities.

Welfare, time poverty and income poverty indicators improve at the national level despite deterioration of the indicators for urban household in the first experiment. These indicators deteriorate in the second and third experiments though domestic liberalisation reduces negative effects of welfare and poverty incidence in urban households.

The overall results show the dire need to prepare a policy framework to boost textile as Pakistan does not benefit from quota abolition against all countries. The policy framework should take into account cotton and energy supply constraints, which are necessary to make the country competitive in a quota-free world.

A limitation of the study is the aggregation of textile into one sector which may hide many facts. A disaggregated analysis is necessary to reveal the hidden realities. In addition, quota restricted exports and unrestricted exports should be treated separately. Theses aspect can be the focus of future research.

Appendix

A2.1: Structure of the Social Accounting Matrix

Institutions	I. Households: Rural and Urban, II. Enterprises, III Government, IV. Rest of the World
Activities and commodities	**Market Sectors:** I. Agriculture: 1. Crop, 2. Cotton, 3. Forestry, II. Industry: 4. Mining, 5. Food, 6. Text, 7. Petroleum 8. Other Manufacturing, III. Services: 9. Construction, 10. Housing, 11. Whole sale and Retail Trade, 12. Energy 13. Services
	Non-Market Sectors:
	1. Households Social Reproduction Sectors (Rural and Urban) 2. Leisure (Rural and Urban)
Factors of production	I. Capital, II. Land and III. Labor — Male unskilled (below five years of education), Male skilled (5 or above), Female unskilled (below five years of education), Female skilled (five and above)

Notes

1. Major exports of textile groups include raw cotton; cotton yarn; cotton cloth; cotton combed; yarn other than cotton yarn; knitwear; bed wear; towels; tents; canvas; tarpulin; readymade garments; art, silk and synthetic textile; made up articles; and other textile material.
2. Social reproduction and household production are interchangeably used.
3. Empirical work on time allocation traces its roots to Becker, who first formulated a utility-maximizing model of Z goods that were produced by both time and market goods inputs. Later, Gronau (1977) and others extended the model by including home production and leisure.
4. National poverty line is PKR 748 per adult per month.

5. Here textile sector includes spinning, weaving, processing and knitting, garment/clothing manufactures (PSIC-32011-32290).
6. SNA = system of national accounts. The SNA defines productive activities that produce goods and services for sale and for personal consumption and are included in GDP. The extended SNA (ESNA) defines services that could be provided by others within households such as cooking, cleaning, collecting wood, fetching water, and looking after children and the elderly. These activities are defined as economic but not 'productive'. Leisure (non-SNA) is non-economic and non-productive as it cannot be delegated to someone else.
7. Martin et al. (2004) has conducted the analysis in global model - GTAP.
8. To the best of my knowledge, this type of analysis has not been conducted with latest version of GTAP, which contain Pakistan as a separate region.
9. In reality, a country faces two or multiple types of demand for their commodities — the restricted markets and unrestricted markets. For instance, EU and US markets are quota restricted and more than 50 per cent exports from Pakistan are to these markets. Rest of the 50 per cent exports of textile goes to unrestricted markets.

References

Cororaton, Caesar B., Abdul Salam, Zafar Altaf, David Orden, Reno Dewina, Nicholas Minot and Hina Nazli. 2008. 'Cotton-Textile-Apparel Sectors of Pakistan: Situations and Challenges Faced'. International Food Policy Research Institute (IFPRI) Discussion Paper 00800, Washington, D.C.: IFPRI.

Decaluwe, B., A. Patry, L. Savard and E. Thorbecke. 1999. 'Poverty Analysis within a General Equilibrium Framework'. CREFA Working Paper no. 9909. Quebec: University of Laval.

Dorosh. P., M. K. Niazi and H. Nazli. 2006. 'A Social Accounting Matrix for Pakistan, 2001–02: Methodology and Results'. PIDE Working Paper no. 9. Islamabad: Pakistan institute of Development Economics.

Fofana. I, J. Cockburn and B. Decaluwe. 2005. 'A Gender-aware Macroeconomic Model for Evaluating Impacts of Policies on Poverty Reduction in Africa: The Case for South Africa, Part II: Construction of the Model and Policy Simulation Results'. African Centre for Gender and Development (ACGD). Washington, D.C.: United Nations.

Fontana, M. 2001. 'Modelling the Effects of Trade on Women: A Closer Look at Bangladesh', IDS Working Paper no 139, Institute of Development Studies. Brighton: University of Sussex.

Fontana, M. and A. Wood. 2000. 'Modelling the Effects of the Trade on Women, At Work and At Home', *World Development*, (28) 7: 1173–90.

Foster, James, Joel Greer and Erik Thorbecke. 1984. 'A Class of Decomposable Poverty Measures', *Econometrica*, 52 (3): 761–66.

Gronau, R 1977. 'Leisure Home Production and Work — Theory of the Allocation of Time', *Journal of Political Economy*, 85 (6): 1099–123.

Martin, Will, Vlad Manole and Dominique Van Der Mensbrugghe. 2004. 'Dealing With Diversity: Analysing the consequences of the Textile quota Abolition'. Paper presented at the 7th Annual GTAP Conference, Washington, DC.

Government of Pakistan. 2002a. *Labor Force Survey (LFS)*. Islamabad: Federal Bureau of Statistics.

———. 2002b. *Pakistan Integrated Household Survey (PIHS.)* Islamabad: Federal Bureau of Statistics.

———. 2009a. *Pakistan Economic Survey 2008–9*. Islamabad: Planning Commission.

———. 2009b. *Time Use Survey 2006–7*. Islamabad: Federal Bureau of Statistics.

Siddiqui, Rehana, Shehnaz Hameed, Rizwana Siddiqui, Naeem Akhtar and Ghulam Yasin Soomro. 2006. *Gender and Empowerment: Evidence from Pakistan*. Islamabad: Pakistan Institute of Development Economics.

Siddiqui, Rizwana. 2005. 'Modelling Gender Dimensions of the Impact of Economic Reforms on Time Allocation among Market Work, Household Work, and Leisure', *Pakistan Development Review*, 44 (4): 615–42.

———. 2007. 'Modelling Gender Dimensions of the Impact of Economic Reforms', MPIA Working Paper no. 2007–13, Poverty and Economic Policy, IDRC. Montreal: University of Laval.

———. 2008. 'Welfare and Poverty Implications of Global Rice and Agricultural Trade Liberalisation for Pakistan', in M. A. Razzaque and Edwin Laurent (eds), *Global Rice and Agricultural Trade Liberalisation: Poverty and Welfare Implications for South Asia*, pp. 131–69. New Delhi: Commonwealth Secretariat, London, United Kingdom and Academic Foundation.

Siddiqui, Rizwana. 2009. 'Modeling Gender Effects of Pakistan's Trade Liberalisation', *Feminist Economics,* 15 (3): 287–321.

Siddiqui, Rizwana and Kemal Abdur-Razzaque. 2006. 'Remittances, Trade Liberalization, and Poverty in Pakistan: The Role of Excluded Variables in Poverty Change Analysis', *The Pakistan Development Review*, 45(3): 383–415.

Social Policy and Development Centre (SPDC). 2005. 'The Elimination of Textile, Quotas and Pakistan — EU Trade, European Union Project', SPDC Project No. ASIE/2005/115-591. http://www.spdc-pak.com/pubs/pubdisp.asp?id=rr66b (accessed 19 November 2009).

3

Quantitative Assessment of India–EU FTA: A CGE Analysis

Shahid Ahmed

Indian suppliers can substantially increase their exports to the European Union (EU) in response to any meaningful trade concessions. On the other side, EU suppliers may also gain significant market access to the Indian market as India has high tariff protection on a range of products. However, the overall impact of proposed India–EU Free Trade Agreement (FTA) will depend on the relative strength of the trade creation and trade diversion. Turning to its potential implications for developing countries, since the EU has been one of the principal export destinations for most of the other low income countries, where many of these countries also receive significant trade preferences, extension of similar preferences to India might result in their loss of competitiveness.

India is the fourth largest economy by Purchasing Power Parity (PPP) while the economy of the EU generates a Gross Domestic Product (GDP) based on PPP of over $16,523.78 billion, making it the largest economy in the world. Also, EU is the largest exporter in the world and as of 2008 the largest importer of goods and services. Both India and EU share a strong and rapidly growing trade and economic relationship. Further strengthening and deepening this relationship, India and the EU have launched negotiations for a Bilateral Trade and Investment Agreement.

The High Level Trade Group recommended that under any possible future FTA, the ambition shall be to achieve elimination of duties on 90 per cent of tariff lines and trade volume within 7 years of the entry into force of the agreement. There can be both gainers and losers as a result of India–EU FTA. Hence, it is important to undertake a comprehensive assessment of the potential implications of India–EU FTA for India, EU and other low-income developing countries in Asia and Africa. This chapter adds in identifying gainers and losers as a result of tariff liberal-isation using a computable general equilibrium model called the GTAP model.

The remainder of this chapter is structured as follows. Section 2 reviews bilateral trade relations between India and EU. Section 3 discusses selected theoretical and empirical literature. Section 4 provides research methodology and databases. Section 5 presents various simulation scenarios. Section 6 reports and discusses GTAP results. Section 7 discusses the systematic sensitivity analysis of GTAP results. Section 8 presents results of SMART model while section 9 provides concluding remarks.

2. Bilateral Trade Relations

India's exports to EU-27 increased from US$ 10 billion in 2001 to US$ 38 billion in 2008, registering a growth of 40 per cent per annum. On the other hand, EU's exports to India increased from US$ 9 billion in 2001 to US$ 42 billion in 2008, recording a growth of 51 per cent per annum. As revealed, EU provides a substantial market for India's exports and has always been an important supplier for India's imports, though the balance of trade has always been in EU's favour. The EU-27 accounts for around one-fifth of India's total trade (21.5 per cent in 2008) whereas India contributes around 0.81 per cent of the total EU-27 trade.

On the basis of GTAP commodity classification, India's top 10 exports to the EU in 2008 are shown in Figure 3.1. These were mainly chemical, rubber, plastic products (14 per cent); petroleum and coal products (12 per cent); wearing apparel (11.5 per cent); textiles (9.5 per cent); machinery and equipment (8 per cent); manufactures (7.5 per cent); ferrous metals (6.1 per cent); leather products (5.4 per cent), motor vehicles and parts (5.2 per cent); and metal products (3.6 per cent). These products account for 83 per cent of India's exports to EU. EU's top 10 exports to India in 2008 are shown in Figure 3.2. These consisted mainly of machinery and equipment (34.4 per cent); minerals (15.9 per cent); chemical, rubber, plastic products (11 per cent); transport equipment (7 per cent); ferrous metals (5.9 per cent); metals (5.9 per cent); electronic equipment (5.5 per cent); motor vehicles and parts (3.8 per cent); paper products and publishing (2.7 per cent); and metal products (2 per cent). These products account for 94 per cent of EU's exports to India.

Figure 3.1: Percentage of India's Export to EU in 2008

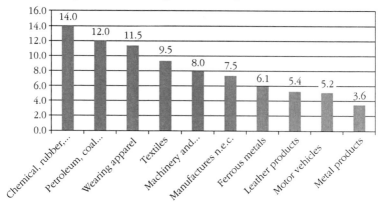

Source: UNCOMTRADE (2009).
Note: GTAP Commodity Classification.

Figure 3.2: Percentage of EU's Export to India in 2008

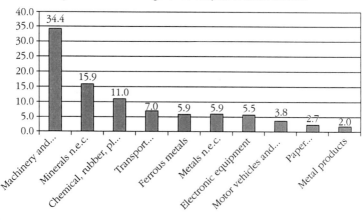

Source: UNCOMTRADE (2009).
Note: GTAP Commodity Classification.

Despite substantial increase in trade between India and EU, it can be seen that the trade Intensity for India and EU has been below optimum. The value of trade between the two countries indicates that the extent of trade between the economies is lower than expected on the basis of their importance in world trade. Trade intensity index[1] has been estimated to capture the intensity of trade and presented in Table 3.1.

Table 3.1: Trade Intensity Index

Year	Trade Intensity Index of India with EU-15	Trade Intensity Index of India with EU-27	Trade Intensity Index of India with EU-25	Trade Intensity Index of EU-25 with India	India's Export Intensity Index with EU-25	India's Import Intensity Index with EU-25	EU-25's Export Intensity Index with India	EU-25's Import Intensity Index with India
1965	0.602	0.647	0.634	0.686	0.514	0.589	0.282	0.012
1970	0.446	0.511	0.488	0.636	0.439	0.449	0.262	0.007
1975	0.526	0.605	0.577	0.738	0.502	0.690	0.355	0.007
1980	0.565	0.594	0.576	0.835	0.501	0.445	0.293	0.007
1985	0.496	0.533	0.506	0.917	0.456	0.665	0.409	0.008
1990	0.486	0.501	0.497	0.961	0.454	0.479	0.379	0.008
1995	0.730	0.707	0.709	0.961	0.696	0.652	0.469	0.012
2000	0.684	0.653	0.656	0.752	0.651	0.547	0.408	0.013
2005	0.627	0.588	0.593	0.633	0.543	0.461	0.325	0.016
2006	0.604	0.558	0.564	0.590	0.576	0.437	0.300	0.017
2007	0.609	0.563	0.567	0.596	0.541	0.402	0.319	0.018
2008	0.610	0.561	0.566	0.570	0.543	0.375	0.249	0.019

Source: Author's Calculations based on UNCOMTRADE (2009).

Table 3.1 reveals that Trade Intensity Index (TII) of India with EU-15 and 25 is less than 1 and has remained so since 1965. Similarly, TII of EU-25 with India is also less than 1. TII indicates a bilateral trade flow that is smaller than expected, given the partner country's importance in world trade. India's export intensity and import intensity with EU is less than 1 and Import Intensity Index (III) is less than Export Intensity Index (EII). India's III has declined over a period of time. EU-25's EII and III with India are also less than one which implies exports and imports are below the expected level. It implies that India's exports and imports are not intense with EU countries compared with its trading pattern with rest of the world. On the basis of above, we can conclude that neither the extent of trade between the economies is large nor there has been a substantial increase in trade between India and EU economies.

3. Review of Literature

Economic theory suggests that the most desirable trading bloc is one that is the most trade-creating, and that bloc is global which is expected to be materialised if free, transparent and non-distorting trade flows of goods and services take place under WTO rule-based regime. Such a bloc comprises countries with the most diverse range of comparative advantage, which affords the greatest scope for trade creation and the least scope for trade diversion. The earliest work on the theory of regional integration was presented by Viner (1950). Subsequently Meade (1955), Kemp and Wan (1976), Baldwin (1995), Ethier (1998), Lazer (1999) and Albertin (2008) made substantial improvements in the theory of regional integration.

When it comes to empirical analysis of trade, researches have different opinion regarding the effects of RTAs and PTAs. In particular, ex-post analysis[2] of trade based on gravity equations has been unable to convincingly disentangle the effects of regional trade agreements from other effects occurring simultaneously (e.g., Brada 1994; Krueger 1999). The recent literature in examining RTA's trade impacts shows that different studies come out with different trade effects for the same RTAs. This is due to the use of different estimation methods, different databases and time periods to measure these trade effects. Hence, it is not possible to arrive at firm conclusions about potential impact of preferential trading agreements. As a result, some researchers has opted for ex ante analysis[3] of preferential trading agreements using global general equilibrium model like the GTAP models to explain the welfare and other macro effects. Computable general equilibrium (CGE) models are simulations that combine the abstract general equilibrium structure formalised by Arrow and Debreu with realistic economic data to solve numerically for the levels of supply, demand and price that support equilibrium across a specified set of markets. CGE models are a standard tool of empirical analysis, and are widely used to analyse the aggregate welfare and distributional impacts of policies whose effects may be transmitted through multiple markets, or contain menus of different tax, subsidy, quota or transfer instruments. Examples of their use may be found in areas as diverse as fiscal reform and development planning (e.g., Perry et al. 2001), international trade (e.g., Harrison et al. 1997), and increasingly, environmental regulation (e.g., Goulder 2002).

In the existing literature, there are few empirical studies so far on the proposed EU–India FTA. Action Aid (2008) suggests that there is little scope for trade creation, and indicates more likelihood of trade diversion. Meincke (2008) indicates that far-reaching tariff elimination and liberalisation of government procurement can have negative effects on the most vulnerable and marginalised groups in Indian society and hamper rather than foster human development. However, Winters et al. (2009) conclude that the dissimilarities of composition of export structures between the partners' exports to each other and excluded countries' exports to them suggests that the scope for negative effects arising from the EU–India agreement is relatively limited.

4. Methodology and Databases

The present study has applied a computable general equilibrium model called the GTAP model for assessing welfare and other macro effects of India–EU FTA. Revenue effect has been estimated using SMART model of World Bank/UNCTAD. The theory of the GTAP model is documented in Hertel (1997). The brief summary of theoretical framework is given here.

4.1. Theoretical Framework of the GTAP Model

GTAP model is a comparative static model, and is based on neo-classical theories. All markets are assumed to be perfectly competitive. The price received by the producer is the same as the producer's marginal cost. By imposing taxes and subsidies on commodities and primary factors, regional government can drive wedges between prices paid by purchasers and prices received by producers. These policy interventions are modelled as ad valorem taxes, tariffs and subsidies, or quantitative restrictions. International trade is linked through Armington substitution among goods differentiated by country of origin (Armington 1969).

The production technology in GTAP is represented by a set of nested Constant Elasticity of Substitution (CES) and Leontief functions. At the first level, intermediate input bundles and primary-factor bundles are used in fixed proportions according to a Leontief function. At the second level, intermediate input bundles are formed as combinations of imported bundles and domestic goods, and primary-factor bundles are obtained according to a CES form. At the third level, imported bundles are formed as CES composites of imported goods with the same name from each region.

Each region in GTAP has a single representative household that collects all the regional income. This income is exhausted through constant share to private household consumption, government expenditures and national savings. The private household buys bundles of commodities to maximise utility, subject to its expenditure constraint. The constrained optimising behaviour of the private household is represented by Constant Difference Elasticity demand system. The bundles are CES combinations of domestic goods and import bundles, with the import bundles being CES aggregations of imports from each region.

The share of aggregate government expenditure in each region's income is held fixed. Government expenditure is allocated across commodities by a Cobb-Douglas distribution. The allocation of total expenditure on each good to domestically produced and imported versions is based on the same nesting scheme used to allocate total household expenditure on each good. Investment in each region is financed from a global pool of savings. Each region contributes a fixed proportion of its income to the savings pool. Two alternative ways can be used to allocate the savings pool. The first way is where each region's share increases by the proportion in which aggregate pool increases. The second way is where the investment allocation is done according to the relative rates of return. Regions which experience increases in their rate of return relative to the global average will receive increased shares of the investment budget, whereas regions experiencing reductions in their rate of return relative to the global average will receive reduced shares.

In each region, there are five types of factors of production. First, the model recognises two types of labour (skilled and unskilled) and a single, homogenous capital good. Then there is land and other natural resources that also form part of the set of the factors of production. In the typical closure of the model, there is clear distinction between those factors that are perfectly mobile and those that are sluggish to adjust. In the case of the mobile factors, they earn the same market return regardless of the use location. As for the sluggish factors, returns in equilibrium may be different across sectors.

The model relies on country and regional input–output tables for each region and bilateral trade data derived from United Nations trade statistics. This is supplemented with individual country's global trade information and aggregate bilateral trade statistics such as from the International Monetary Fund (IMF), Food and Agriculture Organisation (FAO) and World Bank. Another important sub-component of the GTAP database is the protection data which has been taken from the MacMap database at the 6-digit Harmonised Systems (HS6) level. These are then aggregated to GTAP concordance using trade weights compiled from the COMTRADE database.

4.2. The GTAP Database and the Study Aggregation

In the present study, GTAP database version 7, covering 113 countries/regions and 57 sectors, with a base year of 2004, have been used (Narayanan and Walmsley 2008). All the trade flows for the 57 commodity categories are distinguished by their countries/regions of origin and destination, and on the basis of agents such as intermediate demand, final demand by private households, government and investment. The tariff data is mainly in the form of applied ad valorem rates. In the present analysis, 113 countries/regions are aggregated into five countries/regions and 57 commodities are aggregated into 14 commodity groups. Details of sectoral and regional aggregation are presented in Appendix.

4.3. The Revenue Effects using SMART Model

Revenue effects have been estimated using UNCTAD/World Bank SMART model (Jammes and Olarreaga 2005). The tariff revenue is given as the product of the tax rate (tariff rate in this case) and the tax base (the value of imports). Thus, before the change in the ad valorem incidence of the trade barriers, the revenue is given for country j from country k of commodity g as:

$$R_0 = \sum_g \sum_k t^0_{gjk} \, p_{gjk} \, m_{gjk}$$

After the change in the tariff rate, the new revenue collection will be given by:

$$R_1 = \sum_g \sum_k t^1_{gjk} \, p_{gjk} \, m_{gjk}$$

The revenue loss as a result of the implementation of RTAs/FTAs would then be the net between R_1 and R_0 which is the same as:

$$R_L = \sum_g \sum_k \Delta^t_{gjk} \, p_{gjk} \, m_{gjk}$$

5. Simulation Scenarios

To examine potential economic effects as a result of tariff removal by India and EU on imports from each other, four hypothetical scenarios are simulated:

- Scenario I consider 50 per cent tariff cut by India on imports from EU and 100 per cent tariff cut by EU on imports from India. In this scenario, capital has been treated as sluggish factor for short-run simulations.[4]
- Scenario II consider 50 per cent tariff cut by India on imports from EU and 100 per cent tariff cut by EU on imports from India. In this scenario, capital has been treated as mobile factor to capture long run effects.
- Scenario III consider 100 per cent tariff cut by India and EU on imports from each other. In this scenario, capital has been treated as sluggish factor for short-run simulations.
- Scenario IV consider 100 per cent tariff cut by India and EU on imports from each other. For long-run effects, capital has been treated as mobile factor.

These simulations are undertaken on the basis of modified standard closures for India. In India, there is typically an excess supply of unskilled labour, which can be drawn on by industries in the event of increased production. An assumption of full employment is inappropriate for countries like India. Hence, real wage rate has been fixed exogenously and the supply of labour is endogenised. This allowed us to take the effect on unemployment in India. However, full employment for EU is assumed as per the standard assumption of GTAP. The outcomes of the simulations are reported in terms of its effect on prices, welfare, output, imports, exports and employment.

6. GTAP Model Simulation Results

The results for welfare effects are reported in Table 3.2. In GTAP, welfare effects are measured using the equivalent variations (EV).[5] In scenario I, GTAP results reveal that welfare gains for India and EU are US$ 2704.6 million and US$ 1124.6 million respectively and net global welfare increases by US$ 2169 million. In India, employment for unskilled labour will be increasing by US$ 909.8 million. Terms

Table 3.2: Welfare and its Components (US$ Millions)

Country Groups	Allocative Efficiency Effects	Unskilled Employment Effects	Change in Terms of Trade	Change in Capital Stock	Total
Scenario I					
INDIA	301.8	909.8	1298.5	194.5	2704.6
EU_27	699.2	0	472.2	−46.8	1124.6
ODCs	8.5	0	223.4	−77.6	154.3
EBA	−54	0	−163.4	−7.5	−224.9
Rest of world	316.9	0	−1842.3	−64.3	−1589.7
Total	**1272.4**	**909.8**	**−11.5**	**−1.7**	**2169**
Scenario II					
INDIA	224.5	1138.8	1143.9	172.8	2680.1
EU_27	1058.5	0	174.8	−45.3	1188.1
ODCs	−49	0	−197.5	−116	−362.4
EBA	−44.4	0	−94.1	−9.1	−147.5
Rest of world	308	0	−1035.8	−3.7	−731.5
Total	**1497.7**	**1138.8**	**−8.6**	**−1.3**	**2626.6**
Scenario III					
INDIA	−612.7	2066.9	482.1	1.8	1938.2
EU_27	1283.2	0	2264.2	16.3	3563.6
ODCs	−15.3	0	126.7	−58.2	53.3
EBA	−47.5	0	−175	−13.9	−236.4
Rest of world	900.5	0	−2691.7	54.5	−1736.7
Total	**1508.2**	**2066.9**	**6.3**	**0.5**	**3581.9**

(Table 3.2 Continued)

(Table 3.2 Continued)

Country Groups	Allocative Efficiency Effects	Unskilled Employment Effects	Change in Terms of Trade	Change in Capital Stock	Total
		Scenario IV			
INDIA	−566.1	2299.6	347	−12.8	2067.7
EU_27	1506.7	0	1935.5	15	3457.1
ODCs	−83.4	0	−331	−109.5	−523.9
EBA	−37.8	0	−100	−16.6	−154.4
Rest of world	848	0	−1855.6	124.1	−883.5
Total	**1667.4**	**2299.6**	**−4.1**	**0.1**	**3962.9**

of trade improve significantly for both India and EU. In scenario II, welfare effect is similar in direction except Other Developed Countries (ODCs). However, India gains more in terms of employment while EU gains more in terms of allocative efficiency compared to scenario I. In scenario III, welfare gains for India and EU are US $ 1938.2 million and US $ 3563.6 million respectively. For scenario 4, broadly results remain invariant except ODCs which may be affected negatively.

From the discussion, it is explicit that welfare gains for India and EU are positive in both partial and full liberalisation scenarios. The decomposition of the welfare suggests that India's gain from the FTA is primarily driven by terms of trade and employment for unskilled labour, whereas for the EU's gain is mainly due to the rise in allocative efficiency and terms of trade. India would incur loss in allocative efficiency because of the loss in tariff revenue. India's terms of trade gain is because of rise in the prices of her export items relative to the prices of imports. However EU, because of elimination of tariff protection on many of her inefficient production process, would experience large gains in allocative efficiency as resources will divert from the inefficient sectors to the more efficient sectors. The EBA countries in Asia and Africa under consideration would suffer from losses in allocative efficiency and terms of trade. However, negative terms of trade shocks are the dominant factor behind welfare loss. Capital stock effect appears mixed for India and EU.

To identify broad categories of gaining and losing sectors, sectoral output effects are reported in Table 3.3. In India, the result of GTAP model reveal that aggregate output is expected to be increased by 0.249, 0.200, 0.585 and 0.593 in percentage terms in scenario I, II, III and IV respectively. Sectoral output effects are mixed.

Table 3.3: Percentage Change in Output

Commodity Groups	Scenario I		Scenario II		Scenario III		Scenario IV	
	INDIA	EU_27	INDIA	EU_27	INDIA	EU_27	INDIA	EU_27
Grains crops	0.32	-0.2	0.66	-0.34	0.38	-0.23	0.7	-0.38
Vegetables and fruits	-0.33	0.07	-0.14	0.07	-0.35	0.08	-0.19	0.08
Meat and livestocks	4.45	-0.48	5.85	-0.69	4.57	-0.5	5.95	-0.72
Fishing	0.06	0	0.17	-0.01	0.02	0	0.04	-0.01
Extraction	-0.35	0.04	-1.92	0.42	-0.42	0.13	-2.67	1.09
Dairy milk	0.13	0	0.29	-0.02	-0.2	0.01	-0.14	-0.01
Beverages and tobacco	-0.45	0.03	-0.46	0.03	-1.63	0.1	-1.83	0.11
Processed food	-0.62	0.01	-0.54	-0.01	-0.65	0.03	-0.72	0.01
Texiles	2.02	-0.34	3.62	-0.53	2.92	-0.4	4.55	-0.61
Wearing apparel	11.4	-0.25	19.45	-0.41	13.84	-0.32	22.63	-0.51
Leather	0.02	-0.01	2.06	-0.08	0.79	-0.06	3.5	-0.18
Light manufacturing	-1.08	0.03	-1.58	0.04	-0.48	0.02	-0.87	0.01
Heavy manufacturing	-0.76	0.05	-1.51	0.08	-0.37	0.06	-0.92	0.1
Services	0.11	0	0.13	0	0.35	0	0.4	0
CGDS	1.62	-0.01	1.27	-0.01	2.47	0.02	2.3	-0.01
Total	**0.249**	**-0.001**	**0.200**	**0.001**	**0.585**	**0.002**	**0.593**	**0.000**

India's gains are concentrated in textile, meat and livestocks and wearing apparel. In case of EU, aggregate output broadly remains invariant with an increase in output of light manufacturing, heavy manufacturing, processed food, beverages and tobacco, extraction, and vegetable and fruits. In case of scenario II, III and IV, the direction of effect broadly remains invariant with greater intensity of effects in either direction. Intensity of sectoral effects on either direction for India is higher.

Sectoral employment effects are reported in Table 3.4. The employment of unskilled labour in India will increase by 0.471, 0.59, 1.07 and 1.19 in percentage terms in scenario I, II, III and IV respectively, with an increase in grain crops, textile, meat and livestocks and wearing apparel sector. In case of EU, labour is fully employed by assumption. However, sectoral redistribution of unskilled labour indicate an increase in labour absorption in light and heavy manufacturing sectors while unskilled labour may lose their jobs in textile, meat products and wearing apparel sectors. Broadly the direction of effects remains invariant; however, intensity of effect in either direction varies. The present study also indicates that employment gains are larger in the full liberalisation (scenario III and IV) than in the partial liberalisation (scenario I and II).

Table 3.5 provides percentage change in global imports. The study reveals an increase in India's global imports by 3.73, 3.80, 6.80 and 7.06 in percentage terms in scenario I, II, III and IV respectively. In EU, GTAP model results indicate an increase in EU's global imports by 0.11, 0.12, 0.26 and 0.25 per cent in scenario I, II, III and IV respectively. In Table 3.6, global exports gains are reported. The study reveal an increase in India's global exports by 1.75, 2.38, 6.43 and 7.04 per cent in scenario I, II, III and IV respectively. The results also indicate an increase in EU's global exports by 0.11, 0.12, 0.20 and 0.21 per cent in scenario I, II, III and IV respectively. Low percentage change for EU and higher percentage change for India merely reflect low base value for India compared to EU.

Table 3.7 reports change in bilateral exports. The results of scenario I indicate an increase in EU's exports of various commodity groups to Indian market in the range of 3.12–119.32 per cent, with an aggregate increase by 39.12 per cent. While India's exports of various commodity groups to EU's market increases in the range of 2.29–1887.22 per cent, with an aggregate increase by 17.52 per cent. For the long run scenario II, the results indicate similar direction of

Table 3.4: Percentage Change in Employment

Commodity Groups	Scenario I		Scenario II		Scenario III		Scenario IV	
	INDIA	EU_27	INDIA	EU_27	INDIA	EU_27	INDIA	EU_27
Grains crops	1.06	-0.29	1.28	-0.39	1.20	-0.34	1.39	-0.43
Vegetables and fruits	0.15	0.06	0.38	0.05	0.17	0.07	0.38	0.05
Meat and livestock	8.12	-0.75	7.84	-0.75	8.41	-0.78	8.09	-0.78
Fishing	0.2	-0.01	0.23	-0.01	0.08	-0.01	0.13	-0.01
Extraction	-1.05	0.14	-2.42	0.57	-1.26	0.51	-3.28	1.48
Dairy milk	0.31	0	0.30	-0.02	-0.32	0.03	0.27	0.00
Beverages and tobacco	-1.13	0.07	-0.45	0.03	-4.08	0.24	-1.39	0.12
Processed food	-1.32	0.02	-0.53	-0.01	-1.27	0.06	-0.29	0.01
Texiles	2.71	-0.5	3.64	-0.53	4.01	-0.60	4.85	-0.60
Wearing apparel	15.3	-0.41	19.47	-0.41	18.74	-0.51	22.96	-0.50
Leather	0.08	-0.02	2.08	-0.08	1.96	-0.09	4.00	-0.17
Light manufacturing	-2.16	0.05	-1.56	0.04	-0.86	0.03	-0.43	0.02
Heavy manufacturing	-3.07	0.08	-1.50	0.09	-1.38	0.10	-0.32	0.11
Services	0.31	0.01	0.17	0.01	1.06	0.01	0.99	0.01
CGDS	2.8	-0.03	1.35	-0.01	4.45	0.02	2.78	-0.01
Total	**0.471**	**0.000**	**0.59**	**0.00**	**1.07**	**0.00**	**1.19**	**0.00**

Table 3.5: Percentage Change in Imports

Commodity Groups	Scenario I		Scenario II		Scenario III		Scenario IV	
	INDIA	EU_27	INDIA	EU_27	INDIA	EU_27	INDIA	EU_27
Grains crops	15.52	0.43	14.13	0.59	17.76	0.54	16.62	0.71
Vegetables and fruits	8.21	−0.03	7.93	−0.05	9.02	0.02	8.99	0
Meat and livestock	23.11	1.38	16.72	1.6	25.76	1.47	19.59	1.68
Fishing	4.63	0	3.87	−0.02	4.56	0.04	4.48	0.02
Extraction	0.42	0.82	0.42	0.75	2.59	2.07	3.1	1.86
Dairy milk	59.8	0.07	56.36	0.07	163.99	0.11	161.94	0.11
Beverages and tobacco	8.16	0.01	8.18	0.01	23.58	0.04	24.54	0.04
Processed food	5.59	0.04	5.4	0.04	6.86	0.1	7.11	0.1
Textiles	11.71	0.32	10.73	0.33	15.11	0.42	14.3	0.42
Wearing apparel	18.47	0.64	14.2	0.83	30.16	0.8	25.28	1.01
Leather	16.17	0.13	15.31	0.16	28.19	0.24	26.98	0.29
Light manufacturing	8.03	0.02	8.26	0.03	14.62	0.08	14.91	0.08
Heavy manufacturing	4.14	0.05	4.58	0.05	8.16	0.13	8.55	0.13
Services	3.15	−0.02	2.61	−0.01	2.58	0.05	2.26	0.06
Total	**3.733**	**0.115**	**3.803**	**0.123**	**6.810**	**0.261**	**7.068**	**0.257**

Table 3.6: Percentage Change in Exports

Commodity Groups	Scenario I		Scenario II		Scenario III		Scenario IV	
	INDIA	*EU_27*	*INDIA*	*EU_27*	*INDIA*	*EU_27*	*INDIA*	*EU_27*
Grain Crops	4.36	-0.18	8	-0.57	6.69	-0.23	10.01	-0.64
Vegetables and fruits	-10.26	0.2	-9.63	0.21	-8.93	0.28	-8.66	0.3
Meat and Livestock	211.14	-1.68	254.08	-2.36	219.07	-1.79	261.1	-2.49
Fishing	-3.58	-0.01	-2.18	-0.01	-1.25	-0.04	-1.13	-0.05
Extraction	7.35	4.24	4.19	5.05	20.39	11.18	15.05	13.22
Dairy milk	19.02	0.03	24.45	-0.02	25.51	0.07	27.37	0.02
Beverages and tobacco	2.31	0.09	2.24	0.1	5.7	0.36	3.8	0.37
Processed food	-2.32	0.1	-1.9	0.04	-0.03	0.21	-0.57	0.16
Textiles	7.2	-0.31	10.66	-0.62	11.24	-0.34	14.58	-0.67
Wearing apparel	12.86	-0.48	22.47	-0.86	16.16	-0.68	26.64	-1.13
Leather	2.29	0.08	5.44	-0.03	5.51	0.04	9.7	-0.16
Light Manufacturing	-2.35	0.09	-3.52	0.1	2.38	0.08	1.34	0.07
Heavy Manufacturing	0.82	0.13	-1.41	0.2	7.85	0.23	6.06	0.29
Services	-5.53	0.04	-4.6	0.02	-4.06	-0.08	-3.43	-0.1
Total	**1.756**	**0.106**	**2.378**	**0.117**	**6.432**	**0.196**	**7.044**	**0.212**

Table 3.7: Percentage Change in Bilateral Exports

Commodity Groups	Scenario I		Scenario II		Scenario III		Scenario IV	
	EU'S Exports to India	India's Exports to EU_27	EU'S Exports to India	India's Exports to EU_27	EU'S Exports to India	India's Exports to EU_27	EU'S Exports to India	India's Exports to EU_27
Grains crops	96.32	108.95	92.91	117	249.75	114.08	244.49	121.52
Vegetables and fruits	95.95	−9.13	95.4	−8.43	297.14	−7.53	297.19	−7.25
Meat and livestock	60.83	1887.22	51.23	2153.7	110.56	1937.12	98.61	2198.03
Fishing	34.62	2.41	33.71	3.91	77.79	5.04	77.76	5.14
Extraction	80.89	10.48	81.9	6.88	205.56	26.9	210.79	20.55
Dairy milk	113.07	215.09	108.43	230.68	310.93	234.11	307.69	239.62
Beverages and tobacco	105.11	47.38	105.16	47.27	451.18	52.6	455.54	49.73
Processed food	119.32	20.94	118.69	21.51	415.98	23.98	416.76	23.35
Textiles	78.45	45.95	76.44	50.78	191.37	51.67	188.63	56.32
Wearing apparel	61.09	50.44	55.11	63.24	131.88	54.97	122.91	68.97
Leather	59.74	12.91	58.36	16.39	132.36	16.54	130.20	21.18
Light manufacturing	45.78	2.29	46.07	1.08	104.84	7.48	105.30	6.42
Heavy manufacturing	47.85	4.11	48.6	1.75	113.49	11.77	114.41	9.83
Services	3.12	−6.32	2.57	−5.25	2.42	−4.58	2.08	−3.85
Total	**39.12**	**17.52**	**39.36**	**19.99**	**93.98**	**22.21**	**95.13**	**24.69**

effect as reported in scenario I. For scenario III, the results indicate an increase in EU's bilateral exports of various commodity groups to Indian market in the range of 2.42–451.18 per cent, with an aggregate increase by 93.98 per cent. In case of India's exports to EU, the results indicate an increase in bilateral exports in the range of 5.04–1937.12 per cent, with an aggregate increase by 22.21 per cent. For the long run scenario IV, broadly results are similar to the results of scenario III. However, intensity varies in the short and long run.

7. Systematic Sensitivity Analysis

Results from simulation models are sometimes highly dependent on parameter values such as substitution elasticities. In GTAP, the values of key economic parameters in the disaggregated database are derived from a survey of econometric work. Such estimates are most appropriately viewed as random. To address this issues, we conduct formal Systematic Sensitivity Analysis[6] (SSA) using the multivariate order three Gaussian Quadrature (GQ) procedure (Arndt 1996). This analysis is an attempt to show how uncertain we are about modelling results given that there is some uncertainty over model inputs. It is a way of testing the robustness of the model results to these inputs.

While undertaking SSA, we kept the default relation in the Armington structure, ESUBM=2ESUBD. The 95 per cent confidence intervals (CI) are constructed using Chebysshev's Inequality $(\hat{\mu}_{EV} - 4.5\,\hat{\sigma}_{EV}, \hat{\mu}_{EV} + 4.5\hat{\sigma}_{EV})$. This method of determining CI does not require any assumptions about the distribution of Equivalent Variations (EV). However, the CI computed in this way is wider than if we knew its distribution. They should thus be treated as conservative estimates. The mean and standard deviation columns are obtained via SSA for scenario IV only and reported in Table 3.8.

The SSA results for (+/–) 50 per cent shock around the default value of ESUBD indicate that welfare gains for EU will remain positive in prospective India–EU FTA and lies within 95 per cent confidence interval. The SSA results for India indicate both possibilities, negative and positive, with greater chance of having positive welfare gains. The SSA results for (+/–50 per cent) shock around the default value of ESUBVA indicates positive welfare gains for both partners and lies within 95 per cent confidence interval. The SSA results for (+/–) 50 per cent shock around the default value of ESUBD and ESUBVA (vary independently) reveal that welfare gains for EU will remain

Table 3.8: Systematic Sensitivity Analysis (Welfare Changes in US$ Million)

Country Groups	ESUBD (+/-50% shock)					ESUBVA (+/-50% shock)				
	Default	Mean	SD	95% CI		Default	Mean	SD	95% CI	
INDIA	1953.05	1969.43	504.81	-302.215	4241.075	1953.05	1939.15	290.64	631.27	3247.03
EU_27	3457.1	3502.99	387.33	1760.005	5245.975	3457.1	3459.57	53.85	3217.245	3701.895
ODCs	-522.15	-526.38	89.94	-931.11	-121.65	-522.15	-518.82	24.83	-630.555	-407.085
EBA	-154.43	-158.09	19.63	-246.425	-69.755	-154.43	-155.12	3.18	-169.43	-140.81
Rest of World	-887.59	-887.05	244.52	-1987.39	213.29	-887.59	-895.07	15	-962.57	-827.57

EV	ESUBD and ESUBVA-vary independently (+/-50% shock)					ESUBD and ESUBVA- vary together (+/-50% shock)				
	Default	Mean	SD	95% CI		Default	Mean	SD	95% CI	
INDIA	1953.05	1948.09	574.6	-637.61	4533.79	1953.05	1980.96	573.73	-600.825	4562.745
EU_27	3457.1	3505.54	392.85	1737.715	5273.365	3457.1	3544.26	532.53	1147.875	5940.645
ODCs	-522.15	-522.51	94.61	-948.255	-96.765	-522.15	-531.21	101.13	-986.295	-76.125
EBA	-154.43	-158.78	19.93	-248.465	-69.095	-154.43	-158.69	11.26	-209.36	-108.02
Rest of World	-887.59	-894.29	244.33	-1993.78	205.195	-887.59	-902.07	161.46	-1628.64	-75.5

positive in prospective India–EU FTA and lies within 95 per cent confidence interval but not necessarily true for India. The SSA results for (+/−) 50 per cent shock around the default value of ESUBD and ESUBVA (vary together) indicate similar results. Thus, the SSA results for welfare gains remain positive for EU irrespective parameter values. However, it is not true for India. Hence, the welfare gains for EU are more stable compared to India.

8. Revenue Effect using SMART

Revenue loss for India has been measured using SMART model. Simple average and weighted average tariff have also been used for verification. India is expected to lose US $ 4057.27 million in perfect tariff liberalisation respectively (Table 3.9). Broadly similar results are revealed by using weighted and simple average tariffs. Given the development needs, India must consider revenue loss and re-look to alternative make up strategies. The results for revenue loss indicate that India should opt for partial and selective tariff liberalisation in case of prospective India–EU FTA.

Table 3.9: Revenue Effect of India–EU FTA (US$ Million)

Country	100 Per cent Tariff Cut India Using SMART Model	100 Per cent Tariff Cut India: Using Weighted Average	100 Per cent Tariff Cut India: Using Simple Average
India	−4057.27	−3654.479	−4349.763

Source: Author's estimates.

9. Conclusion

The study reveals that the EU–India FTA would result in welfare gains for both India and EU. In absolute terms, the gains of EU would be much higher than that of India. India's welfare gain is mainly driven by the gain in terms of trade and employment whereas EU's welfare gain is primarily driven by the gains in allocative efficiency. In case of the EBA countries, a decrease in welfare may be likely due to India–EU FTA losses in allocative efficiency and terms of trade. However, negative terms of trade shocks are the dominant factor behind welfare loss. The SSA results reveal that the welfare gains for EU remain positive, irrespective of parameter values, while SSA results reveal mixed possibilities for India. Hence, the welfare gains for EU are more stable compared to India. It is safe to conclude that zero-tariff regimes on imports from EU may not be profitable to India at this stage and partial or selected tariff liberalisation is the best strategy in India's interest while negotiating prospective India–EU FTA.

It is also important to recognise that the predicted outcomes may not be materialised due to number of economic and non-economic constraints. For instance, Indian export gains may not be materialised, despite tariff removal, due to the presence of non-tariff barriers. It should be noted that the GTAP results may also be underestimated as the present analysis is based on comparative static CGE framework rather than dynamic CGE. To garner the dynamic gains, the FTA between India and EU must be comprehensive, including issues to trade in goods and services, and investment, as well as other cross-cutting issues such as technical barriers to trade, sanitary and phytosanitary measures, the movement of service providers, agreements on the mutual recognition of qualifications, etc. Hence, the fruitful area of future research may be to identify non-tariff barriers in both markets and to estimate potential trade at more disaggregated regional and sectoral level.

Appendix: GTAP Model Aggregations

Table A3.1: Regional Aggregation

Number	Code	Region Description	Comprising
1	INDIA	India	India
2	EU_27	European Union	Austria; Belgium; Cyprus; Czech Republic; Denmark; Estonia; Finland; France; Germany; Greece; Hungary; Ireland; Italy; Latvia; Lithuania; Luxembourg; Malta; Netherlands; Poland; Portugal; Slovakia; Slovenia; Spain; Sweden; United Kingdom; Bulgaria; Romania
3	ODCs	Other Developed Countries	New Zealand; Hong Kong; Japan; Korea; Taiwan; Singapore; Canada; United States of America; Switzerland; Norway; Rest of EFTA
4	EBA	EBA countries	Rest of Oceania; Cambodia; Lao People's Democratic Republic; Bangladesh; Rest of South Asia; Caribbean; Senegal; Rest of Western Africa; Central Africa; South Central Africa; Ethiopia; Madagascar; Malawi; Mozambique; Tanzania; Uganda; Zambia;

(Table A3.1 Continued)

(*Table A3.1 Continued*)

Number	Code	Region Description	Comprising
			Rest of Eastern Africa; Rest of South African Customs
5	Rest of world	Rest of world	China; Rest of East Asia; Indonesia; Myanmar; Malaysia; Philippines; Thailand; Viet Nam; Rest of Southeast Asia; Pakistan; Sri Lanka; Mexico; Rest of North America; Argentina; Bolivia; Brazil; Chile; Colombia; Ecuador; Paraguay; Peru; Uruguay; Venezuela; Rest of South America; Costa Rica; Guatemala; Nicaragua; Panama; Rest of Central America; Albania; Belarus; Croatia; Russian Federation; Ukraine; Rest of Eastern Europe; Rest of Europe; Kazakhstan; Kyrgyztan; Rest of Former Soviet Union; Armenia; Azerbaijan; Georgia; Islamic Republic of Iran; Turkey; Rest of Western Asia; Egypt; Morocco; Tunisia; Rest of North Africa; Nigeria; Mauritius; Zimbabwe; Botswana; South Africa

Source: Author's aggregation from GTAP database compiled by Badri Narayanan G. and Terrie L. Walmsley (2008).

Table A3.2: Sectoral Aggregation

Number	Code	Description	Comprising
1	Grains Crops	Grains and crops	Paddy rice; Wheat; Cereal grains nec; Oil seeds; Sugar cane, sugar beet; Plant-based fibers; Crops nec; Processed rice
2	Vegetables and Fruits	Grains and crops	Vegetables, fruit, nuts.
3	Meat and Livestock	Livestock and meat products	Cattle, sheep, goats, horses; Animal products nec; Raw milk; Wool, silk-worm cocoons; Meat: cattle,sheep, goats, horse; Meat products nec
4	Fishing	Extraction	Fishing
5	Extraction	Mining and extraction	Forestry; Coal; Oil; Gas; Minerals nec
6	Dairy Milk	Dairy products	Dairy products
7	Beverages and Tobacco	Beverages and tobacco	Beverages and tobacco products

(*Table A3.2 Continued*)

(*Table A2 Continued*)

Number	Code	Description	Comprising
8	Processed food	Processed Food	Vegetable oils and fats; Sugar; Food products nec
9	Textiles	Textiles and clothing	Textiles
10	Wearing Apparel	Textiles and clothing	Wearing apparel
11	Leather	Light manufacturing	Leather products
12	Light Manufacturing	Light manufacturing	Wood products; Paper products, publishing; Metal products; Motor vehicles and parts; Transport equipment nec; Manufactures nec
13	Heavy Manufacturing	Heavy manufacturing	Petroleum, coal products; Chemical, rubber, plastic products; Mineral products nec; Ferrous metals; Metals nec; Electronic equipment; Machinery and equipment nec
14	Services	Other Services	Electricity; Gas manufacture, distribution; Water; Construction; Trade; Transport nec; Sea transport; Air transport; Communication; Financial services nec; Insurance; Business services nec; Recreation and other services; PubAdmin/Defence/Health/Educat; Dwellings

Source: Author's aggregation from GTAP database compiled by Badri Narayanan G. and Terrie L. Walmsley (2008).

Notes

1. The trade intensity index (T) is used to determine whether the value of trade between two countries is greater or smaller than would be expected on the basis of their importance in world trade. It is defined as the share of one country's exports going to a partner divided by the share of world exports going to the partner. It is calculated as, $T_{ij} = (x_{ij}/X_{it})/(x_{wj}/X_{wt})$, where x_{ij} and x_{wj} are the values of country i's exports and of world exports to country j and where X_{it} and X_{wt} are country i's total exports and total world exports respectively. An index of more (less) than one indicates a bilateral trade flow that is larger (smaller) than expected, given the partner country's importance in world trade.
2. Analysis of the effects of a policy, such as trade liberalisation or formation of a PTA, based on information available after the policy has been implemented and its performance has also been observed.

3. Ex-ante analysis helps to give an idea of the future impact of a newly implemented policy.
4. GTAP database arrays H7 and H8 divide the endowment commodities into two groups. The mobile endowment commodities (H8) are perfectly mobile across industries within each region; the sluggish endowment commodities (H7) are imperfectly mobile or immobile. In the standard database, skilled and unskilled labor and capital are classed as mobile, and land and natural resources as sluggish. This is suitable for long-run simulations. For short-run simulations, users may wish to move capital from H8 to H7, to treat it as sluggish rather than mobile (Narayanan, Dimaranan and McDougal 2008).
5. The regional household's equivalent variation, resulting from a shock, is equal to the difference between the expenditure required to obtain the new level of utility at initial prices and the initial expenditure. Thus, the EV uses the current prices as the base and asks what income change at the current prices would be equivalent to the proposed change in terms of its impact on utility.
6. Systematic Sensitivity Analysis is an emerging technique that can incorporate information on distributions, as opposed to single point estimates, in computable general equilibrium models. Arndt (1996) developed the SSA technique from recent advances in the area of numerical integration and its application to economic problems. The procedure automates solving the model as many times as necessary, once the user has set up and started it running.

References

Action Aid. 2008. 'An Assessment of the Likely Impact of the India-EU Free Trade Agreement: An ActionAid briefing for UK MPs', ActionAid, London.
Albertin, G. 2008. 'Regionalism or Multilateralism? A Political Economy Choice', IMF Working Papers 08/65, International Monetary Fund. http://www.imf.org/external/pubs/ft/wp/2008/wp0865.pdf (accessed 15 March 2009).
Armington, P. S. 1969. 'A Theory of Demand for Products Distinguished by Place of Production', *International Monetary Fund Staff Papers*, 16: 159–76.
Arndt, C. 1996. 'An Introduction to Systematic Sensitivity Analysis via Gaussian Quadrature', Center for Global Trade Analysis, Purdue University. https://www.gtap.agecon.purdue.edu/resources/download/39.pdf (accessed 20 January 2010).
Badri Narayanan G. and Terrie L. Walmsley. eds. 2008. *Global Trade, Assistance, and Production: The GTAP 7 Database.* West Lafayette: Center for Global Trade Analysis, Purdue University.
Baldwin, R. 1995. 'A Domino Theory of Regionalism', in R. Baldwin, P. Haaparnata and J. Kiander (eds), *Expanding Membership of the EU*, pp. 25–53. Cambridge: Cambridge University Press.
Brada, J. C. 1994. 'Regional Integration in Eastern Europe: Prospects for Integration within the Region and with the European Community', in

J. D. and A. Panagariya (eds), *New Dimensions in Regional Integration*, pp. 319–47. Cambridge: Cambridge University Press.

Ethier, W. J. 1998. 'Regionalism in a Multilateral World', *Journal of Political Economy*, 106 (6): 1214–45.

Goulder, L. ed. 2002. *Environmental Policy Making in Economies with Prior Tax Distortions*. Northampton: Edward Elgar.

Harrison, G.W., T. F. Rutherford and D. G. Tarr. 1997. 'Quantifying the Uruguay Round', *Economic Journal*, 107 (444): 1405–30.

Hertel, T. W. ed. 1997. *Global Trade Analysis: Modeling and Applications*. Cambridge: Cambridge University Press.

Jammes, O. and M. Olarreag. 2005. 'Explaining SMART and GSIM', The World Bank. http://wits.worldbank.org/witsweb/download/docs/Explaining_SMART_and_GSIM.pdf (accessed 20 January 2010).

Kemp, M. C. and Henty Y. Wan Jr. 1976. 'An Elementary Proposition Concerning the Formation of Customs Unions', *Journal of International Economics*, 6 (1): 95–98.

Krueger, A. 1999. 'Trade Creation and Trade Diversion under NAFTA', NBER Working Paper No. 7429. Cambridge: National Bureau of Economic Research.

Lazer, D. 1999. 'The Free Trade Epidemic of the 1860s and Other Outbreaks of Economic Discrimination', *World Politics,* 51 (4): 447–84.

Meade, J. E. 1955. *The Theory of Customs Unions*. Amsterdam: North-Holland.

Meincke, B. 2008. 'The EU–India-FTA: Development and Growth for Each and Everybody?', Briefing Paper, Heinrich Böll Foundation, Berlin.

Narayanan, G. Badri and Terrie L. Walmsley. eds. 2008. *Global Trade, Assistance, and Production: The GTAP 7 Database*. West Lafayette: Center for Global Trade Analysis, Purdue University.

Narayanan, G. B., B. V. Dimaranan and R. A. McDougal. 2008. 'Guide to the GTAP Database', in Badri N. G. and Terrie L. W. (eds), *Global Trade, Assistance, and Production: The GTAP 7 Database*, Center for Global Trade Analysis, Purdue University. https://www.gtap.agecon.purdue.edu/resources/download/4177.pdf (accessed 10 November 2009).

Perry, G., J. Whalley and G. McMahon. eds. 2001. *Fiscal Reform and Structural Change in Developing Countries*. New York: Palgrave-Macmillan.

UNCOMTRADE. 2009. 'United Nations Commodity Trade Statistics Database', World Integrated Trade Solution (WITS). http://wits.worldbank.org/WITS (accessed 12 March 2009).

Viner, J. 1950. *The Customs Union Issue*. New York: Carnegie Endowment for International Peace.

Winters, L.A., M. Gasiorek, J. L. Gonzalez, P. Holmes, M. M. Parra and A. Shingal. 2009. *Innocent Bystanders: Implications of an EU-India Free Trade Agreements for Excluded Countries*. London: Commonwealth Secretariat.

Part 2

Regional Integration in South Asia

4

South Asian Integration: Dream or Reality

Rajan Sudesh Ratna

Established in 1985, South Asian Association for Regional Cooperation (SAARC) is a grouping of seven countries — Bangladesh, Bhutan, India, Maldives, Nepal, Pakistan and Sri Lanka. Afghanistan has also become a member of SAARC. Recognising its great economic strength in terms of its market potential, rich natural resources and capable human resources, and the possibility of enhanced intra-regional trade and investment flows, a trade block among SAARC members was formed with the signing of SAARC Preferential Trading Arrangement (SAPTA) during the Seventh Summit held in Dhaka in April, 1993. The Agreement reflected the desire of the member states to promote and sustain mutual trade and economic co-operation within the SAARC region through the exchange of concessions.

Since SAPTA was a preferential trade agreement, during each round, the negotiations for SAPTA were held on the basis of 'request and offer' approach, where the exporting party came up with a 'country-specific' request list of its exportable (real as well as potential) items on which it would seek preferential market access. The other party would then make an offer on items from 'request-list' and indicate the extent of tariff concessions in terms of Margin of Preference (MoP) which were multilateralised.[1] In each round, the coverage of products under tariff concessions were expanded and the MoP on products under concessions was also deepened. The Least Developed Country (LDC) members got concessions on a large number of products with deeper MoP, without reciprocating with equivalent concession to other developing countries under the Special and Differential Treatment (S&DT) provision of SAPTA. In four rounds of negotiations, tariff concessions on around 5,000 products at 6-digit Harmonised System (HS) level were exchanged. The opportunity to expand the basket of products for exports to

SAARC Member Countries (SMC) was not fully utilised. Few attribute this to the Non Tariff Barriers (NTBs) imposed by other members, some cite the supply-side constraints of LDC members, and some others cite the lack of intra-regional investment flows and the absence of backward–forward linkages amongst the industries. However, contrary to the belief of many, the rule of origin of SAPTA was much liberal, as a product would be originating if it generates a local value added content of 40 per cent (30 per cent for LDCs) in the exporting country.

To enhance trade integration, the South Asian Free Trade Area (SAFTA) was signed on 6 January 2004 during the Twelfth SAARC Summit in Islamabad and was implemented with effect from 1 January 2006, though the tariff liberalisation started from 1 July 2006. Despite the delay in its start, it was also agreed that the time frame for reduction of tariffs would remain unchanged.

In this context, it is important to critically examine potential of SAFTA. This chapter is an attempt to decompose various constraints involved in SAFTA and recommend policy suggestions to convert the dreams into reality. It is structured as follows. Section 2 discusses various SAFTA provisions. Section 3 discusses selected empirical literature and Section 4 argues integration possibilities. Section 5 presents various policy suggestions and finally section 6 provides concluding remarks.

2. South Asian Free Trade Area (SAFTA)

The salient features of the agreement on SAFTA are as follows:

2.1. Trade Liberalisation Programme (TLP)

The agreement provides for the following schedule of tariff reductions.

(a) Non-Least Developed Country (Non-LDC) Members of SAARC (India, Pakistan and Sri Lanka)

Non-LDC countries would reduce their existing tariffs (for Most Favoured Nation or MFN tariffs more than 20 per cent) to 20 per cent within a time frame of two years from the date of coming into force of the agreement. If the actual MFN tariff rates are below 20 per cent, then there shall be an annual reduction of 10 per cent on MoP basis for each of the two years. The subsequent tariff reductions from 20 per cent or below to 0–5 per cent shall be done within the next five years by India and Pakistan and six years by Sri Lanka. Therefore the TLP allowed the tariffs to be reduced to 0–5 per cent in a total time frame of seven years to India and Pakistan, and eight years to Sri Lanka.

(b) Least Developed Country (LDC) Members of SAARC (Bangladesh, Bhutan, Maldives and Nepal)

The LDC member countries would reduce their existing tariff (for MFN tariff more than 30 per cent) to 30 per cent within a time frame of two years from the date of coming into force of the agreement. If the MFN tariff rates are below 30 per cent, there will be an annual reduction of 5 per cent on MoP basis for each of the two years. The subsequent tariff reductions from 30 per cent or below to 0–5 per cent shall be done within the next eight years, thus allowing them a time frame of a total of 10 years to reduce their tariffs to 0–5 per cent.

2.2. Sensitive Lists

The agreement provides member countries to maintain sensitive lists consisting of items which are not subject to tariff reduction. It also provides that LDCs can seek derogation for removal of items of their export interest from the sensitive list of developing country members. Only three members, namely Bangladesh, India and Nepal maintain different sensitive lists for LDCs and Non-LDCs. Besides, the LDCs were allowed to maintain a bigger size of sensitive lists than the Non-LDCs. The sensitive lists are subject to review after every four years or earlier with a view to reducing the number of items which are to be traded freely among the SAARC countries (Table 4.1).

Table 4.1: Sensitive Lists among the SAFTA Members[2]

Country	Total number of sensitive list		Coverage of sensitive list as per cent of total HS lines	
	For non-LDCs	For LDCs	For non-LDCs	For LDCs
Bangladesh	1,254	1,249	24.0	23.9
Bhutan	157	157	3.0	3.0
India	865	744	16.6	14.2
Maldives	671	671	12.8	12.8
Nepal	1,335	1,299	25.6	24.9
Pakistan	1,191	1,191	22.8	22.8
Sri Lanka	1,079	1,079	20.7	20.7

Source: SAARC Secretariat.

2.3. Rules of Origin

The rules of origin agreed under SAFTA are general (i.e., one criterion for all products) barring 191 products for which product specific rules are applied. Thus, SAFTA rules of origin prescribes for an application of twin criteria of sufficient transformation through a Change in Tariff Heading (CTH: change at 4-digit HS level between the non-originating inputs and the final export product) and achieving a local value added content of at least 40 per cent as a percentage of Free on Board (FoB) value. However, local value added content requirement is lower for Sri Lanka and LDCs, which is 35 per cent and 30 per cent respectively. There is also a provision relating to regional cumulation wherein inputs from other SAARC members can be sourced. Under this provision, a higher value added content of 50 per cent for entire region has been prescribed out of which 20 per cent valued added content should be done in the exporting country.

2.4. Non-Tariff and Para-Tariff Barriers

The agreement provides that no quantitative restrictions would be maintained by SAARC members if they are not allowed under GATT 1994. With respect to other non-tariff measures and para-tariff measures, the agreement prescribes that the countries notify their measures to SAARC Secretariat on an annual basis and SAFTA Committee of Experts (CoE) will review them and make necessary recommendations for their elimination. For its implementation, a sub-group on non-tariff measures has already been established, which is engaged in addressing the non-tariff barriers.

2.5. Mechanism for Compensation of Revenue Loss

A mechanism has been established to compensate the revenue loss to be incurred by the LDCs due to reduction of tariffs. The Mechanism for Compensation of Revenue Loss (MCRL) for the SAARC LDCs prescribes:

a. The compensation to LDCs would be available for four years. However, for Maldives it would be available for six years.
b. The compensation would be in the form of grant in US dollar.
c. The compensation shall be subject to a cap of 1, 1, 5 and 3 per cent of customs revenue collected on non-sensitive items under bilateral trade in the base year, i.e., average of 2004 and 2005.
d. The compensation shall be administered by the CoE.

This scheme initially generated a lot of attention when the SAFTA was signed but upon its finalisation, it did not appear to have met the expectations of LDC members due to limited scope and period. By the time the LDCs would grant duty-free market access to other members of SAFTA, thereby incurring major revenue losses, the mechanism will no longer be in place.

2.6. Technical Assistance for LDCs

There are provisions for technical assistance for LDCs at their request. Areas of technical assistance as agreed upon are as follows:

- Capacity building (trade related).
- Customs procedures related measures.
- Development and improvement of tax policy and instruments.
- Legislative and policy related measures, assistance for improvement of national capacity.
- Studies on trade related physical infrastructure development, improvement of banking sector and development of export financing.

In addition to the above core areas, the agreement also provides for trade facilitation, institutional mechanism, safeguard measures and dispute settlement mechanism (See SAFTA agreement, SAARC Secretariat).

3. Selected Literature Review

The existing literature reveals diverse views on SAFTA. Despite having vast natural resources in this region, the failure to utilise them optimally and efficiently has led some analysts to believe that no trade complementarities exist among the SAARC nations. Another reason that substantiates this argument is the belief that SAFTA is in existence due to political objectives of SAARC and not due to the economic logic. For instance, Baysan et al. (2006), Pitigala (2005) and Srinivasan (2001) draw from both existing literature and own analysis to argue that an economic case for a free trade area in South Asia is relatively weak due to reasons like the small size of the economies (other than India), lack of openness and higher transaction costs of doing formal trade. Baysan et al. (2006) holds the view that political rather than economic reasons were behind the creation of the SAFTA, a view which finds echo in other studies as well (e.g., World Bank 2006). Krueger et al. (2004) put forward a largely pessimistic view which indicates that although potential gains exist from SAFTA, the South Asian region does not meet most of the theory-based criteria for successful trade agreements. Therefore, it is unlikely that large welfare gains will be realised from this agreement.

World Bank Study (1997) analyses the static welfare consequences of preferential liberalisation. Using an integrated general equilibrium model of the world economy (Global Trade Analysis Project, GTAP), it shows that regional trade liberalisation would increase the welfare between 0.5 per cent of GDP for India and one per cent for the rest of South Asia. RIS (2004) reports the result of studies conducted in the framework of gravity model. It suggests that complete elimination of tariffs under SAFTA may increase the intra-regional trade 1.6 times. It further suggests that in the dynamic frame work, the gains from liberalisation are at least 25 per cent higher than the static gains.

Further, an ex-post analysis by Kelagama and Mukherji (2007) on the Indo-Sri Lanka Bilateral FTA (ISLFTA) records increase in two-way trade during the period of analysis. The boom in preferential exports under ISLFTA resulted in India becoming the third largest export destination for Sri Lanka since 2003, whereas it was only 16th largest in 2000. According to the authors, there is trade creation and entry of new goods into the Indian market through the preferential route offered by the ISLFTA.

4. Is Integration Possible?

It has been recognised that trade and investment flows have played a crucial role in the economic integration of various regions of the world, and it could have been true for South Asia even. The case in point is India–Sri Lanka FTA which has been able to integrate the two economies through enhanced trade and investment flows and backward-forward integration of the industries. India's Foreign Direct Investment (FDI) to Sri Lanka had been low. One could observe a dramatic increase of FDI flow from India to Sri Lanka after the signing of the bilateral FTA in 1998. A major attraction for Indian investors has been the ability to re-export to India while benefiting from lower tariffs on raw materials in Sri Lanka. India became the biggest FDI investor in Sri Lanka in 2002 and 2003.

India and Sri Lanka have also signed an agreement on the US$100 million line of credit in January 2001 to enable Sri Lankan importers to source goods and services from India under soft loan terms. The credit is only for items of Indian manufacture and services. The credit covers import of capital goods; import of consumer durables; and five specified food items, i.e., sugar, wheat flour, rice, red split lentils and wheat grains, as well as consultancy services.

The bilateral agreement provided opportunity to both sides to diversify their export basket of products and increase their bilateral trade. Most of the Sri Lankan exports may have created trade diversion rather than trade creation due to high import duties in India. Post-FTA, however, several new items were traded and it allowed Sri Lanka to replace Nepal being the largest exporter to India (Ratna and Sidhu 2007). The Sri Lankan government provided a more lucrative investment and tax policies to attract investments and it could have been utilised by any investor, either from India or other country (3rd party). However, this provided a wider economic space to the Indian industry to diversify and aspire for going global on one side and utilise the tariff concessions for exports to Indian market on the other side. Therefore, the Indian businessmen invested in Sri Lanka.

5. Policy Recommendations

SAARC with its FTA in goods alone through SAFTA would not be able to achieve its goal of strengthening intra-SAARC economic co-operation to maximise the realisation of the region's potential for trade and development for the benefit of their people. To be a truly integrated economic region, it would need to expand its areas of co-operation and activities. If SAARC has to integrate, several measures would be necessary to be taken.

The present size of the sensitive list is much bigger than any successful RTA. It has been understood that in the last Ministerial Council meeting held on 3 March 2008 in New Delhi, the ministers have decided that the COE will start negotiations for the removal of items from the sensitive list. To facilitate the intra-regional trade and investment flows, it is important that the size of the sensitive list of each SAFTA member is reduced drastically, especially those items which are either being traded bilaterally or comprise major global export items of member countries.

Given the time frame for liberalisation of their tariffs in other FTAs (India–ASEAN, India–Singapore, India–Thailand, Pakistan–China, etc.), the current time frame for tariff liberalisation (seven to 10 years) needs to be shortened, implying advancement in the tariff liberalisation schedule.

The present SAFTA treaty allows the members for bringing duties to the level of 0–5 per cent and not necessarily a duty-free market access. The duty reduction to 5 per cent may deny adequate preferential market access to the members and if the Doha Round succeeds, then a possibility of erosion of the SAFTA preferences cannot be ruled out. It is important that all members decide to make it a duty-free agreement.

The present Rules of Origin (RoO) of SAFTA provides that in order to utilise the regional cumulation benefits, the total regional value addition should be 50 per cent (10 per cent higher than the normal value addition) and the exporting party should have a minimum value addition of 20 per cent. A similar provision which existed in SAFTA did not stimulate intra-regional trade; hence a concept of full cumulation without any value addition obligation to the exporting party should be explored.

Many exporters from South Asia allege that the NTBs have been put in place with the intention to restrict the trade from neighbouring countries. Though such measures may be totally WTO compatible, the fact that it creates difficulty to the exporters of neighbouring countries cannot be denied, causing irritation in the region. Taneja et al. (2003) pointed out that the cost of doing business through formal channels in the region is higher than through informal channels in SAARC. Moves should be initiated for standard setting and mutual recognition of standards through accredited testing laboratories. Therefore, even if these are WTO compliant standards or regulations, a fast track procedure for establishing equivalence, Mutual Recognition Agreements (MRAs), conformity assessment procedures, accreditation, etc., in a time bound manner should be put in place.

SAFTA is an agreement covering only goods. Given the fact that worldwide the negotiations are held for comprehensive coverage of issues like services, investments, Intellectual Property Rights (IPRs), competition policy, Sanitary and Physio Sanitary Measures (SPS), Technical Barriers to Trade (TBT) etc., it is high time that SAARC catches up with the pace of these agreements.

There is a historical existence of services trade in the SAARC region, most of which is through informal channels. There is no official statistics on sector-wise services trade but the fact that SAARC nationals travel to other SAARC countries, especially to India for education or medical treatment, is well known. Studies have shown that SAARC member countries have revealed comparative advantage in different sectors covering transport, travel and other services (Mukherji 2005). It is understood that the Ministerial Council meeting on 3 March 2008 in New Delhi decided to include the agreement in services in SAARC and a road map is being drawn for the negotiations. This is a positive and welcome step and negotiations should be started as soon as possible.

To enhance the intra-SAARC trade and investment flows as well as backward-forward linkages between the investors of the region, it is essential that a blueprint for SAARC Investment Area is prepared and negotiations are held to finalise the agreement. The agreement will not only bring transparency and predictability in the respective regimes but would also ensure that investors' rights are protected and the reforms are 'locked-in'.

The members of SAARC are at different levels of economic development and so are their infrastructural supports to promote trade and investment flows. The countries in the region have common interest in the areas of road and railway construction, building of bridges and telecommunication development. Joint projects for development of ports and land customs infrastructure for facilitating movement of goods should be initiated on priority. SAARC involves some member countries which are landlocked and therefore they face problems relating to accessibility to sea ports for their trade. There is a need for a regional framework or treaty for promoting transit to promote unhindered movement of goods across borders.

Though the SAFTA provides for S&D treatment to be accorded to LDC members and liberalisation of tariffs by the developing countries in three years, the TLP is for bringing the duties to 0–5 per cent. There is no such commitment to grant duty-free treatment to SMCs or LDCs at the end of TLP. As per the announcement by its Prime Minister at the 14th SAARC Summit, India eliminated its tariffs to zero (duty-free) for LDC members with effect from 1 January 2008. India has also unilaterally reduced its sensitive list for LDCs. It is important that other developing members like Pakistan and Sri Lanka also announced providing a duty-free market access to LDC members for non-sensitive items. Secondly, the SAARC LDCs also do not compete with each other in their respective markets and therefore, even the LDCs should decide for grant of duty-free market access to each other at the end of the TLP.

SAARC Chamber of Commerce should aim at enhancing B2B interactions and ensure that suggestions made by it are accommodated by each member. Given the success of the line of credit that India has opened with Sri Lanka and its positive effect on trade and investment flows, one of the actions that can be recommended is to replicate the same with other members.

6. Conclusion

In order to make SAARC a cohesive and integrated block, it would be essential that the member countries share this vision for which a strong political commitment would be necessary. It has been seen that most of the regional blocks have integrated due to strong political commitment which has superseded often raised conflicting issues which at times pose threat to such efforts for integration.

The complementarities on different dimensions need to be explored so that the entire region progresses and the benefits are balanced. Therefore, broadening the current SAFTA agreement beyond trade in goods to include areas of services and investment is equally important. While free trade alone will yield gains, these are unlikely to be great. However, dynamic long-term effects can be significant, particularly if combined with aggressive trade-facilitation measures, removal of NTBs, opening up the services sectors and, in particular, liberalisation of the investment regime. Unless a serious attempt to address these issues are taken, it would be very difficult for the region to integrate.

Notes

1. 'Margin of Preference' (MoP) means the percentage difference between the Most-Favoured-Nation (MFN) rate of duty and the preferential rate of duty for the product on which tariff concession is offered.
2. This changed subsequently after Afghanistan acceded to SAFTA and India reduced its sensitive list for LDCs on a later date.

References

Baysan, Tercan, Arvind Panagariya and Nihal Pitigala. 2006. 'Preferential Trading in South Asia', *World Bank Policy Research Working Paper 3813*. Washington DC: World Bank.

Krueger, E., R. Pinto, V. Thomas and T. To. 2004. 'Impacts of the South Asia Free Trade Agreement'. Paper presented at Policy Analysis Workshop, Public Affairs 869, University of Wisconsin–Madison.

Mukherji, I. N. 2005. 'Regional Trade Agreements in South Asia', *South Asian Yearbook of Trade and Development*, pp. 363–93. Delhi: CENTAD.

Pitigala, Nihal. 2005. 'What Does Regional Trade in South Asia Reveal about Future Trade Integration?: Some Empirical Evidence', World Bank Policy Research Working Paper 3497. Washington DC: World Bank.

Ratna, R. S. and Geetu Sidhu. 2007. 'Making SAFTA a Success: The Role of India', *Commonwealth Secretariat*. http://www.thecommonwealth.org/files/178426/ FileName/SAFTA %20and%20India%20-%20Final%20doc1. pdf (accessed 25 November 2009).

Research and Information System for the Non-Aligned and Other Developing Countries (RIS). 2004. *South Asia Development and Cooperation Report 2004*. Delhi: RIS.

Saman Kelegama and Indra Nath Mukherji 2007. India–Sri Lanka Bilateral Free Trade Agreement: Six Years Performance and Beyond, Research and Information Systems for Non-Aligned and Other Developing Countries, Discussion Paper 119. New Delhi: RIS.

SAARC Secretariat. 2009. 'SAFTA Agreement'. http://www.saarc-sec.org/userfiles/saftaagreement.pdf (accessed 25 November 2009).

Srinivasan, T. N. 2001. Preferential Trade Agreements with Special Reference to Asia. http://www.econ.yale.edu/~srinivas/PrefTrade Agreements.pdf (accessed 25 November 2009).

Taneja, Nisha, Muttukrishna Sarvanathan and Sanjib Pohit. 2003. 'India–Sri Lanka Trade: Transacting Environments in Formal and Informal Trading', *Economic and Political Weekly*, 38 (29): 3095–98.

World Bank. 1997. *World Development Report 1997*. Washington DC: World Bank.

———. 2006. *India-Bangladesh Trade, Trade Policies and Potential Free Trade Agreement*. Washington DC: World Bank.

5

Fostering Regional Trade in South Asia: Prospects and Challenges*

Kazi Mahmudur Rahman, Syed Saifuddin Hossain, Asif Anwar and Md. Tariqur Rahman

Trade regimes of countries in South Asia have gone through significant changes over the recent years through liberalisation of tariff structure with increasingly deeper integration with the global economy. However, although bilateral trade relations among a number of South Asian Association for Regional Cooperation (SAARC) countries have registered some growth over time, intra-regional trade in South Asia has continued to remain rather insignificant, particularly when compared to other regional trading blocs. Thus, in spite of the fast pace of global integration of these economies, manifested in their increasing degree of openness, potentials of intra-regional trade opportunities have tended to remain largely underutilised. Poor trade and investment linkages at the regional level, coupled with various structural, infrastructural and political constraints, have severely limited the scope and opportunity for development of integrated production network within the region. In this backdrop, this chapter aims to confine its scope only with trade in goods.

Section 2 of this chapter discusses South Asia's trade regime focusing especially on structure, composition and trend of regional trade. An analysis of relevant regional trading agreements has also been presented in this section. In the section 3, analysis of the state of intra-industry and inter-industry trade in South Asia has been carried out and attempt has been made to identify ways and means to realise the potentials in this area. Section 4 explores the implications of trade barriers as impediments to realising the potentials of intra-regional trade in South Asia. Section 5 takes the discussion a bit further by specifically dealing with issues related to trade facilitation in the context of the region. The overall discussion is then concluded in the final section.

2. Structure and Composition of Trade in South Asia

South Asia's global trade stood at US$628.9 billion in 2008 of which 4.8 per cent was accounted for by intra-regional trade. The region is far behind most other regions in terms of share of overall trade: Europe (36.8 per cent), North America (15.3 per cent) and South East Asia (6.1 per cent). Extra-regional trade dominates South Asia's overall trade structure accounting for 93.7 per cent of her total export and 96.1 per cent of import (Table 5.1). Although small economies such as Afghanistan and Nepal maintain relatively higher level of trade within the region, overall trade is skewed up due to low level of intra-regional trade of large economies like India and Pakistan. Most of region's export is destined to developed countries: European countries accounted for 23 per cent of region's export while the US for 16 per cent during 2008 (Table 5.2). However, the share of export to these two regions registered a decline over time (from 53 per cent in 2000 to 39 per cent in 2008) while export to other regions has considerably increased.

Leading export destinations of the region such as Europe and North America involve large markets, offer diversified export opportunities and provide preferential market access for Least Developed Countries (LDCs) of the region. India, and in some cases Pakistan, are two of the major export destinations for Afghanistan, Nepal, Bhutan and Sri Lanka mainly because of geographical proximity, common borders and bilateral trading agreements. The region's sources of import, on the other hand, are widely diversified among countries of Europe, North America and East Asia.

Structure of intra-regional trade has changed over time with a marginal fall in the region's share since 2005. India holds the lion's share in terms of intra-regional export, experiencing a high level of growth between 2005 and 2008 (27 per cent), whilst share of most of the other countries registered considerable fall over time (Table 5.3). Limited country-specific export basket and high export similarity have been the major concerns for narrowing down the scope for export and proliferation of production network among countries

Table 5.1: South Asia's Intra- and Extra-regional Trade in 2008

	Export			Import		
	Total export (million US$)	Share of intra-regional export (%)	Share of extra-regional export (%)	Total import (million US$)	Share of intra-regional import (%)	Share of extra-regional import (%)
Afghanistan	421.95	41.75	58.25	5734.71	40.65	59.35
Bangladesh	13907.4	3.1	96.9	23756.9	16.93	83.07
India	187405	5.1	94.9	300539	0.8	99.2
Maldives	202.63	8.78	91.22	1426.17	15.13	84.87
Nepal	1179.67	73.89	26.11	3540.44	59.59	40.41
Pakistan	21762.9	13.36	86.64	46292.8	2.75	97.25
Sri Lanka	8688.02	8.39	91.61	14051.1	22.87	77.13
Total	**233567.57**	**6.29**	**93.71**	**395341.12**	**3.94**	**96.06**

Source: Authors' estimate based on DOTS (IMF 2009).

Table 5.2: South Asia's Export to Different Regions

	2000	2004	2005	2006	2007	2008	Exports of South Asia — average growth rate (2004–2008)
South Asia	4.6	6.4	6.6	6.2	6.3	6.3	29.00
South East Asia	5.3	7.8	8.2	6.6	6.8	7.3	27.52
Europe	26.6	25.6	24.7	23.5	23.7	23.0	21.76
North America	26.4	20.8	20.5	20.9	18.2	16.0	16.40
Others	37.2	39.4	40.0	42.7	45.1	47.3	29.41
Share (%) Total	100.0	100.0	100.0	100.0	100.0	100.0	24.63

Source: Authors' estimate based on DOTS (IMF 2009).

Table 5.3: South Asian Intra-Regional Export (% Share)

	1980	1990	2000	2005	2008	% change per year between 2005 and 2008
Afghanistan	13.92	1.97	2.08	1.19	1.2	24.2
Bangladesh	9.07	6.49	3.23	2.18	2.93	43.4
India	42.57	57.7	62.98	61.46	65.08	27.1
Maldives	0	0.77	0.48	0.2	0.12	1.2
Nepal	0	1.71	10.68	6.38	5.93	19.7
Pakistan	24.46	23.77	13.98	20.95	19.78	20.6
Sri Lanka	9.99	7.6	6.56	7.64	4.96	3.7
Total	**5.66**	**3.45**	**4.56**	**6.6**	**6.29**	**23.8**

Source: Authors' estimates based on DOTS (IMF 2009).

within the region (ESCAP 2008). High level of export similarities has led countries to follow similar kinds of tariff structure reducing the scope of enhanced trade between the countries. This is reflected in the negative lists of member countries of South Asian Free Trade Area (SAFTA), as discussed later.

As is known, South Asia's major share of import is sourced outside the region. Since two major economies of the region, India and Pakistan, have insignificant level of bilateral trade, the region has yet to emerge as a major source of import for procuring raw materials and intermediate products. A low level of trade intensity for most countries of South Asia, both as source as well as destination, corroborates with the fact of poor intra-regional trade.

In view of the above, it is evident that strengthening intra-regional trade integration largely lies on the region's combined efforts. Without enabling trade policies leading to deeper market integration, establishment of vertical and horizontal integration of production networks within the region will be difficult to establish.

2.1. Regional Trading Agreements

South Asia's intra- and extra-regional trade has been more or less influenced by various preferential trading agreements/arrangements. All eight countries of South Asia are members of SAFTA. Other than SAFTA, member countries are also involved in various other regional, sub-regional and bilateral integration initiatives where trade is included as major component. Barring the Maldives, almost all countries are currently in negotiation for bilateral trading arrangements within and outside the region (Table 5.4).

Table 5.4: South Asian Countries in Different Trade Arrangements

South Asian countries	Bilateral FTAs	Regional trade arrangements								
		SAPTA (1993)	SAFTA (2006)	BIMSTEC (1997)	D-8 (1997)	IOR-ARC (1997)	Bangkok agreement (1975)	SAGQ (1997)	ASEAN (1993)	APTA (1975)
Bangladesh	India*	✓								
	Pakistan*		✓	✓	✓	✓	✓	✓		✓
	Sri Lanka*									
Bhutan	India	✓	✓	✓				✓		
India	Bangladesh*	✓	✓	✓						
	Bhutan									
	Nepal					✓	✓	✓	✓	✓
	Sri Lanka									
Nepal	India	✓	✓	✓				✓		
Maldives		✓	✓							
Pakistan	Bangladesh*	✓	✓		✓					
	Sri Lanka									
Sri Lanka	Bangladesh*	✓	✓	✓		✓	✓			
	India									
	Pakistan									

Source: Rahman and Shadat 2006.

Note: *Indicates bilateral FTAs are in the process of negotiation.

2.2. SAFTA: Looking Forward to Greater Regional Integration

According to the SAFTA accord, the first phase for completion of tariff liberalisation was scheduled to end in 2008. Non-LDC members were supposed to reduce their maximum tariff rates to 20 per cent (or less) and LDCs to 30 per cent (or less) by this time. It remains unclear as to what extent member countries have been able to fulfil their commitments. The deadline for the completion of the second phase on tariff liberalisation is 2013 for India and Pakistan, 2014 for Sri Lanka and 2016 for LDCs. The non-LDC members agreed to reduce their import tariffs to 5 per cent or less in 5 years (i.e., by 1 January 2013) with the exception of Sri Lanka (Table 5.5). LDCs have agreed to do the same in eight years (by 2016). Henceforth, SAFTA's full operation will not start before 2016 and more importantly, its effectiveness will largely depend upon members' compliance with their commitments on reduction of tariff as mandated in the agreement.

The SAFTA tariff liberalisation programme allows members to maintain a sensitive/negative list of items that are not to be offered for concessional treatment. It also has the provision for its members to offer two sensitive/negative lists, one for LDCs and the other for non-LDCs (see Annex 1, SAFTA Agreement 2004). Till date, three countries have taken advantage of this provision though no signs of differential treatment can be observed.

The limited product coverage and the extensive nature of negative lists decrease the scope for intra-regional trade in South Asia (Rahman and Shadat 2006). Although India has a moderately low number of items on the sensitive list for non-LDCs, a sector-wise distribution of these items reveals that it has the largest per cent of tariff lines in categories for vegetable products (20.2 per cent) and textile products (34.2 per cent) — the two most important items of export interest of most South Asian countries. India's import of these items from South Asian countries constitutes only 12 per cent of its world imports (Taneja and Sawhney 2007). Among the member countries, India and Sri Lanka have restricted respectively up to 38 and 52 per cent of their total imports by value from other SAFTA members under the sensitive list category (Sawhney and Kumar 2008). The negative lists, thus, continue to significantly curtail the scope for a South Asian 'free trade' entity.[1]

After the operationalisation of SAFTA in July 2006, time has passed without making any progress in the context of intra-regional trade

Table 5.5: Differentiating Tariff Liberalisation Programme (TLP)

	Countries	Existing tariff rates	Tariff rates proposed under SAFTA	Year to be completed
First Phase	India, Pakistan and Sri Lanka	20% and above	20% maximum	2008
	Bangladesh, Bhutan, Maldives and Nepal (LDCs)	30% and above	30% maximum	2008
Second Phase	India, Pakistan	20% or below	0–5%	2013
	Sri Lanka	20% or below	0–5%	2014
	Bangladesh, Bhutan, Maldives and Nepal (LDCs)	30% or below	0–5%	2016

Source: SAFTA Agreement (2004).

under the accord. Most of the intra-regional trade in South Asia has taken place under various bilateral trading arrangements or under Most Favoured Nation (MFN) rates. Henceforth, SAFTA's effectiveness has been undermined at least during the first two years of its operation.

3. Intra-industry and Inter-industry Trade in South Asia

Intra-regional export of South Asian countries appears to be primary and resource-based products with a small share of low tech products (Table A5.1). Although export structure in general has specialised in low end operations (UNIDO 2009), their share has declined over time in view of faster growth of export of manufactured products. Export of resource-based products of the region has experienced some encouraging changes, mainly due to large amount of export from India. Within the region, India has been successful in improving its specialisation in terms of production and export of medium-technology products, while export of high-technology products has changed at a slow pace.[2]

It is widely acknowledged that expansion of intra-industry trade is conducive to make international trade more competitive (Ruffin 1999), and it helps boost regional integration (Kemal 2004). Intra-industry trade among South Asian countries is estimated by using 'Grubel-Lloyd (GL) Index', which captures trade in products under the same product line or industry. In case of the GL Index, the values vary between 0 to 1 where any value of 0 means only unidirectional trade and any value of 1 denotes full scale trade for that industry within the region. Following the approach of Austria (2004), the GL Index is estimated for selected set of industries of South Asian countries. The selected set of industries is termed here as 'Priority Goods Sector' which maintained the highest intra-regional trade during 2008 at Standard International Trade Classification (SITC) 2 digit level (top ten sectors; see Table 5.6), which we then divided into two groups, namely '**Priority Goods Sector-A and B**'. For this analysis, SAARC region has been considered as a whole as the partner country for any reporting country within the region.

As can be seen from Table 5.6, smaller economies possess relatively higher share of their trade in the priority sectors; for example, Bhutan's 83 per cent trade within the region consists of trade of these sectors. India and Pakistan, however, traded at a lower level for these priority sectors.

Table 5.6: Share of Intra-regional Trade for the 'Priority Goods Sector' within SAARC in 2008

SITC level	Description	Bangladesh*	Bhutan	India	Maldives	Pakistan	Sri Lanka
6	Manufactured goods	14.38	74.43	3.38	20.20	8.01	17.60
0	Food and live animals	25.89	98.68	12.57	27.46	13.72	17.95
7	Machinery transport/equipment	8.83	53.01	1.65	10.04	1.20	18.55
65	Textile yarn/fabric/art	15.69	NA	10.89	NA	6.13	19.88
26	Textile fibres	34.62	18.63	21.38	NA	31.91	1.11
5	Chemicals/products n.e.s.	18.52	NA	2.96	29.74	11.34	17.92
2	Crude matter. Ex food/fuel	26.07	95.69	3.78	45.37	20.43	21.31
4	Cereals/cereal preparation	40.24	NA	14.99	NA	7.33	11.87
33	Petroleum and products	13.99	NA	1.48	NA	4.21	32.66
3	Mineral fuel/lubricants	13.92	99.86	1.44	NA	4.03	31.17
Total		**18.61**	**83.34**	**2.83**	**13.59**	**7.42**	**21.81**

Source: World Integrated Trade Solution (WITS), World Bank (2009).

Note: *Bangladesh's 2008 data is not available in World Bank WITS website: http://wits.worldbank.org/witsweb/, and hence percentages of the same products of year 2007 for Bangladesh has been used in this analysis.

The fact that overall pattern of the intra-industry trade (IIT) index among the countries, even for the trade under 'Priority Goods Sector', is very low and somewhat erratic, corroborates with low level of integration of the South Asian economies (Tables A5.2 and A5.3). IIT index for most of the industries experienced a deceleration over time and in some industries, it has alarmingly declined. Between 1995 and 2008, Pakistan's IIT index has declined in textile yarn, textile fibres, chemical products, crude materials and cereal products which show Pakistan's relatively less linkage with the production networks within the region. Low and declining IIT index was also registered in case of the Maldives for manufactured goods, India for textile fibres, India and Sri Lanka for Chemical products, and India and Nepal for crude materials.

It is argued that developing vertical specialisation through production-sharing arrangements would help the smaller economies of the region capture benefits from the cooperation initiative (Kemal 2004). Hence, the region can promote trade by formulating devices which will enhance intra-industry trade on the basis of the competitive advantages of each country in such areas as tariff rates, wages, technological structure, transportation cost, human and natural resources. According to Moazzem and Rahman (2009), countries of the region should take initiative to specialise in parts of the value chain within specific sectors where they enjoy the strongest comparative advantages. The sector specific potential of different countries could be converted into complementarities by using areas of comparative advantage in terms of resource and skill endowments that could create vertically linked regional production chains. Therefore, tapping the potentials of IIT would be the most challenging part for enhancing intra-regional trade in South Asia.

4. Challenges for Promoting Trade

Analysis shows that more than 55 per cent of South Asia's intra-regional trade potential has not been tapped adequately with bilateral trade between most countries of the region remaining unused as high as 100 per cent (ADB and UNCTAD 2008). Most importantly more than US$1.8 billion worth of trade potentials be-tween India and Pakistan has been unutilised, which is more than 80 per cent of existing bilateral trade between these two countries. As for Bangladesh and India, it is equivalent to US$1.6 billion. Bangladesh's maximum trade potential lies at least in relative sense with Bhutan, Nepal and Pakistan. Similarly Bhutan's trade potentials are relatively high with Pakistan and the Maldives. Prospect of enhancement of trade has not only suffered from lack of trade complementarity among the member countries, but also because of other challenges which surfaced due to non-tariff and other barriers.

4.1. Non-Tariff Barriers (NTBs)

It is evident that as tariff measures went down during 1990s, NTBs faced by SAARC member states accelerated at the same time. Most of the NTBs imposed are related to Sanitary and Phyto-sanitary Measures (SPS) and Technical Barriers to Trade (TBT), Quota restrictions, anti-dumping measures, licensing requirements and countervailing measures (Table 5.7). Documentation procedures and SAFTA certification have been strong forms of NTBs amongst SAARC countries.

SAFTA has not been effective in dealing with NTBs. Though SAFTA requires member states to notify to the Committee of Experts (CoE) regarding any NTBs and para-tariff measures, the CoE can only recommend their removal, which does not imply a binding commitment.[3] Although India is the major export destination of most countries in the region, strong prevalence of large number of NTBs has adversely affected export of other countries to India. A number of examples can be put forward regarding prevalence of NTBs in South Asia. In Indo-Sri Lanka FTA (ISFTA), for example, tea and garment exports from Sri Lanka to India can only be cleared at specified ports. Similarly, the customs entry points along India's land borders with Bangladesh, Nepal, Bhutan and Pakistan cannot be used to clear items on the sensitive list — SPS measures taken by India that are said to be compatible with international standards. Pakistan has low NTBs but it applies technical and safety regulations under World Trade Organisation (WTO) rules on trade in goods. Bangladesh continues to maintain quantitative restrictions on eggs, poultry and salt, for which the government has obtained waivers from the WTO. Sri Lanka bans import of tea and spices on the grounds of low quality imports. Some of these NTBs such as certain

Table 5.7: Percentage Share of NTBs to All NTBs by SAARC Countries

Non-tariff measures	Share
SPS, TBT, and other related measures	86.3
Tariff quota	9.8
Anti-dumping measures	7.4
License requirement	5.3
Countervailing measures	1.2

Source: ADB (2008).

items of national security, health and cultural interest are genuine and legitimate. However, a majority of them are simply political measures to protect the 'vote bank'.

If SAFTA fails to phase out NTBs within a stipulated timeframe, tariff liberalisation will have little positive impact. Alburo (2004, cited in ADB 2008) highlighted that though there is potential for regional cooperation in addressing NTBs, there is little scope for resolving the barriers since it is a matter of negotiation amongst the governments.

4.2. Specific Duties, Para-tariffs and Port-specific Destinations — Other Variations of NTBs

The regulatory infrastructure poses several other NTBs in South Asia including para-tariffs in addition to the basic customs duties. These constitute domestic taxes charged either by the central government or the state governments which could, for instance, be the countervailing duty of 16.3 per cent levied by India on most goods to adjust for the Central Excise Duty and the Special Countervailing Duty of 4 per cent that compensates for the Central Sales Tax and another 2 per cent to cover the education *cess*.[4] Other SAARC members also actively practice imposition of para-tariffs.[5]

4.3. Infrastructure Constraints

One reason behind the subdued trade figures between the South Asian nations is the weak nature of physical, industrial and communication infrastructure. Land, air and maritime ports are deemed to be less efficient and thus lag behind in competition with their counterparts in East Asia (Jones 2006). Compared to a couple of hours it takes in Singapore and Laem Chabang, Thailand, to clear a vessel, Chittagong port in Bangladesh takes 2–3 days. Similarly, Delhi airport has an average cargo dwelling time of 2.5 days. Several studies and estimates have been conducted to calculate the magnitude of NTBs emanating from infrastructural deficiencies. World Bank (2004), for example, computed an estimation of saving in terms of transport cost from road to rail along the Kolkata–Kathmandu corridor at 22–33 per cent of road cost. Similarly, UNESCAP approximated transit charges at 0.45 per cent of Cost, Insurance and Freight (CIF) values for private cargo (ADB 2008). Nevertheless, despite these grim developments, some South Asian countries have been moderately successful in introducing and augmenting IT infrastructure at some important border crossings in the last few years.

Most of the border crossings between South Asian countries are not designed to manage the volumes of traffic that currently passes through them, which results in severe congestion and causes delay in handling the shipments. Land ports have open storage and closed godowns within the customs controlled area. For example, at the Petrapole–Benapole border, it takes longer time to unload vehicles than the physical clearance time. Not surprisingly, due to lack of thorough-transport arrangements, there are transport inefficiencies at the borders.

4.4. Extra-regional Free Trade Agreements (FTAs)

There is an increasing tendency of South Asian countries towards signing bilateral trading/economic partnership with economically strategic regional blocs. India and Pakistan in particular have been especially keen towards fostering bilateral cooperation with other regional blocs. As a result, a number of agreements were either signed, such as India–ASEAN FTA or in the process of negotiation, such as India–EU FTA. Analysis shows that if this initiative is successful, the other South Asian countries (especially Bangladesh) will suffer from trade preference erosion in the EU market. Bangladesh will suffer more because nearly 60 per cent of her total exports are concentrated towards the EU market (for which India will also receive preferential access), followed by Pakistan and Sri Lanka. Such initiatives, therefore, would deter development of an effective regional trading area within the South Asian bloc (Winters et. al. 2009).

4.5. Bilateral FTAs in the Region Versus SAFTA

Analysis shows that compared to bilateral trading agreements signed by South Asian countries within the region, SAFTA is more structurally rigid. Rules of Origin (RoO) set forth under the SAFTA seems stringent where LDCs are required to comply with 30 per cent of domestic value addition criteria.[6] In contrast, a low level of domestic value addition criteria have been set forth under the Bilateral Free Trade Agreements (BFTAs)[7] which helped promote bilateral trade between the concerned parties. Tariff Liberalisation Programme (TLP) under the SAFTA is relatively slow and less attractive since no commitment for immediate duty reduction to zero per cent has been made whereas bilateral FTAs agreed upon reduction of duties at zero level for a substantial number of products. Even the full implementation of SAFTA will be completed as per schedule by 2016, whereas the comparable period for bilateral FTAs are no later than 2010. The long negative list of member countries for trading under SAFTA accord has been a deterrent factor for enhancing regional trade. Overall, SAFTA's structural rigidities have helped to incentivise member countries to negotiate for signing bilateral trading agreements both within and outside the region.

4.6. Other Barriers

South Asian countries often specify the port of entry for all or selective products. While this approach has been implemented to curb illegal flow, it also appears to have been supplemented by inadequate administrative capacity. The port-specific restrictions have increased transaction costs for trading across border, and have sometimes led to a virtual blockage of imports. Other restraints include sanitary standards, undocumented/illegal money, documentation requirements for trade transactions (as well as the average amount of time spent in fulfilling these requirements), procedural delays,[8] limited vehicle access, and inefficient rail links and transport through third ports.[9] The cost of trading has increased significantly by the virtue of these indirect costs. In broader perspective, enabling factors, governance issues, infrastructural constraints and institutional barriers have provided an avenue to carry out huge amount of informal trade within the region.

Entrepreneurs of the region suffer from a dearth of information and restrictions in their mobility and interaction. Timely and accurate information on trade-related matters are difficult to obtain. The Geneva based World Economic Forum identified the enabling factors and constructed an Enabling Global Trade Index ranking 120 countries around the globe. Barring India and Sri Lanka, all other South Asian countries have been ranked below 100 overshadowing the magnitude of restrictiveness in their national policies, inadequate physical infrastructure, cumbersome border administration procedure and a strong reluctance to grant access to their respective markets (Table A5.4).

5. Trade Facilitation in South Asia

With the evolving nature of complexity of trade among nations, costs associated with moving goods across international borders is now as important as tariffs in determining the cost of landed goods. The ability of countries to deliver goods and services in time and at low costs is a key determinant of their participation in the global economy.

For individual members of the SAARC, the priority issues relating to trade facilitation are heavily influenced by the perspective of the concerned country. For example, if a country is landlocked (e.g., Afghanistan, Nepal and Bhutan), the focus of trade facilitation is likely to be on the need for an efficient and effective transport mechanism that services its trade needs, regardless of distance and the number of borders to be crossed. The importance and forms of trade facilitation in the context of South Asia is thus multifaceted, given the mix of geostrategic positions of its member countries.[10]

According to Chaturvedi (2007), focus of major South Asian regional trading arrangements are still falling short of addressing some of the core issues with regard to facilitating trade for development purpose. These include, among others, provisions related to automation of customs procedures, establishing single window, border agency cooperation and exchange of information among relevant agencies operating in different countries. Such factors impose higher cost on doing business across the borders. Coupled with these is the lack of an integrated multimodal transport system (road, rail and waterway) which fattens the cost of import and export within the region.

Although a core objective of trade facilitation is to reduce such barriers as use of excessive documentation in customs clearance procedure and bringing down the costs related to export and import, studies show that South Asia, both as a region and its individual member states, lags significantly behind the best performers in the world (Table 5.8).

It is in the above context that simplification of customs procedures is of high relevance for South Asian countries. Statistics reveal that whereas standard time required for completion of export and import procedures in Bangladesh is 28 days and 32 days respectively (Table A5.5), the corresponding figures for Singapore is 5 and 3 days, and for Sweden 8 and 6 days.[11]

As has been noted earlier, lack of adequate infrastructure and logistics support is a major obstacle in facilitating trade in South Asia. According to a report,[12] only one of the eight South Asian countries (India) managed to claim a position among the top 50 performers in terms of Logistics Performance Index (LPI).[13] Logistics in terms of customs, infrastructure and international shipment of the South Asian countries lags behind competing countries (e.g., China and Thailand) of neighbouring regions (see Table A5.6). Further, Wilson and Otsuki (2007) has argued that development of required capacity in facilitating trade might result in US$2.6 billion worth of

Table 5.8: Trading Across Borders: South Asia vis-à-vis other Regions

	South Asia	East Asia and Pacific	Sub-Saharan Africa	OECD
Documents for export				
2008	8.5	6.8	7.9	4.6
2009	8.5	6.7	7.8	4.5
Documents for import				
2008	9.0	7.4	8.9	5.2
2009	9.0	7.1	8.8	5.1
Time for export (days)				
2008	32.5	23.4	35.5	10.9
2009	33.0	23.3	34.7	10.7
Time for import (days)				
2008	32.0	24.7	43.4	11.4
2009	32.5	24.5	48.1	11.4
Cost to export ($ per container)				
2008	1179.9	882.0	1660.1	936.5
2009	1339.1	902.3	1878.8	1069.1
Cost to import ($ per container)				
2008	1331.9	954.1	1985.9	1016.7
2009	1487.3	948.5	2278.7	1132.7

Source: World Bank (2009).

gain for South Asia as a region, with India having the lion's share equivalent to more than US $1 billion (Table A5.7).

However, attaining such results hinge critically on addressing a number of factors such as establishing SAARC single window (similar to Asia-Pacific Economic Cooperation (APEC) or single window initiative), strengthening customs-to-customs cooperation, introducing authorised economic operator (see WCO, 2007), strengthening regulatory framework and assuring enhanced risk management procedures which are important prerequisites towards meaningfully facilitating trade in the regional context.

6. Conclusion

Existing regional economic integration instruments such as SAFTA has so far failed to enhance intra-regional trade. More importantly, regional trade has been extensively influenced by various intra- and extra-regional FTAs and various other preferential initiatives provided by the developed and a number of developing countries. There is also an increasing tendency of South Asian countries towards signing bilateral trading/economic partnership agreements with economically strategic regional blocs. Nevertheless, analyses demonstrate that South Asia as a region as well as on a bilateral basis possesses enormous export potentials. No doubt that an effective regional integration initiative would expedite those prospects.

It seems that South Asian integration should be effective and possible only when it can perform as a regional trading block which could meet the growing demand of major economies, both as a source of input as well as a destination for export. The region can promote trade by formulating devices which will enhance intra-industry trade on the basis of the competitive advantages of each country in such areas as wages, technological structure, transportation cost, human and natural resources.

Realising intra-industry trade potentials would require significant amount of intra-regional and extra-regional investment targeting both regional and extra-regional markets. Signing of SAARC investment treaty and establishment of integrated production network within the region based on comparative advantages will be essential to stimulate intra-regional and extra-regional trade of individual SARRC countries. Many of the initiatives suggested in this chapter would require strong political will, which at the moment, leaves much to be desired.

Appendix

Table A5.1: Export Pattern of South Asian Countries According to Technological Classification (As Percentage of Total Export)

	2000	*2001*	*2002*	*2003*	*2004*	*2005*
Product type	60.6 (15.4)	63.4 (19.3)	72.4 (20)	86.3 (23.8)	106.2 (26.9)	125 (22.2)
Primary	15.51 (11.69)	15.62 (13.47)	14.92 (13.00)	13.56 (11.76)	12.62 (11.15)	13.28 (15.32)
Resource-based	21.45 (2.60)	21.29 (4.15)	23.48 (5.00)	23.75 (5.46)	27.50 (6.32)	31.76 (10.36)
Low-technology	49.01 (78.57)	48.74 (76.17)	46.69 (75.50)	46.47 (75.63)	43.88 (76.21)	37.44 (67.57)
Medium-technology	10.40 (6.49)	10.09 (5.18)	10.50 (5.00)	11.82 (5.88)	11.96 (4.83)	13.28 (5.41)
High-technology	3.63 (0.65)	4.26 (1.04)	4.42 (1.50)	4.40 (1.26)	4.05 (1.49)	4.24 (1.35)

Source: Calculated based on UNIDO data (UNIDO 2009).

Note: Figures in the parentheses indicate South Asia excluding India.

Table A5.2: Pattern of Intra-industry Trade Under 'Priority Goods Sector-A'

Country	1995	2000	2005	2006	2007	2008
Manufactured goods (SITC Level: 6)						
Bangladesh	0.049	0.031	0.212	0.204	0.263	–
Bhutan	–	–	–	–	–	0.105
India	0.121	0.298	0.548	0.543	0.575	0.507
Maldives	–	0.000	0.000	–	–	0.000
Nepal	–	0.398	–	–	–	0.608
Pakistan	0.217	0.253	0.277	0.309	0.334	0.296
Sri Lanka	–	–	0.688	–	–	0.274
Food and live animals (SITC Level: 0)						
Bangladesh	0.095	0.230	0.333	0.208	0.088	–
Bhutan	–	–	–	–	–	0.371
India	0.210	0.399	0.435	0.271	0.283	0.319
Maldives	0.755	0.675	0.596	0.539	0.429	0.280
Nepal	–	0.959	0.609	0.738	0.831	0.791
Pakistan	0.631	0.899	–	–	–	0.434
Sri Lanka	–	–	0.543	–	–	–
Machinery transport/equipment (SITC Level: 7)						
Bangladesh	0.022	0.159	0.040	0.098	0.131	–
Bhutan	–	–	–	–	–	0.000
India	0.023	0.046	0.120	0.182	0.153	0.329
Maldives	–	0.001	0.000	0.000	–	0.000
Nepal	–	–	–	–	–	–
Pakistan	0.821	0.782	0.578	0.653	0.790	0.924
Sri Lanka	–	–	0.197	–	–	0.375

Textile yarn/fabric/art (SITC Level: 65)

Bangladesh	0.039	0.048	0.328	0.297	0.336	–
Bhutan	–	–	–	–	–	–
India	0.078	0.304	0.395	0.455	0.448	0.382
Maldives	–	–	0.528	–	–	–
Nepal	–	0.027	0.085	0.058	0.056	–
Pakistan	0.085	–	0.139	–	–	0.071
Sri Lanka	–	–	–	–	–	0.143

Textile fibers (SITC Level: 26)

Bangladesh	0.584	0.664	0.795	0.540	0.978	–
Bhutan	–	–	–	–	–	0.069
India	0.562	0.587	0.386	0.221	0.206	0.109
Maldives	–	–	–	–	–	–
Nepal	–	–	–	–	–	–
Pakistan	0.821	0.963	0.620	0.389	0.123	0.253
Sri Lanka	–	–	0.621	–	–	0.927

Source: World Bank (2009).

Table A5.3: Pattern of Intra-industry Trade Under 'Priority Goods Sector-B'

Country	1995	2000	2005	2006	2007	2008
Chemicals/products n.e.s (SITC Level: 5).						
Bangladesh	0.645	0.335	0.479	0.425	0.511	–
Bhutan	–	–	–	–	–	–
India	0.743	0.543	0.406	0.334	0.308	0.264
Maldives	–	–	0.001	–	0.000	0.001
Nepal	–	–	0.845	–	–	–
Pakistan	0.747	0.653	0.598	0.412	0.186	0.251
Sri Lanka	–	–	0.410	–	–	0.122
Crude matter. Ex food/fuel (SITC Level: 2)						
Bangladesh	0.746	0.565	0.716	0.522	0.945	–
Bhutan	–	–	–	–	–	0.278
India	0.989	0.914	0.532	0.492	0.451	0.321
Maldives	0.089	0.059	0.137	0.132	0.107	0.107
Nepal	–	–	–	–	–	–
Pakistan	0.396	0.626	0.341	0.292	0.132	0.215
Sri Lanka	–	–	0.492	–	–	0.520
Cereals/cereal products (SITC Level: 4)						
Bangladesh	0.000	0.002	0.003	0.001	0.060	–
Bhutan	–	–	–	–	–	–
India	0.010	0.045	0.027	0.019	0.054	0.038
Maldives	–	–	–	–	–	–
Nepal	–	0.146	–	–	–	–
Pakistan	0.000	0.000	0.053	0.007	0.007	0.241
Sri Lanka	–	–	0.108	–	–	0.069

Petroleum and products (SITC Level: 33)

Bangladesh	0.006	–	0.060	0.226	0.683	–
Bhutan	–	–	–	–	–	–
India	–	0.072	0.000	0.205	0.071	0.181
Maldives	–	–	0.000	–	–	–
Nepal	–	–	–	–	–	–
Pakistan	–	0.004	0.003	0.013	0.009	0.000
Sri Lanka	–	–	0.003	–	–	0.003

Mineral fuel/lubricants (SITC Level: 3)

Bangladesh	0.000	–	0.059	0.226	0.682	–
Bhutan	–	–	–	–	–	0.540
India	0.005	0.810	0.000	0.186	0.067	0.166
Maldives	–	–	0.000	–	–	–
Nepal	–	–	–	–	–	–
Pakistan	0.000	0.453	0.017	0.014	0.018	0.034
Sri Lanka	–	–	0.003	–	–	0.003

Source: World Bank (2009).

Table A5.4: Enabling Global Trade Index 2009

South Asian countries	Overall index	Market access	Border administration	Transport and communications infrastructure	Business environment
India	76	116	58	64	53
Sri Lanka	78	64	67	69	90
Pakistan	100	111	63	80	102
Nepal	110	29	113	107	117
Bangladesh	111	57	104	108	110

Source: World Economic Forum (2009).

Table A5.5: Performance of Individual South Asian Countries in Trading Across Borders

Year	Afghanistan	Bangladesh	Bhutan	India	Maldives	Nepal	Pakistan	Sri Lanka
Rank								
2008	177	104	153	81	116	157	67	60
2009	179	105	151	90	121	157	71	66
Documents for export								
2008	12	7	8	8	8	9	9	8
2009	12	6	8	8	8	9	9	8
Documents for import								
2008	11	9	11	15	9	10	8	6
2009	11	8	11	9	9	10	8	6
Time for export (days)								
2008	67	28	38	18	21	43	24	21
2009	74	28	38	17	21	41	24	21
Time for import (days)								
2008	71	32	38	21	20	35	19	21
2009	77	32	38	20	20	35	18	20
Cost to export ($ per container)								
2008	2500	844	1150	820	1200	1600	515	810
2009	3000	970	1210	945	1348	1764	611	865
Cost to import ($ per container)								
2008	2100	1148	2080	910	1200	1725	1336	844
2009	2600	1375	2140	960	1348	1900	680	895

Source: World Bank (2009).

Table A5.6: Country Rankings as Per the LPI

Country	Rank	Customs	Infrastructure	International shipment
India	39	47	42	39
Pakistan	68	69	71	65
Bangladesh	87	125	82	96
Sri Lanka	92	91	106	112
Bhutan	128	134	127	134
Nepal	130	141	144	131
Afghanistan	150	150	150	150
China	30	35	30	28
Thailand	31	32	32	32

Source: World Bank (2007).

Table A5.7: Trade Gains from Capacity Building in Trade Facilitation

(US$ millon)

Country/ Region	Port efficiency	Customs modernisation	Regulatory reforms	Service-sector infrastructure	All
Bangladesh	228	144	71	339	782
India	314	193	123	519	1149
Pakistan	74	29	42	191	336
Sri Lanka	97	63	41	175	376
South Asia	712	429	278	1224	2643

Source: Wilson and Otsuki (2007).

Notes

* This chapter draws on a Centre for Policy Dialogue (CPD) report titled *Regional Trade in South Asia*.
1. Products included in each country's sensitive list are being traded according to the MFN tariff rates which are often quite significant, especially for agricultural products. Since agricultural products dominate the export baskets of South Asian countries, prevailing high tariff rates on these items have seriously discouraged intra-regional trade.
2. India's export of electrical machinery and apparatus, iron and steel, and chemicals grew at a faster rate. One striking feature in the case of the export structure of South Asia is her high dependency on imported intermediate inputs compared to their production targeted to the domestic market (UNIDO 2009).

3. A wide range of WTO consistent NTBs are still in place in India. These include Tariff Rate Quotas (TRQs) on 14 tariff lines (HS 8-digit level), import restrictions, licensing and limited port availability.
4. Taxation with the specific objective of using the revenues in building local educational infrastructure.
5. For example, industrial development surcharges and supplementary duties.
6. In case of cumulative RoO, the minimum aggregate content required to be 50 per cent though input from domestic sources is required to be 20 per cent.
7. Such as India–Sri Lanka BFTA and Pakistan–Sri Lanka BFTA.
8. Such as absence of staff, administrative inefficiencies, excessive department clearances and signatures.
9. For instance, India allows the entry of tea from Sri Lanka through four specified ports excluding Chennai which is one of the nearest ports of entry to India. Similarly, India has limited the entry of drugs and chemicals from Bangladesh through three land customs stations only, excluding Kolkata port and Petrapole land custom station — the two closest trading points for facilitating Indo-Bangladesh trade.
10. Out of eight South Asian countries, three are landlocked (Afghanistan, Bhutan and Nepal), two are water-locked (Maldives and Sri Lanka) and three have both land and maritime boundaries (Bangladesh, India and Pakistan).
11. 'Doing Business', World Bank (2009).
12. World Bank (2007).
13. Logistics Performance Index (LPI) is the simple average of the country scores on the seven key dimensions: (i) efficiency and effectiveness of the clearance process by customs and other border control agencies; (ii) ability of transport and IT infrastructure for logistics; (iii) ease and affordability of arranging shipments; (iv) competence in the local logistics industry (e.g., transport operators, customs brokers); (v) ability to track and trace shipments; (vi) domestic logistics costs (e.g., local transportation, terminal handling, warehousing); and (vii) timeliness of shipments in reaching destination.

References

Asian Development Bank (ADB). 2008. 'Report on the South Asia Department: Economists Annual Conference'. Manila: Asian Development Bank.

Asian Development Bank (ADB) and United Nations Conference on Trade and Development (UNCTAD). 2008. *Quantification of Benefits from Economic Cooperation in South Asia*. New Delhi: Macmillan.

Austria, Myrna S. 2004. 'The Patterns of Intra-ASEAN Trade in the Priority Goods Sectors'. Report prepared for the ASEAN Secretariat under the

AADCP–Regional Economic Policy Support Facility. Jakarta: ASEAN Secretariat.

Chaturvedi, S. 2007. 'Trade Facilitation Measures in South Asian FTAs: An Overview of Initiatives and Policy Approaches', Asia-Pacific Research and Training Network on Trade (ARTNeT) Working Paper Series No. 28. New York: United Nations.

ESCAP. 2008. *Emerging Trade Issues for the Policymakers in Developing Countries Asia and the Pacific*. New York: United Nations.

International Monetary Fund (IMF). 2009. *Direction of Trade Statistics* (DOTS). Washington, D.C.: IMF.

Jones, S. 2006. 'Infrastructure Challenges in East and South Asia'. Paper presented at Promoting Growth, Ending Poverty, Asia 2015 Conference, 6–7 March, London.

Kemal, A. R. 2004. 'SAFTA and Economic Cooperation in SAFMA'. Paper presented at Regional Conference on Regional Cooperation in South Asia organised by SAFMA, Dhaka. http://www.centad.org/relatedinfo12.asp (acessed 14 August 2009).

Moazzem, Khondaker Golam and Md. Tariqur Rahman. 2009. 'Bangladesh Country Investment Study', in Asian Development Bank, *Study on Intra-regional Trade and Investment in South Asia*, pp. 87–113. Manila: Asian Development Bank.

Rahman, M. and Wasel Bin Shadat. 2006. 'NAMA Negotiations in the WTO and Preference Erosion: Concerns of Bangladesh and Other Asia-Pacific LDCs', *South Asia Economic Journal*, 7 (2): 179–203.

Ruffin, Roy J. 1999. 'The Nature and Significance of Intra-Industry Trade', *Economic and Financial Review*, 4: 2–9, Federal Reserve Bank of Dallas, Dallas.

SAFTA Agreement. 2004. 'Agreement on South Asian Free Trade Area (SAFTA)'. http://www.saarc-sec.org/userfiles/saftaagreement.pdf (accessed 20 August 2009).

Sawhney, A. and Kumar, R. 2008. *Why SAFTA?* London: Commonwealth Secretariat and CUTS International.

Taneja, N. and A. Sawhney. 2007. 'Revitalising SAARC Trade', *Economic Political Weekly*, 42 (13): 1081–1084.

UNIDO. 2009. *Industrial Development Report 2009. Breaking in and Moving Up: New Industrial Challenges for the Bottom Billion and the Middle-Income Countries*. Vienna: United Nations Industrial Development Organisation.

Wilson, John S. and Tsunehiro Otsuki. 2007. 'Regional Integration in South Asia: What Role for Trade Facilitation?', Policy Research Working Paper Series 4423. Washington, DC: World Bank.

Winters, L. A. et al. 2009. *Innocent Bystanders: Implications of an EU-India Free Trade Agreement for Excluded Countries*. London: Commonwealth Secretariat.

World Bank. 2004. *Promoting Regional Integration in South Asia: A Private Sector Perspective,* Washington D.C.: World Bank.

————. 2007. *Connecting to Compete: Trade Logistics in the Global Economy.* Washington D.C.: World Bank.

————. 2009. *Doing Business.* www.doingbusiness.org World Bank. 2009a. *World Integrated Trade Solution (WITS).* http://wits.worldbank.org/witsweb/ (accessed 5 August, 2009).

World Customs Organisation (WCO). 2007. 'WCO SAFE Framework of Standards'. http://www.wcoomd.org/files/1.%20Public%20files/PDFand Documents/SAFE%20Framework_EN_2007_for_publication.pdf (accessed 5 August 2009).

World Economic Forum. 2009. *The Global Enabling Trade Report 2009.* Geneva: World Economic Forum (WEF).

6

A Study of Economic Feasibility of Optimum Currency Area in South Asia

Mirza Allim Baig

In the global scenario, there has been a growing trend towards regional economic integration. Now all countries are members of at least one regional trading block and many belong to more than one (Schiff and Winters 2003). These regional groupings are still in the process of intensifying the regional economic integration and are open to enlarge the union. Developed countries account for the functioning of major Regional Trade Agreements (RTAs). They are stronger than the blocks consisting of developing countries as they have high levels of intra-regional trade. RTAs among industrialized countries are also expanding themselves to integrate select developing countries implying trade diversion away from other developing countries.

In such a scenario, it is important for developing countries to build up a framework for stronger economic cooperation within the region. The East Asian Crisis of 1997 has heightened the importance of regional economic cooperation, especially in the area of money and finance. Again, the recent financial crisis of 2008–2009 originating from developed countries reinforce the importance of regional monetary cooperation in the form of Optimum Currency Area (OCA).

During the crisis, the problems with the IMF conditionality to provide financial assistance prompted regional groups to seriously think about strong regional monetary and financial cooperation. At the time, the notion of a sovereign nation giving up its national currency to adopt a common regional currency was unthinkable. However, the recent adoption of the euro has dispelled all doubts about the reality of monetary unions. Other regions for such economic integration have been analysed by researchers, for example,

Bayoumi and Eichengreen (1994), and Bayoumi and Mauro (2001) for Association of Southeast Asian Nations (ASEAN) and North American Free Trade Agreement (NAFTA); Masson and Pattillo (2001) for West Africa; and Bhowmik (1998), Maskay (2003), Saxena (2002), and Saxena and Baig (2004) for South Asia.

In Asia, ASEAN and South Asian Association for Regional Co-operation (SAARC) are emerging as important regional groupings. South Asian countries are also engaged in a number of bilateral, sub-regional and regional trading agreements with the purpose to increase trade and other areas of economic cooperation. Though the progress of SAARC in strengthening economic integration has been very slow — the operationalisation of South Asian Free Trade Area (SAFTA), bringing Afghanistan under its umbrella, among others — SAARC has made some convincing advancement. The commitments of member countries to reduce tariffs in phased manner under the tariff liberalisation programme and reduction of items under negative list will further enhance trade/economic cooperation in the region.[1] The region even went to the extent to have a talk on optimum currency area — a single currency zone — the strongest form of monetary cooperation.

With this backdrop, the specific objectives of the study are as follows: (i) to understand the rationale and benefits of optimum currency area in South Asia, (ii) to examine the economic conditions and study the feasibility of OCA in the region, and (iii) to suggest alternatives for exchange rate arrangements and a roadmap for OCA in the region. The conclusion of the study is presented in the last section of this chapter.

The Rationale and Benefits of Optimum Currency Area

The concept of OCA stems from the seminal work of Mundell (1961) and McKinnon (1963). The idea was to have fixed exchange rates based on regional currencies rather than national currencies. According to this view, any region that has high intra-regional trade, fiscal transfers, high labour and capital mobility, and that experience the same economic shocks should have a common currency. This common regional currency should float against other currencies.

The literature also discusses the macroeconomic criteria as a pre-requisite condition for forming an OCA. Most of the literature recognises the following interrelationships between the countries that would impinge on the benefits of adopting a common currency (for example, see Frankel and Rose 1998). If the potential members of a union trade a lot with each other, OCA would reduce transaction costs. The cost of giving up monetary policy independence would decrease if the member countries experience similar shocks. High labour mobility across borders can be a useful mechanism for adjusting to asymmetric shocks that leads to high unemployment in a subset of the members of the union. If region-specific shocks prevail, a federal fiscal system would provide regional insurance thereby attenuating the impact of regional shocks on inter-regional income differentials. There would be low fiscal deficits and public debts.

The greatest benefit of a common currency can be experienced through intra-regional trade. Rose (1999) finds that the countries sharing same currency have trade three times greater than what they would have with different currencies. Glick and Rose (2001) show that under ceteris paribus, bilateral trade rises (falls) by about hundred per cent as a pair of countries forms (dissolves) a currency union. Frankel and Rose (2000), by using economic and geographic data, show that trade triples for each of the members belonging to a currency union. They also find that every one per cent increase in trade relative to Gross Domestic Product (GDP) raises income per capita by roughly one-third of a per cent over 20 years. They suggest that the beneficial effects of currency unions on economic performance come through promotion of trade, rather than through a commitment to non-inflationary monetary policy or other macroeconomic influences.

Since members of an OCA give up their independent monetary policies to stabilise their domestic economies, it is recognised that they experience a synchronised business cycle for a single monetary policy in the region to be effective. Rose and Engel (2002) find that members of international currency unions tend to experience more trade and less volatile exchange rates. They also find that business cycles are more tightly synchronised for members of a currency union suggesting closer trade links among themselves; and the members of common currency areas tend to be more specialised. Frankel and Rose (1998) find that countries with closer trade links tend to have more tightly correlated business cycles.

Full monetary integration, in whatever form it takes, implies that there exists a fixed exchange rate and perfect coordination of monetary policy among countries. Monetary union avoids competitive devaluation of regional currencies. Financial policy cooperation/ coordination reduces the spillover effects of exchange rate changes. Stable exchange rate promotes international trade and investment. In the presence of capital mobility, differing monetary policies can lead to differential real returns and volatile exchange rates. However, if the exchange rates are fixed, such capital flows make the economies vulnerable to financial crises. Hence, coordinated financial policies can reduce the risk of financial crises.

A fixed exchange rate arrangement among the member countries on the lines of Exchange Rate Mechanism in Europe has the advantage that it reduces the volatility in exchange rates and hence promotes trade and investment. In addition, the countries retain their monetary independence (howsoever limited it may be due to the fixed exchange rate system) and preserve their national currencies (which may be a symbol of national pride). The member countries retain an escape clause of abandoning the fixed exchange rate system if it is the adequate policy response to avert a financial crisis or revive a slowing economy. This is evident from the European crisis in 1992, when Britain and Italy opted out of the system to prevent further speculative attack on their currencies.

The biggest advantage of adopting a common currency as opposed to the fixed exchange rate system discussed above is the expectations about its permanence and the resolve by the policymakers. This advantage outweighs the cost of renouncing an independent monetary policy. As Mussa (1997) argues, the European crisis of 1992 could have been prevented if the European countries were using the same currency. Under a common currency, all countries follow the common monetary policy and it eliminates any divergence in returns that may exist in national currencies. This could prevent speculative attacks. In addition, the high cost of reverting back to national currencies (if that is even permissible, which is not the case for the European Union) and losing face in the international community encourage economic co-ordination among the member states.

Feasibility of OCA in South Asia

It might seem at first that the question on the appropriate domain of a currency area is purely academic since it hardly appears within the realm of political feasibility that national currencies would ever be abandoned in favour of any other arrangement (Mundell 1961). On the other side, European Union finally got the Euro, most probably for political reasons (Flandreau and Maurel 2005). Though the fate of monetary integration in South Asia largely lies on the political domain, a convincing economic feasibility of such a union must be investigated. Here, we must mention a caveat to the literature on OCA. It suffers from the famous Lucas Critique — even if the conditions for OCA do not exist ex-ante, which does not necessarily mean that the countries should not adopt a common currency. These countries may be more likely to satisfy the criteria after the adoption of the common currency than before (Frankel and Rose, 1997). This is because entering a monetary union induces structural changes that may imply that those countries become an OCA ex-post.

Macroeconomic Indicators

If the member countries could achieve low inflation, low interest rates and fiscal discipline, and control the volatility of exchange rate, then it will facilitate the formation of a monetary union in the region. Again, if the differences in inflation, interest rates, exchange rates and fiscal positions, among other factors, are very high within the member countries, then an exchange rate area may involve greater costs. Hence, we closely examine these macroeconomic variables for the SAARC region.

The SAARC countries exhibit a similar demographic structure. The population growth varies between 1.5 and 2.4 per cent per annum. South Asia has emerged as one of the fastest growing regions of the world. The SAARC countries grew at 6.3 per cent per annum on an average in 2008, and are projected to grow at the rate of 5.6 and 6.4 per cent per annum respectively for the next two years. Through the growth rate of Gross Domestic Product (GDP) or per capita GDP is not very similar, the structure of production is reasonably similar across the SAARC countries (ADO 2009). The correlations of growth rates are calculated and presented in Table 6.1.

Most of the countries experience average rate of inflation of SAARC (9.6 per cent in 2008). Afghanistan and Sri Lanka registered very high rate of inflation of 26.7 and 22.6 per cent respectively in 2008. The OCA criterion for European Union on inflation does not satisfy for SAARC countries[2]. The inflation rates based on Consumer Price Index, CPI (Wholesale Price Index, WPI for India only) are very low in the recent years as compared to that of 1990s. The volatility has also reduced significantly and the rates are converging for most of

Table 6.1: Correlation of Growth Rate of Real GDP in South Asia (Percentage per Annum), 1995–2008

	Afghanistan	Bangladesh	Bhutan	India	Maldives	Nepal	Pakistan	Sri Lanka
Afghanistan	1.00	0.76	0.47	0.57	0.04	-0.22	0.67	0.44
Bangladesh	0.76	1.00	0.31	0.35	0.23	0.19	0.34	0.61
Bhutan	0.47	0.31	1.00	0.02	-0.05	-0.10	-0.03	0.24
India	0.57	0.35	0.02	1.00	0.03	-0.73	0.53	0.73
Maldives	0.04	0.23	-0.05	0.03	1.00	-0.03	-0.49	0.44
Nepal	-0.22	0.19	-0.10	-0.73	-0.03	1.00	-0.33	-0.45
Pakistan	0.67	0.34	-0.03	0.53	-0.49	-0.33	1.00	0.04
Sri Lanka	0.44	0.61	0.24	0.73	0.44	-0.45	0.04	1.00

Source: ADB Key Indicator 2009.

the countries in the region, which is a sign of convergence. There are high correlations of inflations for cross countries and vary from 0.5 to 0.9 over the period 2000–2008 (see Table 6.2).

The national exchange rates vis-à-vis the US dollar is considered in the study. The exchange rate of Maldives' currency stands at rufiyaa 12.8 whereas that of Sri Lanka at Sri Lankan rupees 108.3 per US dollar in 2008. The correlations of exchange rates are very high and vary from 0.689 to 0.998 over the period 1997–2008 (see Table 6.3). It is clear that though there is a wide difference in the value of different national currencies, the movements are very smooth and steady, and are moving together.

The current account balance as a percentage of GDP varies from −51.7 (Maldives) to 3.9 (Bhutan). All the countries experienced fiscal deficits ranging from 2 per cent (for Nepal) to 13.6 per cent (for Maldives) in 2008 (Table 6.4). It can be observed from the table that except for Nepal and Bhutan, fiscal balance figures for other countries are unsatisfactory.

As far as the value of domestic currency and flow of Foreign Direct Investment (FDI) is concerned, the SAARC countries have experienced significant differences. While India received US$ 20700 million FDI in 2008, Nepal received an insignificant amount of US$ 5 million and Maldives received only US$ 16 million. There are divergent growth rates in money supply varying from 2.3 per cent (Bhutan) to 34.6 per cent (Afghanistan) in 2008 (ADO 2009). However, most of the countries have comfortable levels of foreign exchange reserves.

Extent of Intra-regional Trade

The benefits from an OCA accrue from a high level of intra-regional trade in the form of lower transaction costs. The volume of intra-regional trade in South Asia is quite insignificant (around 5 per cent), resulting in a limited interdependence among the South Asian countries.[3] Maldives and Nepal trade a lot within the SAARC region. The high trade figures for Nepal are due to its trade with India, which is not surprising, given a nearly free trade treaty between India and Nepal since 1996. India has started exporting a lot more to the SAARC nations in the 1990s, while Bangladesh and Sri Lanka have started importing a lot more.

The low level of intra-regional trade stands at odds with the openness of these economies to trade. Bhutan and Maldives trade more than their GDP. The degree of trade openness for India has

Table 6.2: Correlation of Inflation in South Asia (Percentage per Annum), 2000–2008

	Afghanistan	Bangladesh	Bhutan	India	Maldives	Nepal	Pakistan	Sri Lanka
Afghanistan	1.00	0.91	0.76	0.73	0.78	0.46	0.83	0.95
Bangladesh	0.91	1.00	0.87	0.80	0.82	0.77	0.89	0.95
Bhutan	0.76	0.87	1.00	0.64	0.86	0.67	0.95	0.86
India	0.73	0.80	0.64	1.00	0.85	0.46	0.60	0.75
Maldives	0.78	0.82	0.86	0.85	1.00	0.47	0.75	0.89
Nepal	0.46	0.77	0.67	0.46	0.47	1.00	0.62	0.61
Pakistan	0.83	0.89	0.95	0.60	0.75	0.62	1.00	0.85
Sri Lanka	0.95	0.95	0.86	0.75	0.89	0.61	0.85	1.00

Source: ADB Key Indicator 2009.

Table 6.3: Exchange Rates to US Dollar (Annual Average), 1997–2008

	Afghanistan	Bangladesh	Bhutan	India	Maldives	Nepal	Pakistan	Sri Lanka
Afghanistan	1.00	-0.19	0.07	0.07	-0.45	-0.03	0.08	-0.07
Bangladesh	-0.19	1.00	-0.33	-0.33	0.80	-0.22	0.75	0.88
Bhutan	0.07	-0.33	1.00	1.00	0.10	0.98	0.03	0.01
India	0.07	-0.33	1.00	1.00	0.10	0.98	0.03	0.01
Maldives	-0.45	0.80	0.10	0.10	1.00	0.27	0.66	0.89
Nepal	-0.03	-0.22	0.98	0.98	0.27	1.00	0.08	0.13
Pakistan	0.08	0.75	0.03	0.03	0.66	0.08	1.00	0.80
Sri Lanka	-0.07	0.88	0.01	0.01	0.89	0.13	0.80	1.00

Source: ADB Key Indicator 2009.

Table 6.4: Fiscal Balance (% GDP) of South Asia

Year	Bangladesh	Bhutan	India	Maldives	Nepal	Pakistan	Sri Lanka
1996	−3	2.2	−4.1	−2.5	−5.2	−6.5	−8.4
2000	−4.5	−3.8	−5.7	−4.4	−4.3	−5.4	−9.3
2006	−3.3	−0.8	−3.5	−6.8	−1.6	−4.3	−7
2007	−3.2	0.6	−2.7	−4.7	−1.8	−4.4	−6.9
2008	−5.3	...	−6	−13.6	−2	−7.6	−7

Source: ADB Key Indicator 2009.

increased from 18 per cent (1991) to 45.7 per cent (2007). Overall, SAARC countries are fairly open to trade (Table 6.5). However, further liberalisation and intra-regional trade may be needed in order to gain the benefits of low transaction costs and elimination of exchange rate risk that accrue from using a common currency.[4] With the operationalisation of SAFTA, the region is expected to realise the expansion in intra-regional trade, both in terms of official trading and new trade creation. The region is also expected to gain in terms of cost reduction, which further encourages intra-regional trade.

Nature of Disturbances/Pattern of Shocks

On the basis of nature of shocks criteria, the present study does not make any serious empirical investigation. The correlation of GDP growth rates (See Table 6.1) shows that there is no systematic growth pattern. This may give an indication of asymmetric nature of growth in output. In the literature, no study finds the possibility of forming an OCA for the whole region as they do not follow similar shocks. Some of the studies (for example, Saxena 2002 and Maskay 2003) however find that different sub-groups may qualify as suitable candidates for an OCA.

Table 6.5: Degree of Openness of South Asia

Year	Country Bangladesh	Bhutan	India	Maldives	Nepal	Pakistan	Sri Lanka
1991	19.16	85.83	18.04	153.33	33.1	39.58	68.01
2001	37.12	91.32	29.1	158.79	59.66	38.87	83.75
2007	37.71	115.06	45.76	178.3	41.16	36.17	68.75

Source: International Financial Statistics Year Book & WDI CD-ROM, World Bank.

Note: $\text{Openness} = \dfrac{(\text{Export of Goods and Services} + \text{Imports of Goods and Services})}{\text{GDP}} \times 100$

Labour Mobility

The OCA literature argues that labour mobility helps the members of a monetary union to adjust to asymmetric shocks by allowing labour to move from areas of high unemployment to low unemployment: 'With low labour mobility and sticky prices, the cost of losing monetary weapon is huge' (Flandreau and Maurel 2005). While labour mobility varies across the SAARC region, it may be hindered by differences in language and culture. However, labour is more mobile between India and Nepal, but very little official mobility occurs between India and Pakistan. Bangladesh has a very porous border with India that results in a substantial, but mostly illegal, flow of labour from Bangladesh to India. Given the geopolitical situation in the region, we do not expect high labour mobility at present. It took the European Union a long time to achieve the current levels of labour mobility and this can be enhanced through integrated labour laws in South Asia.

Fiscal Federalism

The overall fiscal deficits for the South Asian countries stood at high level but it is showing a declining trend (see Table 6.4). The fiscal deficit as a percentage of GDP is more than 3 per annum, the level required by EU for a member country. There is a need for maintaining fiscal disciple. If region-specific shocks prevail, a federal fiscal system would provide regional insurance (in the form of federally funded unemployment insurance benefits), thereby attenuating the impact of regional shocks on interregional income differentials. While no official fiscal transfer mechanism exists at present (except in the form of official aid), this issue can be addressed when formal negotiations for adoption of common currency start. These fiscal transfers may not be a panacea for all troubles, as Eichengreen (1997) argues against fiscal federalism, which may discourage factor mobility and may encourage national labour unions to demand higher wages as the burden of unemployment benefits falls on the entire union (and this may create more socially inefficient unemployment).

While examining the macroeconomic convergence criteria, the study finds that inflation rates are very low and they are converging for most of the countries. The exchange rate movements are showing very smooth pattern.[5] While India, Pakistan and Sri Lanka have a managed float, all the other countries have a pegged exchange rate regime, with Bhutan and Nepal pegged against the Indian rupee.

There is one-to-one convertibility of Indian rupee and Bhutanese ngultrum over the last 20 years and there is a little adjustment in the exchange rate between India and Nepalese rupees since last early 1990s.

It is argued that under free trade, smaller countries are expected to experience more trade gains that will bring all the economies in the region to converge in terms of macroeconomic performance.[6] Also, in recent years, the region is doing well in terms of macroeconomic performance. The key macroeconomic variables like inflation rates, exchange rates and fiscal deficits are converging in recent years. The ongoing macroeconomic reforms and increasing openness of capital account are positive steps in the direction of monetary co-operation in the region.

From the above discussion, there is no clear indication of fulfilment of macroeconomic convergence criteria for forming an OCA in the region. The countries have to work hard in the direction of containing fiscal deficit. The broad economic structure of the SAARC countries is not very similar in all aspects, which we can expect since no move towards any kind of convergence has been initiated yet. However, solid macroeconomic policies and performances are required for countries in a potential monetary union in order to prevent a poor performer from imposing externalities on the union. Since most of the members of SAARC currently have low inflation, low budget and current account deficits, similar growth, trade and production structure, it prods us to think of the possibility of monetary cooperation in the region. A road map for forming an OCA in the region may be prepared.

A Roadmap for OCA in South Asia

Once the countries agree to monetary cooperation among themselves, then the question arises on the practical operation of the system. An important issue arises on the design of a monetary and exchange rate policy framework for the unified system. At the operational level, there are many issues to be looked at like the distribution of seignorage revenue across countries, the role of each country's central bank for monetary policy, the harmonisation of banking supervision and regulations on monetary matters, etc. And, at the strategic level, the most important question is about the proper monetary/exchange rate co-ordination within the region, and between the region and the rest of the world.

Once a region decides to form an OCA, then it is left with two possibilities for the exchange rate coordination — the member countries can either adopt a fixed exchange rate or a single currency for their exchange rate management. However, they can have the option of a flexible exchange rate arrangement with the rest of the world. In a fixed exchange rate system, the member countries can have their own currency but their value will be fixed with the currencies of the other member countries. A single currency system is an extreme form of monetary arrangement where there will be one currency for all the member countries. Both arrangements have their own costs and benefits.

While adoption of a common currency leads to economic integration, the same level of integration could also be achieved through policy coordination — like between Canada and the United States or Switzerland and Germany. However, movement to a common currency is a political commitment to ensure regional integration and hence it might be desirable in the SAARC region.

This chapter proposes to appraise certain aspects of monetary and financial coordination and cooperation in the region. The goal of optimum currency area can only be achieved over time in a gradual process. Particularly after the East Asian currency crisis, different alternative exchange rate arrangements were proposed as intermediate steps towards the ultimate goal of achieving common currency in the region. The literature also suggests the adoption of parallel currency in the region.

The relationship between exchange rate coordination and macroeconomic coordination is more asymmetric in nature. The general macroeconomic coordination can be justified in the absence of explicit exchange rate coordination, but exchange rate coordination typically requires coordination in other macroeconomic policies, such as monetary and fiscal policies. Inflation targeting as a monetary policy goal may precede to exchange rate coordination.

To support any kind of chosen exchange rate coordination, the region should have sufficient reserves pool to revert any kind of unprecedented crisis. The region has made some progress in this direction. Although a more ambitious proposal to set up an Asian Monetary Fund did not take off due to the opposition by the US and the IMF, the crisis led to the launch of a regional initiative, namely the Chiang-Mai Initiative in 2000, involving creation of a network of bilateral swaps among the ASEAN and the plus three countries as a way to ensuring exchange rate stability.

This chapter recognises that economic integration is essential for growth and prosperity in the region. Some efforts have been made in this direction though not enough. There is a need for greater and free mobility of factors of production in the region which will work as a shock absorber in case of asymmetric shocks. Deeper economic reforms with increasing current and capital account openness and removal of trade restrictions will facilitate in establishing a single market in the region. Trade integration can be thought of as a first step for moving towards monetary cooperation and it can be facilitated through elimination of tariff and non-tariff barriers. To reduce the cost of exchanging currencies for intra-regional trade, the Asian Clearing Union (ACU) can be strengthened further to help such transactions. The other Asian countries may be invited to join ACU.

The convergence of macroeconomic indicators like inflation rate, interest rate, exchange rate, public debt, fiscal deficits, etc., are prerequisites for common monetary arrangements in the region. The countries have to bring down their fiscal deficit to the minimum possible level to use fiscal policy effectively for stabilisation purpose. SAARC countries could build a federal budget on the line of the EU, which collects a euro-wide VAT. It is important to understand the nature of shocks and the sources of shocks so that appropriate policy can be adopted. Fiscal positions need to be strengthened through deficit and debt reduction. There is a need to establish greater harmony in monetary policies in order to reduce currency misalignment and achieve full convertibility within the region. The central banks could share informations relating to central bank policies. The SAARCFINANCE could serve to coordinate the monetary fiscal and monetary policy in the region.

The countries should be working towards achieving macroeconomic stability and full convertibility in both current and capital account before moving to adopt a common currency in the region. A gradual move towards capital account convertibility, at least within the region, can be thought of seriously. The member countries should have some sort of pegged exchange rate system among themselves with wider band initially. However, the currencies could float against the other major currencies like the dollar, yen and euro. There must be availability of sufficient regional funds to act if a financial crisis happens to hit the region. In this context, the proposal to establish Reserve Bank of Asia needs to be considered more seriously. The purpose of pulling reserves can be widened beyond to that of Chiang-Mai initiatives, to include financing developmental expenditure and attaining macroeconomic stability. The criteria of surplus foreign exchange reserves can be decided on the basis of liquidity-at-risk principle rather than trade weights.

Finally, strong political cooperation and constant efforts are needed for monetary cooperation in the region. It is very much necessary to remove irritants and build extreme level of confidence and trust before thinking about common currency in the region. Lastly, the member countries should form a final road map for monetary cooperation, and proceed gradually to achieve the full form of monetary cooperation in the region to derive benefits from it.

Conclusion

Though monetary integration in South Asia is at present in its infancy stage with limited coordination among SAARC countries on monetary and exchange rate policy, there exists potential for monetary and financial cooperation. The study finds that the member countries have more or less similar pattern of human and economic development in terms of GDP growth, per capita income, inflation rates and sectoral contribution to GDP. There is a high and stable growth of out-put in the region. The key macroeconomic variables like inflation rates, exchange rates and fiscal deficits are converging. The ongoing macroeconomic reforms and increasing openness of capital account are the positive steps in the direction of monetary cooperation in the region. The study finds that though the level of intra-regional trade is very low, of late it has increased among most of the SAARC countries and trade is likely to increase with the implementation of SAFTA.

There has been growing realisation in the last decade among the South Asian leaders that the future of SAARC, like any other regional group, lies in concentrating on economic cooperation in specific areas. The conscious efforts made at the political level and demonstration of political will by the South Asian leaders will strengthen the regional economic cooperation. With cooperation already in place and progressing in terms of trade, social issues, regional investment promotion, WTO issues, tourism, tea council, steel front, promotion of internet, finance and network of SAARC researchers, the prospects for greater economic integration through coordination of macroeconomic policies seems to be brighter.

✳

Notes

1. The number of tariff lines in negative list is very high and hence restricts the scope of intra-regional trade.
2. The OCA criterion for EU on inflation was that inflation for a member country should be no more than 1.5 percentage points higher than the average of the three best performing (lowest inflation) member states of EU.
3. The low intra-regional trade figures might not be very representative of the total 'actual' trade that takes place among these countries. This is partly due to the non-accountability of high illegal cross-border trade and official restrictions. Recently intra-regional trade has increased among most of the SAARC countries and it is likely to increase further with the implementation of SAFTA. The complete elimination of tariffs under SAFTA may increase the intra-regional trade by 1.6 times the existing level (Mehta and Bhattacharya 1999). For example, the magnitude of formal and informal trade between Bangladesh and India is roughly the same, while informal trade forms almost a third of the value of formal trade between India and Sri Lanka (Taneja and Pohit 2001). Estimates on illegal trade between India and Pakistan vary from $100 million to $1 billion per year. If only India's informal trade with Bangladesh, Bhutan, Nepal and Sri Lanka is included, it is found that the intra-SAARC trade as a proportion of SAARC's total trade with the world stands at 6.48 per cent in 1999, which is much higher than the official figure 4.46 per cent (RIS, 2002).
4. The effect of openness on the net benefits is ambiguous, contrary to the usual argument that more open economies are better candidates for a currency area (Ricci 2008).
5. Maskay (2003) finds a similarity in the movement in the Nominal Effective Exchange Rate (NEER) and Real Effective Exchange Rate (REER) of all the countries.
6. Under SAPTA, it is the smaller countries that have experienced trade gains. For evidences, see RIS (2004: 48–49).

References

ADO. 2009. *Asian Development Outlook*. Manila: Asian Development Bank.
Bayoumi,Tamim A. and Barry Julian Eichengreen. 1994. 'One Money or Many? Analysing the Propects of Monetary Unification in Various Parts of the World', *Princeton Studies in International Finance No. 76*, pp. 76. New Jersey: Princeton University Press.

Bayoumi,Tamim A. and Paolo Mauro 2001. 'The Suitability of ASEAN for a Regional Currency Arrangement', *The World Economy*, 24 (7): 933–54.

Bhowmik, Debasis. 1998. 'Monetary Cooperation of SAARC: A Plan for a Single Currency', *Indian Economic Journal*, 45 (1): 138–45.

De Brito, Jose Brandao. 2004. 'Monetary Integration in East Asia: An Empirical Research', *Journal of Economic Integration*, 19 (3): 536–67.

Dasgupta, Amit and N. M. Maskay. 2003. 'Financial Policy Cooperation in SAARC: A First Step towards Greater Monetary Integration in South Asia', *South Asia Economic Journal*, 4 (1): 133–43.

Eichengreen, Barry. 1997. *European Monetary Unification: Theory, Practice and Analysis*. Massachusetts: MIT Press.

Flandreau, Marc and Mathilde Maurel. 2005. 'Monetary Union, Trade Integration, and Business Cycles in 19th Century Europe', *Open Economies Review*, 16 (2): 135–52.

Frankel, Jeffrey A. and Andrew K. Rose. 1997. 'Is EMU More Justifiable Ex Post Than Ex Ante?', *European Economic Review*, 41: 753–60.

———. 1998. 'The Endogeneity of the Optimum Currency Area', *The Economic Journal*, 108 (449): 1009–25.

———. 2000. 'Estimating the Effects of Currency Unions on Trade and Output', NBER Working Paper No. 7857. Cambridge: National Bureau of Economic Research.

Glick, R. and A. Rose. 2001. 'Does a Currency Union Affect Trade? The Time Series Evidence', National Bureau of Economic Research (NBER) Working Paper No. 8396. Cambridge: NBER.

Krugman P. R. and M. Obstfeld. 2000. *International Economics: Theory and Policy*. Delhi: Addison Wesley Longman Pte. Ltd.

Maskay, N.M. 2003. 'Patterns of Shocks and Regional Monetary Cooperation in South Asia', IMF Working Paper 03/240. Washington: International Monetary Fund.

Masson, Paul R. and Catherine A. Pattillo. 2001. 'Monetary Union in West Africa (ECOWAS)', IMF Occasional Papers 204. Washington: International Monetary Fund.

McKinnon, Ronald I. 1963. 'Optimum Currency Areas', *American Economic Review*, 53 (4): 717–24.

Mehta, R. and S. K. Bhattacharya. 1999. 'The South Asian Preferential Trading Arrangement: Impact on Intra-regional Trade', *The Asia Pacific Journal*, 4 (1): 92–111.

Mundell, R. 1961. 'A Theory of Optimum Currency Areas', *American Economic Review*, 51 (4): 657–64.

Mussa, Michael. 1997. 'Political and Institutional Commitment to a Common Currency', *The American Economic Review*, 87 (2): 217–20.

Ricci, Luca Antonio. 2008. 'A Model of an Optimum Currency Area', *Economics E-Journal*, 2: 1–31.

RIS. 2002. *South Asia Development and Cooperation Report 2001/02*. New Delhi: RIS.

———. 2004. *South Asia Development and Cooperation Report*. New Delhi: RIS.

Rose, A. 1999. 'One Money, One Market: Estimating the Effects of Common Currencies on Trade', NBER Working Paper No. 7432. Cambridge: National Bureau of Economic Research.

Rose, A. and C. Engel. 2002. 'Currency Unions and International Integration', *Journal of Money, Credit and Banking*, 34 (4): 1067–89.

Saxena, S. C. 2002. 'South Asia Monetary Integration in Light of the OCA Criteria Pattern of Shocks: A Comment', *South Asia Economic Journal*, 3 (2): 265–80.

Saxena, S. C. and M. A. Baig. 2004. 'Monetary Cooperation in South Asia: Potential and Prospects', RIS Discussion Paper 71/2004. New Delhi: RIS-DP.

Schiff, M. and L. A. Winters. 2003. *Regional Integration and Development*. Washington DC: Oxford University Press.

Taneja, Nisha and S. Pohit. 2001. 'Informal Trade in SAARC Region', *Economic and Political Weekly*, 36 (11): 17–23.

Part 3

Trade Integration in Africa and Arab States

7

Regional Integration and Small Resource-based Economies: An African Perspective

Narain Sinha, Imogen Bonolo Mogotsi and Anthony Kimotho Macharia

Conventional theoretical underpinning of regional integration does not hold in Africa in general and Sub-Saharan Africa in particular, for most of the economics there are resource-based and landlocked. Moreover, these economies have significant influence of a large neighbouring economy that is South Africa which happens to be a transit economy for all trade. According to Foroutan and Pritchett (1993), though situated amidst natural resources, these economies are poorly endowed with human and physical capital. On the contrary, small economies in East Asia (for example ASEAN), as in Europe, are not resource based but their growth is driven by both human and physical capital. Another feature that makes these Sub-Saharan economies different is poor infrastructure and low domestic savings. Besides, these economies are least diversified in the sense they are highly dependent on export revenue from one or two commodities. Thus, lack of complementarities makes the pace of economic integration in this region slower.

Economic integration with small or island economies has a different perspective. The unique characteristics of small or island economies have attracted the attention of many economists exploring among other things different pattern of economic development, systems of governance, and other socio-cultural practices. In the literature, islands have been looked at as representative of small population, small areas and remote countries. By extension, several authors have treated island countries similar to small, remote or landlocked countries (Srinivasan 1986; Perkins and Syrquin 1989). On the other hand, Selwyn (1980) argues that small islands are not distinct category from small countries although he does not present satisfactory analysis to support this position. The existing literature on small economy effect does not distinguish between island and small-country effects (Cleland and Singh 1980). In this chapter, we disagree with this argument because landlocked countries tend to have higher cost of transportation than the island countries. In this context, small and large refers to population rather than area or per capita income, because the size of population determines the economies of scale in domestic production.

In this chapter, we first examine the sustainability of regional integration involving resource-based economies in section 2 followed by some evidence of growth explanation and presence of small-country effect on growth in resource-based economy. Review of literature on Curse of Natural Resources (CNR) is given along with analysis of the effect of natural resources. Section 3 describes literature on small economy or landlocked economy effect. We attempt to link small economy effect to inflation and growth for the sustainability of regional integration. The lessons with special reference to Botswana are presented in section 4. Main results documenting these two effects are presented in this section. The conclusions are given in section 5.

2. Regional Integration and Natural Resources

The evidence on poor growth experience of resource-rich countries has been provided in the studies by Auty (2001), Gelb (1988), Sachs and Warner (1997) and Gylfason et al. (1999). Empirical observation that countries rich in natural resources tend to perform badly has been termed as the 'curse of natural resources (CNR)' in the literature (Sachs and Warner 2001). In Africa countries like Botswana, Zambia, Angola, etc., are unique in the sense these are all small in terms of population and landlocked in terms of location with mineral resources. For example, Botswana is sandwiched between two extreme economies namely South Africa and Zimbabwe — the former is a leader and the latter a lagard in the region. CNR can be converted into cure if sufficient Foreign Direct Investment (FDI) targeted at institutional support is designed appropriately and made available timely.

2.1. Resource Rich Economy — Curse or Cure and FDI

The role of FDI in resource-based small landlocked developing economies is very limited, particularly when the economy is based on only one or two mineral resources. In a resource-based small economy, it is observed that the FDI is basically in the mining sector which has very high share in total Gross Domestic Product (GDP) but very small multiplier effect in terms of employment. In such countries, apart from mining sector, new technology is required for production of goods either meant for domestic consumption or for exports. In case of economy with limited market size, domestic consumption is not a relevant argument for production because of the absence of economies of scale. Exports are also not a viable argument because of higher transportation cost for a landlocked country. FDI can be attracted in such economies through agriculture sector or infrastructure. It has been done in Kenya where agriculture land has been leased to some Gulf countries (particularly Qatar).

New theory of growth is another reason for considering the small-country effect. Higher transportation cost, absence of economies of scale in production and proximity of a big economy are some of the factors responsible for their slow growth. After controlling for other important factors, Sachs and Warner (2001) have shown that the countries' rates of economic growth in the 1970s and 1980s were strongly and negatively affected by their natural resource dependence, measured as the share of primary commodities in exports. This observation has since been endorsed by a series of studies (Gylfason 2001; Leite and Weidmann 1999). Considering Nigeria, Sala-i-Martin and Subramanian (2003) observe that 'oil corrupts and excess oil corrupts more than excessively'. Measuring the resource dependence in terms of the share of natural resource wealth (rather than exports) in total national wealth, Gylfason (2001) observes similar phenomenon. However, if the policy for attracting FDI is appropriately designed and targeted towards agriculture and commercial farming, it will result in sustainable growth of resource-based economies.

Notion of the CNR is based on crowding out argument as it crowds out other activities (say industrialisation or agriculture) as a result most of such economies, especially in Africa, have skipped the second stage of development and have entered directly into the third stage wherein the service sector has grown. This phenomenon is never sustainable because the industrialisation drives the growth rate but small market size and landlocked nature of the economy hamper the growth. Thus abundance of natural resources has harmed the sustainability of the growth in Africa. Effect of natural resources has resulted in the decline of the agriculture sector without any sustainable increase in the share of manufacturing sector.

2.2. Role of Institutions in Resource Rich Economies

Natural resources need not be a curse if institutions are good enough to discourage corruption and graft. Curse becomes cure if institutional support is provided before the growth due to natural resources starts plummeting. Mehlum et al. (2002) find the effect of resource abundance on growth ambiguous because it is influenced by the amount of resources and quality of governing institutions. Their conclusion was that when institutions are sufficiently good, larger share of primary commodities in exports is associated with a faster, not slower, growth. Low levels of resource abundance 'help' growth, but at sufficiently high levels, resource abundance generally 'hurt' growth. Relationship between growth, volume of natural resources exploited and institutional support is given in Figure 7.1.

There is an inverted U-curve relationship between growth and volume of natural resources in the economy. Role of good institutional support, if provided timely, would prevent the economic growth from falling. As institutions become more 'producer-friendly' and less 'grabber friendly', the threshold for a negative effect expands, so that natural resources are growth enhancing for a wider range of abundance. Mehlum et al. (2006) show that the interaction of natural resource abundance with high-quality institutions measured by an aggregate indicator has a positive growth effect. The direct negative growth effect of resource wealth seems to persist. However, these results are based on resource exports data which suffer from severe inconsistencies for developing countries, especially in

Figure 7.1: Economic Growth, Natural Resources and Institutional Support

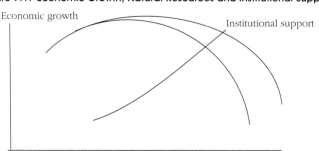

Volume of natural resources

Africa (Yeats 1990). Notwithstanding the growth winners among the resource-rich countries thereby rejecting the claim suggested by Sachs and Warner (1997) and Leitie and Weidmann (1999), there is a negative relationship between resource abundance and average growth provided some institutional link is taken into consideration.

A prominent example of a growth winner in Africa is diamond-rich Botswana with the world's highest growth rate since 1960. Another growth winner is Norway, the world's third largest oil exporter where oil extraction started as late as 1973, and has since had high economic growth as compared to the other Scandinavian countries (Larsen 2004). Chile, Brazil and Australia are other examples where the mineral sector has contributed positively to the economy (Wright and Czelusta 2002). Peru, Malaysia and Thailand are developing countries that can be added to the list of resource-rich countries that have avoided the curse (Abidin 2001). Resource abundance can be a cure (blessing) for countries with good institutions and a curse for countries with bad institutions (Mehlum et al. 2006).

It is evident that economic growth in countries with abundant natural resources is sustainable only with strong institutional back-up. Most of the African economies do not have required institutional backup for sustainable economic growth because of geopolitical factors. Botswana has the best African score on the Groningen Corruption Perception Index and that was the reason why its performance has been better. In order to make economic growth sustainable and keep the economy growing, Botswana has to have required institutional support. From the data presented for Botswana, it is obvious that declining share of agriculture and manufacturing sectors need to be reversed.

3. Economic Integration and Small Economies — SADC Countries

In the literature on small economy and islands, effects are considered either in terms of area or population. A distinction may be drawn between islands and small economy as the former are nations surrounded by water, whereas small economies are small either in terms of area or population. In the present chapter, we deviate from these definitions and consider a country small where population is small not in absolute sense but in relation to resource endowment or income. There are many developed countries which have small population but high income in spite of lower growth. In such countries, income inequality is lower with very high human development. On the other hand, Africa countries have higher income. However, population is small and income inequality is higher with lower human development. Abundance of natural resources puts them in the list of middle-income countries with very high income. Most of these countries are surrounded by land resulting in very high transportation cost.

From the economic integration perspective, two similar and developed economies can impact a permanent increase in the worldwide growth. The objective behind every regional integration is first to achieve economic growth, enlarge the market size, reduce inequalities in incomes, bridge gap between rich and poor, move towards free and fair trade through reduction in marketing barriers, pooling of resources both human and nonhuman, etc. The Declaration and Treaty establishing the Southern African Development Community (SADC) was signed on July 17 1992, in Windhoek, Namibia. South Africa joined SADC in 1994 followed by Mauritius (1995), the Democratic Republic of Congo or DRC (1997) and Seychelles (1997) which subsequently pulled out in 2004. Currently Angola, Botswana, DRC, Lesotho, Malawi, Mauritius, Mozambique, Namibia, South Africa, Swaziland, Tanzania, Zambia and Zimbabwe are members of the SADC with national economies which are structurally diverse and at varying stages of development.

South Africa, the region's most developed economy, has a GDP of \$213.1 billion, which is more than double the combined GDP of the other Southern African countries. However, Botswana and Mauritius have higher per capita income, and Malawi and DRC have lower per capita income. Similarly, DRC and South Africa have higher population. An explicit attempt has been made in this section to establish various transmission channels of the economic integration among the SADC countries and to explore the possibility of any 'contagion effect' in regional integration. Broadly, various transmission mechanisms have been considered but for the sake of space only two are presented, namely growth transmission and inflation transmission.

3.1. Growth Convergence in the Region

Generally for small landlocked economies, both the economic growth and inflation are determined more by exogenous rather than the endogenous factors. In other words, there is a relationship between inflation/growth of an economy and the size of the economy and other exogenous factors such as exchange rate, small population, etc.

Table 7.1: Economic and Demographic Indicators in SADC, 2004

Country	GDP (Billions of US$)	Real GDP Growth Rate, 2004 Estimate (%)	Real GDP Growth Rate, Projection (%)	Per Capita GDP (US$)	Population (Millions)
Angola	20	12.2	14.4	1,381	14.8
Botswana	9	5.4	4.8	4,852	1.7
Democratic Republic of Congo	6.0	5.7	6.0	110	54.8
Lesotho	1.5	4.4	4.8	682	2.1
Malawi	2.8	3.6	4.5	248	11.2
Mauritius	6.3	4.1	4.3	5174	1.2
Namibia	5.0	4.4	3.8	2,524	1.9
South Africa	213.1	3.7	4.0	4,562	46.7
Swaziland	2.0	2.1	1.8	1,772	1.1
Tanzania	11.0	5.7	5.8	266	42.1
Zambia	5.0	4.6	4.8	489	10.7
Zimbabwe	3.9	-4.3%	-1.4%	296	13.2

Source: African Development Report, 2007.

Barro and Sala-i-Martin (1992, 1995) find unconditional β convergence when the countries are homogeneous and regions within country always exhibit convergence. Idea of convergence performs better with cross-sectional data.

The small economy effect is defined as the difference between growth/inflation rate in small-country and in non-small country with the same level of per capita income. Theory gives no clue about the functional form, but inflation and growth rate should be positively correlated. The share of mining income in total income, which measure the intensity of natural resources, is another variable included in the explanation of inflation. A parsimonious representation of the model will have following specification

$$\Delta y_{it,\,t+t+T} = \alpha - \beta y_{i,t} + \gamma DUM_{i,t} + \varepsilon_{i,t}$$

If the estimate of $\beta > 0$, it implies an absolute β.

Landlockedness and Growth Rate

In SADC, there are six countries which have no direct access to sea; these are Botswana, Lesotho, Swaziland, Malawi, Zambia and Zimbabwe. Cost of imports being inclusive of cost, insurance and freight (cif) is expected to be high in these countries as compared to those which have direct access to the sea port. The higher cost of import puts constrain on the growth of the economy. Based on the shipping data, Limãu and Venables (2001) observe that the transportation cost is high in the median landlocked countries as compared to the median coastal countries and this cost can be reduced if own infrastructure is improved to the level of best 25th percentile among landlocked countries. Irrespective of the magnitude, one thing that is evident is that improvement in infrastructure either in landlocked countries or in transit countries or in both always leads to decline in transport cost. The transport cost affects the trade volume and available literatures suggest that the trade volume of the landlocked countries is 40 per cent of the trade volume of the median coastal countries for the same income level and distance. Improvement is infrastructure in the landlocked country, transit country and both countries increases the trade volume by 13 per cent, 2 per cent and 15 per cent, respectively.

Apart from landlockedness, trade within African economies and also between African and outside Africa is much lower as compared to other continents. The poor trade performance is not because of protectionist policies but more because of high transport cost due to

Table 7.2: Regression Results [Dependent Variable — Real GDP Growth Rate, 2004]

S. No.	Constant	PCI-2004	DUM	SACU	R^2
1	0.050661	−0.00000095			0.0027
	(0.003813)	(0.864905)			
2	0.035693	−0.000002	0.032927		0.2357
	(0.04245)	(0.630011)	(0.111382)		
3	0.032167		0.031262		0.2168
	(0.032392)		(0.108742)		
4	0.053909	0.000001		−0.02029	0.0690
	(0.004121)	(0.799117)		(0.418384)	
5	0.055625			−0.01723	0.0627
	(0.000951)			(0.409262)	

Source: Authors' calculations.
Note: p-values are given below estimated coefficient in parantheses.

poor infrastructure and inappropriate transport policies among the African economies. Sachs and Warner (1997) believe that poor trade performance in African economies is due to low income growth. Poor communication infrastructure in Africa also leads to higher transport cost per kilometer, particularly within Sub-Saharan African economies. Under such situations, the infrastructure development among African countries will help lower the transport cost. Foreign investment in infrastructure has to be accelerated.

Considering the SADC economies, we have estimated the effect of landlockedness on growth and the growth regressions have been estimated with initial level of income. The growth equations have been estimated with a cross section of 13 countries in the SADC region with and without dummy variable. Besides, dummy variables have been introduced, one each for landlockedness and South Africa Customs Union (SACU) membership. The dummy takes the value zero if the country is landlocked and one if it is not landlocked. The regressions have been estimated (Equations 1 and 2) and results are given below (Table 7.2). Growth rate is lower in landlocked countries than non-landlocked countries in SADC region by 0.03 points and is significant at 10.8 per cent level of significance as indicated by p-value.[1] Here the base category is landlocked economies. Dummy for the SACU has also been tried in the growth

Table 7.3: Regressive Results [Dependent Variable — Growth Rate and Inflation in SADC Countries, 1991–2007]

Dependent Variable-GROWTH RATE		
Country	*Intercept*	*Growth-SA*
Angola	−11.4627379	5.5591647
	p-value	0.0026505
Zimbabwe	0.43582677	−0.4346894
	p-value	0.5184642
Mozambique	3.28910146	1.212406
	p-value	0.0880443
Mauritius	5.23078312	−0.0854396
	p-value	0.7043177
DRC	−7.35778203	2.1384792
	p-value	0.0003545
Namibia	4.1451727	−0.1837873
	p-value	0.4945792
Tanzania	3.23778578	0.5689708

Dependent Variable-ANNUAL INFLATION		
Country	*Intercept*	*Inflation-SA*
Angola	65.9169614	81.1741179
	p-value	0.3838463
Zimbabwe	Data	incomplete
Mozambique	2.489598	1.976448
	p-value	0.324291
Mauritius	5.170744	0.227941
	p-value	0.193846
DRC	74.58356	18.39766
	p-value	0.582842
Namibia	Data	incomplete
Tanzania	−3.61893734	2.5606807

	p-value		p-value	
	0.07573285	0.0221004		0.00025479
Zambia	p-value		Zambia	2.5606807
	0.9830408	0.0039355	-3.61893734	0.00025479
Malawi	2.2808934		p-value	-0.31798647
	p-value	0.5358481	MALAWI	0.80192212
Lesotho	3.25745688	0.4680657	27.6652433	0.93739545
	p-value	0.287086	p-value	0.0000009
Botswana	7.04014195	0.409143	LESOTHO	0.44695787
	p-value	-0.4555277	1.77547652	0.00346294
Swaziland	Data	0.2852927	p-value	0.47318973
		incomplete	Botswana	0.02351897
			6.01735751	
			p-value	
			Swaziland	
			4.6238206	
			p-value	

Source: Authors' calculations with data from SADC (2009).

equation taking one if the country is a member and zero otherwise. The results (Equations 3 and 4 in Table 7.2) show that the dummy is not significant and at the same time, its sign is negative. Thus the growth rate is lower in the SACU countries. Our results indicate the absence of conditional convergence among the countries in the SADC region. Even the SACU group of countries does not exhibit any convergence. This finding does not support the existence of a 'contagion effect' with South Africa in terms of convergence as indicated in African Development Bank (2000).

3.2. Growth and Inflation in the SADC Region

For econometric analysis of contagian effect, we consider the time series data for each of the member countries for the period 1991–2007 taken from SADC (2009). The models explaining the growth rate and inflation estimated for each member country in the SADC region are given in Table 7.3. The estimated models seek to explain the growth process and inflation in each country taking natural resources into consideration. In the following analysis, we estimate the influence of bigger country on smaller countries also. The set of equations given in the right panel of Table 7.3 have the growth rate of the member country explained in terms of growth rate of South Africa. Interestingly, the growth rate of Angola, Mozambique, DRC, Tanzania and Zambia are significantly and positively determined by the growth rate of South Africa. In all these economies, structural adjustments were introduced almost simultaneously in early 1990s and with the opening up of these economies, foreign investment in these countries, particularly from South Africa, increased substantially during 1991–2007.

In other countries like Malawi, Botswana and Lesotho the factors influencing the growth rate are different. For example for Malawi, the growth rate is driven by domestic factors such as share of Agriculture in GDP; for Zambia it is construction, exchange rate and domestic inflation, while for Botswana it is income from the mining sector.

Set of equations with inflation rate as the dependent variable is given in the left panel of Table 7.3. Like economic growth, inflation in small landlocked countries is not endogenously determined; rather the external factors are responsible for high inflation and lower growth. Another factor influencing the inflation is high transport cost both within and in the transit country. The landlocked countries have no sea port and hence are at more disadvantageous position than the islands nations. In view of this, inflation in the landlocked country is generally higher than in island nations. From this respect, the small country effect has been distinguished in this chapter from the island effect.

Results on estimates of econometric model explaining inflation and incorporating small-economy effect presented in right panel in Table 7.3 explain parsimoniously the inflation in each of the SADC member country in terms of inflation in SA. Our results show that effect of inflation rate in South Africa on the inflation in the member country is more pronounced in Botswana, Tanzania, Zambia, Lesotho and Swaziland. Out of these countries, three are members of SACU and data are not available for Namibia, the other member. In other words, the impact of SACU is felt more on inflation. In other countries, inflation in South Africa does not have significant impact on inflation. This could be described as 'contagion effect' with South Africa — in terms of growth, it is positive whereas in terms of inflation, it is negative on SACU countries. From our analysis, it is clear that given the diverse nature of the member states' economies, any attempt at economic integration aiming at macroeconomic convergence that covers the conventional stability indicators may not be perceived as credible at this stage of SADC's development. The less ambitious aim of focusing on inflation and poverty alleviation will be more credible and supportive of the process of deepening integration.

4. Lessons from Botswana

In the African continent, Botswana is a small landlocked country not in terms of area but in population. The country is endowed with diamond and has been resource rich for a long time with stable political system. Much of the Botswana's unprecedented growth in the 1990s has been attributed to its endowment in diamonds (Acemoglu et al. 2002). In recent years, Botswana has been experiencing very high inflation (Table 7.4). The small-country effect and island-effect influence the inflation and growth of the economy of Botswana. The small-country effect is measured in terms of the difference in growth rate keeping the income level constant.

Both the higher migration of people from Zimbabwe and higher transport cost of imports through South Africa put extra pressure on

Table 7.4: Economic Parameters for Botswana, 2006

Economic Characteristics	
GDP (current US $) (billions)	11.0
GNI per capita, Atlas method (current US $)	5,680
Share of Mining in GDP (%)	40.6
External debt, total (% of GNI)	4.1
Foreign Direct Investment (% of GNP)	14
Life expectancy at birth, total (years)	50
Growth Rate (%)-Botswana	3.4
Annual Inflation (%)	15.6
Population, total (millions)	1.9
Population growth (annual %)	1.2
Surface area (sq. km) (thousands)	581.7

Source: World Bank (2008).

the growth of the economy of Botswana. These factors dampen her growth advantage. Higher mortality rate and low population growth due to HIV/AIDS also limit the economic growth in the country.

An overview of the dimensions along with resource-abundant winners and losers has been given in Torvik (2009). According to him, Botswana could escape the Dutch disease phenomenon due to its better institutional support. If the economy has abundant resources, growth will still be higher. But none of the earlier studies has considered the growth disadvantages of Botswana with respect to diversification and higher transportation cost because of small market size and landlocked nature. Smallness and landlocked nature affects inflation because of goods. Amidst the spectacular growth of the economy, lower inflow of FDI into non-mining sectors has constrained diversification and job creation (Siphambe 2007).[2] This is the reason why inflation in Botswana is higher and growth is lower in the category of middle income countries.[3] Annual increase in the cost of tradeable goods and services rose from 17.5 to 18.3 per cent while that for non-tradeables eased from 7.3 to 7.0 per cent. The trimmed mean core inflation measure rose from 12.5 to 12.7 per cent while core inflation excluding administered prices increased from 9.8 to 11.1 per cent (Bank of Botswana 2008). During July 2008, the pula appreciated against major trading partner currencies with the exception of the South African rand. On annual basis, the Pula depreciated against most of the currencies except the rand and the pound. The largest year-on-year depreciation was 14.2 per cent against the euro and the least was 2.3 per cent against the US dollar;

against the rand, the year-on-year appreciation against the rand was 1.6 per cent. (Bank of Botswana 2008). According to World Bank, growth rate of the economy has declined from 8.2 per cent in 2000 to 4.9 per cent in 2005 and 3.4 per cent in 2006, but inflation has declined from 12.0 per cent in 2000 to 11.1 per cent in 2005 and then increased to 15.6 per cent in 2006. Higher inflation and lower growth in spite of the higher per capita income in the country may be attributed to small market size and higher transport cost. Due to these two constraints, the economy has not been able to diversify which has led to lower integration of the economies in the SADC region.

5. Conclusion

We have examined the prospects and strategy for economic integration when the economy of the countries is based on one or few mineral resources and most of the countries are landlocked and small in size. Negative relationship that country size has with openness and government size has been put forth by Alesina and Wacziarg (1998) and is supported by Ram (2009). This argument is based on the premise that small countries cannot have economies of scale because of limited domestic demand. Moreover if the country is landlocked, then transit cost is another constraint for FDI. From this chapter, we find that this phenomenon is real for most of the African economies because of their landlocked location and dependence on natural resources as is the case with the economy of Botswana, Zambia, etc. The 'contagion effect' with South Africa is predominant in terms of growth and negative in terms of inflation, particularly for SACU countries. Under this situation, the economic integration should provide the remedy which lies in diversification in agriculture targeting the poor through commercialisation through FDI which may help sustain the tgrowth strategy. For instance in Botswana, share of mining in the total GDP at constant prices has been increasing from 38.1 per cent in 1997–1998 to 42.4 per cent in 2000–2001 but later, it started fluctuating around 40 per cent and was 40.6 per cent in 2006–2007. The current global financial crisis has reduced it. Fall in the share of mining sector in GDP is much lower than the fall in growth rate and hence may not be held responsible for higher inflation or slower growth rate. Finally an appropriate institutional support, which is not evident in most of the African economies, in terms of better and speedy governance and increased investment in infrastructure, will assist the growth trajectory to expand leading to sustainable economic development in the continent. The economic integration of such economies should place high importance on the development of infrastructure, particularly in transport and communication and diversification in agriculture sector which has direct link with the issues of food security and poverty in the African region.

❊

Notes

1. Steven (1996) has suggested that the level of significance needs to be adjusted and set the cut-off of 10 per cent or 15 per cent rather than conventional 5 per cent so as to compensate for small sample. In small samples, non-significant result may be due to insufficient power when the degrees of freedom are very small.
2. The overall employment elasticity has declined from 0.89 during 1980–1991 to 0.34 during 1991–2005.
3. Headline inflation in Botswana is measured by the Consumer Price Index (CPI). In July 2008 the inflation was 15.0 per cent, an increase of 0.5 percentage points over the June figure. This was the result of higher year-on-year rates of price increase in several categories of goods and services including transport (from 35.6 per cent to 37.4 per cent); food and non-alcoholic beverages (from 18.3 per cent to 18.5 per cent), furnishing, household equipment and routine maintenance (from 4.4 per cent to 6.1 per cent); and health (from 15.4 per cent to 15.6 per cent).

References

Abidin, M. Z. 2001. 'Competitive Industrialisation with Natural Resource Abundance: Malaysia', in R. M. Auty (ed.), *Resource Abundance and Economic Development*, pp. 147–64. Oxford: Oxford University Press.

Acemoglu, D., S. Johnson and J. A. Robinson. 2002. 'An African Success: Botswana', in Dani Rodrik (ed.), *Analytic Development Narratives*. Princeton: Princeton University Press.

Adelman, I. and C. T. Morris. 1997. 'Editorial: Development History and its Implications for Development Theory', *World Development*, 25 (6): 831–40.

African Development Bank. 2000. *African Development Report*. New York: Oxford University Press.

African Development Bank. 2007. *African Development Report 2007*. Oxford: Oxford University Press.

Alesina, A. and R. Wacziarg. 1998. 'Openness, Country size and Government', *Journal of Public Economics*, 69 (3): 305–21.

Auty, Richard M. 2001. 'The Political Economy of Resource-driven Growth', *European Economic Review*, 45 (4–6): 839–46.

Bank of Botswana. 2008. *Botswana Financial Statistics*. Gaborone: Bank of Botswana.

Barro, R. J. and X. Sala-i-Martin. 1992. 'Regional Growth and Migration: A Japan-U.S. Comparison', NBER Working Paper No. 4038, National Bureau of Economic Research, Inc. http://ideas.repec.org/p/nbr/nbe rwo/4038.html (accessed 12 January 2010).

Barro, R. J. and X. Sala-i-Martin. 1995. *Economic Growth*. New York: McGraw-Hill.

Carmignani, Fabrizio. 2005. 'The Road to Regional Integration in Africa: Macroeconomic Convergence and Performance in COMESA', *Journal of African Economies*, 15 (2): 212–50.

Cleland, J. and S. Singh 1980. 'Islands and the Demographic Transition', *World Development*, 8 (12): 969–93.

Foroutan, F. and L. Pritchett 1993. 'Intra-Sub-Saharan African Trade: Is It Too Little?', *Journal of African Economies*, 2 (1): 74–105.

Gelb, A. H. 1988. *Windfall Gains: Blessing or Curse?* New York: Oxford University Press.

Gylfason, T. 2001. 'Natural Resources, Education and Economic Development', *European Economic Review*, 45 (4): 847–59.

Gylfason, T., T. T. Herbertson, and G. Zoega 1999. 'A Mixed Blessing: Natural Resources and Economic Growth', *Macroeconomic Dynamics*, 3: 204–25.

Larsen, Erling Røed. 2004. 'Escaping the Resource Curse and the Dutch Disease? When and Why Norway Caught up with and Forged ahead of Its Neighbors', Discussion Papers No. 377. Oslo: Statistics Norway, Research Department.

Leite C. and J. Weidmann. 1999. 'Does Mother Nature Corrupt? Natural Resources, Corruption and Growth', International Monetary Fund Working Paper No. 99/85. Washington DC: International Monetary Fund.

Limão N. and A. J. Venables 2001. 'Infrastructure, Geographical Disadvantage, Transport Costs, and Trade', *The World Bank Economic Review*, 15 (3): 451–79.

Lockhart, D., D. Drakakis-Smith and J. Schembri. (eds). 1993. *The Development Process in Small Island States*. London: Routledge.

Mehlum, H., K. Moene and R. Torvik 2002. 'Plunder & Protection Inc.', *Journal of Peace Research*, 39 (4): 447–59.

———. 2006. 'Cursed by Resources or Institutions?', *The World Economy*, 29 (8): 1117–131.

Perkins, D. and M. Syrqui. 1989. 'Large Countries: Influence of Size', in H. Chenery and T. N. Srinivisan (eds), *Handbook of Development Economics*, pp. 1691–1753. Amsterdam: Elsevier.

Ram, R. 2009. 'Openness, Country Size and Government Size: Additional Evidence from a Large Cross-section Panel', *Journal of Public Economics*, 93 (1–2): 213–18.

Sachs, Jeffrey D. and Andrew M. Warner. 1997. 'Sources of Slow Growth in African Economies', *Journal of African Economies* 6 (3): 335–76.

———. 2001. 'Natural Resources and Economic Development: The Curse of Natural Resources', *European Economic Review*, 45: 827–38.

SADC. 2009. 'The Committee of Central Bank Governors in SADC'. www.sadcbankers.org (accessed 12 January 2010).

Sala-i-Martin, X. and A. Subramanian. 2003. 'Addressing the Natural Resource Curse: An Illustration from Nigeria', NBER Working Paper No. 9804. Cambridge: National Bureau of Economic Research.

Selwyn, P. 1980. 'Smallness and Islandness', *World Development*, 8 (12): 945–51.

Siphambe, H. K. 2007. *Growth and Employment Dynamics in Botswana: A Case Study of Policy Coherence*, Working Paper No. 82. Geneva: International Labour Office.

Srinivisan T. N. 1986. 'The Cost and Benefits of being a Small, Remote, Island, Landlocked, or Mini-state economy', *World Bank Research Observer*, 1 (2): 205–18.

Stevens, J. 1996. *Applied Multivariate Statistics for Social Sciences*. Mahwah, NJ: Lawrence Erlbaum.

Torvik, Ragnar. 2009. 'Why do Some Resource-abundant Countries Succeed while others do not?', *Oxford Review of Economic Policy*, 25 (2): 241–56.

Yeats, A. 1990. 'On the Accuracy of Economic Observations: Do Sub-Saharan Trade Statistics mean Anything?', *The World Bank Economic Review*, 4 (2): 135–256.

World Bank. 2008. *World Development Indicators Database*. Washington DC: World Bank.

Wright, G. and J. Czelusta. 2002. 'Exorcising the Resource Curse: Minerals as a Knowledge Industry, Past and Present', Working Papers 02008. Palo Alto, CA: Stanford University.

———. 2004. 'The Myth of the Resource Curse', *Challenge*, 47 (2): 6–38.

8

Trade Agreements and Exports: A Case of Africa–China and the European Union Trade Relations

Olayinka Idowu Kareem

The potential of developing countries to achieve rapid and sustainable economic growth and reduction in the level of poverty in part depend on their integration into global markets. These potential gains from global trade could be achieved if all participating countries can limit their barriers to trade through effective trade agreements, so as to encourage the free flow of goods and services. In reality, this is often not the case as there are various market access barriers to some key exports of developing countries, which make it difficult for them to take full advantage of the opportunities that abound in global trade.

In international trade theory of comparative cost advantage, countries are advised to specialise in the production of commodities in which they have comparative cost advantage over other countries. This will make countries to gain from international trade. African exports prior to 1970s have performed well in terms of the volume and number of products, while the issue of market access barriers to their exports in the markets of their trading partners did not arise. Though Africa has its strength in the production of primary products that attract fewer restrictions in the developed nations' markets (especially in the markets of their colonial masters), the continent has however gained from trade in which the returns serve as the bulk of their foreign exchange during these periods.

However, recently, the developed countries found it appropriate to engage in backward integration (that is, to encourage the production of primary products for the use of the industrial sector of their economies) that will reduce the import bills they pay to their trading partners. It is as a result of this that the developed countries started encouraging the production of primary products, especially agricultural products, which attracted some supports and subsidies that distort international prices of these commodities. These subsidies and supports in the developed countries made imports from African countries less competitive. Also, in order for developed countries to encourage domestic producers, they imposed trade restrictions on agricultural exports coming to their markets.

So far, there has been a divergence of opinions as to what extent has the regional trade agreements been able to minimise the trade barriers on Africa's exports, which will thereby enhance her exports in global trade. While a school of thought believes that the trade agreements have not contributed to Africa's exports to both developed and developing countries, thereby reducing the income level and employment rate. However, another school argues that even if Africa's exports are allowed free access to the developed countries' markets through trade agreements, the continent lacks the ability to produce to meet the demand due to Africa's supply constraints.

Some studies[1] have been carried out on the effects of regional trade agreements in the North–South and South–South markets, many of which ascertained the extent to which Africa has gained from these trade agreements. For instance, Mayda and Steinberg (2008) examined and opined that there has been proliferation of trade agreements between South–South countries, yet the impact of these agreements is largely unknown. Abdoulahi (2005) presents an overview of efforts made by African countries and their regional economic communities to promote intra-African trade through the implementation of trade liberation schemes as well the corresponding impact on intra-regional trade. Schiff and Wang (2006) found that both North-South and South-South trade related R&D stocks have a positive impact on Total Factor Productivity (TFP) growth. Bussiere, Fidrmuc and Schnatz (2005) analysed the rapid trade integration of the Central and Eastern European Countries (CEECs) with the euro area in the past 10 years and draws implications for further integration. El-Rayyes (2007) examines the trade and regional integration between Mediterranean Partner Countries (MPC) and concludes that there is potential for increased trade between MPCs. It is against this background that this study intends to determine the effects of trade agreements in the European Union (EU) and China on Africa's exports.

The remainder of this chapter is structured as follows. Section 2 discusses Africa's export performance. Some selected trade agreements in Africa have been discussed in Section 3. Section 4 provides research model and Section 5 reports research findings. Section 6 provides concluding remarks.

2. Africa's Exports Performance

Table 8.1 shows Africa's exports to the rest of the world in absolute terms between 1980 and 2006. Though Africa's exports are high in absolute terms, its share of world exports is relatively low. In 1980, African countries exported about US$119 billion worth of commodities, representing about 6 per cent of world exports in that year. However in 1990, the value of exports dropped to about US$107 billion, or 3 per cent of the world exports. The continent's exports regained an upward trend in 1995, and recorded up to over US$112 billion. However this represented 2 per cent of world exports. Africa's exports value increased to US$147.2 billion in 2000 and later rose to US$332.8 billion in 2006, which is 2.28 per cent and about 2.8 per cent, respectively, of the global exports. Thus, the share of Africa's exports in world exports is not only very low but it depicts an unstable trend.

2.1. Africa's Exports to the EU and China

This section presents the trend in Africa's exports to China and the EU. Figure 8.1 indicates that in 1990, Africa exported over $47 billion

Table 8.1: Exports Value by Region (US$ Billion)

Region	1980	1990	1995	2000	2005	2006
World	2032.1	3478.6	5168.9	6444.1	10440.8	11982.9
Developed Countries	1327.6	2506.4	3606.6	4229.8	6291.9	7085.0
Developing Countries	597.6	842.9	1427.0	2044.6	3780.5	4409.0
Developed America*	293.5	521.8	777.0	1058.9	1267.0	1442.6
Developed Asia**	136.0	299.2	462.2	510.7	639.7	691.0
EU	870.7	1636.3	2300.7	2583.1	4259.7	4805.4
Africa	119.0	107.0	112.5	147.2	298.0	332.8
Developing America	111.2	143.8	225.2	361.1	566.8	680.0
Developing Asia	365.0	589.3	1084.8	1532.3	2879.7	3389.5
Oceania	233.5	280.3	454.5	405.7	591.1	668.8

Source: Author's Compilation from UNCTAD Handbook of Statistics (2007).
Note: *This includes Bermuda, Canada, Greenland, Saint Pierre and Miquelon and US.
**It includes Israel and Japan.

Figure 8.1: Africa's Exports to the European Union and China

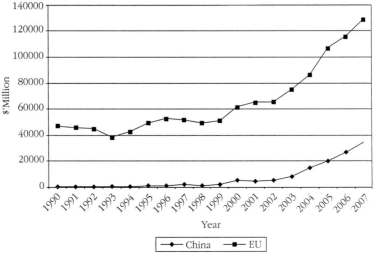

Year

China   EU

Source: IMF (2008).

worth of commodities to the EU, while only $357 million worth of commodities were taken to China. Due to crises that engulfed most African countries in the 1990s, Africa's exports to the EU dropped to about $39 billion in 1993, while that to China increased relatively to $740 million. However by the year 2000, Africa's exports to the EU have gotten to about $62 billion, while that to China have reached $5 billion. This increasing trend continued and seven years after, Africa's exports to the EU recorded about $129 billion, while that to China has gotten to over $34 billion in the same period. The interesting thing to note in this trend is that Africa has been exporting to the EU more than China and it was just in recent years that there has been tremendous and significant increase in the continent's exports to China. However, the rate of this increase in Africa's exports to China is remarkable, particularly after 1999 when it doubled, which is an indication of gradual shift in Africa's exports direction.

In terms of the EU and China's exports to Africa, Figure 8.2 shows that China exported over $1 billion worth of commodities to Africa in 1990, while the correspondence EU exports to the continent was about $42 billion. By 2000, China exported over $4 billion to Africa, while EU brought $50 billion worth of commodities. Furthermore, China recorded about $32 billion worth of exports to Africa, while the EU in the same year recorded about $120 billion worth of exports.

Figure 8.2: China and European Union's Exports to Africa

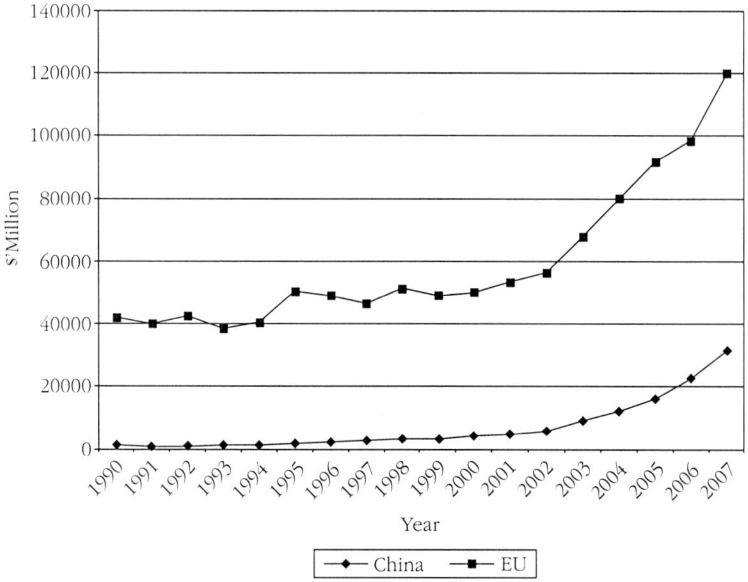

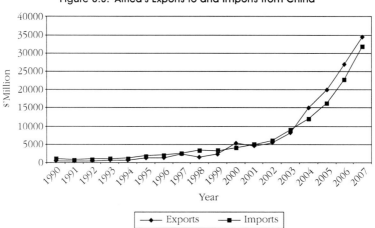

Source: IMF (2008).

Figure 8.3 presents both Africa's exports to China and her imports from China. It could be seen that in 1990 to around 1999 and 2000, Africa imported more from China than it exported to the Chinese

Figure 8.3: Africa's Exports to and Imports from China

Source: IMF (2008).

market, which means that Africa has trade deficit with China for the period. However, from 2003 to 2007, Africa's exports to China superseded her imports, which indicate that the continent recorded trade surplus with respect to her trade with China.

For the EU markets, Figure 8.4 shows that there has been oscillation between Africa's exports and imports to and from the EU. From 1990 to 1993, Africa's exports superseded her imports from the EU, which indicates trade surplus. The trade surplus that Africa recorded with the EU was vivid from the year 2000 to 2007. This means that exports to the EU has been on the increase right from 2000, which were due to the non-reciprocity trade preference granted to most African countries to the EU markets.

Figure 8.4: Africa's Exports to and Imports from European Union

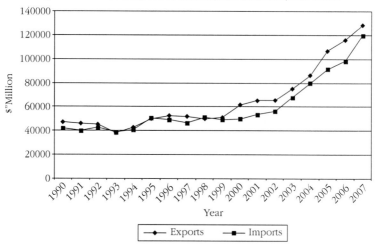

Source: IMF (2008).

3. Some Trade Agreements with Africa

Trade preference is an arrangement or agreement between countries, whereby they agreed within themselves to allow trade to flow with little or no trade restrictions. Generally, it is developed countries that often grant trade preferences to developing economies. Many developing countries, especially Africa, enjoy easier access to developed markets through preferential trade schemes. These are traded either through unilateral, bilateral, non-reciprocal schemes such as Generalised System of Preferences (GSP), or through reciprocal free trade agreements or regional integration agreements such as the EU Mediterranean agreements.

3.1. Generalised System of Preferences (GSP)

These are preferential access schemes that allow products coming from developing countries at lower tariffs than those under Most Favoured Nation (MFN) status. Under the GSPs, the developing countries are not allowed to reciprocate, unlike the preferential trading agreements such as North America Free Trade Agreements (NAFTA) — a regional free trade agreement. There are several types of GSP:

i. The basic GSP scheme;
ii. Special trade preferences with selected group of developing countries; and
iii. 'Super GSP' for LDCs.

In the GSP scheme, the EU grants important concession to 180 developing countries. In the EU, the degree of reduction of the MFN rate varies with the level of 'sensitivity' of the product. In other words, this depends on the degree to which an import competes with EU temperate products like dairy produce, beef, cereals and oil seeds. The 2001–2004 case provides an additional 5 per cent tariff reduction for countries who meet additional environmental and labour conditions. Even so, an expulsion provision has also been built in for those countries that seriously and systematically violate minimum labour standards.

3.2. EU Trade Preference

The EU has a complex and intricate web of trade preference in addition to GSP. Among them are the Global Mediterranean Policy, Europe Agreements and EU–ACP or African, Carribean and Pacific Countries Cotonou Partnership Agreement. These concessions are granted to different countries, products, markets and sessions. Preference access may involve tariff preferences within Tariff Rate Quotas (TRQs), tariff preferences outside allocated TRQs and/or tariff preferences with no quantitative restrictions. There are three classifications of EU grants preferences to different groups of countries.

(a) LDCs that are not African Caribbean and Pacific (ACP) members.
(b) ACP countries (this is divided into LDC and non–LDC countries).
(c) Non–ACP developing countries that benefit from GSP treatment and Free Trade Agreement (FTA) preferences, granted to Eastern Europe and Mediterranean countries.

The EU has been the largest market for Africa's exports. Given this, they have granted two special preferences that are significant. They are:

3.3. Everything but Arms (EBA) for LDCs

The EU council adopted the EBA proposal on the 5 March 2001, which is the most generous trade preference scheme in their portfolio: duty and quota-free access is granted to 49 LDCs for all imports except arms and ammunitions (25 lines of arms trade was left out). Moreover, preference access was extended for 919 agricultural products including fruits and vegetables (fresh as well as processed), meat, cereals, vegetable oils, beverages and dairy products (919 tariff lines). This concession has made the EBA a more attractive scheme than the EU–ACP Cotonou preferences in terms of tariff treatment, product coverage and tariff advantages. The EBA initiative will also provide LDCs with greater stability. This is because the EU undertook to maintain this special preferential treatment for an unlimited period of time. This scheme is not subject to periodic reviews as occurs with the basic GSP scheme.

Banana, rice and sugar were initially excluded from EBA schemes because they were considered to be sensitive (these products of particular interest to Africa). These products were not given immediate unlimited duty-free treatment, but it was planned that gradual liberalisation will be given to them by stages. The duties on banana will be eliminated by using a 20 per cent annual reduction, starting from 1 January 2002 and eliminated at the latest on 1 January 2006. Imports of sugar and rice by EU from LDCs are subject to transition arrangements until 2009. Then after 2009, the option of a safeguard will exist if imports become a significant threat to domestic products EU–ACP Lome Convention (now Cotonou Partnership Agreement).

Under the successor agreement to the Lome Convention, the preferential tariff rates to developing countries are referred to as the EU–ACP Cotonou Partnership Agreement, which was signed in June 2000. They are applicable to 77 African, Caribbean and Pacific countries. This current trade regime will cease to exist by 31 December 2007, and the proposed Economic Partnership Agreement (EPA) will come on bound if finally agreed upon by all the stakeholders in the negotiation.

Within the EU–ACP Cotonou Partnership Agreement, African countries were granted 80 per cent duty-free access for most agricultural products (UNCTAD 2002). For example, they include exotic fresh fruits and vegetables, as well as raw/semi-processed tropical beverages. The exception is for a limited number of agricultural products that are subject to the common market organisation of the EU. Based on these, they allowed only a reduction of the ad valorem component of the tariff, e.g., some higher valued processed products (i.e., some types of fruit juice such as orange and grape juice). This agreement also provides significant tariff advantages to Africa in the form of MFN and GSP rates, but excluding the EBA. There is about 25 per cent average tariff advantages for MFN rates to Africa, especially Sub-Saharan Africa (SSA). Thus, there was a request from the EU to the World Trade Organisation (WTO), for a waiver for the continuation of these preferences up till the end of 2007, before they replace it with a new reciprocal arrangement in January 2008 (EPA).

The EU–ACP Cotonou Partnership Agreement makes provision for the introduction of a new Regional Economic Partnership Agreements (REPAs) that must be negotiated between EU and the regional grouping of ACP countries in 2008. These EPAs will provide for free reciprocal trade exchanges, compatible with WTO rules (Jabati 2003). This agreement (EU–ACP Cotonou Partnership Agreement) allows for co-operation between EU and ACP in trade related areas such as competition policy, intellectual property rights, standards of certification, sanitary and phytosanitary measures, trade and environment, trade and labour standards, consumer policy and public health.

3.4. EU–South Africa Free Trade Development and Cooperation Agreement (TDCA)

This agreement was signed by the EU and South Africa on 11 October 1999 with the aim of gradually establishing FTA. It was agreed that there will be elimination of tariffs on 83 per cent of current EU agricultural exports to the Southern African Customs Union Market (SACU) within the time frame of 12 years. South Africa was also granted duty-free access for 61 per cent of current agricultural products to the EU market, while the EU has been given a 10-year phasing-in period for tariff reductions.

3.5. EU–ACP Economic Partnership Agreement

This intends to be a reciprocal agreement between the EU and ACP countries on areas of mutual agreements. These agreements ought to have taken effect from 2008 when the non-reciprocal agreements would have ended. However, there are contentious clauses that are still debated, which must be agreed upon before the signing of the agreements. Thus, in order for exports to the EU not to face the MFN rates, some countries like Ghana and Cote d'Ivoire, temporarily signed these agreements with the EU despite the fact that the agreements are still being negotiated.

4. The Model

In this study, we take a specific form of a gravity-type model. The model for this study is adapted from the empirical work of Mayer and Zignago (2005) that modelled market access in global and regional trade through trade agreements using a border-effect methodology. The modifications that our study has done to the work of Mayer and Zignago (ibid.) is by including trade agreements variable as well as trade policy variables with which trade agreements tend to adjust. The theoretical underpinning of the gravity type will occur in almost every trade model with full specialisation, as shown by Evenett and Keller (2003).

Let us assume that the consumers in country i is assumed to have a two-level utility function where the upper level is a Cobb-Douglas with expenditure parameter u_i, which gives rise to a fixed expenditure share out of the income, y_i. The lower level utility function on the other hand is a Constant Elasticity of Substitution (CES) aggregate of differentiated varieties produced in the considered industry, with σ representing an inverse index of product differentiation.

$$U_i = \left(\sum_{j=1}^{N} \sum_{b=1}^{Nj} \left(a_{ij} c_{ijb} \right)^{\frac{\sigma-1}{\sigma}} \right)^{\frac{\sigma}{\sigma-1}} \tag{1}$$

The CES structure usually indicates the love for variety based on the fact that the consumers are willing to consume all the available varieties. Our study shall deal with a situation where the consumers have different preferences over varieties depending on bias. The consumers' preference parameter in country i for varieties produced in j is denoted a_{ij}.

Given the fact that most of these varieties are produced in foreign countries, there is need to model trade cost, τ_{ij} that ought to be *ad valorem*, and incurred by the consumer when the good is transported from country j to country i. The delivered price p_{ij} faced by consumers in i for products from j is therefore the product of the mill price p_j and the trade cost. The trade costs include all transaction costs associated with the movement of goods across the space and natural borders. The demand for a representative variety produced in j is denoted as c_{ij}, which the demand function derived from this system gives the bilateral total imports by country i from country j for a given industry.

$$ M_{ij} = \eta_j P_{ij} C_{ij} = \eta_j a_{ij}^{\sigma-1} P_j^{1-\sigma} \tau_{ij}^{1-\sigma} \mu_i Y_i P_i^{\sigma-1} \qquad (2) $$

where $P_i = \left(\sum_\kappa \eta_\kappa a_{i\kappa}^{\sigma-1} P_\kappa^{1-\sigma} \tau_{i\kappa}^{1-\sigma} \right)^{1/(1-\sigma)}$ is the "price index" in each location.

From equation (2), one could see that trade costs influence demand when there is a high elasticity of substitution, σ. Based on Head and Mayer (2000), we take the ratio of m_{ij} over m_{ii}, country i's imports from itself, the $\mu_i y_i p_i^{\sigma-1}$ term then drops and we are left with relative numbers of firms, relative preferences, and relative costs in country i and j.

$$ \frac{m_{ij}}{m_{ii}} = \left(\frac{n_j}{n_i} \right) \left(\frac{a_{ij}}{a_{ii}} \right)^{\sigma-1} \left(\frac{P_j}{P_i} \right)^{1-\sigma} \left(\frac{T_{ij}}{T_{ii}} \right)^{\sigma-1} \qquad (3) $$

In order to estimate equation (3), the model must be specified fully by adopting the supply side features of the monopolistic competition model. Hence, the firms producing q_j in country j employ l_j workers in an IRS production function $l_j = F + rq_j$, where F is fixed (labour) costs, and r is the inverse productivity of firms. The profits are $\tilde{\lambda}_j = p_j q_j - w_j (F + rq_j)$, where w_j is the wage rate in j.

Thus, equilibrium output of each representative firm is, $q_j = \dfrac{F(\sigma-1)}{r}$.

We assume an identical technology that is $q_j \equiv q$, $v_j = 1 \cdots N$ and V_j is the value of production for the considered industry in j, $v_j = qp_jn_j$, from equation (3):

$$\frac{n_j}{n_i} = \frac{v_j}{v_i}\frac{p_i}{p_j} \tag{4}$$

Also, the functional forms of trade cost (τ_{ij}) and preferences (a_{ij}) have to be specified in order to get an estimable equation. The trade costs are function of distance $(d_{ij}$, which proxies for transport cost) and 'border-related costs' that consist of tariffs and Non-tariffs Barriers (NTBs) (these include quantitative restrictions, administrative burden, sanitary measures, etc). The *ad valorem* equivalent of all border-related costs brc_{ij} is given as:

$$\tau_{ij} \equiv d_{ij}^\delta (1 + brc_{ij}) \tag{5}$$

We shall allow the border-related costs to be flexible in this study since our aim is to assess a possible North–South divide in market access; we then need to allow for different levels of broadly defined protection in each (North–South and South–South) direction. Also, of importance is the issue of effect of regionalism, which we are going to control in the assessment of North markets' access by Southern exporters. Further, we observed some of the actual protection that is taking place between importing and exporting countries (tariffs and NTBs). We shall include measures of market access initiatives in order to determine the extent to which these initiatives would impact on African exports.

Generally, we assume that the following structure for border-related costs that vary across country pair and depend on the direction of the flow of a given pair:

$$1 + brc_{ij} \equiv (1 + t_{ij})(1 + ntb_{ij})(\exp[\eta E_{ij} + \theta RTA_{ij} + \vartheta NS_{ij} + \varphi SN_{ij}]) \tag{6}$$

From this specification, t_{ij} denotes the *ad valorem* bilateral tariffs, ntb_{ij} is a frequency index of NTBs. RTA_{ij} is a dummy variable set equal to 1 when $i (\neq)$ and j belongs to a regional integration agreement. We expect all the parameters to be positive which denote tariff equivalent of NTBs. We also expect $\theta > 0$ to be the lowest of those parameters which will be true if all national borders impose transaction costs, with the minimum burden of those costs being between RTA members.

The preferences have a random component e_{ij}, and a systemic preference component for goods produced in the home country, β. The home bias is assumed to be mitigated by the share of a common language.

$$a_{ij} \equiv \exp\left[e_{ij} - (\beta - \lambda L_{ij})\,(E_{ij} + NS_{ij} + SN_{ij})\right] \tag{7}$$

L_{ij} is set equal to 1 when two different countries share the same language. When L_{ij} switches from 0 to 1, home bias changes from β to $\beta - \lambda$.

Therefore, based on all these above, we obtain an estimable equation from the monopolistic competition equation of Krugman (1980) with home bias:

$$\ln\left(\frac{m_{ij}}{m_{ii}}\right) = -(\sigma - 1)\,[\beta + \eta] + \ln\left(\frac{\upsilon_j}{\upsilon_i}\right) - \sigma \ln\left(\frac{P_j}{P_i}\right) - (\sigma - 1)$$

$$\ln(1 + t_{ij}) - (\sigma - 1)\,\ln(1 + ntb_{ij}) - (\sigma - 1)\delta$$

$$\ln\left(\frac{d_{ij}}{d_{ii}}\right) + (\sigma - 1)\,\lambda L_{ij} - (\sigma - 1)\,[\theta_3 - \eta_3]\,RTA_{ij} + \in_{ij} \tag{8}$$

where $\in_{ij} = (\sigma - 1)(e_{ij} - e_{ii})$

$(-(\sigma - 1)[\beta + \eta])$ is the constant of equation (8) and it gives the border effect of the international trade for countries that belong to the same group, the south for instance. This includes both the level of protection of the importing country (η) and the home bias of consumer (β). The coefficients of measures of RTA indicate the effect that the regional and multilateral trade agreements had on African exports.

4.1. Estimation Techniques

As we have said earlier, this study shall make use of generalised method of moment panel data analytical methods with the test of the panel data properties and panel granger causality. These methods would allow us to estimate our regression equations for the whole of Africa and the sub-groups as identified earlier.

The reason for the use of panel data technique in the gravity model is based on the several benefits of the technique as identified by Hsiao (1985), Klevmarken (1989) and Solon (1989). They believed it could be used to control for individual heterogeneity, and that it provides more informative data, more variability, less collinearity among the chosen variables, more degree of freedom and more efficiency. Also, panel data technique is a better option when one intends to study the dynamics of adjustment and duration of economic states like poverty and employment, and if these panels are long enough, they can shed light on the speed of adjustments to economic policy changes. Panels are necessary for the estimation of intertemporal relations, life-cycle and intergenerational model and they can easily relate an individual's experiences and behaviour at another point in time. They are better able to identify and measure effects that are simply not detectable in pure cross section or pure time-series data, such as Ordinary Least Square (OLS).

The basic class of specification of these models is given as:

$$Y_{it} = f(X_{it}, \beta) + \delta_i + \gamma_t + \in_{it} \qquad (9)$$

This leading case involves a linear conditional mean specification, so that we have:

$$Y_{it} = \alpha + X_{it}\,\beta_{it} + \delta_i + \gamma_t + \in_{it} \qquad (10)$$

Where Y_{it} stands for the dependent variable, X_{it} is a K-vector of regressors and $\in_{it}$ are the error terms for i = 1, 2, …, M cross-sectional units observed for dated periods t = 1, 2, …, T. The α represents the model constant, while the δ_i and γ_t represent the fixed and random effects, respectively. Identification obviously requires that the β coefficients have restrictions placed upon them. They maybe divided into sets of common (cross-section and periods), cross-section specific and period specific regressor parameters.

This panel estimation technique will enable us to estimate panel equations using linear or non-linear squares or instrumental variables (system of equations), with correction for the fixed or random effects in both the cross section and period dimensions, AR errors, Generalised Least Square (GLS) weighting, and that of robust standard error. In addition to the above, the Generalised Method of Moment (GMM) will be used to estimate the specification with various system weighting matrices. It should be noted that apart from the above basis for panel data analysis, panel equations allow us to specify equations in general form and also permits specification of non-linear coefficients mean equations with additive effects. Panel equations do not automatically allow for β coefficients that vary across sections or period, but one may create interaction variables that permit such variation.

5. Research Findings

The results of the panel-gravity models used in this study are presented below. The estimates of the panel-gravity models are done through GMM. Using the GMM to estimate the models, we present two different estimates of the GMM, vis-à-vis, no effect and random effect. We have decided to estimate the random effect due to the fact that the models for this study are gravity models that have dummy variables of which fixed effect estimator will be inappropriate. According to Baltagi (2001) and Greene (2003) fixed effect, also known as Least Squares Dummy Variables (LSDV), suffers from a large loss of degree of freedom, in which when it involves estimating $(N - 1)$ extra parameters and too many dummy variables, it will aggravate the problem of multicollinearity among the regressors. Also, the fixed effect estimator cannot estimate the effect of any time-invariant variable like sex, race, language, religious, colonial links, schooling, etc., because they will be wiped out by the Q transformation, the deviations from means transformation. Thus they concluded that any regression attempting to use this estimator will fail. It is on this basis that in this study we have used the random effect estimator.

In the Africa-EU trade relations using the no effects, relative output between EU and Africa is an important variable to consider when modelling their trade relations. The result shows relative output has a significant positive slope in the model and it indicates that the absorptive capacity of the EU to exports from Africa is about 12 per cent, which is higher than that of China. The relative price conform with the a priori expectation, indicating that an increase in the relative prices will reduce the access of African exports to the EU, though statistically insignificant (see Table 8.2).

Tariffs and the NTBs have the required slopes, that is, it conforms to the a priori expectation. These results indicate that the EU allowed African exports greater access than any other country chosen in this study. This is because the slopes of tariffs and NTB show that the EU encourages the importation of African product to their domestic economies by lowering down the tariffs and the NTBs to such products. The reason behind these encouraging trade

Table 8.2: Panel GMM Result (Africa–EU)

Variable	No effects	Random effects
Routput	0.1172	0.1247
	$(11.17)^c$	$(2.10)^b$
Rprices	−1.77E-05	−2.15E-05
	(−0.75)	(−1.10)
Tariffs	−0.0002	−0.0002
	(−0.78)	$(−1.96)^b$
NTB	−0.0001	−7.72E-05
	(−0.33)	$(−8.25)^c$
Distance	−4.30E-08	−4.91E-08
	$(−12.05)^c$	$(−4.69)^c$
Language	−0.0005	−0.00004
	$(−8.71)^c$	$(−4.63)^c$
RTA	−0.0006	−0.0005
	(−0.60)	$(−16.03)^c$
Colonial	1.02E-05	−4.95E-05
	(0.09)	$(−6.80)^c$
Constant	0.0024	0.0021
	(1.06)	(2.83)
Adj. R^2	0.74	0.49
Std. Error	0.0004	0.0003
D. Watson	0.31	0.43
J. Statistic	52.19	41.72

Source: Author's computation.
Note: The Figures in parentheses are the t-statistic. The superscript c, b, a indicate 1 per cent, 5 per cent and 10 per cent level of significant, respectively.

relations is that the EU has signed some agreements, particularly non-reciprocal trade preference, in which it will allow African products access to the EU without mandating African countries to reciprocate. Distance here is significant to the model and shows that it could discourage trade if the trading partners are far away from each other. Language also shows that if the trading partners do not speak the same language, this might cause a barrier that will affect trade. Though the magnitude of the reduction in trade is small, 0.05 per cent, but it is statistically significant. Colonial affiliation between Africa and the EU will propel trade among them. This means that the EU often trade more with those countries in Africa with which they have same colonial affiliation to or that they colonised. This could be seen in the relationship between francophone African countries and France.

We discovered that there has been a considerable level of integration among African countries in this model. Though insignificant, its magnitude is over 0.2 per cent. However, the regional trade agreement within the continent and between EU as a trading partner has not yielded any genuine trade to the continent. This essentially might be due to Africa's supply constraints.

The random effects estimate confirms the results of the least square estimator. However, the random effect was able to establish significance of some variables that were hitherto insignificant. For instance, tariffs and NTB were not significant in the least square model, but are now significant. Also, RTA and level of integration (constant) were not significant until now. Lastly, a major difference is that the colonial affiliation that is before now positively sloped is now having statistically significant negative relationship with trade, indicating that it is not a determined of trade between the EU and Africa — a good reason being that all African countries colonial masters were from the EU, so it should not be a factor that will determine their trade with Africa.

Furthermore, in the trade between Africa and China, the result is shown in Table 8.3 where a relative output is significant and positively related to China's imports from all African countries. What this means is that as relative output increase, there will be additional African products access to the Chinese markets. Relative prices also depict some trend, as it is significantly positively related to Chinese imports from Africa.

Tariffs, which are measures of trade restrictions, indicate that as more of Africa's products gained access to Chinese market, there will be a rise in the rate of tariffs imposed on these exports. The reason for the increment in tariffs might be due to revenue generation purpose or in order to protect the domestic producers from the influx of foreign products. However, NTBs reduce with increase in access of products from Africa to China. This might be due to the fact that some of the NTBs have been quantify tariffs so as to reduce the difficulties associated with NTBs that is acknowledged to be more painful and inhibit trade than tariffs.

Language is an enhancing factor that will propel trade if both trading parties speak similar language. Distance has the required sign

Table 8.3: Panel GMM Result (Africa–China)

Variable	No effects	Random effects
Routput	2.25E-06	−3.03E-06
	(6.27)^c	(−4.67)^c
Rprices	2.75E-07	1.94E-04
	(55.74)^c	(24.20)^c
Tariffs	1.47E-05	4.15E-05
	(0.69)	(0.85)
NTB	−1.22E-05	−3.31E-07
	(−0.68)	(−0.83)
Distance	−4.41E-05	−2.64E-06
	(−0.84)	(−1.07)
Language	9.04E-05	3.89E-05
	(1.76)^a	(1.70)^a
RTA	1.15E-05	3.37E-06
	(0.69)	(0.98)
Colonial	2.62E-06	−1.74E-06
	(2.25)^b	(−2.16)^b
Constant	−2.05E-05	−3.02E-05
	(−0.70)	(−0.37)
Adj. R^2	0.89	0.48
Std. Error	0.9926	3.00E-06
D. Watson	1.97	1.58
J. Statistic	0.0318	0.09

Source: Author's Computation.
Note: The Figures in parentheses are the t-statistic. The superscript c, b and a indicate 1 per cent, 5 per cent and 10 per cent level of significant, respectively.

and show that is a factor to consider in any trade relation because it could serve as hindrance to trade. Colonial link also propels trade between Africa and China, that is, any country in Africa that has colonial affiliation with China will have more access to her markets.

The estimate of regional integration (constant) indicates that there is no integration with African countries that trade with China, while their involvement and participation in regional trade agreements have brought about additional trade and market access to the countries in Africa. In terms of the random effects, the estimator shows that there is an inverse relationship between relative output and China imports of African products, that is, the more the relative outputs increase, the lower the level of market access to African products in Chinese markets, and it is statistical significant. A relative price is significant and it conforms with the a priori expectation. The positive slope of its coefficient indicates that the higher the market access of African products to the Chinese market, the more the relative prices paid by the consumers of the products in China.

The degree of association between tariffs and China's imports of African products is positive and insignificant, which demonstrates that as the products of African increase in its access to the Chinese economy, the products were then confronted with higher tariffs. This reason for the increase in tariffs might be to reduce the volume of the products coming into China so as not to make Chinese economy a dumping ground for frivolous products. However, NTBs for African products are reduced and minimised as the imports of China increase from Africa, suggesting that this reduction in NTB might be due to multilateral negotiation and agreements between African countries and China.

Distance serves as hindrance to the market access of African products in the Chinese economy. This means that the more the distance between African countries and China, the more discouraged African exporters are to trade with China and this ultimately reduces market access. This is statistically significant and conforms to the a priori expectation of the study. Language similarity between African and China will increase the trade and market access of products from Africa in the Chinese markets. This also means that there is no language barrier between Africa and China in the course of transacting business. However, colonial link between Africa and China has nothing to do with their trade relations or the entrance of African products in to the Chinese markets.

In another words, with Africa's market access quest in China, there has been disintegration with African countries, which imply that there has been intra-trade within the continent that could lead to trade and regional integration. However, the regional trade agreements that African countries have assented to have had positive impact in their access to Chinese markets.

6. Conclusion

This study has tried to evaluate the effects of Africa's trade agreements with the EU and China on Africa's exports. We have shown empirically, using descriptive analysis and econometrics method, the effects of these trade agreements on Africa's export products access to both the North and South markets. Thus, at this juncture, it is important to note that the objective of this study has been adequately achieved and accomplished, that is, we have shown the effect of trade agreements on Africa's exports in the North (EU) and South (China) countries.

Therefore, we conclude that African exports have not been gaining access to both the North and South countries not only because of inadequate implementation of the trade agreements which had led to the trade restrictions imposed on their products, but due to the fact that Africa has low and inadequate production capacity that will enable her to meet up with the market access allowed to her products despite the potentiality of her output gaining access to these trading partners markets. We also conclude that products of relevance to African countries are confronted with higher trade restrictions, mostly in the South countries than in the developed countries, due to the fact that these South countries have not granted appropriate trade preference to African countries for the continent commodities to gain access to these markets. The implication of this is that there are more market access conditions in South–South trade than North–South trade, which confirm the results of Mayer and Zignago (2005), and Hammouda, Karingi and Perez (2005).

The policy implication of the outcome of the study is that African countries need to increase their export products base so that there will be variety of export products for the continent. Also, African countries should re-strategize and redefine the trade agreements they had with the EU. This is an important issue because it was discovered that the trade agreements, as they were, are not too market access enhancing, especially the imposition of NTBs that have been inhibiting Africa's exports access to China and the EU markets. Therefore, there is the need to re-negotiate these trade agreements so that it could bring about enhanced access of African exports to these markets.

Note

1. See Sanguinetti, Traistaru and Martincus (2000); Schiff and Wang (2006); Mayda and Steinberg (2007); El-Rayyes (2007).

References

Abdoulahi, Mahamat. 2005. 'Progress Report on Regional Integration Efforts in Africa towards the Promotion of Intra-african Trade', ATPC Report No. 30. Addis Ababa: Economic Commission for Africa.

Bussière,Matthieu, Jarko Fidrmuc and Bernd Schnatz. 2005. Trade Integration of Central and Eastern European Countries: Lessons from a Gravity Model. Working Paper Series 545, European Central Bank. http://ideas.repec.org/p/ecb/ecbwps/20050545.html (accessed 10 July 2007).

Baltagi, B. H. 2001. *Econometric Analysis of Panel Data*. West Sussex: John Wiley & Son.

Dixit, A. K. and J. E. Stiglitz. 1977. 'Monopolistic Competition and Optimum Product Diversity', *American Economic Review*, 67: 297–308.

El-Rayyes, T. 2007. 'Trade and Regional Integration between Mediterranean Partner Countries', Go-EuroMed Working Paper 8, Deliverable No. 10, Six Framework Programme, Contract No. 028386. Jordan: Center for Strategic Studies.

Evenett, S. and W. Keller 2003. 'On Theories Explaining the Success of the Gravity Equation', *Journal of Political Economy*, 1(10): 281–316.

Gary, S. 1989. 'Biases in the Estimation of Intergenerational Earnings Correlations', *The Review of Economics and Statistics*, 71 (1): 172–74.

Greene, W. H. 2003. *Econometric Analysis*. New Jersey: Prentice Hall.

Hammouda, H. B., Karingi, S. and R. Perez. 2005. 'Can Market Access help African Agriculture', ATPC Working Paper No. 42. http://www.uneca.org/atpc/Work%20in%20progress/42.pdf (accessed 6 July 2007).

Hsiao, C. 1985. 'Benefits and Limitations of Panel Data', *Econometric Reviews*, 4 (1): 121–74.

Head, K. and T. Mayer 2000. 'Non-Europe: The Magnitude and Causes of Market Fragmentation in Europe', *Weltwirtschaftliches Archive*, 136 (2): 285–314.

International Monetary Fund (IMF). 2008. *Direction of Trade Statistics*. Washington, DC: IMF.

Jabati, M. C. 2003. 'Market Access for Developing Countries of Africa: The Reality', AGSF Occasional Paper No. 1. Rome: United Nations Food and Agriculture Organisation.

Klevmarken, N. A. 1989. 'Introduction', *European Economic Review*, 33 (2–3): 523–29.

Krugman, P. R. 1980. 'Scale Economics, Product Differentiation and the Pattern of Trade', *American Economic Review*, 70: 950–59.

Mayda, A. M. and C. Steinberg. 2007. 'Do South–South Trade Agreements Increase Trade? Commodity-Level Evidence from COMESA', IMF Working Papers 07/40. Washington, DC: International Monetary Fund.

———. 2008. 'Do South–South Trade Agreements Increase Trade? Commodity-Level Evidence from COMESA', Centro studi luca d'agliano Development

Studies Working Papers, No. 247. www. DAGLIANO.UNIMI.IT (accessed 7 February 2009).

Mayer, T. and S. Zignago 2005. 'Market Access in Global and Regional Trade', CEP II Working Paper, No. 2005-02. www.cepii.fr/anglaisgraph/workpap/pdf/2005/wp05-02.pdf (accessed 15 December 2005).

Sanguinetti, P., I. Traistaru and C. Martincus. 2000. 'Economic Integration and Location of Manufacturing Activities: Evidence from Mercosur', ERSA conference papers ersa04p609, European Regional Science Association.

———. 2004. 'The Impact of South–South Preferential Trade Agreements on Industrial Development: An Empirical Test'. Paper Presented at the 3rd Workshop of the Regional Integration Network (RIN), World Congress of the Regional Science Association International (RSAI), Port Elizabeth.

Schiff, M. and Y., Wang 2006. 'North–South and South–South Trade Related Technology Diffusion: How Important are they in Improving TFP Growth?', World Bank Seminar Paper. Wahington DC: World Bank.

Solon, G. S. 1989. 'The Value of Panel Data in Economic Research', in D. Kasprzyk, G. J. Duncan, G. Kalton and M. P. Singh (eds), *Panel Surveys*, pp. 486–96. New York: John Wiley.

United Nations Conference on Trade and Development (UNCTAD). 2002. 'Back to Basics: Market Access Issues in the Doha Agenda'. New York: United Nations.

———. 2007. *Handbook of Statistics*. New York: United Nations.

Weerahewa, J. 2007. 'Regional Trade Integration Options for South Asia: A Welfare Analysis', Proceedings of the Peradeniya University Research Sessions, Sri Lanka, 30 November.

9

The Contribution of Trade to Growth of Arab Countries

Hossam Younes and
Abd El-Wakil Mohammed Abo-Taleb

During the late 1980s and early 1990s, many developing countries entered into new regional agreements, strengthened old ones, or investigated the potential for one. The existing literature provides mixed evidence regarding the contribution of integration on economic growth. For example, studies of the European Union show that regional integration and its effects on trade and growth have been positive in some analyses (Italianer 1994; Henrekson et al. 1997), while in others, EU membership appears insignificant in explaining Gross Domestic Product (GDP) growth rates (Vamvakidis 1999; Vanhoudt 1999). In this debate, this chapter has made an attempt to analyse the composition of trade within an Arab integration and investigate whether intra-regional trade spurs higher output growth compared to extra-regional trade. We use data from Arab countries comprising the 13 member states during the period 1990–2007.

The remainder of the chapter is organised as follows. Section 2 provides an overview of the relationship between trade and growth in general and in Arab Countries. Section 3 reviews the economics of the Arab countries. Section 4 describes the data. Section 5 presents the empirical framework. Results of the empirical estimation are discussed in Section 6. Finally, Section 7 provides concluding remarks.

2. Review of Literature

2.1. Trade and Growth

The literature discusses several channels through which trade can affect economic growth. First, trade is a vehicle through which technological innovations and knowledge are transmitted between trading partners (Grossman and Helpman 1991; Sala-i-Martin and Barro 1997). Second, higher trade openness also increases competition in the local market which in turn increases productive efficiency and economic growth (Vickers and Yarrow 1991). Finally, countries that can access larger markets through trade can also benefit economically. For example, Alcalá and Ciccone (2003) demonstrate that trade mattered more for growth where domestic markets were smaller suggesting that countries with small domestic markets benefit more from trade openness. The positive effect of trade openness on growth has not, however, found consistent support in the literature (Rodriguez and Rodrik 1999). Although some studies point to gains from trade, trade liberalisation may have a negative effect on growth for countries in transition from controlled to market economies (such as most countries in Eastern Europe, Asia and sub-Saharan Africa). For example, Parikh and Stirbu (2004) find that on average, liberalisation is associated with deterioration in the trade balance implying that countries would have difficulty reaching potential or planned growth in the subsequent periods after liberalisation.

The empirical literature on openness and growth is voluminous indeed. Broadly speaking, however, a number of findings appear to emerge from this literature. First, there is no strong unconditional or conditional correlation between economic growth and a number of direct measures of trade policy such as weighted or unweighted tariffs, import quotas, or other non-tariff barriers. This point was first made by Rodríguez and Rodrik (2009) that generated some surprise in the literature. It has since been confirmed by among others who argue that there may be a non-linear relationship where the effect of tariffs on growth depend on the initial level of a country's income and may be positive or negative (DeJong and Ripoll 2006). Second, there appears to be a reasonably strong correlation between growth or productivity and the ratio of trade in GDP, especially when the latter is measured in prices of a constant base year (Dollar and Kraay 2002).

Thirlwall and Santos-Paulino (2004) found that the impact of liberalisation differs between highly protected countries and less protected countries. The positive effect of trade liberalisation on import growth is far greater in the industries that were highly protected during the period before liberalisation. Dollar and Kray (2004) have shown that the growth pattern of countries who have liberalised have shown acceleration in their real income and in the 1990s, globalising developing countries grew at 5 per cent per capita, rich countries at 2.2 per cent and non-globalising developing countries at only 1.4 per cent. Their view is that the countries which have gone on globalisation path are catching up with rich countries while non-globalisers are lagging behind. Irwin and Tervio (2002) following Frankel and Romer (1999) conclude that the countries those trades more as a proportion of their GDP have higher incomes even after controlling for the endogeniety of trade. Overall, it appears that trade contributes to improvement in real income and per capita growth. However, if trade is not combined with adequate policies to balance imports against exports, it could generate the balance of trade and balance of payments deficits leading to deterioration in the growth of real incomes.

In the literature of terms of trade and economic growth, many studies are mainly examined using cross-country evidence. The study that uses time series evidence is relatively scarce. Bleaney and Greenaway (2001) investigate the impact of terms of trade on economic growth of Malaysia using time series data over the period 1965–2002. Moreover, the study examines Granger causality between terms of trade and economic growth. An increase in terms of trade could lead to an increase or a decrease in economic growth (Prebisch 1950; Singer 1950; Blattman et al. 2003). Thus, it is an empirical issue.

2.2. Regional Trade and Growth in Arab Countries

The great bulk of the existing literature related to the economic effects of the Greater Arab Free Trade Area (GAFTA) remains very descriptive (Sekouti 1999; Tahir 1999; Zarrouk 2000; Hadhri 2001; Bayar 2005). A few ex-ante studies are more analytical, but focus on a small number of countries. For example, Neaime (2005) considers the impact of monetary and financial integration, especially Foreign Direct Investment (FDI) liberalisation, across Arab countries. With regard to GAFTA trade provisions, CATT (2005) assesses the GAFTA welfare effect on specific countries, mainly Morocco and Tunisia. This assessment is achieved through Computable General Equilibrium (CGE) modelling. Results show positive or negative welfare effects, depending on the terms of trade.

Drawing on the evidence in the empirical growth literature, recent studies have identified a diverse set of potential structural causes behind the poor growth performance in the Middle East and North Africa (MENA) region. Dasgupta, Keller, and Srinivasan (2002) suggest that the MENA region lags behind other regions in macroeconomic and trade reforms. Salai-Martin and Artadi (2002) argue that while the level of investment in the region has remained high by international and historical standards, too large a fraction of this overall investment has been unproductive public investment.

3. An Overview of the Economics of Arab Countries as a Region

3.1. Basic Economic Indicators and Development

Despite many attempts to promote economic integration, co-operation among states in the Arab region (Box 9.1), economic interactions have remained limited. Increasing attention has been focused on the region's economic potentials due to the steps taken by several countries toward external economic liberalisation. This attention comes at a time of renewed global interest in regional arrangements, whether among industrial countries (such as the EU), a mixture of industrial and developing countries (North American Free Trade Agreement or NAFTA and Asia-Pacific Economic Cooperation or APEC), or developing countries alone.

Being located near a large and developed neighbourhood leads to faster growth. Obviously, North–South regional trade agreements fulfill such a condition. Regarding South–South regional trade agreements with a less optimistic view is in order. In the past, these agreements clearly existed among small and very similar economies, but things have changed insofar as nowadays a differentiation in the level of economic development among developing countries is apparent and it is no longer unusual to find countries on different levels of development in the same region. Therefore, it is possible to build South–South regional integration schemes clustering less developed and smaller countries around a larger neighbouring country. The Arab region, to some extent, fulfills this condition (Shams 2003).

3.2. Direction of Arab's Foreign Trade

Despite the elimination of tariffs between GAFTA, The Cooperation Council for the Arab States of the Gulf (GCC) and The Arab Mediterranean Free Trade Agreement (AGADIR) members, intra-Arab trade is still hampered by a number of non-tariff obstacles that are preventing it from reaching its full potential and are also limiting the beneficial effects of trade liberalisation. More precisely, two factors stand as significant obstacles facing the expansion of intra-GAFTA trade:

Box 9.1: Arab Region at a Glance

Coverage: The Arab region is defined to cover the 21 economies of the Arab League (Algeria, Bahrain, Djibouti, Egypt, Iraq, Jordan, Kuwait, Lebanon, Libya, Mauritania, Morocco, Oman, Palestine, Qatar, Saudi Arabia, Somalia, Sudan, Syria, Tunisia, the UAE and Yemen).

Size: The Arab region covers an area of more than 14 million sq. km represent 10.2 per cent of area of the world, with more than 330 million inhabitants — roughly 5 per cent of the world's population. The populations of individual countries vary from about less than one million (Bahrain, Djibouti, and Qatar) to some 75 million (Egypt). Nominal GDP in the region amounted to over USD 1,476 billion in 2007, which was about 2.7 per cent of world GDP. None of the national economies of the Arab region is especially large on a global scale; this is certainly true if the oil sector is excluded. Moreover, there is great variance in the relative size of national economies, from Djibouti's 0.8 billion US$ and Jordan's 16 billion US$ to Algeria's 132 billion US$ and Saudi Arabia's 377 billion US$, with several steps in between.[1]

Population Growth: Many Arab countries experience rapid population growth, with a high proportion of young dependants in their population. The average population growth rate in recent years has been about 2.1 per cent, although a group of countries (Jordan, Yemen, UAE, Qatar, Saudi Arabia, and the UAE) show a higher growth rate around 3.0 per cent. Bahrain, Egypt, Sudan, Oman, Qatar and Saudi Arabia have relatively low rates of population growth (about 2 per cent).[2]

Per capita income: Great disparities also exist in the region's GDP per capita distribution, from very high (Qatar — 75,978 US$; UAE — 43,709 US$; Kuwait — 38,574 US$; Bahrain — 26,127 US$; Saudi Arabia — 15255 US$) to low (Somalia — 291 US$; Mauritania —874 US$; Yemen — 967 US$; Djibouti — 1,002 US$; Palestinian — 1,359 US$; Sudan — 1,443 US$; Egypt — 1,770 US$; Syria — 1,883 US$).[3]

Regional sub-groupings: There are many sub-groupings in the region. The most common include nine oil-exporting economies (Algeria, Bahrain, Iraq, Kuwait, Libya, Oman, Qatar, Saudi Arabia and the UAE). Although some other Arab countries such as Egypt, Syria, Tunisia and Yemen also export oil, the role of this sector in their economies is limited. The member countries of the Cooperation Council of the Arab States of the Gulf (GCC) are Bahrain, Kuwait, Oman, Qatar, Saudi Arabia and the UAE. The members of the Arab Maghreb Union are Algeria, Libya, Mauritania, Morocco and Tunisia. The Mashreq group consists of Egypt, Jordan, Lebanon, Syria, and the West Bank and Gaza Strip.

cumbersome bureaucratic and institutional frameworks, as well as high transportation and communication costs, in part due to weak infrastructures.

As shown in Table 9.1, intra-Arab exports represent on average merely 8.5 per cent of total Arab exports in 2007. This ratio is strikingly low when compared to other blocs such as Southern Common Market (MERCOSUR) and EU where intra-member exports were equal to 21 per cent and 22 per cent of MERCOSUR's and EU's total exports in 2007. It should be noted that the picture is less gloomy when oil exports are excluded — since oil accounts for the greatest share of many Arab countries' exports and is largely exported to non-Arab countries, oil tends to bias the real magnitude of intra-Arab trade. A substantial share of intra-Arab imports is directed to other Arab countries, the share represents 11.3 per cent in 2007.

Table 9.1: Direction of Arab Trade, 2007

	Export		Import	
	Value (billions of US$)	Share %	Value (billions of US$)	Share %
Arab Countries	58.5	8.2	51.3	11.3
European Union 25	82.0	11.6	137.9	30.3
USA and Canada	69.0	9.7	40.3	8.9
Asia	158.4	22.3	99.8	21.9
Japan	124.2	17.5	27.8	6.1
Others	217.6	30.7	98.5	21.6
Total	**709.7**	**100**	**455.5**	**100.0**

Source: Calculated from United Nations (2009c).

Asia (excluding Japan) is the largest trading partner of most states in the Arab region. Asia (excluding Japan) is a major trading partner for Arab region exports with 22.3 per cent of total exports from the Arab region during 2007, followed by Japan (17.5 per cent) and EU 25 (11.6 per cent). Destinations of imports presented in Table 9.1 shows concentration of Arab region's imports from EU and Asia (excluding Japan). About 52 per cent of the Arab region's imports are from these two regions.

4. Theoretical Framework

4.1. Granger Causality Tests

Our empirical analysis begins with an effort to statistically determine the direction of causality between trade and growth in our sample.

To this end, we estimate a series of Granger causality tests for Arab countries. In general, if Granger causality is found to run only in one direction, say from trade to growth, then the case for linear prediction can be made. In addition, lagging trade variables when estimate their effect on output ensures that observations on trade precede growth effects. Thus, if a significant relationship exists, then the case for linear prediction is strengthened.

Table A9.2 in Appendix show the results of the tests for Granger causality between trade and per capita output growth in two ways. Extra-regional trade granger causes growth in 2 of the 13 countries, while intra-regional trade Granger causes growth in 3 countries. Jointly the trade variables Granger cause growth in 2 of the 13 countries. The two countries for which Granger causality holds are Kuwait and Morocco. It should be noted that the Granger causality results here should not be viewed true causally. Rather, they can be best interpreted as an attempt at specifying a necessary condition for a causal relation.

4.2. Estimation Methodology

Following Bassanini et al. (2001), and Wooster et al. (2007), we consider a specification which includes the basic determinants of output growth. Specifically, we include the accumulation of physical capital and population growth as well as a set of policy and institutional factors potentially affecting economic efficiency. These include: the size of government (which we measure as government consumption spending); inflation; and trade intensities — intra-regional and extra-regional trade (the variables of interest for the study). Thus, the equation can be written as follows:

$$\Delta \ln y_{it} = \beta_0 + \beta_1 \ln k_{it} + \beta_2 n_{it} + \beta_3 \ln r_{it-1} + \beta_4 \ln w_{it-1} + \beta_5 \ln G_{it} + \beta_6 \ln \pi_{it} + \alpha_1 \Delta \ln k_{it} + \alpha_2 \Delta n_{it} + \alpha_3 \Delta \ln r_{it} + \alpha_4 \Delta \ln w_{it} + \alpha_5 \Delta \ln G_{it} + \alpha_6 \Delta \ln \pi_{it} + \varepsilon_{it} \qquad (1)$$

where k is the share of investment in GDP; n is population growth; r is the ratio of intra-regional trade to GDP; w is the ratio of extra-regional trade to GDP; G is government consumption expenditure relative to GDP; π is inflation; the α-regressors capture short-term dynamics; and ε is the usual zero-mean error term.

The β-coefficients measure the long-term growth effects of the respective explanatory variables. To control for short-run adjustments in growth, the model also includes regressors (α–coefficients) that are intended to proxy for cyclical components inherent in year-to-year variations in output. However, it should be noted that the α–coefficients in the model may not necessarily represent transitory growth effects, but may indicate more permanent effects (Bassanini et al. 2001). A priori expectations of the model coefficients are presented in Table A9.3 in Appendix. The expected sing on population growth rate is negative indicating that increases in the population growth rate will lead to a lower average income. We expect that higher investment shares in GDP and higher intra and extra-regional trade intensities will be associated with higher output growth. Finally, we expect government size and inflation to be inversely associated with output growth.

Based on the summary statistics in Table A9.1 and the Granger causality results in Table A9.2, we estimate several specifications of the model to verify the robustness of our results (we use the entire sample of 13 countries). Finally, we use lagged values for our trade intensity variables to ensure that trade observations precede growth effects.

Separating out the effect of intra-regional and extra-regional trade is very difficult and perhaps not possible practically in Arab countries, but under the current conditions of research, it is considered a hypothesis. Also, many factors affecting the rate of GDP growth are not included in the model because the model is subject to certain conditions being valid in the case of achieving these conditions.

4.3. Data Set

This section describes the data used in the empirical analysis below. Our focus variables, intra-regional and extra-regional trade, were constructed using data from the United Nations COMTRADE database which was available for all countries over the period 1990–2007. The import, export and total trade values were scaled by GDP in each year to obtain intra-regional, Arab–EU and extra-regional trade shares relative to the size of the economy for each country. Data on growth rates for GDP per capita expressed in 2,000 purchasing power parities for the period 1990–2004 were obtained from the Penn World Tables 6.2 and calculated from National Accounts Main Aggregates database (United Nation) for the period 2005–2007. Data on investment as a share of GDP were obtained from the Penn World Tables 6.2 for all countries. Government consumption expenditures were also scaled by GDP to obtain the relative size of government with respect to the economy for each country and obtained from Earth Trends Database. GDP for all countries is taken from National Accounts Main Aggregates database (United Nation). The difference in logs was used to approximate growth rates for GDP per capita, population and inflation. The data on population and inflation are taken from World Bank World Development Indicators (WDI) Online Databases.

Table A9.1 presents descriptive statistics for each sample country which highlight the variation in trade patterns between countries. Overall, countries with large trade shares exhibited higher mean growth rates. Specifically, United Arab Emirates stands out as a leader in growth and extra-regional trade with mean GDP per capita growth of 3.7 per cent and mean extra-regional trade intensity of 115.4 per cent of GDP over the sample period.

5. Empirical Results

We report fixed effects estimation results in Table A9.4 with t value for each coefficient are shown in parenthesis. With the exception of population growth and total intra-regional trade as a percentage of GDP, the signs of the regression coefficients are consistent with theoretical predictions and robust across specifications for the full sample (13 countries). On the other hand, all consistent coefficients are not statistically significant. The coefficients on the rate of change variables (short-run regressors) are both positive and significant except intra-regional trade and the rate of change of the GDP deflator (inflation) that have inverse sings. These non-similarities are a likely indication that these variables do not have similar structural linkages to growth.

In the same Table A9.4 in the Appendix, we report fixed effects estimation results for sample excluding all negative effect countries. With exception of intra-regional trade and inflation, the estimated coefficients of all the inputs are consistent with theoretical predictions and robust across specifications. The coefficient on the log of investment is small, while the rate of change in the share of investment has a strong and significant effect on growth. This suggests that growth responded more strongly to the rate at which investment levels changed. Conversely, the rate of government consumption spending has a significant negative effect on growth in both the short and long-run and these effects are statistically significant.

Our focus variables, extra-regional and intra-regional trade, are both significant and but only extra-regional trade has a positive effect on output growth per capita. Conversely, the coefficients on the rate of change variables (short-run regressors) are positive but only intra-regional trade is significant. The coefficient on extra-regional trade (1.71) is about 17 per cent higher than the coefficient on intra-regional trade (−5.48). This suggests that all else equal, with a 1 per cent increase in each of these variables, extra-regional trade will increase growth by 0.02 percentage points while intra-regional trade will decrease growth by 0.055 percentage points. To test whether the difference in the trade coefficients is statistically significant, we perform a difference-in-means test. Our null hypothesis is that the difference-in-means of the estimated coefficients on lnrt-1 and lnwt-1 is zero. The computed test statistic is 37.30 (P-value = 0.000) which rejects the null hypothesis, implying that extra-regional trade has a significantly greater effect on growth than intra-regional trade in the sample countries (column 2, Table A9.4).

Results show that the impact of extra-regional trade on GDP growth is greater than the impact of intra-regional trade in this case, and this is a logical consequence in view of the failure to establish a Arab common market since the establishment of the Arab League in 1945 accompanying the emergence the European union, which developed during the same period to the current situation.

Our results support empirical findings in previous literature on trade, regionalism and growth. With respect to trade and growth, Bassanini et al. (2001) conclude that 1 percentage point increase in trade exposure results in a 4 per cent increase in steady-state output per capita in 21 OECD countries between 1971 and 1998. Regarding the effects of different trade patterns on growth, previous literature provides some insights as to likely explanations. Vamvakidis (1999) found that participation in Regional Trade Agreements (RTAs) was on average associated with slower growth rates than following a policy of broad liberalisation and Wooster et al. (2007) show that intra-regional trade has had a lesser impact on growth in output per capita than extra-regional trade by almost 30 per cent over the period 1980–2003.

A number of other factors could be responsible for the observed difference in trade effects on growth. These could include market size, different structural relationships between growth and trade patterns, or the composition of commodities in the respective trade patterns. For example, Alcalá and Cicone (2003) found that the effect of trade on growth depended on country (market) size. With respect to the composition of commodities, conventional knowledge would suggest that higher proportions of capital goods in extra-regional trade may be responsible for its greater effects.

6. Conclusion

This study seeks to investigate whether intra-regional trade among Arab member countries has been a stronger source for growth in output per capita relative to extra-regional. The analysis here represents a significant departure from most previous studies that have assessed growth effects of RTAs by use of dummy variables which do not capture dynamic effects and some that treat trade as having the same effect regardless of trade partners involved. Specifically, our empirical framework uses intra-regional and extra-regional trade intensities to estimate the differential contribution of these two types of trade on growth in 13 Arab countries over the period 1990–2007.

The empirical results show that with sample excluding negative effect countries, extra-regional trade has had a lesser impact on output growth than intra-regional trade by almost 17 per cent, holding all other factors constant. This suggests that, all else equal, a 1 per cent increase in each of these variables, extra-regional trade will increase growth by 0.02 per cent points. This is likely due to the fact that extra-regional trade exposes countries to a larger and more diverse global market, which implies more possibilities for transfer of skills and technology. The global market also implies larger economies of scale and greater competition leading to higher efficiency in production.

Yet, the contribution of intra- and extra-regional trade to growth is only one element in the set of arguments on the globalisation versus regionalism debate. In particular, the formation of regional trade agreements is often a combination of both economic and political arguments. There may be perceived benefits from using regional economic integration as a basis for increasing regional security, promoting bargaining power and creating a 'commitment mechanism' for domestic policy reform.

Given that the focus of this research is on the economic objectives of RTAs and on the Arab's experience in particular, the results should not be interpreted as evidence that the benefits of multilateral trade liberalisation outweigh those of regional integration. Such evidence may be possible with time as the accumulation of data on the performance of more recent RTAs will allow for a richer picture

Appendix

Table A9.1: Summary Statistics by Country, 1990–2007

Variables	GDP per capita growth (Y)		Population growth (n)		Investment (k)		Intra-regional trade (r)		Extra-regional trade (w)		Indicator of government size (G)		Inflation (π)	
Statistics	Mean	Standard deviation	Mean	Standard deviation	Mean	Standard deviation	Mean	Standard deviation	Mean	Standard deviation	Mean	Standard deviation	Mean	Standard deviation
Algeria	0.5%	2.4	1.8%	0.4	11.3%	1.4	1.2%	0.3	48.7%	9.2	15.6%	1.6	16.5%	13.8
Bahrain	1.4%	7.4	2.5%	0.5	8.6%	2.3	24.7%	13.0	113.5%	16.7	20.0%	2.9	2.5%	6.1
Egypt	2.7%	2.2	1.9%	0.1	5.4%	0.6	2.3%	1.3	24.1%	6.9	11.4%	0.9	8.7%	5.3
Jordan	-0.4%	4.4	3.5%	2.1	15.2%	4.3	26.2%	8.5	63.0%	8.5	23.3%	1.5	3.6%	3.0
Kuwait	2.0%	14.8	-0.1%	12.8	11.2%	8.8	4.2%	1.4	65.3%	5.7	32.0%	15	5.4%	12.4
Lebanon	5.0%	11.1	1.9%	0.9	20.2%	8.7	9.8%	3.6	50.1%	14	16.5%	2.5	15.2%	29.2
Morocco	1.0%	5.6	1.5%	0.3	11.1%	1.2	3.9%	0.8	41.8%	7.2	17.6%	1.1	3.1%	3.2
Oman	1.5%	2.7	2.1%	1.0	7.7%	1.0	15.5%	3.2	66.2%	6.1	23.3%	1.8	4.0%	10.4
Qatar	1.8%	7.2	3.4%	1.3	14.6%	4.4	7.4%	1.3	73.0%	7.2	23.5%	8.5	10.8%	12.0
Saudi Arabia	0.1%	4.9	2.4%	0.6	8.5%	0.8	4.9%	2.0	55.2%	10.5	26.3%	2.9	4.8%	7.6
Syria	2.1%	3.5	2.7%	0.2	7.4%	0.8	8.6%	3.8	46.3%	8.2	12.9%	1.4	7.7%	5.2
Tunisia	3.2%	1.3	1.4%	0.5	13.0%	1.0	5.8%	1.2	69.5%	6.6	15.8%	0.6	3.8%	1.3
UAE	3.7%	6.0	5.0%	0.9	19.6%	2.0	7.2%	1.6	125.4%	14.5	16.0%	2.1	5.0%	7.6

Source: Authors' calculations.

Table A9.2: Granger Causality Wald Test Results

Dependent variable → Explanatory variable ↓	GDP per capita growth		
	Intra-regional trade	Extra-regional trade	Total trade
Algeria	–	–	–
Bahrain	–	–	–
Egypt	+	–	–
Jordan	–	–	–
Kuwait	+	–	+
Lebanon	–	–	–
Morocco	–	+	+
Oman	–	+	–
Qatar	–	–	–
Saudi Arabia	–	–	–
Syria	–	–	–
Tunisia	–	–	–
United Arab Emirates	+	–	–

Notes: "+" indicates the explanatory variable Granger causes the dependent variable at either the 1% or 5% level.

"–" indicates the explanatory variable does not Granger-cause the dependent variable at either the 1% or 5%, level.

Table A9.3: Explanatory Variables and Expected Signs

Variable	Expected sign
Population growth (n)	Negative (–)
Investment (lnk)	Positive (+)
Intra regional trade (lnr)	Positive (+)
Extra regional trade (lnw)	Positive (+)
Indicator of government size (lnG)	Negative (–)
Inflation ($ln\pi$)	Negative (–)

Note: Expectations are not implied for short-term explanatory variables.

Table A9.4: The Contribution of Intra- and Extra-Regional Trade to Output Growth — Fixed Effects Estimation

	Estimated coefficients	
Variables	Full sample (N = 233)	Sample excluding negative countries (N = 89)
Investment (ln$k$)	**0.052**	**0.635**
	(0.828)	(4.626)**
Population growth (**n**)	**0.066**	**– 0.702**
	(2.516)*	(–7.297)**

(*Table A9.4 Continued*)

(*Table A9.4 Continued*)

Variables	Estimated coefficients	
	Full sample (N = 233)	Sample excluding negative countries (N = 89)
Lagged intra-regional trade ($\ln r_{t-1}$)	−0.142	−0.548
	(−3.807)**	(−3.387)**
Lagged extra-regional trade ($\ln w_{t-1}$)	0.021	1.712
	(0.267)	(6.875)**
Indicator of government size ($\ln G$)	−0.201	−1.383
	(−1.681)	(−3.358)**
Inflation ($\ln \pi$)	−0.040	0.052
	(−1.643)	(1.593)
Short-run regressors:		
$\Delta \ln k$	3.453	−3.544
	(7.608)**	(−5.516)**
Δn	−0.504	10.701
	(−3.511)**	(6.276)**
$\Delta \ln r$	−0.047	0.853
	(−2.839)**	(6.183)**
$\Delta \ln w$	4.036	2.939
	(4.783)**	(2.018)
$\Delta \ln G$	−5.106	−20.775
	(−4.363)**	(−8.129)**
$\Delta \ln \pi$	0.058	0.020
	(7.096)**	(1.621)
F	9.337	19.225
R^2	0.17	0.57

Notes: N = no. of observations; **, * denote significance at the 1%, and 5% respectively. t values in parentheses.

to emerge regarding the differential impact of intra- and extra-regional trade. With advancements in the liberalisation of trade in services, it would also be possible in future research to investigate the differential impact of service and merchandise trade on growth.

Finally, the impact of intra-regional trade on output growth is negative and less than extra-regional trade because the intra Arab trade still represents less than 10 per cent of total Arab trade. The very low conventional figure for Arab countries' intra-regional trade as a proportion of their total trade reflects the huge predominance of oil in the latter: if oil is excluded, intra-regional trade is a quite respectable proportion of total trade. Although there is negative effect of intra-regional trade on output growth, GAFTA is needed for Arab because it aims at liberalising trade and increasing economic growth based on trade as an engine for development and growth. In addition, the area represents a step towards the economic integration among the Arab countries.

*

Notes

1. United Nations, National Accounts Main Aggregates database, Statistics Division, 2009.
2. World Bank, WDI Online Databases, 2009.
3. United Nations, National Accounts Main Aggregates database, Statistics Division, 2009.

References

Alcalá, Francisco, and Antonio Ciccone. 2003. Trade, Extent of the Market, and Economic Growth 1960 – 1996." UPF Economics and Business Working Paper 765. http://ideas.repec.org/e/pci47.html (accessed 20 August 2009).

Bassanini, Andrea, Stefano Scarpetta and Philip Hemmings. 2001. 'Economic Growth: The Role of Policies and Institutions. Panel Data Evidence from OECD Countries', OECD Economics Department Working Papers 283. Paris: Organisation for Economic Cooperation and Development.

Bayar, Ali. 2005. 'An Evaluation of the Benefits and Challenges of the South–South Integration among the Mediterranean Partner Countries', FEMISE Report No. FEM-22–27. Marseille: FEMISE.

Blattman, Christopher, Jason Hwang and Jeffrey G. Williamson. 2003. 'The Terms of Trade and Economic Growth in the Periphery 1870–1983', NBER Working Paper 9940. Cambridge: National Bureau of Economic Research.

Bleaney, Michael and David Greenaway. 2001. 'The Impact of Terms of Trade and Real Exchange Rate Volatility on Investment and Growth in sub-Saharan Africa', *Journal of Development Economics*, 65 (2): 491–500.

CATT. 2005. 'Obstacles to South-South Integration, to Trade and to Foreign Direct Investment: the MENA Countries Case', FEMISE Report No. FEM-22–36. Marseille: FEMISE.

Dasgupta, Dipak, Jennifer Kelle and T. G. Srinivasan. 2002. Reforms and Elusive Growth in the Middle East. What Has Happened in the 1990s?', Middle East and North Africa Working Paper Series 25. Washington, DC: World Bank.

DeJong, David, and Marla Ripol. 2006. 'Tariffs and Growth: An Empirical Exploration of Contingent Relationships.', *The Review of Economics and Statistics*, 88 (4): 625–40.

Dollar, David and Aart Kraay. 2002. 'Growth is Good for the Poor', *Journal of Economic Growth*, 7: 195–225.

———. 2004. 'Trade, Growth, and Poverty', *Economic Journal*, 114 (493): F22–49.

Frankel, Jeffrey, A. and David Romer, 1999. 'Does Trade Cause Growth?', *American Economic Review*, 89 (3): 379–99.

Grossman, Gene and Elhanan Helpman. 1991. *Innovation and Growth in the Global Economy*. Cambridge, MA: MIT Press.

Hadhri, Mohieddine. 2001. 'La Grande Zone Arabe de Libre-Echange et les Perspectives d'Intégration Sud-Sud en Méditerranée', Conférence FEMISE. Marseille: FEMISE.

Henrekson, Magnus, Johan Torstensson and Rasha Torstensson. 1997. 'Growth Effects of European Integration', *European Economic Review*, 41 (8): 1537–57.

Irwin, Douglas andMarko Terviö. 2002. 'Does Trade Raise Income?: Evidence from the Twentieth Century', Journal of International Economics, 58 (1): 1–18.

Italianer, Alexander. 1994. 'Whither the Gains from European Economic Integration?', *Revue Economique*, 45 (3): 689–702.

Neaime, Simon. 2005. 'South South Trade, Monetary and Financial Integration and the Euro-Mediterranean Partnership: An empirical Investigation', FEMISE Report No. FEM-22–39. Marseille: FEMISE.

Parikh, Ashok and Corneliu Stirbu. 2004. 'Relationship between Trade Liberalisation, Economic Growth and Trade Balance: An Econometric Investigation', HWWA Discussion Paper 282. Hamburg: HWWA.

Prebisch, R. 1950. 'The Economic Development of Latin America and Its Principal Problems', UN document no. E/CN.12/89/Rev.1. New York: United Nations.

Rodriguez, Francisco and Dani Rodrik. 1999. 'Trade Policy and Economic Growth: A Skeptic's Guide to Cross-National Evidence', NBER Working Paper 7081. Cambridge: National Bureau of Economic Research.

Sala-i-Martin, Xavier and J. Robert Barro. 1997. 'Technological Diffusion, Convergence, and Growth', *Journal of Economic Growth*, 2 (1): 1–26.

Sala-i-Martin, Xavier and Elsa Artadi. 2002. 'The Economic Tragedy of the XXth Century: Growth in Africa', NBER Working Paper Series 9865. Cambridge: National Bureau of Economic Research.

Sekouti. Natik. 1999. 'The Arab Free Trade Area (AFTA): Potentialities & Effects', in *New Economic Developments and their Impact on Arab Economies*, pp. 257–8.1 New York: Elsevier.

Shams, Rasul. 2003. 'Regional Integration in Developing Countries: Some Lessons Based on Case Studies', HWWA Discussion Paper 251. Hamburg: HWWA.

Singer, William. 1950. 'The Distribution of Gains between Investing and Borrowing Countries', *American Economic Review*, 40: 473–85.

Tahir, Juana. 1999. 'Free Economic Zones in Arab Countries in the Context of Arab Free Trade Areas and World Trade Organization Arrangements: Trends and Future Prospects', in *New Economic Developments and Their Impact on Arab Economies*, pp. 331–403. New York: Elsevier.

Thirlwall, Anthony and Amelia U. Santos-Paulino. 2004. 'Trade Liberalisation and Economic Performance in Developing Countries – Introduction', *Economic Journal*, 114 (493): F1–3.

United Nations (UN). 2009a. 'National Accounts Main Aggregates Database', Statistics Division. http://unstats.un.org/unsd/snaama/selbasicFast.asp (accessed 5 September 2009).

———. 2009b. 'National Accounts Main Aggregates Database', Statistics Division. http://unstats.un.org/unsd/snaama/selbasicFast.asp (accessed 5 September 2009).

United Nations (UN). 2009c. 'COMTRADE Database', Statistics Division. http://comtrade.un.org/db/dqQuickQuery.aspx (accessed 5 September 2009).

Vamvakidis, Athanasios. 1999. 'Regional Trade Agreements or Broad Liberalization: Which Path Leads to Faster Growth?', *IMF Staff Papers 46*, 46 (1): 42–68.

Vanhoudt, Patrick. 1999. 'Did the European Unification Induce Economic Growth? In Search of Scale Effects and Persistent Changes', *Weltwirtschaftliches Archive*, 135 (2): 193–220.

Vickers, John and George Yarrow. 1991. 'Economic Perspectives on Privatization', *Journal of Economic Perspectives*, 1991 (5): 111–32.

Wooster, Rossitza B., Smile Dube and Tepa M. Banda. 2007. 'The Contribution of Intra-Regional and Extra-Regional Trade to Growth: Evidence from the European Union'. Paper presented at the Globalisation and Regional Economic Integration conference, Gyeong Ju, South Korea.

World Bank. 2009. WDI Online Databases. http://data.worldbank.org/data-catalog/world-development-indicators (accessed 2 September 2009).

Zarrouk, Jameil. 2000. 'The Greater Arab Free Trade Area: Limits and Possibilities', in B. Hoekman and Z. Jameil (eds), *Catching Up with the Competition: Trade Opportunities and Challenges for Arab Countries*, pp. 285–305. Ann Arbor: University of Michigan Press.

Part 4

Sectoral Dimensions of International Trade

10

Comparison of Trade Complementarities and Similarities between India and ASEAN Countries

B. P. Sarath Chandran and P. K. Sudarsan

India–ASEAN Free Trade Agreement (IAFTA) generated intense debate on its likely fallout on India's economy, particularly on certain agricultural sub-sectors on which the livelihoods of large number of people are depended upon. For any Regional Trade Agreement (RTA) to be successful, it is imperative on partner countries to have complementary trade structure to be exploited for mutual benefits. RCA indices, despite their limitations, provide a useful guide to demonstrate the underlying comparative advantage and offer a further insight into the competitiveness of participating countries and hence reveal the possibility of increased trade cooperation between them. In this context, this chapter tries to identify complementary and competing sectors of trade between India and Association of South East Asian Nations (ASEAN) to consolidate their strengths and to overcome the deficiencies. Identification of synergies between India and ASEAN is important for further cementing the economic cooperation and deepening the relationship.

The proliferation of large number of RTAs in the international trading environment in the recent past is mainly due to the failure of the world trading system to provide a quick and acceptable solution to the problems it encountered during its existence. Multilateral trade negotiations are protracted and delayed as it encompasses large number of countries with diverse economic, political and social background leading to higher transaction costs and lost economic opportunity. The inability to arrive at consensus at the multilateral trade negotiations made countries to gang up under fiercely competing trade blocks such as European Union (EU), North American Free Trade Agreement (NAFTA), Southern Common Market or Mercosur and

ASEAN to benefit from discriminatory trade liberalisation and to get short-term market access.

Realising the importance of the Asian region for sustaining high trade growth, India initiated the 'Look East' policy in the early 1990s. India's sustained interest in and focused attention on improving economic relationship with the region resulted in the India–ASEAN Free Trade Agreement. The India–ASEAN total trade which was 2.9 billion US $ in 1993 which rose rapidly to 37.23 billion US $ in 2007. For the period 2003–2008, ASEAN exports to India grew at an average annual rate of 28.90 per cent while imports grew at 33.68 per cent.

2. Theoretical Developments and Empirical Studies

Theoretical studies on regionalism focused two important issues, namely how formation of regional trade blocks impact the welfare of the members and world at large and secondly whether regionalism helps or hinders the process of multilateral trade liberalisation. In his seminal work, Viner (1950) developed the theory of Customs Union (CU) which later received substantial theoretical improvement from Meade (1955), Lipsey (1960), Vanek (1965) and Ohyama (1972). Baldwin (1993, 1997) developed Domino theory of Regionalism and, along with Juggernaut theory, tried to answer the question of why countries prefer regional integration than multilateral liberalisation. The political economy dimension of regional trade agreements were empirically looked into by Krishna (1998), Bird and Rajan (2002), Albertin (2008), etc.

Balassa (1965) introduced the concept of 'Revealed Comparative Advantage' (RCA) as a way to approximate Comparative Advantage (CA) in autarky and suggested that CA is 'revealed' by observed trade pattern. Balassa Index tries to identify whether a country has a RCA rather than to determine the underlying sources of CA. The advantage of using the CA index is that it considers the intrinsic advantage of a particular export commodity and is consistent with changes in an economy's relative factor endowment and productivity. The index of revealed CA (RCAij) is simple to interpret: it takes a value greater than one if a country is having revealed CA in that product.

There have been many studies that used RCA index developed by Balassa (1965). Chow (1990) and Leu (1998) assessed the shift in CA of Japan and the Asian Newly Industrialised Countries (NICs).

Lim (1997) in his study based on the RCA index showed if North Korea's CA had moved up from Ricardo goods[1] to Heckscher Ohlin[2] (HO) goods, it would be difficult for the country to move into the terrain of Product Cycle (PC) goods[3]. Vollrath (1991) made improvement in Balassa index and offered three alternative ways of measurement of a country's RCA, namely the Relative Trade Advantage (RTA), the logarithm of the relative export advantage (ln RXA), and the Revealed Competitiveness (RC). Ferto and Hubbard (2002) used these modifications of the RCA index in the context of agricultural trade between Hungary and EU.

3. Methodology

This chapter uses Trade Intensity Index (TII) and RCA Index to see trade complementarity and similarity between India and ASEAN countries. The TII is used to determine whether the value of trade between the two is greater or smaller than would be expected on the basis of their importance in world trade. It is defined as the share of one country's exports going to a partner divided by the share of world exports going to the partner. It is calculated as:

$$T_{ij} = \frac{(x_{ij}/X_{it})}{(x_{wj}/X_{wt})}$$

Where x_{ij} and x_{wj} are the values of country i's exports and of world exports to country j and where X_{it} and X_{wt} are country i's total exports and total world exports respectively. An index of more (less) than one indicates a bilateral trade flow that is larger (smaller) than expected, given the partner country's importance in world trade.

TII is further divided in to Export Intensity Index (EII) and Import Intensity Index (III) for looking at the pattern of exports and Imports. Following Kojima (1964) and Drysdale (1969), the index of trade intensity is restated as follows:

$$EII \text{ between India and ASEAN} = \frac{X_{IA}/X_I}{(M_A/(M_W - M_I)}$$

X_{IA} = India's Export to ASEAN; X_I = India's total Export; M_A = Total Import of ASEAN; M_w = Total World imports M_I = Total Imports of India.

$$III\ between\ India\ and\ ASEAN = \frac{M_{IA}/M_I}{(X_A/(X_W - X_I)}$$

M_{IA} = Import of India from ASEAN; M_I = Total Import of India; X_A = Total Export of ASEAN; X_W = Total World Export; X_I = Total Export of India.

TII is calculated for India and ASEAN countries for the period 1990 to 2007 taking data from COMTRADE (UN 2008) of UN and accessed through World Integrated Trade Solutions (WITS). Both EII and III are calculated for India and ASEAN taking partners' position in world trade. An index value of one indicates bilateral trade is following the pattern of rest of the world and the value above one shows there is higher trade intensity between partners.

RCA Index shows how competitive is a product in countries' export compared to the products share in world trade. A product with high RCA is competitive and can be exported to countries with low RCA. Measures of RCA have been used to assess a country's export potential. It can also provide useful information about potential trade prospects with new partners. Countries with similar RCA profiles are unlikely to have high bilateral trade intensities unless intra-industry trade is involved. RCA measures, if estimated at high levels of product disaggregation, can focus attention on other non-traditional products that might be successfully exported. The RCA index of country 'i' for product 'j' is often measured by the product's share in the country's exports in relation to its share in world trade:

$$RCA_{ij} = \frac{x_{ij}/X_{it}}{(x_{wj} - X_{wt})}$$

Where x_{ij} and x_{wj} are the values of country i's exports of product j and world exports of product j and where X_{it} and X_{wt} refer to the country's total exports and world total exports. A value of less than unity implies that the country has a revealed comparative disadvantage in the product. Similarly, if the index exceeds unity, the country is said to have a RCA in the product.

In this chapter, RCA for ASEAN countries are calculated at three different levels namely Commodity Group level, HS-2 and HS-4, and compared then against India's RCA to see trade complementarity. WTO provide trade data at the commodity group level and based on this classification, RCA is calculated for eight ASEAN countries across 16 major commodity groups for 17 years to identify specific trade advantage. The product groups for which RCA has been computed include agricultural products, food, fuels and mining, fuels, manufactures, iron and steel, machinery and transport equipment, office and telecom equipments, electronic data processing and office equipments (EDP & OE), telecom equipments, information communication and electronic components (IC & EC), pharmaceuticals, chemicals, automotive, textiles and clothing. Data for calculating RCA are also collected from IMF, WTO and ASEAN Statistical Yearbook.

In order to get RCA at the disaggregate level, RCA index at HS-2 digit level of classification are calculated for India and ASEAN countries for the period 2003 to 2006. RCA for four years are calculated for India and combined ASEAN countries (Cambodia, Malaysia, Philippines, Singapore and Thailand) and a mean RCA is arrived at for comparison. Export–Import data for India and ASEAN Countries at HS-2 level classification are extracted from COMTRADE of UN through WITS. The absolute difference in RCA between India and ASEAN is calculated to understand the extent of complementarity in commodities. This is supplemented with trade performance under HS-4 digits classification to know finer specialisation of products by India and ASEAN countries.

4. Trade Intensity Index between ASEAN and India

India's export intensity (1.49 in 2007) as well as import intensity (1.61 in 2007) with ASEAN is above one in the recent past. This means India is trading more intensely with ASEAN countries compared with its trading pattern with rest of the world. The natural trading partner theory reveals countries tend to trade more with neighbours and close proximate partners. ASEAN countries being geographically closer to India, value of these indices are likely to come down once it is adjusted for geographical distance. ASEAN's EII (1.48 in 2007) is higher than III (1.40 in 2007) as it exports more to India compared to its imports.

Country-wise look at the trade intensity showed India's export intensity is above one for Indonesia, Malaysia, Myanmar, Singapore, Thailand and Vietnam. For others (Brunei, Laos, Cambodia and Philippines), the export intensity is fluctuating over the years. Myanmar, Singapore and Vietnam are the three countries with whom India got high export intensity. For the year 2007, except Cambodia, Laos and Philippines, India got high trade intensity with all ASEAN countries.

Table 10.1 gives the country-wise export and import intensity of India with ASEAN countries.

India is importing smaller volumes from the less developed countries of ASEAN which is reflected in the low III with Brunei, Cambodia and Lao PDR. Imports are also restricted with Philippines and Vietnam with import intensity well below one.

Table 10.1: India's Export and Import Intensity Index with ASEAN Countries

Year		BRU	CAM	INDO	LAO	MAL	MYA	PHI	SING	THAI	VIET
1990	EII	0.05	4.58	0.82	0.10	0.84	0.42	0.32	0.99	1.18	0.57
	III	0.00	0.00	0.94	0.82	2.60	30.93	0.07	1.83	0.38	3.30
1995	EII	0.28	0.20	2.06	0.09	0.77	1.52	0.72	1.08	1.00	1.95
	III	0.00	11.84	1.24	0.00	1.53	19.62	0.12	1.20	0.36	0.40
2000	EII	0.30	0.85	1.77	1.11	1.06	2.43	0.84	0.94	1.26	2.04
	III	0.01	0.12	1.87	0.00	1.78	11.40	0.20	1.35	0.61	0.11
2005	EII	2.17	0.95	2.56	0.40	1.08	3.37	1.08	2.80	0.94	1.93
	III	0.01	0.02	2.54	0.01	1.28	10.17	0.37	1.03	0.77	0.28
2006	EII	2.05	0.83	1.80	0.35	0.92	3.58	0.70	1.84	1.13	1.74
	III	0.01	0.01	2.01	0.01	2.23	8.86	0.18	1.97	0.98	0.24
2007	EII	1.21	0.53	1.77	0.32	1.19	3.07	0.59	1.90	1.25	1.49
	III	0.01	0.01	1.85	0.01	2.03	8.75	0.13	2.03	1.06	0.22

Source: Computed from COMTRADE (UN 2008).

India's import intensity was small with Thailand for many years but improved strongly after signing the bilateral trade agreement. India's imports from ASEAN was traditionally confined to Singapore and Malaysia. Import intensity is markedly high with Myanmar as it shares geographical border with India and is in close proximate with northeastern states of India. This exceptionally high import intensity is also due to Myanmar's low imports from the rest of the world due to political reasons. For all other countries, the index is stable without much deviation except for Cambodia in the year 1995.

5. Analysis of Revealed Comparative Advantage (RCA) between India and ASEAN

RCA at Product Groups Level

Table 10.2 gives the mean RCA of ASEAN countries and India for the period 1990 and 2006 for 16 product categories. The mean RCA for agricultural commodity is above one for India, Indonesia, Malaysia,

Table 10.2: Mean RCA for India and ASEAN in Major Commodity Groups

Commodity Categories	INDIA	BRU	CAM	INDO	MALA	PHI	SING	THA	VIET
Agriculture	**1.62**	0.01	0.34	**1.57**	**1.34**	**1.01**	0.40	**2.09**	**3.01**
Food	**1.84**	0.02	0.13	**1.38**	**1.07**	**1.18**	0.40	**2.25**	**3.47**
Fuel and mining	0.66	**7.33**	0.01	**2.63**	0.91	0.40	0.95	0.25	**1.77**
Fuels	0.41	**7.76**	0.00	2.96	**1.09**	0.17	1.13	0.23	**2.27**
Manufacture	**1.06**	0.09	**1.35**	0.66	**1.02**	**1.16**	**1.19**	**1.01**	0.66
Iron and steel	**1.28**	0.06	0.001	0.34	0.34	0.10	0.26	0.37	0.12
Chemicals	**1.04**	0.01	0.01	0.41	0.37	0.19	0.84	0.50	0.13
Pharmaceutical	**1.32**	0.01	0.07	0.04	0.03	0.41	0.07	0.02	
Machinery and transport equipment	0.23	0.10	0.02	0.27	**1.40**	**1.57**	**1.70**	0.98	0.21
Office and telecom equipments	0.09	0.03	0.004	0.48	**3.64**	**4.17**	**4.33**	**1.87**	0.30
EDP and office equipments	0.12	0.01	0.01	0.70	**3.63**	**3.95**	**3.53**	**2.21**	0.49
Telecom equipments	0.12	0.04	0.01	**1.05**	**2.53**	0.65	**1.50**	**1.26**	0.20
IC & EC products	0.07	0.00	0.00	0.29	**5.00**	**10.64**	**6.43**	**1.71**	0.14
Automotive	0.20	0.02	0.02	0.07	0.05	0.19	0.08	0.33	0.01
Textiles	**4.88**	0.12	0.48	**2.03**	0.49	0.41	0.37	**1.22**	0.92
Clothing	**4.07**	0.86	**24.46**	**2.23**	0.93	**3.52**	0.48	**2.29**	**4.81**

Source: Computed from WTO database (WTO 2008).

Philippines, Thailand and Vietnam and below one for Brunei, Cambodia and Singapore. This means there is a scope to trade agricultural commodities between India and low-RCA countries of ASEAN such as Brunei, Cambodia and Singapore. Food items form part of agricultural products and resemble the same pattern of RCA that of agricultural products. RCA for food is high for India, Indonesia, Malaysia, Thailand and Vietnam and low for Brunei, Cambodia, Philippines and Singapore. The average RCA showed that the two ASEAN countries namely Vietnam and Thailand are having a strong RCA of above two. But Brunei, Cambodia and Singapore got a very low RCA in food and India, which got a mean RCA of 1.8374, can export food articles to these nations.

Fuel and mining are resource-based products depending on the natural endowments of the country. However, industries can be established to process and refine these products. For mining and fuels, RCA is high in Brunei, India, Indonesia, and Vietnam and low in Cambodia, Malaysia, Singapore and Thailand. The mean RCA shows that Brunei and Indonesia and Vietnam have got RCA for fuel and mining products and they can export fuel products to Cambodia, Philippines, Thailand, Malaysia, Singapore and India who have revealed comparative disadvantage. This shows that there is complementarity in trading fuel products in the ASEAN region. With regard to the mining products alone, India got the comparative advantage in many product categories and can export them to most of the ASEAN countries.

Manufactured commodities are value-added products and exports of these products depend on the industrial development of the country. The computation of RCA for manufacture products showed India, Cambodia, Malaysia, Philippines, Singapore and Thailand had RCA above one where as Brunei, Indonesia and Vietnam have got RCA below one. But the disaggregation of manufacture products into different categories showed that countries enjoy clear RCA in specific product categories. In the case of iron and steel industry, all the ASEAN countries got comparative disadvantage whereas India enjoys a high RCA in this product. This industry depends on the availability of natural resource in a country and India has got huge iron ore reserve in the country. India can export iron and steel to most of the ASEAN countries.

The computation of RCA for chemicals showed that India developed comparative advantage in this product category over the period of time. Currently India is exporting different chemical products and increasing the share in its export basket. India has got RCA in chemicals whereas all the other ASEAN countries have revealed comparative disadvantage pointing out that India can improve trade in chemical products with the ASEAN countries. With regard to pharmaceutical products, the mean RCA suggests that India has got comparative advantage in this important category. India's comparative advantage in this knowledge-based industry is the reflection of the capacity developed over the period of time. All the ASEAN countries have comparative disadvantage in this category even though Philippines is slowly increasing its share over time. There is a prospect of higher trade between India and ASEAN countries in pharmaceutical products.

Singapore, Malaysia, Philippines and recently Thailand have been exporting more machinery and transport equipment and showing comparative advantage in this skill-based product category. The disadvantaged countries in the product group include India, Brunei, Cambodia, Indonesia and Vietnam. This reveals that there is scope for trading machinery and transport equipment within ASEAN countries and between ASEAN and India. In this high technology industry, Singapore, Malaysia, Philippines and Thailand have developed competencies and are exporting large share of products to other countries. The mean RCA is above two for Singapore, Philippines and Malaysia where as it is above one for Thailand. On the other hand, countries like India, Brunei, Cambodia, Indonesia and Vietnam have to go a long way in developing comparative advantage and exporting these products to other countries. This gives scope for higher intra-regional trade for office and telecom equipment and between Singapore, Malaysia, Thailand and India. If we take the electronic data processing and office equipment separately, it follows the same pattern. Singapore, Malaysia, Philippines and Thailand had higher mean RCA and rest of ASEAN and India have got comparative disadvantage.

Malaysia enjoys high export performance of telecom equipment and thereby possesses significant comparative advantage, followed by Singapore and Thailand in the region. Indonesia, whose RCA was above one during early 2000, slipped from its position after 2005 when RCA fell below one. The less developed countries of ASEAN, Philippines and India have got comparative disadvantage in this product category giving scope for higher trade among these countries. Integrated circuits and electronic components are an important input for the development of electronics and communication industry which is growing at a rapid rate in this information age. East Asian countries like Singapore, Malaysia, Philippines and Thailand have developed competencies in this sector and have a strong RCA. The high mean RCA of Philippines (10.64), Singapore (6.43), Malaysia (5.00) and Thailand (1.71) shows the strong export performance of this high-value technology sector. On the other hand, the remaining East Asian countries like Brunei, Cambodia, Indonesia, Vietnam and India have got revealed comparative disadvantage in this category. This shows that large potential exists for bilateral trade for this important input component and increased trade among ASEAN countries and between India and ASEAN.

Automotive is an important component in the manufacturing sector with strong backward linkage and employment potential. But ASEAN countries as well as India do not have comparative advantage in this sector. This is because of the dominance of Japanese companies for long and Korea recently. India has been attracting foreign entry and investment in this sector and exporting cars manufactured by multinational (Maruti Suzuki, Hyundai), particularly to European nations but is yet to develop RCA for sizable export share and market dominance.

Textiles is labour-intensive sector with high employment potential and most of the developing countries of Asia depend on their export to earn their foreign exchange. India traditionally exported large quantity of textile products and revealed significant comparative advantage. Indonesia and Thailand also have high RCA as their textile export shares are much above the world textile export share. The mean RCA computed in the study is 4.88 for India, 2.03 for Indonesia and 1.22 for Thailand. Most of the ASEAN countries have low RCA showing the complementarity existing in the sector and they can trade more with India for their requirement. But the dismantling of MFA (Multi Fibre Agreement) brought in strong players like China who dominate the market and India needs to equip itself to take care of this advantage. There is increased competition in the clothing sector in the East Asian region as most of the developing countries having strong comparative advantage along with India. The mean RCA for Cambodia (24.46), Vietnam (4.81), Philippines (3.52), Thailand (2.29), and Indonesia (2.23) are high and these countries are major exporters of clothing to the rest of the world. India is also a major exporter of clothing to the world and there is limited complementarity between India and ASEAN countries for increased trade in this sector.

RCA greater than or less than one is the classification used in the studies to ascertain the comparative advantage for a country in a given product. But the degree of comparative advantage is useful in getting the relative position of the commodity in the country's export basket. If the RCA index is slightly lower than one, the country can make concentrated efforts to move towards comparative advantage compared to a commodity whose RCA is closer to zero. This facilitates easy comparison of relative position of comparative advantage across countries and product groups. For this purpose, mean RCA of countries are classified into four categories based on their export performance. These categories are high comparative disadvantage (RCA 0 to 0.5), low comparative disadvantage (RCA 0.5 to 1), high comparative advantage (RCA 1 to 2) and strong comparative advantage (RCA above 2). RCA above one in the Table 10.2 is given in bold showing comparative advantage enjoyed by the country. High and low revealed comparative disadvantaged countries cannot trade as they do not have efficiency in commodity production. High and strong RCA countries have comparative advantage but face similar export structure. Finer specialisation in production can lead to possible intra-industry and increased trade between these categories of countries. But trade is genuinely possible between countries with complementary trade structure like High Disadvantage–Strong Advantage, High Disadvantage–High Advantage, Low Disadvantage–Strong Advantage and Low Disadvantage–High comparative advantage.

India's Comparative Advantage with ASEAN Countries — Product Category-wise

For agricultural commodities, India has got a high RCA and can export to Brunei, Cambodia and Singapore who have disadvantage in this product category. Food products are part of agricultural products and follow the same pattern as that of agricultural products. For fuel and mining products Brunei, Indonesia and Vietnam have comparative advantage and can trade with India. India has got comparative disadvantage in fuel and can import it from Brunei, Indonesia and Vietnam who are the oil exporters of ASEAN, or from Malaysia and Singapore who refine crude oil and export it to other countries.

India's RCA for manufacture is high and there is a possibility to trade with Indonesia and Vietnam who have got low comparative advantage. All the ASEAN countries have weak comparative advantage

Table 10.3: Country Classification Based on Mean RCA of Commodities

Commodity classification	High comparative disadvantage RCA<0.5	Low comparative disadvantage 0.5<RCA<1	High Comparative Advantage 1<RCA<2	Strong Comparative Advantage RCA>2
Agricultural products	Brunei, Cambodia, Singapore	–	**India**, Indonesia, Malaysia, Philippines	Thailand, Vietnam
Food	Brunei, Cambodia, Singapore	–	**India**, Indonesia, Malaysia, Philippines	Thailand, Vietnam
Fuels and MP	Cambodia, Philippines, Thailand	**India**, Malaysia, Singapore	Vietnam	Brunei, Indonesia
Fuels	**India**, Cambodia, Philippines, Thailand	–	Malaysia, Singapore	Brunei, Indonesia, Vietnam
Manufacture	Brunei	Indonesia, Vietnam	**India**, Cambodia, Malaysia, Philippines, Singapore, Thailand	–
Iron and steel	Brunei, Cambodia, Indonesia, Malaysia, Philippines, Singapore, Thailand, Vietnam	–	**India**,	–
Chemicals	Brunei, Cambodia, Indonesia, Malaysia, Philippines, Vietnam	Singapore, Thailand	**India**	–
Pharmaceuticals	Brunei, Cambodia, Indonesia, Malaysia, Philippines, Singapore, Thailand	–	**India**	–
Machinery and transport equipments	**India**, Brunei, Cambodia, Indonesia, Vietnam	Thailand	Malaysia, Philippines, Singapore	–

Office and telecom equipments	India, Brunei, Cambodia, Indonesia, Vietnam	–	Thailand	Malaysia, Philippines, Singapore
EDP and OE	India, Brunei, Cambodia, Vietnam	Indonesia	–	Malaysia, Philippines, Singapore, Thailand
Telecom	India, Brunei, Cambodia, Vietnam	Philippines	Indonesia, Singapore, Thailand	Malaysia
IC and EC	India, Brunei, Cambodia, Indonesia, Vietnam	–	Thailand	Malaysia, Philippines, Singapore
Automotive	India, Brunei, Cambodia, Indonesia, Malaysia, Philippines, Singapore, Thailand, Vietnam	–	–	–
Textiles	Brunei, Cambodia, Malaysia, Philippines, Singapore	Vietnam	Thailand	India, Indonesia
Clothing	Singapore	Brunei, Malaysia	–	India, Cambodia, Indonesia, Philippines, Thailand, Vietnam

Source: Computed from WTO database (WTO 2008).

in iron and steel and there is a trade complementarity between them and India. India's export of chemical products is increasing and reveals a high comparative advantage. RCA for chemicals is weak for Brunei, Cambodia, Indonesia, Malaysia, Philippines and Vietnam and low for Singapore and Thailand. This complementarity in trade structure gives opportunity for India to export more chemical products to ASEAN countries. Similarly, India has got high RCA in pharmaceutical products and export them to weak RCA ASEAN countries.

Table 10.4 highlights the complementary sectors between India and ASEAN for trade promotion. For iron and steel and chemical and pharmaceuticals, India has got complementarity with all ASEAN countries. For textiles and fuels, India has got trade complementarity with four ASEAN countries. With regard to countries, India's complementarity is highest with Singapore (13 sectors), followed by Malaysia (11), Brunei (10), Philippines (8), Indonesia (07), Thailand (7), Cambodia (6) and Vietnam (6). With regard to machinery and transport equipment, India has got comparative disadvantage and can import them from high RCA ASEAN countries such as Malaysia, Philippines and Singapore.

Revealed Comparative Advantage for HS-2 Digits Classification

In order to get RCA at a disaggregated level, an attempt is made to calculate RCA at the HS-2 digits level taking data from the COMTRADE. The 97 HS-2 digits are grouped into seven categories, namely agricultural commodities, chemical products, manufactured products, textile products, industrial inputs, mineral products and electrical machinery and parts. With regard to agricultural commodities, of the 24 HS-2 digits commodities, 9 categories showed trade complementarity between India and ASEAN. These include edible vegetables and certain roots (HS-07), edible fruits and nuts; peel of citrus fruit or melon (HS-08), products of the milling industry; malt; starches; inulin; wheat gluten (HS-11); oil seed, oleagi fruits; miscellaneous grain, seed, fruit etc (HS-12); animal/vegetable fats and oils and their clea (HS-15); preparation of meat, fish or crustaceans (HS-16); residues and waste from the food industry (HS-23); and tobacco and manufactured tobacco (HS-24). The highest RCA for India in agricultural products is in vegetable plaiting materials (HS14) and coffee, tea, mati and spices (HS-09) and for ASEAN is Animal or vegetable fats, oils and waxes (HS15) and preparation of meat, fish or crustaceans

Table 10.4: India–ASEAN Trade Complementarity from Computed RCA

INDIA — Product groups	Brunei	Cambodia	Indonesia	Malaysia	Philippines	Singapore	Thailand	Vietnam
Agricultural products	H-W	H-W	H-H	H-H	H-H	H-W	H-S	H-S
Food	H-W	H-W	H-H	H-H	H-H	H-W	H-S	H-S
Fuels and MP	L-S	L-W	L-S	L-L	L-W	L-L	L-W	L-H
Fuels	W-S	W-W	W-S	W-H	W-W	W-H	W-W	W-S
Manufacture	H-W	H-H	H-L	H-H	H-H	H-H	H-H	H-L
Iron and steel	H-W	H-W	H-W	H-W	H-W	H-W	H-W	H-W
Chemicals	H-W	H-W	H-W	H-W	H-W	H-L	H-L	H-W
Pharmaceuticals	H-W	H-W	H-W	H-W	H-W	H-W	H-W	H-W
Machinery and transport equipments	W-W	W-W	W-W	W-H	W-H	W-H	W-L	W-W
Office and telecom equipments	W-W	W-W	W-W	W-S	W-S	W-S	W-H	W-W
EDP and OE	W-W	W-W	W-L	W-S	W-S	W-S	W-S	W-W
Telecom	W-W	W-W	W-H	W-S	W-L	W-H	W-H	W-W
IC and EC	W-W	W-W	W-W	W-S	W-S	W-S	W-H	W-W
Automotive	W-W	W-W	W-W	W-W	W-W	W-W	W-W	W-W
Textiles	S-W	S-W	S-S	S-W	S-W	S-W	S-H	S-L
Clothing	S-L	S-S	S-S	S-L	S-S	S-W	S-S	S-S

Source: Computed from WTO database (WTO 2008).

(HS-16). The highest absolute difference in RCA is for vegetable plaiting materials (HS-14) and coffee, tea, mate and spices (HS-09).

For chemical products, the trade complementarity is present in salt, sulphur, earth and stone; plaste (HS-25); ores, slag and ash (HS-26); mineral fuels, oils & product (HS-27); tanning/dyeing extract; tannins (HS-32) and explosives; pyrotechnic prod; match (HS-36). Interestingly, India has a higher RCA than ASEAN for all product categories. India's highest RCA is for ores, slag and ash (5.66) and salt, sulphur, earth and stone, lime and cement (HS-25) and these two products have highest absolute difference in RCA.

For other manufactured products, the complementarity is present in rubber and articles thereof (HS-40), raw hides and skins (HS-43) and articles of leather, saddlery/harne (HS-43). India has strong comparative advantage in articles of leather, saddlery/harne and raw hides and skins (other than fu) where ASEAN has got high comparative advantage in rubber and articles thereof. India's strong comparative advantage in textiles and related products include silk (HS-50), cotton (HS-52), vegetable textile fibers nesoi, yarns and woven, etc, (HS-53), man-made filaments (HS-54), carpets and other textile floor coverings (HS-57), art of apparel and clothing access (HS-61), articles of apparel and clothing accessories, not knitted or crocheted (HS-62) and other made-up textile articles (HS-63) and these products have export markets in ASEAN countries. The mean RCA for ASEAN countries taken together do not reveal comparative advantage in textiles and related products even though individual countries show high revealed comparative advantage.

In the category of industrial inputs, the complementarity is present in prepared feathers and down; artificial flower (HS-67) and natural/cultured pearls, precious stone (HS-71) in which India has got very strong comparative advantage. Pearls and precious stones are important items of export as these are used in jewellery and artifacts.

India enjoys comparative advantage in many mineral products compared to ASEAN countries. These include iron and steel (HS-72), articles of iron or steel (HS-73), copper and articles thereof (HS-74) and zinc and articles thereof (HS-79) in which India has got high RCA against ASEAN. ASEAN's comparative advantage lies in tin and articles thereof (HS-80) and India can import this from ASEAN as the absolute difference is highest in this category.

ASEAN has strong RCA for electrical machinery, equipments, parts thereof (HS-85) and high RCA for nuclear reactors, boilers, machinery (HS-84) against India and exports lots of these items to India. On the other hand, India's RCA include ships, boats and floating structure (HS-89), clocks and watches and parts thereof (HS-91) and works of art, collectors' pieces etc. (HS-97).

RCA under HS-4 Digits Classification

RCA is calculated for four ASEAN countries, namely Malaysia, Philippines, Singapore and Thailand for the year 2008 and compared against India's RCA to see trade complementarity at the more disaggregated level. The exercise could not be done for other ASEAN countries due to non-availability of data at the HS-4 digits level. The following section gives the analysis of RCA of ASEAN and India in HS-4 digits commodity classification.

The top five HS-4 commodities in terms of export share for India are petroleum oils and oils obtained from bituminous minerals (17.35 per cent with a RCA of 3.84); diamonds, whether or not worked, but not mounted or set (8.19 per cent with a RCA of 15.13); iron ores and concentrates included (3.10 per cent with a RCA of 46.30); rice (1.56 per cent with a RCA of 10.05); and other organic compounds (1.31 per cent with a RCA of 46.30). Among agricultural commodities, India has got comparative advantage in coconuts, pepper, vanilla, seeds of anise, badian, fennel, rice, groundnut, copra and oil cakes and other residues.

For Malaysia, the top five HS-4 commodities in terms of export share are automatic data processing machines (7.20 per cent with a RCA of 3.37), petroleum gases and other gaseous hydrocarbons (7.07 per cent with a RCA of 3.56), petroleum oils and oils obtained from bituminous minerals (6.65 per cent with a RCA of 1.21), palm oil and its fractions, whether or not refined, but not chemically modified (6.41 per cent with a RCA of 47.18) and parts and accessories, other than covers, carrying cases and the like (5.47 per cent with a RCA of 6.30).

The top five HS-4 commodities in terms of export share for Philippines are electronic integrated circuits and (9.73 per cent with a RCA of 6.28); automatic data processing machines (7.65 per cent with a RCA of 3.58); parts and accessories of the motor (4.19 per cent with a RCA of 2.24); diodes, transistors and similar items

(3.67 per cent with a RCA of 6.75); and parts and accessories, (other than covers, carrying cases and the like (3.35 per cent with a RCA of 3.85).

Singapore's top five export items are petroleum oils and oils obtained from bituminous minerals (24.16 per cent with a RCA of 5.35), electronic integrated circuits and parts (11.26 per cent with a RCA of 7.28), parts and accessories (other than covers, carrying cases and the like) suitable for use solely or principally with machines of headings 8469 to 8472 (4.28 percent with a RCA of 4.92); automatic data processing machines (3.77 per cent with a RCA of 1.77) and prepared unrecorded media for sound (1.72 per cent with a RCA of 9.61).

The top five HS-4 export for Thailand include automatic data processing machines (7.62 per cent with a RCA of 3.57); petroleum oils and oils obtained from bituminous minerals (5.05 per cent with a RCA of 1.12); electronic integrated circuits and parts (4.07 per cent with a RCA of 2.63); natural rubber, balata, gutta-perch (3.82 per cent with a RCA of 37.09); and rice (3.47 per cent with a RCA of 22.31).

6. Conclusion

Inferences from the trade indices computed for understanding the trade structure between India and ASEAN reveal that there are complemetary sectors and products available for enhancing trade cooperation between the trading partners. ASEAN countries are in different stages of economic development and India can have trade cooperation with some of them in all product categories. While India can export food grains to small and developed countries of ASEAN, it can import edible and other agricultural products from other ASEAN countries. India enjoys advantage in minerals whereas it can import crude oil from ASEAN. India possesses advantage in some manufactured items like chemicals, iron and steel, jems and jewellery and can export them to many ASEAN countries. ASEAN has comparative advantage in electrical and electronic components and India can import them from ASEAN. With regard to textiles and clothing, there is intense competition between ASEAN and India to increase market share. India's average tariff is higher than ASEAN countries and reduction of tariffs from RTA will have short-term adverse impact on India's exports but can consolidate in the medium term through productivity gains and efficiency. Also, emerging global economic structure warrants greater cooperation from India in the regionalisation efforts of Asia.

❋

Notes

1. 'Ricardo' goods incorporate those goods which use natural resources for their production.
2. 'HO' goods are produced using standard technology and are characterised by lower costs in R&D.
3. 'PC' goods essentially are technology-intensive and are characterised by high R&D.

References

Albertin, Giorgia. 2008. 'Regionalism or Multilateralism? A Political Economy Choice', IMF Working Paper WP/08/65.. Washington, D.C.: International Monetary Fund.

Balassa, Bela. 1965. 'Trade Liberalization and Revealed Comparative Advantage', *The Manchester School of Economic and Social Studies*, 33 (1): 99–123.

Baldwin, Richard. 1993. 'A Domino Theory of Regionalism', NBER Working Paper, 4465. Cambridge: National Bureau of Economic Research.

Baldwin, R.E. 1997. 'The Causes of Regionalism', *The World Economy*, 20 (7): 865–88.

Bird, Graham and Ramkishen S. Rajan. 2002. 'The Political Economy of a Trade-First Approach to Regionalism', Institute of Southeast Asian Studies, Visiting Researchers Series No. 2. Adelaide: Centre for International Economic Studies.

Chow, Peter C. Y. 1990. 'The Revealed Comparative Advantage of the East Asian NICs', *The International Trade Journal*, 5 (2): 235–62.

Drysdale, P. 1969. 'Japan, Australia, New Zealand: The Prospect for Western Pacific Economic Integration', *Economic Record*, 45 (11): 321–42.

Ferto, Imre and Lionel J. Hubbard. 2002. 'Revealed Comparative Advantage and Competitiveness in Hungarian Agri-Food Sectors', Discussion Paper Series 2002/8, Institute of Economics. Budapest: Hungary Academy of Sciences.

Kojima, K. 1964. 'The Pattern of International Trade among Advanced Countries', *Hitotsubashi Journal of Economics,* 5 (1): 62–84.

Krishna, P. 1998. 'Regionalism and Multilateralism: A Political Economy Approach', *Quarterly Journal of Economics*, 113 (1): 227–50.

Leu, Gwo-Jiun Mike. 1998. 'Changing Comparative Advantage in East Asian Economies', Working Paper Series 3-98, School of Accounting and Business Research Center, NTU. Singapore: Nanyang Technological University.

Lim, Kang-Taeg. 1997. 'Analysis of North Korea's Foreign Trade by Revealed Comparative Advantages', *Journal of Economic Development*, 22 (2): 97–117.

Lipsey. 1960. 'The Theory of Customs Unions: A General Survey', *Economic Journal*, 70: 496—513.

Meade, J. E. 1955. *The Theory of Customs Unions*. Amsterdam: North-Holland.

Ohyama, M. 1972. 'Trade and Welfare in General Equilibrium', *Keio Economic Studies*, 9: 37–73.

United Nations (UN). 2008. *COMTRADE Database*, WITS (World Integrated Trade Solution). http://wits.worldbank.org/WITS (accessed 10 November 2009).

Vanek, J. 1965. *General Equilibrium of International Discriminaton: The Case of Customs Unions*, Cambridge: Harvard University Press.

Viner, J. 1950. *The Customs Union Issue*. New York: Carnegie Endowment for International Peace.

Vollrath, T. L. 1991. 'A Theoretical Evaluation of Alternative Trade Intensity Measures of Revealed Comparative Advantage', *Weltwirtschaftliches Archiv*, 130: 265–79.

World Trade Organisation (WTO). 2008. *International Trade Statistics*, Geneva. http://www.wto.org/english/res_e/statis_e/statis_e.htm (accessed 10 November 2009).

11

ASEAN–India Free Trade Agreements and Plantations: Beyond Casual Observations and Common Sense

K. J. Joseph

The signing of ASEAN–India Free Trade Agreement on 13 August 2009 in Bangkok may be considered as a landmark in the evolution of India–ASEAN relationship. For the enthusiasts of Asian Economic Integration, this is a milestone in the progress towards Asian Economic Community. Since the initiation of look East policy in the early 1990s, India–ASEAN partnership has been progressing at a faster pace — from a sectoral dialogue partner in 1992 to a summit-level interaction in 2002 and the signing of the Framework Agreement on Comprehensive Economic Cooperation in 2003. The journey from Framework Agreement to the Free Trade Agreement (FTA), however, was rather slow. Signed during the Bali Summit, the Framework Agreement envisaged the regional trade liberalisation between 2004 and 2016.

India, being a country of continental size but more diverse than most continents with many sectors inward oriented, while dealing with an outward Association of South East Asian Nation (ASEAN), preferred to keep a list of 1,400 products (HS-6 digit level) in the negative list that accounted for almost 40 per cent of exports from ASEAN to India. ASEAN, however, insisted that products covered in FTA should account for at least 90 per cent of the imports from ASEAN. The six years of negotiations that followed led to the present FTA that was acceptable to the member countries of ASEAN while ensuring many safeguards for the protection of Indian producers.

Important Provisions

The Free Trade Agreement provides for a phased removal of tariff barriers on more than 80 per cent of traded products (about 10,885 tariff lines at HS 8 digit) during January 2010 to December 2019. Of these, duties on 7,788 tariff lines would be eliminated within a period of four years from the current level of 7.5 to 10 per cent by an annual reduction of 1.5 to 2 per cent. On 1,252 tariff lines with current tariff level of 7.5 to 10 per cent, import duty will be eliminated within a period of seven years by an annual reduction of 1 to 1.5 per cent.

The tariff lines subject to tariff reduction/elimination are divided into normal track, sensitive track, highly sensitive lists, special products and the exclusion (negative) list. In case of normal track, applied Most Favoured Nation (MFN) tariff rates will be reduced and subsequently eliminated. While the less developed new ASEAN countries (Cambodia, Lao, Myanmar and Vietnam) and Philippines are given time till 2019, old ASEAN countries will have to accomplish tariff reduction by 2016. Needless to say India has to reciprocate its tariff as per the reduction offered by the member countries. In case of sensitive track, all the applied MFN tariff rates above five per cent will be reduced to five per cent. In case of special products (crude and refined palm oil, coffee, tea and pepper), applied MFN tariff rates will be brought down as follows: for crude palm oil from 80 to 40 per cent, refined palm oil from 90 to 40 per cent, coffee and tea from 100 to 50 per cent and pepper from 70 to 51 per cent in the terminal year.

The highly sensitive list has three categories of products with different reduction commitment. In the first category, the applied MFN tariff rates are to be reduced to 50 per cent, in the second category by 50 per cent, and in the third category applied MFN tariff rates are to be reduced by 25 per cent by 31 December 2019. Finally the Agreement also provides for a negative and exclusion list of 489 products that includes 303 items of agricultural sector, 81 items from textiles, 50 items of auto sector and 17 items of chemicals sector.

The Agreement also provides for safeguard measures in case of imports of a particular product from a partner country exceeds three per cent of the total imports and cause substantial injury to the domestic industry. In case of non-originating products, the Agreement has a fairly strict rule of origin stipulating a value addition of at least 35 per cent or a change in the tariff sub-heading level of the harmonised system.

Predicting the Unpredictable: Likely Impact

It is rather difficult to predict in precise terms how the FTA would impact on different stakeholders. The impact would vary not only between countries but between sectors within the countries and also across time. The conventional theory of customs unions (Viner 1950) tells us that the net welfare outcome of the Preferential Trading Arrangements (like Regional or Bilateral FTA) would depend on the balance between trade creating and trade diverting influences resulting from tariff reduction.

Earlier empirical studies undertaken in the context of PTAs based on the above approach did not entail any definite conclusion on the net welfare effect of such arrangements (Pomfret 1988). Further, according to the above approach, even when there is net welfare gain, such gains can be no better than that of unilateral elimination of tariffs on a non-preferential basis. Thus, according to the conventional theory, preferential trading arrangements are economically irrational, as compared to the first-best option of non-preferential tariff cuts, and therefore, can be explained only by non-economic motives (ibid.). No wonder, many economists considered FTAs as stumbling blocks and not building bocks in world trade.

Developments in the theory of PTAs that followed, however, could break the impasse of the above framework by relaxing its restrictive assumptions and incorporating more dynamic effects of preferential trading arrangements, viz., scale economies, improved technical efficiency, possible terms of trade effects and higher growth rates (Corden 1986). In the absence of major tariff preferences, as argued by Hoekman and Konan (1999) South–South integration could lead to the removal of several invisible trade barriers such as border norms, customs formalities, testing and other trade facilitation measures. Later there were also rich empirical evidences highlighting the gains from PTAs. A study by the United Nations Conference on Trade and Development or UNCTAD (2004) for example, concluded that almost all the South–South Regional Trading Arrangements (S–S RTAs) are not only trade-creating, but also trade expanding, increasing overall trade with third countries outside the RTA. Further, the study suggests that S–S RTAs could be used as a mechanism for the gradual integration of developing countries into the global economy.

Winters and Schiff (2003) argued that the impetus for domestic reforms may be strengthened by the openness initiated through RTAs, particularly South–South ones. Furthermore, beyond these economic effects, RTAs are very much part of a larger framework for regional cooperation aimed at promoting regional stability, sound and coordinated economic policies and a better regional economic infrastructure. Although difficult to quantify, all these improvements would lead to positive spillover effects.

Even while respecting the theoretical arguments and empirical evidence on the positive contribution of FTAs, one cannot ignore the fact that the FTAs create losers and gainers especially in large and diversified countries. This is, inter alia, on account of the differences in the extent of sectoral complimentarity between partner countries. Also, the returns to trade liberalisation induced by FTA is bound to be different in the short and long run. Hence in a context wherein theory-based generalisations have obvious limits, informed policy making should be based on realistic analysis of the specific context in which trade liberalisation takes place under FTA.

Export, Import and Trade Balance

With the entry of Cambodia, Laos, Myanmar and Vietnam (also known as new ASEAN), ASEAN today is a heterogeneous group of countries at varying stages of development. While the old ASEAN (Brunei, Indonesia, Malaysia, Philippines, Thailand and Singapore) have higher per capita income (see Table 11.1) with a long record of outward oriented growth with greater role for FDI, the new ASEAN, with the possible exception of Vietnam, exhibit many characteristics of less developed economies. Also, agriculture in new ASEAN continues to be the prime sector as the manufacturing sector is at its infancy. In contrast, the old ASEAN countries have been highly successful in developing production base and export competitiveness in a wide range of medium and high technology industries. Particularly notable are their production capabilities in electronics and telecommunication equipment, heavy engineering, capacity in the construction and management of infrastructure — to list a few (RIS 2004). These characteristics are bound to get reflected in the pattern of trade between India and ASEAN.

The FTA takes place in a context wherein India's trade with ASEAN is growing at a higher rate than with rest of the world. To illustrate, during 2001–2007 exports to and imports from ASEAN

Table 11.1: Select Indicators of Development and India's Trade with ASEAN

Development Indicators	India	Cambodia	Laos	Myanmar	Vietnam	Brunei Darussalam	Indonesia	Malaysia	Philippines	Singapore	Thailand
GDP (Billion $)	703.3	6.31	2.53	–	48.43	6.99	219.27	118.436	99.59	121.63	164.99
Agriculture (% of GDP)	17.53	30.1	42.01	–	20.36	0.7	12.9	8.71	14.18	0.09	10.7
Industry (% of GDP)	27.89	26.22	32.46	–	41.56	73.39	47.05	49.94	31.63	34.74	44.62
Manufacturing (% of GDP)	16.28	18.59	20.86	–	21.25	10.48	28.05	29.79	22.9	29.19	35.05
Services etc. (% of GDP)	54.58	43.68	25.53	–	38.08	25.91	40.06	41.35	54.19	65.17	44.68
Population (in Million)	1109.81	14.2	5.76	48.38	84.11	0.38	223.04	26.11	86.26	4.48	63.44
FDI as % of GFCF (2007)	5.8	52.3	26.1	20.4	25.4	11.3	6.4	20.6	14.3	60	14.6
Per capita income (PPP $)	2222	1440	1814		2143	46991	3209	11678	2956	41479	7061

(*Table 11.1 Continued*)

(Table 11.1 Continued)

Development Indicators	Cambodia	Laos	Myanmar	Vietnam	Brunei Darussalam	Indonesia	Malaysia	Philippines	Singapore	Thailand
					Indicators of trade between India and ASEAN					
India's exports (2007)	44.83	2.94	162.76	1241.48	8.81	1878.2	1850.25	571.41	6390.04	1673.34
India's imports (2007)	1.24	0.08	809.07	153.13	234.09	4759.52	5720.29	173.54	6886.73	2191.8
Trade balance (2007)	43.58	2.86	−646.31	1088.34	−225.28	−2881.32	−3870.04	397.88	−496.69	−518.46
Exports growth (2001–07)	25.61	−1.4	17.59	33.37	20.52	23.06	15.43	14.73	36.61	17.37
Import growth (2001–07)	1.66	13.16	13.5	41.46	194.58	28.69	30.74	10.4	31.77	31.31

Source: 1. World Bank (2008).
2. UN (2008).

Note: 1. Development indicators are for the year 2006 GDP is at constant (2000) prices.

recorded an annual average growth rate of 25.7 and 29.5 per cent respectively as compared to 22 and 27 per cent with rest of the world. Similarly, India's trade deficit with ASEAN has also been growing faster. During 2001–2007, it increased more than seven fold from $0.9 billion to $7.1 billion as compared to a little more than 1.5 times increase (from $33.9 billion to $55.5 billion) with rest of the world. Within ASEAN, bulk of the trade deficit was with old ASEAN as they accounted for 89 per cent of exports and 95 per cent of imports of India during the period under discussion.

Of late, India's exports to new ASEAN has been growing at a rate twice (30.3 per cent) than that their exports (15.6 per cent) to India. Hence trade with new ASEAN is in India's favour resulting from a trade surplus of over one billion US dollars mostly on account of trade with Vietnam — the most dynamic among the new ASEAN. Given the ongoing Initiative for ASEAN Integration (IAI) and other measures, the other new ASEAN countries are likely to record a better economic performance in the years to come as happening in Vietnam. In such a context, with FTA, it is likely that that India's export to new ASEAN would increase, especially of industrial capital goods. An increase in the exports from India, needless to say, would lead to a further worsening of their trade balance with India. In such an eventuality, the new ASEAN countries would be left with hardly any option but to increase their exports to India at any cost. Given their current resource endowments, the exports are likely to be agricultural commodities. Being countries with agro-climatic conditions similar to southern states like Kerala, their primary exports would be competing with crops from states like Kerala.

In a context of growing trade deficit with ASEAN, India could have two options: a static approach of raising the tariff barriers or a dynamic approach of liberalising trade in commodities, services and investment. Drawing from her experience under external liberalisation since 1991 that led to a healthy external sector, India opted for the latter strategy. Such a strategy, it is expected, would help harnessing growing synergies between India and the ASEAN (Sen et al. 2004; Cheow 2005) and result in more efficiency seeking investment as has happened in case of India and Sri Lanka (Kelegama and Mukherjee 2007). Also, given India's comparative advantage in services, greater access to growing service market of ASEAN, which is highly restricted at present (Karmakar 2005), would help India offset the deficit in merchandise. Thus, even if FTA results in increased trade deficit with ASEAN in the short run as argued by Pal and Dasgupta (2008), it could be financed by the surplus on account of increased service trade and investment. Here it may be remembered that in 2008–2009, India had a trade deficit of $119 billion. But thanks to surplus in service trade, the current account deficit was only $29.8 billion. It is our service exports that pay for the import of goods. Surplus in invisibles along with foreign investment has contributed towards building foreign exchange reserves of $280 billion today.

Table 11.2 provides applied MFN tariff rates for India and the ASEAN countries for the year 2007. It is evident that the Indian economy is more protected than all the ASEAN countries as the applied MFN tariff for all the products in India (14.5 per cent) is significantly higher than that of the old ASEAN and even higher than the new ASEAN with the possible exception of Vietnam. The observed pattern is similar when it comes to both agricultural and non-agricultural products. To the extent that applied MFN tariff is low at present in old ASEAN and further reduction would be negligible under FTA, one is tempted to argue that India cannot expect much tariff reduction induced increase in export to old ASEAN countries. On the other hand, for the ASEAN, given the higher applied MFN tariff in India at present, further reduction as envisaged under FTA would be helpful in increasing their exports to the Indian market. In the event of such an increased imports to India, the import competing sectors are likely to experience a loss of income and employment. Earlier

Table 11.2: Simple Average Applied MFN Tariff in India and ASEAN (2007)

Countries	All products	Agricultural products	Non-agricultural products
India	14.50	34.40	11.50
Cambodia	14.20	18.10	13.60
Lao PDR	9.70	19.50	8.20
Myanmar	5.60	8.70	5.10
Vietnam	16.80	24.20	15.70
Brunei Darussalam	3.60	7.90	3.00
Indonesia	6.90	8.60	6.70
Malaysia	8.40	11.70	7.90
Philippines	6.30	9.60	5.80
Singapore	0.00	0.10	0.00
Thailand	10.00	22.00	8.20

Source: WTO (2008).

studies (Pal and Dasgupta 2008) also noted that there could be a further worsening of India's balance of trade in the short run due to increased imports and limited scope for export expansion.

The outcome, however, is likely to be different in the medium and long term. Trade between countries is governed by many factors other than tariff rates. Studies (Joseph 2006) have highlighted the complementary relation between trade and investment liberalisation. It was also shown that MNCs play an important role in most of the industries in the old ASEAN that are active in the global production network. The location decision of MNCs is known to be governed, in addition to the traditional factors like incentives and low labour cost, by the availability of complementary capabilities (Ernst and Lundvall 2000). Hence trade liberalisation along with greater access to complimentary capabilities that India provides could lead to efficiency-seeking investments and India's entry into the global production networks of some of the industrial products. This in turn could lead to further increase in trade as happened in the case of India–Sri Lanka FTA (Kelegama and Mukherjee 2007).

Thus far we have argued that the ASEAN being a heterogeneous group of countries the outcomes, to a great extent, would be governed by this heterogeneity. While there could be an increase in India's trade deficit in the short run, the Agreement is likely to be a win-win situation for both parties in the long run from a macroeconomic perspective. To say the least, India should get access to the growing ASEAN market for services to pay for the growing imports from these countries for which FTA is an imperative. But what is true at the macro level need not necessarily be true at the micro level — the fallacy of composition error! Hence any attempt at enabling various sectors to confront new challenges and to harness the new opportunities calls for sector-specific exploration. In what follows, we shall examine the likely implications of the FTA on India's plantation sector.

FTA and Plantation Sector

Analysis of the likely impact on any sector has to begin with an under-standing of the present state of that sector in the country concerned. In India, the plantation sector appears to assume more importance today in the national and regional economies (like Kerala, Tamil Nadu, Karanataka and the Northeastern states) than ever before. While the importance on account of its significant contribution to foreign exchange has been highlighted in the yesteryears, its role in achieving inclusive and environmentally sustainable growth is gaining greater attention toady. Historically, plantation crops have been raised in large estates. Over the years, there has been a trans-formation in the ownership structure and today there are over 4 million growers, mostly small and medium. The sector employs over 1.7 million plantation workers and nearly 2 crore (20 million) farm workers, mostly women. Though this sector accounts for only about one per cent of the total cropped area, it however accounts for over 15 per cent of the agricultural exports.

The prices of plantation commodities are known for their volatility and cyclicality and that got accentuated under WTO. If the available empirical evidence is any indication, as the policy pendulum shifted from protection to greater competition under the aegis of WTO there has been simultaneous decline in the price of most of the crops (Joseph and Joseph 2005) along with heightened volatility in prices (Joseph 2004; Subrahmanian 2008) that induced farmers to resort to such survival strategies that are hostile to ecology (Damodaran 2002) and inhibited investment in plantations (Government of India 2006). These and other related developments made the plantation sector, which generates massive rural employment opportunities and is located largely in economically backward and ecologically fragile regions, unviable. In the context of accumulated debt burden be-yond the paying capacity, many farmers engaged in plantation sector opted to take their lives leading to farmers' suicide in India at a rate unheard of in human history (Jeromi 2007; Reddy and Mishra 2009).

The likely impact of the FTA on plantations could be analysed either using a simple static analytics or a dynamic perspective tempered by reality. Those opposing FTA, by adopting the former approach, fear increased imports on the following grounds. With the ongoing IAI and other measures to level up the development divide among ASEAN, Cambodia, Laos and Myanmar are likely to record a better economic performance in the years to come as is being currently ex-perienced in Vietnam. In such a context, facilitated by FTA, India's export of manufactured and capital goods to these countries would increase. This could further worsen their trade deficit as in case presently with Vietnam where India has a trade surplus of over one billion. In such an eventuality, these countries would be left with hardly any option but to increase their exports to India at any cost. Being countries with primary sector focus and agro-climatic conditions similar to southern states like Kerala, their primary exports would be competing with crops from these states. Competition from Vietnam has already been felt with its full intensity.

In a similar vein, there is a perception of heightened import competition from other ASEAN countries as well. Compared to India, old ASEAN countries like Malaysia, Indonesia and Thailand are having much higher production of plantation commodities like black pepper, natural rubber, coffee and to a lesser extent tea (see Table 11.3). Thanks to a large and growing domestic market, production of these crops in India is increasingly for the domestic consumption. Production of plantation crops in ASEAN, on the other hand, is mostly for the world market as their domestic market is very small. Yet, India accounts for only a negligible share of their total exports while these exports form a substantial part of India's imports (see Table 11.3).

Table 11.3: Importance of India for ASEAN Exports and Their Share in India's Import for Select Plantation Commodities

	2000		2007	
Crops	Share of India in total export	Share in India's import	Share of India in total export	Share in India's import
Vietnam				
Coffee	0.22	28.34	0.24	13.65
Tea	1.31	9.64	0.52	2.39
Pepper	1.05	11.31	3.79	26.98
Natural rubber	0.41	10.12	0.51	2.79
Malaysia				
Coffee	0.07	0.04	0.92	0.09
Tea				0.00
Pepper	1.01	7.33	0.24	0.40
Natural rubber	0.30	29.70	0.52	4.66
Thailand				
Coffee	0.01	0.08	1.83	0.99
Tea			0.01	0.00
Pepper			0.01	0.00
Natural rubber	0.13	28.94	1.93	45.59
Indonesia				
Coffee	19.24	54.64	15.65	36.69
Tea		47.30	32.66	11.89
Pepper	67.62	31.13	72.36	43.58
Natural rubber	3.43	9.20	17.14	38.95

Source: UNCOMTRADE Database (2008).

To illustrate, India accounts for only about 3.8 per cent of Vietnam's export of pepper while their share in India's import is as high as 27 per cent. Similarly, India provides only 1.9 per cent of the export market for Thai natural rubber but it accounts for over 45 per cent of India's imports. Hence, it is feared that given the large domestic market of India and large scale supply of these commodities in the ASEAN countries, the removal of tariff barriers, would result in increased import competition and would lead to fall in domestic prices. The solution lies in doing away with FTA such that the plantation sector could be fortified from external competition. Such simple static analytics might appear appealing for those opposing FTA. But if the objective is to develop a vibrant plantation sector and improving the livelihood of millions involved, there is the need to take a dynamic approach and a more careful analysis.

From Perception to Reality

To appreciate the reality, we need to move out of the simple analytics to a dynamic analysis of real world. Key issue will be the actual (observed) relation between tariff rate and import on the one hand and import and domestic price, on which the fortunes of plantation sector is pegged, on the other. It is found that since the implementation of India–Sri Lanka FTA, import of pepper (black and green) from Sri Lanka to India recorded nearly sixfold increase during 2001 to 2008 ($3.4 to $18.2 million) as predicted by Harilal and Joseph (1999). Similarly, after the FTA with Thailand, the import of natural rubber from Thailand increased nearly tenfold (from $12 million in 2005 to $116 million in 2008). Import from other countries also recorded a similar increasing trend. Thus we find an association between tariff and import. But association cannot be construed as causation and jump into premature conclusions.

Our estimate of the elasticity of import with respect to tariff is not found statistically significant. Thus the negative relationship between tariff and imports predicted in theory is not standing the test of Indian reality. How to account for such a deviation between theory and practice? This has to be seen against India's import policy with provision for duty-free import of raw materials for exports. Bulk of the import of plantation commodities that we have noted above has been through advance licensing route (duty free) for processing and export as noted by George and Joseph (2005). This was further confirmed by my discussion with officials in Commodity Boards. Such a policy has the laudable objective of promoting employment through value addition and aspires to make India a global processing hub for plantation commodities. To the extent that such imports provide backward linkages to the plantation sector abroad and weakens the plantation sector within, it has the unintended effect of robbing Paul to pay Peter. Hence one fails to understand the economic logic of being blissful to duty-free imports while raising voice of dissent against FTA that envisages no tariff reduction in most commodities and only a phased reduction for a few others. If the real concern is with plantations and the millions involved therein, the attempt should be to correct the anomalies in the import regime and help in developing a vibrant processing sector that provides growth impulses to the country's plantation sector. Given this sector's role in inclusive growth and its operation in ecologically fragile regions that are more backward than some of the least developed countries that were exempted from tariff reduction commitment under WTO, we don't need a Kautilya to make the case for subsidising this sector.

Let us now turn to the issue of imports and domestic prices. We have seen that after India–Thailand FTA, there has been a massive increase in imports of natural rubber. But this import was not associated with any decline in prices. Instead the price of natural rubber recorded nearly a threefold increase — a rate of increase unheard of in the history of rubber. Similar instances could be multiplied. The observed pattern needs to be seen against the reality wherein domestic prices are governed by prices in the world market which in turn is shaped by global demand–supply conditions and other factors. In such a context, it is rather myopic is to argue that domestic prices are determined by imports. It is not to argue that imports have no bearing on domestic prices. In fact, even a threat of imports is sufficient to cause short run price fluctuations.

To be fair, threat of such import competition has already been taken into account in the FTA. Hence some of the products are permitted to enjoy the ongoing level of protection (negative list) while in others, tariff reduction has been effected in a phased manner (special products) such that productivity and competitiveness could be built up. More importantly, since the share in India's total import is more than three per cent in all the partner countries, India could resort to safeguard measures in case of substantial injury for the local producers. What is needed is an effective mechanism to monitor prices and markets for which there is no dearth of institutional mechanism at present.

For those opposing FTA since tariff cut under FTA would lead to reduction in protection, tariffs needs to be maintained to shield the domestic industry from import competition. It is productivity along with cost of production and exchange rate that determines the required level of tariff. Table 11.4 presents data on productivity (production per hectare) in competing ASEAN countries as percentage of India's productivity. On the basis of observed productivity difference between India and competing countries in some of the crops, it is evident that even if India reverts to the tariff levels in pre-liberalisation period these crops could not be protected to the level of their satisfaction. To illustrate, the productivity of black pepper in Malaysia and Indonesia is higher by 208 and 451 per cent respectively and that of Vietnam 600 per cent higher. In such a context, it is

Table 11.4: Percentage Productivity in Competing Countries
in Proportion to India

Years	Indonesia	Malaysia	Thailand	Vietnam	India
Natural Rubber					
1995	51.12 (65)	55.68 (63)	103.91 (63)	33.78	1325.80
2007	74.87 (36)	69.60 (36)	128.99 (36)	82.57 (36)	1820.00
Production	2755172	1199600	3024207	601700	819000
Black Pepper					
1995	262.58 (65)	485.96	1137.39	550.48	314.00
2007	208.92 (70)	451.56 (70)	1190.57 (70)	600.35 (70)	280.40
Production	74131	19000	10419	90300	69000
Coffee					
1995	82.66 (10)	115.74	184.92	214.88	654.50
2007	106.65 (100)	115.31 (100)	125.16 (100)	300.99 (100)	839.60
Production	676475	40000	55660	961200	288000
Tea					
1995	77.09 (10)	115.62	17.03	32.23	1761.40
2007	77.16 (100)	46.22 (100)	17.03 (100)	87.42 (10)	1701.10
Production	150224	2850	6000	164000	949220

Source: Estimates based on FAO statistics (FAO 2007). Tariff data is from TRAINS extracted through WITS.

Note: 1. Figures in parenthesis are MFN Applied tariff.
2. Productivity in India is given as kg/hectare. Production figures are in MT and for the year 2007.

rather naïve to believe that it is the tariff (70 per cent at present) that protects black pepper production in India. In other crops like coffee and tea, India's productivity disadvantage is lower and in natural rubber India's productivity is the highest (Table 11.4). Yet, in natural rubber India maintains an effective applied tariff rate of 36 per cent and still faces import competition. Thus viewed, tariff as a measure of protection has its obvious limits. Perhaps product differentiation could be a more powerful means of protection. Number of other factors relating to production conditions, nature and structure of market, import and exchange rate regime are equally influential.

Integration, Competition and Cooperation

Those who oppose FTA consider it only as a source of deadly competition. It is ignored that integration between countries also provides immense scope for cooperation to address common problems. It is generally agreed that while commodity production is a source of foreign exchange and livelihood for millions in both India and ASEAN, the globally determined commodity prices have been historically susceptible to cyclical fluctuations — the so-called commodity problematique. In a context wherein earlier attempts to address the commodity problem failed, the moot question is whether the ASEAN–India integration will help in addressing this problem? Since India and ASEAN together accounts for a significant part of the global production of most of the plantation crops, FTA together with the Agreement on Comprehensive Economic Cooperation leave scope for constructive cooperation to influence the international price and address the commodity problematique. Here it is worth remembering that with respect to plantation sector, India–ASEAN vision 2020 calls for, among others, setting up of India–ASEAN Commodity Boards for price stabilisation through supply management, common brand building, joint marketing and research and other mutually beneficial initiatives (RIS 2004). In a context wherein the earlier attempts at addressing commodity problematique failed, if India and the ASEAN together could make the first step towards addressing this problem, that will be the greatest contribution for the millions who derive their livelihood from plantations. Thus the FTA, contrary to popular arguments, could add a new era in plantation sector and the resultant wellbeing of millions, mostly women and marginal farmers.

Conclusions

ASEAN–India FTA could be celebrated as a landmark in India's integration with Asia and a beginning of an end to the isolation from major trading blocks. FTA could also be considered as part of India's strategy, in the context of newly emerging markets, to diversify her trading partners with greater role for developing countries and an indication of her commitment to South–South cooperation. The FTA, however, had to face vociferous voice of dissent from some sectors in India. In this chapter, we have undertaken a preliminary analysis of the likely impact of the pact with focus on plantation sector.

The extent of gain and loss to the parties involved vary in most agreements. ASEAN–India FTA is no exception. As Jairam Ramesh (2008) rightly observed, along with macro gains there will be micro pains to be felt by specific industries, specific livelihoods and specific regions. Here is no denying fact that given the present state of plantations, it has the potential to be one such affected sector. However, we have argued that the additional threat posed by FTA is not substantial when compared to the threat that the sector has been confronting over the years under the trade policy regime that has the provision for duty free import. Given the current import policy, import is not necessarily caused by tariff reduction and contrary to the common belief, import do not determine domestic price which, in reality, is shaped internationally. Since integration leave scope for both cooperation and competition, there is the potential to collectively address the commodity problematique by harnessing the new possibilities for coordinated action to influence the commodity prices. But for any such actions to be effective and sustainable, there is the need to bridge the efficiency gap in the sector across countries.

Thus viewed, with or without FTA, the plantation sector cannot afford to continue in the current form as economic history reveals that no country has managed to cross $500 per capital income by resorting to the primary production as it exists in India's plantation sector. While trade liberalisation envisaged in plantation sector under the FTA is gradual and in a phased manner, there has to be a concerted effort towards evolving a vibrant system of innovation and production. This would call for addressing various issues in the sphere of production, processing and marketing, labour and employment, agricultural research and extension, diffusion of innovations including the application of new technologies and not to speak of the development of much needed general and specific infrastructure, and human capital for the development of plantation sector and above all a coordination between different actors. This will, inter alia, involve a commitment towards compensating the losers by the gainers under FTA. Given that this sector was adversely affected by WTO, the Ministry of Commerce has been highly proactive with various imaginative steps like large scale replantation scheme, establishment of Spices Parks and others at the instance of Jairam Ramesh, the then Minister in charge of plantations. However, due to various reasons, the progress in some of these projects has not been up to the expectation. The Government of Kerala appointed a Commission on WTO concerns under the Task Force under the Chairmanship of M. S. Swaminathan (Government of Kerala 2002) and has come up with valuable recommendations but with poor record in implementation. It appears that time has come for an 'Action Force' that ensures coordinated action by the Centre and the State along with other stakeholders to ensure the building up of an internationally competitive plantation sector by addressing various issues that plague this sector. At the same time, there is the need to be watchful of trade after FTA so that the safeguard measures could be invoked in case of substantial injury on account of import competition.

❊

References

Cheow, Eric Teo Chu. 2005. 'Strategic Relevance of Asian Economic Integration', RIS Discussion Paper No. 90. New Delhi : Research and Information System for the Non-aligned and Other Developing Countries (RIS).

Corden, Warner Marx. 1986. 'The Normative Theory of International Trade', in R. Jones and P. B. Kennen (eds), *Handbook of International Economics*, pp. 63–130. Amsterdam: Elsevier Science Publications.

Damodaran, A. 2002. 'Conflict of Trade Facilitating Environmental Regulations with Biodiversity Concerns: Case of Coffee Farming Units in India', *World Development*, 30 (7): 1123–35.

Ernst, Dieter and Bengt-Ake Lundvall. 2000. 'Information Technology in the Learning Economy: Challenges for Developing Countries', East–West Centre Working Paper 8. Honolulu: East–West Centre.

Food and Agriculture Organisation (FAO). 2007. 'FAOSTAT'. http://faostat.fao.org/site/339/default.aspx (accessed 12 September 2007).

George, Tharian K. and Joby Joseph. 2005. 'Value Addition or Value Acquisition?', *Economic and Political Weekly*, 40 (26): 2681–87.

Government of India. 2006. 'Report of the Taskforce on Plantation Sector', Department of Commerce. New Delhi: Government of India.

Government of Kerala. 2002. 'Report of the Commission on WTO concerns in Agriculture', M. S. Swaminathan (chair). http://www.kerala.gov.in/agri2/10Main%20report%20Annexure.pdf and http://www.kerala.gov.in/agri2/07Main%20report%20A.pdf (accessed 24 the January 2006).

Harilal, K. N. and K. J. Joseph. 1999. 'India-Sri Lanka Free Trade Accord', *Economic and Political Weekly*, 34 (13): 750–3.

Hoekman, Bernard and Denise Eby Konan. 1999. 'Deep Integration, Non-Discrimination, and Euro Mediterranean Free Trade', World Bank Policy Paper 2130. Washingtom, D.C.: World Bank.

Jeromi, P.D. 2007. 'Farmers' Indebtedness and Suicides', *Economic and Political Weekly*, 42 (31): 3241–47.

Joseph, Brigit. 2004. 'Trade liberalization and Primary Commodity Prices Empirical Evidence from Select Tropical Crops in Kerala, India', GTAP Resource #1537 7th Annual Conference on Global Economic Analysis. http://www.gtap.agecon.purdue.edu/events/conferences/2004/program.asp (accessed 13 September 2007).

Joseph, Brigit, and Joseph, K. J. 2005. 'Commercial Agriculture in Kerala after the WTO', *South Asia Economic Journal*, 6 (1): 37–57.

Joseph, K. J. 2006. *Information Technology, Innovation System and Trade Regime in Developing Countries — India and the ASEAN*. New York: Palgrave Macmillan.

Karmakar, Suparna. 2005. 'India-ASEAN Cooperation in Services — An Overview', ICRIER Working Paper 176. Delhi: Indian Council for Research on International Economic Relations.

Kelegama, Saman and Indra Nath Mukherjee. 2007. *India–Sri Lanka Bilateral Free Trade Agreement: Six Years Performance and Beyond*, RIS Discussion Paper No. 119. Delhi: Research and Information System for Developing Countries (RIS).

Pal, Parthapratim and Mitali Dasgupta. 2008. 'Does a Free Trade Agreement with ASEAN Make Sense?', *Economic and Political Weekly*, 43 (46): 8–12.

Pomfret, Richard. 1988. *Unequal Trade: The Economics of Discriminatory International Trade Policies*. New York: Basil Blackwell.

Ramesh, Jairam. 2008. 'India's Economic Integration with Asia'. Paper presented at the Asian Development Bank, Philippines, Manila.

Reddy, Narashimha and Srijit Mishra. 2009. *Agrarian Crisis in India*. New Delhi: Oxford University Press.

Research and Information System for Developing Countries (RIS). 2004. *ASEAN–India Vision 2020 — Working Together for a Shared Prosperity*. New Delhi: ASEAN–India Network of Think-Tanks and RIS.

Sen, Rahul, Mukul G. Asher and Ramkishen S. Rajan. 2004. 'ASEAN–India Economic Relations: Current Status and Future Prospects', RIS

Discussion Paper No. 73. New Delhi: Research and Information System for Developing Countries (RIS).

Subrahmanian, K. K. 2008. 'Impact of the WTO on Plantation Crops of South India: Export Performance and Price Instability', Mimeo. Thiruvananthapuram: Centre for Development Studies.

UNCOMTRADE. 2008. *Comtrade Database, 2008*, WITS (World Integrated Trade Solution). http://wits.worldbank.org/WITS (accessed 14 November 2008).

UNCTAD. 2004. 'Regionalism and South- South Cooperation: The Case of Mercosur and India', UNCTAD, Geneva. http://www.google.co.in/#hl=en&source=hp&biw=1280&bih=605&q=Regionalism+and+South-+South+Cooperation%3A+The+Case+of+Mercosur+and+India&btnG=Google+Search&aq=f&aqi=&aql=&oq=&gs_rfai=&fp=353305b17292d0d (accessed 28 September 2007).

Viner, Jacob. 1950. *The Customs Union Issue*. New York: Carnegie Endowment for International Peace.

World Bank. 2008. *World Development Indicators 2008*. Washington D.C.: World Bank.

World Trade Organisation (WTO). 2008. *World Tariff Profile (2008)*. http://www.wto.org/english/res_e/booksp_e/tariff_profiles08_e.pdf (accessed on 14 November 2008).

Schiff, Maurice and L. Alan Winters. 2003. *Regional Integration and Development*. Washington, D.C.: World Bank.

12

RTAs: The Way Forward for India

Prahalathan S. Iyer

The proliferating number of Regional Trade Agreements (RTAs) has led to the debate whether they help or hinder the broader process of multilateral trade liberalisation (Ethier 1998; Sampson and Woolcock 2003; Panagariya and Findlay 1996; Krishna 1998). Despite of arguments in favour or against RTAs, there has been a significant increase in the volume of world trade taking place within the framework of such agreements. Countries are engaging in agreements with trading blocs as a whole to access the larger markets and are also transcending geographical borders to rapidly enter into trade relations with distant countries as well. Free Trade Agreements (FTAs) are predominant amongst the RTAs notified under WTO. The predominance of FTAs (most of which are bilateral) is probably due to the fact that they are faster to conclude, and may require lower degree of policy coordination among the contracting parties as compared to plurilateral or multilateral negotiations.

There has been growing interest amongst countries in regional trade agreements since 2000. The trend also reveals that between 2004 and 2006, maximum number of agreements has been concluded. This could be attributed to the failure of the WTO Ministerial Conferences held in Cancun (2003) and Hong Kong (2005). In the initial years, majority of agreements have been signed amongst developing countries. However, there has been a growing tendency amongst developed countries to engage in RTAs, not only with the developed countries, but also with developing countries.

Major Asian economies too have rapidly embraced regionalism in the course of the past decade, which has led to proliferation of several regional trading agreements involving most of the Asian economies. The region is making its presence felt in the global scene with the emergence of significant trade blocs like Association of Southeast Asian Nations (ASEAN), which has contributed to about 27 per cent of Asia's global trade (UNCTAD 2008). ASEAN is also expanding its integration with other major economies in Asia, viz., China, India, Japan and South Korea.

India's Engagements in RTAs

India's endeavour to foster its international trade has been well complemented by its efforts to promote regional trade. This is being reflected in its various initiatives in fostering and facilitating trade with select countries and blocs. India has already entered into bilateral arrangements with countries such as Afghanistan, Bangladesh, Bhutan, Chile, Maldives, Nepal, Mauritius, Mongolia, Singapore, Sri Lanka and Thailand. In addition, Joint Study Groups (JSG) have been established between India and countries such as China, Indonesia, Israel Japan, Korea, Malaysia and Russia to examine the possibilities of expanding trade and economic cooperation. India has recently concluded a FTA with the ASEAN and is also engaged in cooperation arrangements/or in discussions with other regional trading blocs such as Bay of Bengal Initiative for Multi-sectoral Technical and Economic Cooperation (BIMSTEC), South Asian Free Trade Area (SAFTA), Asia Pacific Trade Agreement (APTA), Common Market for Southern America (MERCOSUR), EU, Gulf Cooperation Council (GCC), and Southern African Customs Union (SACU) (Ministry of Commerce and Industry 2009).

India has also been aggressively pursuing its 'Look-East Policy', and many trade-enhancing arrangements are being entered into by India with other Asian nations. The policy received an additional thrust with India becoming a summit level partner of the ASEAN in 2002, and its involvement in regional initiatives like BIMSTEC, Ganga Mekong Cooperation and membership to the East Asia Summit in 2005. Abundance of natural resources, significant technological base in some of the Asian countries and strong base of human capital in India provide immense opportunities to Asian countries to integrate and synergise their trade and investment promotion activities.

INDIA–THAILAND FTA: Lessons from EHS Scheme

A Framework Agreement for establishing a FTA between India and Thailand was signed on 9 October 2003 (Ministry of Commerce and Industry 2009a). The Agreement covers FTA in goods, services, investment and other areas of economic cooperation. It also provides for an Early Harvest Scheme (EHS) under which 82 common items of trade, which are of interest to both the sides, have been agreed for elimination of tariffs on a fast track basis. India–Thailand Trade Negotiating Committee (TNC) has been constituted and discussions are being held on the text of FTA, Rules of Origin, Dispute Settlement Mechanism and Sensitive List. Seventeen Rounds of negotiations for FTA in Goods have so far been held. Negotiations for FTA in Services and Investment have also begun. The India–Thailand FTA on Trade in Goods is expected to be concluded soon.

It may be observed that India's exports to Thailand has increased from US $713 million in 2002–2003 to US $1978.2 million in 2008–2009, Compounded Annual Growth Rate (CAGR) of 19 per cent, whereas India's imports from Thailand has increased from US $380 million in 2002–2003 to US $2655.9 million in 2008–2009, CAGR of 38 per cent. The 82 EHS products, which accounted for about 5 per cent of India's exports to Thailand in 2002–2003, increased its share marginally to around 5.3 per cent of India's total exports to Thailand in 2007–2008. During the period April–February 2008–2009, the 82 EHS products accounted for 6 per cent of the total exports by India to Thailand. However, these products have increased their prominence in India's imports from Thailand. The EHS products, which had a share of around 13 per cent of India's imports from Thailand in 2002–2003, have increased their share to 16 per cent in 2007–2008. During the period April–February 2008–2009, imports form Thailand accounted for a share of 15.2 per cent. The EHS products have witnessed a CAGR of 23 per cent for India's exports to Thailand, and 51 per cent for India's imports from Thailand.

Product-wise analysis shows that the benefits accrued to India and Thailand are concentrated in few products. It may be observed that top 10 EHS products accounted for over 76 per cent in India's total exports and 65 per cent in imports of EHS products from Thailand in 2007–2008 and during April–February 2008–2009 it accounted for 83 per cent in exports, and 73 per cent in imports from Thailand. Top 10 products of India's exports have increased its level of concentration — from around 72 per cent in 2005–2006 to 76 per cent in 2007–2008. Some product groups such as other lighting or visual signaling equipment (CAGR of 324.3 per cent), and parts (HS 841490) (CAGR of 79 per cent), have witnessed greater level of growth in India's exports to Thailand. In terms of India's imports from

Thailand, several product groups have witnessed a CAGR of over 100 per cent. These include other precious metal, whether or not plated (CAGR of 193 per cent), other machinery (CAGR of 153 per cent), compression type refrigerators, household (CAGR of 149 per cent), and aluminium alloys (CAGR of 112.2 per cent).

It may also be inferred that the framework agreement with Thailand has also caused trade diversion, especially in many of the EHS products. Analysis of trade diversion revealed that Thailand has captured the topmost position, as leading supplier to India in respect of EHS product categories, such as aluminum alloys, polycarbonates, other polysters and others (Table 12.1).

Table 12.1: Status of Import of Select Products by India from Thailand

Products (HS Code)	Topmost source country for India's imports in April–February 2006–2007	Rank of Thailand as source country to India's imports — April–February 2006–2007	Rank of Thailand as source country for India's imports — April–February 2008–2009
Aluminium alloys (760120)	Thailand	1	1
Polycarbonates (39074000)	Spain	2	1
Epoxide resins (390730)	Thailand	1	1
Other polysters (390799)	Taiwan	3	1
Other machinery (843780)	Thailand	1	1
Other (720719)	Ukraine	36	2

Source: DGCIS (2009).

INDIA–ASEAN FTA: Implications for Plantation Sector in India

India–ASEAN FTA was signed on 13 August 2009. Through this Agreement, all parties shall gradually liberalise applied MFN tariff rates on originating goods of the other parties in accordance with its schedule of tariff commitments, as set out as part of the Agreement. The Agreement shall enter into force on 1 January 2010. The schedule of tariff reduction may be referred from AIFTA agreement (Ministry of Commerce 2009b).

The Case of Indian Plantation Sector

There are concerns about the impact of the India–ASEAN Free Trade Agreement (FTA), ratified recently, on the plantation sector of India. Prima facie, these apprehensions may seem to have some foundation as many of the ASEAN countries are major producers/exporters of plantation products, and are thus competitors for India in many target countries, as also in the domestic market. The impact of the FTA on the Indian plantation sector may be better revealed by analysing the productivity and trade pattern of India vis-à-vis the ASEAN countries.

The Plantation Sector in the Agreement

It may be mentioned that among the plantation crops such as cashew (shelled), areca nuts, coffee [except for coffee, not roasted, not decaffeinated (HS Code 090111)], tea [except for other black tea (fermented) and other partly fermented tea (HS Code 090240)], pepper (crushed and ground), natural rubber [except for balata, gutta-percha, guayule, chicle and similar natural gums (HS Code 400130)], have been given special protection in the Agreement under the Exclusion (Negative) List, where no tariff concessions (reductions in tariff) have been offered to ASEAN countries (Ministry of Commerce and Industry 2009c).

Even in the case of plantation crops that are included in the list for phased tariff reduction, they are included as part of the Highly Sensitive Lists under Special Products, where only modest and gradual tariff reductions spread over a period of 10 years (up to 2019) are envisaged. Plantation products included under this category include coffee, not roasted, not decaffeinated (HS Code 090111); black tea (fermented) and other partly fermented tea (HS Code 090240); and pepper (neither crushed nor ground). The average annual tariff cuts for these products range between 1.8 and 5 per cent; even after 10 years of implementing the FTA, these plantation products will still have considerably high duties ranging from 45 to 50 per cent, and thereby ensuring necessary protection during the tariff reduction period (2010–2019), as also thereafter.

It may be mentioned that the product under natural rubber category (HS Code 400130) is placed in normal track-1 whose tariff will be reduced and subsequently eliminated in accordance with the following schedule:

Table 12.2: Tariff Reduction Commitments for Special Products

Tariff Line	Base Rate	AIFTA preferential tariffs — Not later than 1 January									
		2010	2011	2012	2013	2014	2015	2016	2017	2018	2019	31.12.2019
Coffee	100	95	90	85	80	75	70	65	60	55	50	45
Black Tea	100	95	90	85	80	75	70	65	60	55	50	45
Pepper	70	68	66	64	62	60	58	56	54	52	51	50

Source: AIFTA (Ministry of Commerce 2009c).

- 1 January 2010 to 31 December 2013 for Brunei, Indonesia, Malaysia, Singapore, Thailand and India.
- 1 January 2010 to 31 December 2018 for Philippines and India.
- 1 January 2010 to 31 December 2013 for India, and 1 January 2010 to 31 December 2018 for Cambodia, Laos, Myanmar and Vietnam.

Table 12.3: Tariff Reduction Under Natural Rubber Category [balata, gutta-percha, guayule, chicle and similar natural gums (HS Code 400130)]

Category	Base Rate	01-Jan-10	01-Jan-11	01-Jan-12	01-Jan-13	31-Dec-13	01-Jan-2019
Normal Track -1	10	7.5	5.0	5.0	2.5	0.0	0.0

Source: AIFTA (Ministry of Commerce 2009c).

Analysis Based on ASEAN Trade and India's Imports in Select Plantation Products

Member countries of ASEAN, other than Indonesia (ranked sixth in the world) are not significant exporters of tea as compared to India, which is ranked as fourth in the world. As regards coffee exports, Vietnam (ranked second in the world) and Indonesia (fourth) are among ASEAN countries ranked ahead of India. Vietnam is the largest exporter of pepper followed by India. Other major ASEAN countries include Indonesia (ranked fourth), Singapore (fifth) and Malaysia (sixth). Member countries of ASEAN like Thailand (ranked first in the world), Indonesia (second), Malaysia (third) and Singapore (fifth) were the largest exporters of natural rubber in the world in 2007, as compared to India's 11th position in the world exporters of natural rubber.

In the last four years, India has imported tea mainly from two ASEAN countries, viz., Indonesia and Vietnam. The share of ASEAN in India's total imports of tea was reduced from 35 per cent in 2005–2006 to 22 per cent in 2008–2009 (up to February). The CAGR of cumulative import of tea from ASEAN countries during the period 2005–2006 to 2008–2009 (up to February) has also declined by (–) 7.7 per cent, as compared to the 7.76 per cent CAGR of imports of tea from the world during the same period.

With regard to coffee, Indonesia and Vietnam are the two major import sources for India in the ASEAN region. The share of ASEAN countries in India's import of coffee was over 95 per cent in 2005–2006, which came down to 66 per cent in 2008–2009 (up to February). The CAGR of cumulative import of coffee by India from ASEAN countries during the period 2005–2006 to 2008–2009 (up to February) has thus been negative at (–) 21.5 per cent, as compared to overall negative CAGR of India's imports of coffee from the world (–10.5 per cent).

Vietnam and Indonesia are the two major suppliers of India's pepper imports among ASEAN countries. Cumulatively, ASEAN countries accounted for around 56 per cent of India's total import of pepper from the world in the year 2008–2009 (up to February). The share has marginally come down from around 60 per cent in 2005–2006. The CAGR of India's import of pepper from ASEAN countries during the period 2005–2006 to 2008–2009 (up to February) has been negative at (–) 19.5 per cent, as compared to India's overall negative import growth of (–) 18 per cent from the world.

Thailand, Indonesia, Malaysia and Vietnam are the leading suppliers of natural rubber for India among the ASEAN countries. Cumulatively, ASEAN countries account for over 90 per cent of India's total imports in 2008–2009 (up to February). India's dependency on imports of natural rubber from ASEAN countries has marginally come down from 95 per cent in 2005–2006. The CAGR of India's import of natural rubber from ASEAN countries has been around 14 per cent during the period 2005–2006 to 2008–2009 (up to February), as compared to the 16 per cent CAGR witnessed by India's import of natural rubber from the world (see Table A12.1 in Appendix).

It may be inferred from the above analysis that Indonesia and Vietnam are the leading source countries for India's import of most of the plantation products analysed. In all these plantation products, India's dependency for imports from ASEAN has come down in the last four years. However, India is still largely dependent on ASEAN countries for import of natural rubber. It has also been reported that Vietnam, which is one of the most competitive producing countries in the ASEAN for the plantation sector, has not fully ratified the FTA (as India has not accorded market economy status to Vietnam), and thus would be ineligible for import tariff concessions under the FTA, until both the countries agrees to that effect.

Productivity of Select Plantation Crops in India and ASEAN

There have been apprehensions about the productivity factor being low in the Indian plantation sector vis-à-vis ASEAN countries, and the resultant negative impact of India–ASEAN FTA. Analyses have been undertaken to review India's productivity vis-à-vis ASEAN

countries for select plantation products for which tariffs have to
be reduced under the FTA, viz., for coffee, tea, pepper and natural
rubber (Table 2 in Appendix). The analyses reveal the following:

- In case of tea, India was ranked first with a productivity of
  1.70 tonnes/ha with Vietnam being second (productivity of
  1.54 tonnes/ha).
- In case of coffee (green), India, with a productivity of 0.84 tonnes
  per hectare was ranked second when compared with other
  ASEAN countries in the year 2007 (Vietnam was first with a
  yield of 1.97 tonnes/hectare).
- In case of natural rubber, India was ranked first with a productivity of 1.82 tonnes/hectare in 2007.
- It is only in the case of pepper that India is ranked at the bottom
  (8th) with a productivity of 0.28 tonnes/ha as against Cambodia
  which was ranked first with a productivity of 6.25 tonnes/ha.

From the above analysis, it may be inferred that productivity is not
a major challenge for India except in the case of pepper (in which
Cambodia is highly competitive). From Cambodia, India's import
of pepper has been insignificant.

The Way Forward for India

It is important for India to assess the long-term implications arising
out of any engagement in RTA and adopt an integrated approach consistent with the long-term interest and potential of the economy. With
many countries entering into RTAs crossing the continents, there
are possibilities that a country may use its FTA with another country as
a corridor to enter into a third country, which is also actively engaged
in RTAs. In such a scenario, it may thus be crucial to give careful
emphasis to the Rules of Origin clauses to protect the domestic
industry. Given the global trend in regionalism and India's increasing
engagements with regional trading arrangements, it is important to
maintain consistency in the negative list so that national interests are
safeguarded effectively.

It is also important to note that RTAs provide opportunities for enhancing international trade in a liberalised environment, and do not
automatically endorse increase in bilateral trade. This is because
many RTAs focus on reduction of tariffs and not on the Non-tariff
Trade Barriers (NTBs). It is therefore important for India to address
the issue of NTBs in free trade negotiations with a view to effectively

promote bilateral trade with the partner countries. It may be observed that elimination of NTBs has been an integral part of the North American Free Trade Agreement (NAFTA), which facilitated growth of Mexico's exports to the United States.

Many RTAs have created positive impact on the trade amongst participating countries. In view of this trend, India could explore possibilities of entering into or enhancing the existing arrangements with major trade blocs in different regions, viz., MERCOSUR in Latin America, NAFTA in North America, EU in Europe, ASEAN in Asia, GCC or Greater Arab Free Trade Area (GAFTA) in West Asia, Southern African Development Community (SADC) and SACU in Africa, and CIS countries. Successful negotiations would lead to substantial enhancement of market access in these blocs, on the one hand, and would widen the choice set for competitive imports on the other. For those, which are customs union or common markets, it may be better to enter into arrangement with the bloc as a whole rather than an individual country to derive maximum gains. If the trade bloc is not a customs union or a common market, but only a free trade area, it may be appropriate to enter into arrangement with at least one of the members, with the objective of simplifying the negotiation process, but with possible enhancement of trade with other countries. To cite an example, India has strategically initiated negotiations for a trade agreement with Russia, which is an important member of the CIS countries. Similarly, India may consider exploring such arrangements with Mexico, which may act as a gateway to NAFTA as well as Central America.

It may be observed that there has been a growing interest among developed countries to enter into free trade agreements with developing countries. The United States and EU have been most active in this regard. India needs to strengthen its trade linkages with developed countries, which is capable of bringing in a quantum jump in India's international trade. Countries such as Mexico and Chile have benefited largely from its FTAs with the USA and EU. While discussions are already on for entering into economic cooperation arrangements with EU and Japan, similar measures could be considered to enhance trade relations with other developed countries such as USA and Australia.

It may be observed that along with an increase in number of bilateral FTAs, there has also been an increase in number of Economic Integration Agreements (EIAs) in recent times. Since 2000, over 35 EIAs have come into force (World Trade Organisation 2010) which primarily look beyond free trade in goods incorporating free trade in services, investment promotion and convergence of regulatory issues. Typically, EIAs relate to greater levels of economic cooperation which are not limited to promotion of free trade in goods. India has also expanded the scope of the negotiations beyond free trade in goods. This trend needs to be sustained as it provides an opportunity for achieving greater levels of global economic integration in goods, services, as also investment. Moreover, by enhancing the scope of negotiations including services and investment, the arrangement is expected to balance the negative impacts on trade in goods through gains from trade in services and investment linkages. In this regard, thrust may also be given to explore independent services trade agreements or investment promotion agreements, giving recognition to the benefits of trade through investment.

In an era of volatile capital flows, emerging economies are increasingly considering regional monetary cooperation as an effective tool to reduce the repercussions of any financial crisis or distress. The Asian Bond Market Initiative launched in 2003, following the Asian financial crisis, envisages deepening regional bond markets in Asia and could be cited as an important development in this direction (Eichengreen, 2004). Other such examples are Central American Monetary Stabilisation Fund (1969), reciprocal credit and payment agreement between the central banks of the members of Latin American Integration Association (1965), the Arab Monetary Fund (1976), and the clearing-house of Common Market for Eastern and Southern Africa (COMESA) members (1984). ASEAN +3 countries have launched Chiang Mai which permits bilateral swap arrangements in member countries.

India is currently a member of Asian Clearing Union (ACU) which facilitates settling of payments for intra-regional transactions on a multilateral basis with select Asian countries. India could consider enhancing its regional monetary cooperation with a view to support and facilitate trade-related transactions. Innovative ways may be considered under the aegis of monetary cooperation. A particular model, which may be replicated in the SAARC region, is that of the MERCOSUR Structural Convergence Fund (FOCEM). FOCEM is an instrument for transferring funds from the relatively advanced countries of MERCOSUR (Brazil and Argentina) to the relatively less developed countries of the bloc (Uruguay and Paraguay). The Fund co-finances individual projects submitted by the members with the predetermined distribution of total resources among the four countries. Such an initiative in the SAARC region could meaning-fully contribute towards economic development of the region and truly capture the essence of regional economic integration.

Transaction costs emerge from the various procedural complex-ities linked with exports, crucial being logistical impediments. Transaction costs of exports are particularly high in case of develop-ing countries encumbering export growth. India could, therefore, consider enhancing regional cooperation in trade logistics and trade facilitation with a view to reduce transaction costs. Several trade blocs have addressed this issue; SADC has a Protocol on Transportation, Communications and Meteorology; Association of Caribbean States have a common agreement on air transport services; and COMESA has a common customs document. While India has already established the SAARC Agreement on Mutual Administrative Assistance with regard to customs-related matters, such possibilities may also be con-sidered with other key Asian blocs such as ASEAN and GCC (Exim Bank of India 2006).

Appendix
Table A12.1: Imports of Select Plantation Products by India (kilograms) and its Growth

Imports of India	2005–06	2006–07	2007–08	2008–09 (upto feb.)	CAGR (%)
Tea, whether or not flavoured (HS code 902)					
from World	18715583	23233847	19586449	23423845	7.77
from ASEAN	6611142	11072659	2956522	5201172	−7.68
Share of ASEAN (%)	35.32	47.66	15.09	22.2	
Coffee, whether or not decaffeinated/roasted (HS code 901)					
from World	38193160	19542284	26540166	27380926	−10.50
from ASEAN	37254074	15596170	13081136	17986821	−21.55
Share of ASEAN (%)	97.54	79.81	49.29	65.69	
Pepper, dried or crushed, including genus of fruits (HS code 904)					
from World	19929431	18537910	14178807	11002613	−17.96
from ASEAN	11864213	10105451	8015339	6198346	−19.46
Share of ASEAN (%)	59.53	54.51	56.53	56.33	
Natural Rubber, in primary form or paste (HS code 4001)					
from World	45288103	89799307	86392886	71023509	16.18
from ASEAN	43456642	81792255	78120088	64417619	14.02
Share of ASEAN (%)	95.96	91.08	90.42	90.7	

Source: Compiled from Directorate General of Commercial Intelligence and Statistics, Ministry of Commerce and Industry, Government of India.

Table A12.2: Productivity Comparison of Select Plantation Crops (Tonnes/ha)

Row labels	2002	2003	2004	2005	2006	2007
Coffee, green						
Vietnam	1.49	1.65	1.68	1.51	2.04	1.97
India	0.93	0.85	0.83	0.84	0.83	0.84
Thailand	0.80	0.81	0.87	0.86	0.68	0.82
Cambodia	0.81	0.81	0.82	0.82	0.82	0.82
Philippines	0.81	0.81	0.78	0.83	0.83	0.79
Malaysia	0.75	0.75	0.75	0.75	0.75	0.75
Lao People's Democratic Republic	0.88	0.75	0.61	0.59	0.59	0.74
Indonesia	0.50	0.48	0.46	0.45	0.70	0.70
Myanmar	0.50	0.51	0.53	0.53	0.55	0.58
Natural rubber						
India	1.59	1.66	1.70	1.80	1.90	1.82
Thailand	1.69	1.79	1.82	1.76	1.76	1.71
Vietnam	0.87	0.82	0.93	1.00	1.06	1.09
Cambodia	1.10	1.10	1.10	0.92	1.04	1.05
Indonesia	0.62	0.67	0.77	0.69	0.97	0.99
Malaysia	0.71	0.75	0.92	0.91	0.92	0.92
Myanmar	0.59	0.58	0.68	0.55	0.59	0.62
Brunei Darussalam	0.06	0.06	0.06	0.06	0.06	0.06
Pepper (Piper spp.)						
Cambodia	6.57	6.86	6.86	6.25	6.25	6.25
Thailand	4.25	4.02	4.15	4.43	4.02	3.74
Vietnam	1.57	2.24	1.44	1.64	1.63	1.89
Philippines	0.00	0.00	2.42	2.37	1.98	1.79
Malaysia	1.76	1.52	1.48	1.42	1.42	1.42
Indonesia	0.69	0.70	0.70	0.70	0.67	0.66
Brunei Darussalam	0.40	0.40	0.40	0.40	0.40	0.40
India	0.28	0.30	0.31	0.32	0.36	0.28
Tea						
India	1.67	1.62	1.69	1.71	1.77	1.70
Vietnam	0.96	1.21	0.99	1.08	1.48	1.54
Indonesia	1.40	1.46	1.47	1.24	1.32	1.36
Malaysia	1.50	1.18	1.11	0.81	0.81	0.81
Myanmar	0.33	0.32	0.34	0.35	0.37	0.37
Lao People's Democratic Republic	0.50	0.44	0.35	0.36	0.36	0.33
Thailand	0.29	0.29	0.29	0.30	0.30	0.30

❖

References

Director General of Commercial Intelligence and Statistics DGCIS). 2009. http://www.dgciskol.nic.in/ (accessed 14 November 2009).

Eichengreen, B. 2004. *Bureau of International Settlements*. http://www.bis.org/publ/bppdf/bispap30a.pdf (accessed 2 April 2010).

Ethier, W. J. 1998. 'Regionalism in a Multilateral World', *Journal of Political Economy*, 106 (6): 1214–45.

Exim Bank of India. 2006. 'Regional Trade Agreements: Gateway to Global Trade', Occasional Paper No 120. Mumbai: Export-Import Bank of India.

Krishna, P. 1998. 'Regionalism and Multilateralism: A Political Economy Approach', *Quarterly Journal of Economics*, 113 (1): 227–51.

Ministry of Commerce and Industry. 2009a. http://commerce.nic.in/trade/international_ta.asp?id=2&trade=i (accessed 14 November 2009).

———. 2009b. 'AIFTA Agreement'. http://commerce.nic.in/pressrelease/pressrelease_detail.asp?id=2506 (accessed 14 November 2009).

———. 2009c. 'Tariff Concession'. http://commerce.nic.in/trade/international_ta_indasean.asp (accessed 14 November 2009).

Panagariya, A. and R. Findlay. 1996. 'A Political Economy Analysis of Free Trade Areas and Customs Unions', in Robert Feenstra, Gene Grossman and Douglas Irwin (eds), *The Political Economy of Trade Reform: Essays in Honor of Jagdish Bhagwati*, pp. 265–87. Cambridge: MIT Press.

Sampson, G. and S. Woolcock. (eds). 2003. *Regionalism, Multilateralism, and Economic Integration. The Recent Experience*. Tokyo: UNU Press.

UNCRAD. 2008. *COMTRADE Database, 2008*. http://wits.worldbank.org/WITS (accessed 14 November 2008).

World Trade Organisation. 2010. 'Welcome to the Regional Trade Agreements Information System (RTA-IS)'. http://rtais.wto.org/UI/PublicMaintainRTAHome.aspx (accessed September 20 2009).

13

ASEAN–India FTA: Sensitivity Analysis of the Textiles and Clothing Sector of India

P. Nayak and Shakeel Ahamed

The rationale behind the ASEAN–India Free Trade Agreement (AIFTA) is clearly in favour of India's entry into the formidable South Asian regional trade block which has greater significance in political manoeuvering than trade. In the angle of trade, the negative trade balance of India with ASEAN has been perpetuity in the recent years. In spite of the fact that India has preferential trade regimes with Thailand, Singapore and Myanmar separately and/or as a part of the Bay of Bengal Initiatives for Multi-Sectoral Technical and Economic Cooperation (BIMSTEC) trade group, the performance of Indian trade has not improved much. India has adverse balance of trade with these partners and over the years it is worsening (see Table 13.1).

The overall Indo-ASEAN bilateral trade deficit during 2007 is around US $15 billion and that too has significantly gone up to this level very recently. In spite of this, economic theory propounds inherent trade creating possibilities of the Free Trade Agreements (FTAs) by better flow of goods and services between the regions, besides helping transfer of technology for better production practices. The combined Gross Domestic product (GDP) of the ASEAN10 is larger than India and has a much larger Per Capita Income (PCI) of the ASEAN indicating economic development of the later (Table 13.2). The PCI of Singapore is approximately 38 times of that of India, Brunei Darussalam about 36 times, Malaysia more than 8 times, Thailand about 4 times and Indonesian's income is double of the Indians. The combined import of the ASEAN from the world during 2008 is US $895 billion, about 4.7 fold of the Indian export to the world.

Table 13.1: India's Trade Surplus/Deficit with ASEAN Member Countries (in Million$)

Country	1999	2000	2001	2002	2003	2004	2005	2006	2007
Brunei Darussalam	1.73	2.63	2.90	3.72	4.22	4.31	32.64	40.34	50.07
Cambodia	6.60	6.88	2.48	16.97	18.55	17.10	21.68	24.43	30.32
Indonesia	−635.65	−536.55	−717.28	−541.06	−883.68	−1160.84	−1492.88	−2450.39	−3975.02
Laos	1.35	5.00	5.52	1.85	0.59	2.00	4.59	5.68	7.05
Malaysia	−1504.35	−820.68	−1032.57	−627.00	−1044.36	−1206.95	−1231.50	−4429.51	−4599.52
Myanmar	−139.05	−131.13	−144.76	−274.11	−304.77	−295.35	−383.30	−473.73	−587.90
Philippines	85.83	126.53	147.41	299.41	236.62	208.86	272.87	233.00	176.98
Singapore	−862.95	−655.53	−2001.17	−92.87	26.29	919.87	2091.95	−4000.42	−5664.81
Thailand	103.33	174.60	81.65	301.66	250.02	72.60	−95.74	−513.20	−1035.06
Vietnam	136.25	195.85	157.36	280.97	356.22	427.08	534.92	648.69	1035.88
Overall Trade Deficit	−2806.93	−1632.41	−3498.46	−630.45	−1340.29	−1011.32	−244.77	−10915.11	−14562.02

Source: Direction of Trade Statistics, IMF, http://www.imf.org/external/pubs/ (accessed 15 May 2009).

Table 13.2: Major Indicators of ASEAN and Indian Economy in 2008

S. No.	Country/Region	GDP (Billion $)	Population (Million)	Per Capita Income, US$	Exports to World (Billion $)	Imports from World (Billion $)
1	Brunei Darussalam	14.6	0.39	37,482	8	2
2	Cambodia	11.3	14	776	5	7
3	Indonesia	511.8	240	2,130	139	116
4	Lao PDR	5.4	6.8	786	1	1
5	Malaysia	221.6	26	8,617	199	155
6	Myanmar	26.2	48	544	7	3
7	Singapore	181.9	5	39,055	343	310
8	Thailand	273.3	66	4,147	175	157
9	Vietnam	89.8	87	1,033	63	75
10	The Philippines	166.9	98	1,703	48	69
	ASEAN	**1503**	**591**	**2,541**	**988**	**895**
	India	**1207**	**1166**	**1,035**	**187**	**315**

Source: World Fact Book, CIA, 2009, http://www.cia.gov/library/publications/the-world-factbook/index.html (accessed 15 May 2009).

Given the economic and development strength of the ASEAN, the FTA between India and ASEAN may trigger a positive trade flow of goods and services in this region.

A large number of studies are strongly pitching in favour of AIFTA (Sen, Asher and Rajan 2004; Joseph 2009). Though overall gain on account of expanded bilateral trade is predicted, there has been widespread skepticism on trade diversion and sensitivity of some sectors (agriculture, textiles, auto and auto components, electronics, etc.) that are vulnerable to the ASEAN imports, the sectors in which the member countries of ASEAN have efficient production systems in place. There is also skepticism that India may not benefit from the tariff liberalisation of ASEAN as most members have low prevailing duty and further lowering of duty will not provide enough room for accelerating exports from India (Pal and Dasgupta 2009).

Indo-ASEAN T&C Trade

Textiles and Clothing (T&C) has been identified as a sensitive sector under the FTA. The sector has its own importance so far as its contribution to the Indian economy is concerned. During 2008–2009, the sector accounted for 13 per cent of Indian exports, contributed 4 per cent to GDP, 26 per cent to manufacturing output, 18 per cent to industrial employment. As the second largest employer, the sector employs as large as 38 million directly and another 53 million indirectly. India is a significant exporter of textiles and clothing to the world covering all products (see Table 13.3). In case of Indo-ASEAN textile and clothing trade, India has been consistently performing better than ASEAN and has favourable trade balances. The moot point is that the Indian share in the ASEAN textiles and clothing imports still remains much lower than the ASEAN share in the Indian imports. (Table 13.4).

The garments being the most sensitive ones, we scrutinised the garment trade of some ASEAN member countries. Major garment exporters of ASEAN are Cambodia, Indonesia, Malaysia, Vietnam and Thailand, who exported clothing worth 3.7, 6.7, 3.6, 4.3 and 9 billion US dollar to world respectively during 2008. Indonesia, Malaysia, Thailand and Vietnam have strong presence in textiles exports also as they exported textiles worth 3.7, 1.6, 3.2 and 1.6 billion US dollar respectively during the same time. Textiles and Clothing industry plays a key role in the economy of Cambodia and Vietnam.

Table 13.3: 2-digit HS Code Descriptions of Textiles and Clothing Products

S.No.	2-Digit HS Code	Description
1	50	Silk
2	51	Wool, fine or coarse animal hair, horse hair yarn and woven fabric
3	52	Cotton
4	53	Other vegetable textile fibres; paper yarn and woven fabrics of paper yarn
5	54	Man-made Filaments
6	55	Man-made staple fibres
7	56	Wadding, felt and non-wovens; special yarns; twine, cordage, ropes and cables and articles thereof
8	57	Carpets and other textile floor coverings
9	58	Special woven fabrics; tufted textile fabrics; lace; tapestries; trimmings; embroidery
10	59	Impregnated, coated, covered or laminated textile fabrics; textile articles of a kind suitable for industrial use
11	60	Knitted or crocheted fabrics
12	61	Articles of apparel and clothing accessories, knitted or crocheted
13	62	Articles of apparel and clothing accessories not knitted or crocheted
14	63	Other made-up textile articles; sets; worn clothing and worn textile articles; rags

Source: Export Import Data Bank, Director General of Foreign Trade, Ministry of Commerce and Industry, Government of India, http://dgft.delhi.nic.in (accessed 15 May 2009).

Table 13.4: Export–Import of Textiles and Clothing Estimated
for 2008 (US$ Million)

S. No.	Countries/Region	India's T&C Export	India's T&C Import	T&C Export to World	T&C Imports from World
1	Brunei Darussalam	2	–	NA	962
2	Cambodia	8	0.2	3766	1449
3	Indonesia	133	80	9959	3583
4	Lao PDR	0.4	0.001	NA	140
5	Malaysia	143	33	5173	1613
6	Myanmar	7	–	391	370
7	Singapore	119	18	2442	3417
8	Thailand	77	105	7452	2837
9	Vietnam	70	10	10610	6494
10	Philippines	25	2	2173	894
	ASEAN10	**584**	**248**	**41965**	**21758**
	India			**21121**	**3022**

Source: DGCIS, Kolkata, http://www.dgciskol.nic.in (accessed 15 May 2009) and WTO, http:www.wto.org/english/res_e/statis_e/statis_e.htm (accessed 15 May 2009).

Garmenting sector constitutes more than 80 per cent of merchandise export earnings of Cambodia and more than 50 per cent of their manufacturing employment depends on it. T&C exports together contributed to around 20 per cent of merchandise exports of Vietnam. However, Vietnam's T&C exports are more import intensive among all ASEAN countries. Vietnam's major import source for textiles is China; and India exported 10 million US dollar worth of textiles out of 6,050 million US dollar worth of textile imports during 2008.

India could be a major source of textiles imports for ASEAN as imports of textiles in ASEAN amount to US$21.76 billion during 2008, but currently India is supplying less than US$400 million worth of textiles. Chapter 52 (cotton including yarn and woven fabrics there of) shows significant growth of exports in the last six years and presently dominating (48.1 per cent) the export basket of India. Other than this, the chapters 54 and 62 (clothing) are also contributing significantly (more than 10 per cent) to the export basket (Table 13.5). Overall Indian export of T&C products to ASEAN by India has been steadily increasing over the years and recorded an export of US$707 during 2008 and at the same time imported an amount of US$250 million leaving a trade balance of about US$457 million (see Figure 13.1). Further, India's share in ASEAN's total textiles and clothing import basket is found to be less

Table 13.5: India's T&C Exports to ASEAN 10 (US $ '000)

Chapter	2003	2004	2005	2006	2007	2008	% Share (2008)
50	15,991.830	21,289.457	22,596.140	17,625.347	13,675.492	11,232.689	1.59
51	1,061.613	2,434.402	5,663.820	5,178.541	9,264.200	12,885.664	1.82
52	97,563.713	134,870.729	134,072.851	226,671.633	280,799.002	339,835.890	48.10
53	1,815.374	2,773.486	3,971.590	2,896.015	2,789.636	5,635.568	0.80
54	135,174.345	132,256.244	84,262.477	59,001.011	62,716.902	61,423.297	8.69
55	31,113.102	38,368.642	46,716.445	54,677.413	78,485.952	82,931.394	11.74
56	3,717.409	5,111.956	9,294.052	7,766.787	9,987.400	18,423.708	2.61
57	6,244.381	13,506.084	12,138.829	29,520.330	16,741.595	15,874.658	2.25
58	2,535.007	2,846.709	2,897.916	3,684.934	3,723.568	11,393.645	1.61
59	3,480.907	3,544.234	9,634.555	5,607.357	7,342.057	8,245.080	1.17
60	186.688	927.335	904.339	701.244	1,033.653	3,223.740	0.46
61	48,902.982	30,413.490	21,738.326	22,095.910	27,726.864	35,921.448	5.08
62	73,897.067	77,180.667	74,788.728	74,077.807	73,780.262	79,103.586	11.20
63	15,804.463	16,468.887	15,041.806	20,805.028	15,713.782	20,418.500	2.89
Total	**437,488.881**	**481,992.322**	**443,721.874**	**530,309.357**	**603,780.365**	**706,548.867**	**100.00**

Source: Compiled from World Integrated Trade Solution (WITS) Database, Reporter ASEAN Secretarial, http://wits.worldbank.org/wits (accessed 15 May 2009).

Figure 13.1: Bilateral Trading Pattern of Textiles and Clothing
(US$ Million)

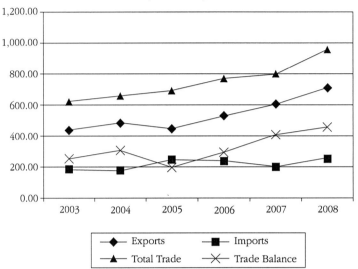

Source: UN Comtrade Database 2009, World Intergrated Trade Solution (WITS), http://wits.worldbank.org/WITS (accessed 15 May 2009).

than 3 percent (Table 13.6). Thus, there could be ample opportunity to increase the presence of Indian T&C exports to ASEAN under AIFTA.

Overall, the T&C exports of India look quite encouraging before the FTA was signed and do not seem to have weakened; in spite of this, the export from more efficient sub-sectors of the T&C of the ASEAN members may inflict sufficient injuries to our industries. Some of the imports to India has been complementary in nature and has been able to support value added Indian exports as well as domestic consumption (see Figure 13.2). Many of the imported items are basic raw materials for the production of technical and non-woven textiles. Tyre-cord fabric of high tenacity yarn of nylon or other polyamides (590210) is the major item being imported from ASEAN in 2008, which has a share of around 17 per cent followed by acrylic of modacrylic staple fibres, not carded, combed or otherwise processed for spinning (550130) with a share of around 9 per cent and synthetic filament yarn (other than sewing thread), not put up for retail sale, including synthetic monofilament of less

Table 13.6: Textiles and Clothing — Bilateral Trade (US$ Million)

Year	Exports	Imports	Total Trade	Trade Balance	India's Share in ASEAN 10's Imports	ASEAN 10's Share in Indian Imports
2003	437.49	184.57	622.06	252.92	3.12	9.54
2004	481.99	176.16	658.15	305.84	2.20	8.53
2005	443.72	246.01	689.73	197.71	2.13	9.22
2006	530.31	236.40	766.71	293.91	2.40	8.61
2007	603.78	196.85	800.63	406.93	2.58	6.48
2008	706.55	249.73	956.28	456.82	3.49	6.97

Source: Same as Table 13.5.

Figure 13.2: India's Exports to and Imports from ASEAN (US$ '000)

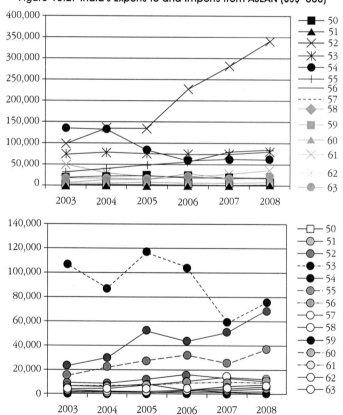

Source: UN COMTRADE Database 2009, World Integrated Trade Solution (WITS), http://wits.worldbank.org/WITS (accessed 15 May 2009).

than 67 decitex (540249) with 7 per cent share. The ASEAN exports to India from 2003 to 2008 clearly brings out that the product groups at HS 2 digit 52, 54, 55, 56, 57, 58 and 59 are figuring dominantly in their product basket in terms of their export shares (Table 13.7). But these sub-sectors' strength in injuring the industry of India cannot be perceived by merely considering this indicator, without an in-depth analysis of their products of exports at a more disaggregated level.

The Objectives

Literature suggests a large number of methods to find out the pos-sible threat and extent of such threat to the concerned products or the product groups from the export surge in a more liberal trading regime such as FTAs. As has been the experience of India, imports from a number of products from HS chapters 54, 55, 56 and 59 have been useful for processing for exports or even for domestic use. These include items mostly from the technical textiles, specialised fabrics and synthetic yarns and so on. While India also exports similar products to the world and ASEAN, it becomes more necessary to examine whether these exports adversely affect the interests of Indian industry. Therefore, ASEAN exports of some product are considered perilous to the industry while some others are complementary in nature that supports value added export. We, in this chapter, propose to examine and identify the product groups at two digit level, which are sensitive and vulnerable to ASEAN and/or member country exports to India using well estab-lished methodologies.

Methodology

The study examines the structure of Relative Comparative Advantages (RCA) enjoyed by ASEAN and India, both bilaterally and globally. Analysis of the comparative advantages such as relative export com-petitiveness and relative trade advantages of product groups are used to identify them as potential competitors and threats. These indices are examined with respect to their structure as well as stabil-ity to arrive at an inference on their latent strength. However, the selection of a product group as a potential predator depends on its competitiveness both globally as well as bilaterally. Besides the above, the product groups in HS chapters 61, 62 and 63 are at the

Table 13.7: ASEAN 10's T&C Exports to India (US$ Million)

Chapter	2003	2004	2005	2006	2007	2008	Share (2008)
50	921.780	777.725	863.061	1,339.511	1,153.228	1,592.818	0.64
51	967.765	1,020.201	1,434.167	557.145	1,123.582	1,784.463	0.71
52	8,995.966	8,517.046	12,385.274	16,352.342	12,177.685	11,342.485	4.54
53	253.735	286.102	365.945	480.922	315.278	338.924	0.14
54	106,761.676	86,622.348	117,166.332	103,873.703	59,197.182	75,298.088	30.15
55	15,437.314	22,372.443	28,229.194	32,731.887	25,371.530	37,931.709	15.19
56	5,927.006	6,370.064	6,947.536	9,292.806	9,800.935	8,647.658	3.46
57	2,771.254	4,463.186	7,737.758	10,469.911	14,135.944	11,922.620	4.77
58	3,102.803	3,177.246	2,481.537	3,971.862	4,911.032	8,574.103	3.43
59	23,692.721	30,111.737	52,318.512	43,400.694	51,173.624	68,601.913	27.47
60	5,310.165	4,741.522	7,774.202	3,428.173	6,233.897	6,157.668	2.47
61	2,994.302	1,705.131	1,899.649	2,783.013	3,174.151	4,387.973	1.76
62	3,261.955	2,363.522	2,598.460	3,680.707	3,743.047	6,362.092	2.55
63	4,171.135	3,627.343	3,810.886	4,041.024	4,336.823	6,785.240	2.72
Total	**184,569.577**	**176,155.616**	**246,012.513**	**236,403.700**	**196,847.938**	**249,727.754**	**100.00**

Source: Same as Table 13.5.

upper end of the value chain and considered very sensitive. Hence these product groups have been taken as sensitive and examined following the above permutations and combinations of RCAs.

The modified revealed comparative advantage developed by Balassa (1977) has been used to measure the competitiveness. Two indices have been used to compare the Bilateral Competitiveness (BC) while three indices have been used to study the global competitiveness. The former two have been defined as follows:

RCA_1 = Ratio of net exports to the total trade; mathematically we represent the measure equal to

$$RCA_1 = (X_{ij} - M_{ij})/(X_{ij} + M_{ij}) \qquad 1$$

Where X and M represents exports and imports respectively, i is a country, j is a commodity (or industry); the index ratios range from −1 ($X_{ij} = 0$ and revealed comparative disadvantage) to +1 ($M_{ij} = 0$ and revealed comparative advantage). However, there exist ambiguities around zero values (Greenaway and Milner 1993).

RCA_2 = Ratio of relative export advantage to relative import advantage; mathematically we represent the measure as:

$$RCA_2 = (X_{ij}/X_{it})/(M_{ij}/M_{it}) \ or \ (X_{ij}/M_{ij})/(X_{it}/M_{it}) \qquad 2$$

Where X and M represents exports and imports respectively. i is a country, j is a commodity (or industry), t is a set of commodities (or industries).

From the foregoing, we simply put a sector or group of the products is revealed competitive if: $RCA_1 > 0$ and so also $RCA_2 > 1$.

For comparing the BC, we adopted more measures developed by Vollrath (1991) and defined as follows:

RXA = Relative Export Advantage, mathematically represented as

$$RXA = (X_{ij}/X_{it})/(X_{nj}/X_{nt}) \ or \ (X_{ij}/X_{nj})/(X_{it}/X_{nt}) \qquad 3$$

Where X represents exports, i is a country, j is a commodity (or industry), t is a set of commodities (or industries) and n is a set of countries. If RXA is less than unity, the country is said to have a comparative disadvantage in the commodity/industry. It is argued that the RCA index is biased due to the omission of imports especially when country size is important (Greenaway and Milner 1993).

The difference between the Relative Export Advantage (RXA) and Relative Import Advantage (RMA) often called as Relative Trade Advantage (RTA).

$$RMA = (M_{ij}/M_{nj})/(M_{it}/M_{ij}) \qquad 4$$

$$RTA = RXA - RMA = (X_{ij}/X_{nj})/(X_{it}/X_{nt}) - (M_{ij}/M_{nj})/(M_{it}/M_{nt}) \qquad 5$$

Where X and M accounts for exports and imports respectively.

The revealed competitiveness is examined on the basis of the following cardinal values of the measures, i.e., RXA > 1 and RTA > 0.

Identification of Threat

We have calculated the alternative measures of the RCAs to examine the global competitiveness of the products of India and ASEAN at HS2 digit level by using RXA and RTA. At the bilateral level, the RCA1 and RCA2 have been used. The stability of these measures has been tested by examining their Coefficients of Variation (CV). Table 13.8 synthesises the overall results of both kinds of RCAs and extends an opportunity to make the initial screening of the sectoral or sub-sectoral strength of the ASEAN versus India. '✓'indicates bilateral or global RCAs while '✗' indicates the group is not in RCA. The sensitivity of any sector is arrived at by using the method of elimination. If the sector for India is bilaterally and globally competitive at a time when ASEAN is not, then the sector is not sensitive or otherwise.

The product groups of 50, 51, 52 and 53 clearly indicate the dominance of India in BC and GC (Table 13.8). ASEAN draws a blank in its RCAs in both BCs and Global Competitiveness (GCs) in these categories. The product groups are silk including yarns and woven fabric thereof; wool and animal hair including yarn; cotton including yarns and woven fabric thereof; and other vegetable textiles fibre, paper yarn and woven fabrics of paper yarn respectively. Except wool and woolen products mentioned in 52, India has strong raw material base to remain competitive in exports to any of the partner countries in ASEAN. All chapters from 50 to 53 are not only BCs in both RCAs but also indicate consistent improvements in their values over the period of consideration, i.e., from 2003 to 2008 excepting 50 whose RCA values are declining. The average values of RCA1 and RCA2 of chapter 50 are 0.87 and 7.34 respectively which are very high. The measures are also stable indicating strong and sustainable competing strength in the markets of ASEAN. As regards to their

Table 13.8: Competitiveness of ASEAN10 and India in Textiles and Clothing

| Chapter | Bilateral Competitiveness | | | | Global Competitiveness | | | | ESI | |
| | ASEAN 10 | | India | | ASEAN 10 | | India | | | |
	RCA_1	RCA_2	RCA_1	RCA_2	RXA	RTA	RXA	RTA	2008	Average
50	✗	✗	✓	✓	✗	✗	✓	✗	0.10	0.49
51	✗	✗	✓	✓	✗	✗	✗	✗	0.18	0.24
52	✗	✗	✓	✓	✗	✗	✓	✗	0.11	0.13
53	✗	✗	✓	✓	✗	✗	✓	✗	0.26	0.18
54	✓	✓	✗	✗	✓	✗	✓	✗	0.16	0.20
55	✓	✓	✓	✗	✓	✗	✗	✗	0.26	0.21
56	✓	✓	✓	✗	✗	✗	✗	✗	0.25	0.20
57	✗	✗	✓	✓	✗	✗	✗	✓	0.15	0.11
58	✗	✓	✗	✗	✗	✗	✗	✗	0.31	0.40
59	✓	✓	✗	✗	✗	✗	✗	✗	0.32	0.22
60	✓	✓	✗	✗	✗	✗	✗	✗	0.33	0.21
61	✗	✗	✓	✓	✓	✓	✗	✓	0.44	0.48
62	✗	✗	✓	✓	✓	✓	✗	✓	0.34	0.35
63	✗	✗	✓	✓	✗	✓	✓	✓	0.31	0.25

Source: Calculations based on a data from World Integrated Trade Solution (WITS) database, Reporter ASEAN Secretariat, http://wits.worldbank.org/wits (accessed 15 May 2009).

Note: '✓' indicates the revealed comparative advantage, '✗' indicates comparative advantage not revealed and ESI stands for Export Similarity Index.
1. The RCA indicators in the above table have been obtained from a compilation of RCAs from 2003 to 2008 for respective partners.

global competing strengths, all product groups in these categories attain the distinction of RXA except Chapter 51 fail the test of competence. As said earlier, India is not a country with good wool production and most of the apparel grade wool is imported from Australia, New Zealand and other countries. Hence, India suffers from competing with many wool exporting countries of the world. Therefore, though the product group remains competitive in BC, it fails in GC. When the matter comes to the issue of the RTA, all the product groups fail to reach the mark.

ASEAN is bilaterally competitive in Chapter 54 (man-made filaments including yarn and woven fabrics) in both the indices and also indicates their global competitiveness in case of relative export advantage. The ASEAN's export to India in this category has the largest share in the export basket (30.15 per cent). India does not figure in bilateral competitiveness but has a small presence in global market and shows their competitiveness in case of export to the world but remains insignificant so far as our relative trade advantage and relative competitiveness are concerned. Though the values of the RCAs do not seem to have a particular trend, they are stable and strong over the period of consideration. The average values of RCA1 and RCA2 of chapter 54 are 0.60 and 6.05 respectively. At the 6-digit product level, other polyester items dominate the imports. These products alone constitute more than 60 per cent of Indian imports from ASEAN. During 2008, India imported about US$0.30 millions worth of other polyester products which belong to chapter 54. Indian polyester industry is highly monopolistic and production is controlled by a very few producers. Though India is enjoying an advantage of importing raw materials for further processing and export, the product group could be a potential threat to the industry as in some products, both India and ASEAN are competing in the international market. In view of the bilateral competitiveness of ASEAN and global presence of both India and ASEAN in Chapter 54, we have considered this product group of India as sensitive in the first level of screening.

In product groups 55 and 56, India and ASEAN are competing with each other though India is not showing consistency in its competitiveness in both the RCAs. These are man-made staple fibres including yarns and woven fabrics; and wadding felt and non-woven special yarn twine cordage, ropes and cables and products thereof. The major product categories at 6 digit level (see Table 13.9) which contribute to the competitiveness of 55 are polyesters (48 per cent), acrylic and modacrylic (19.83 per cent) and other synthetic fibres (7.75 per cent); while the products which invigorates Chapter 56 are other synthetic fibres (29.23 per cent) and made up fishing nets (19.22 per cent). India has been in the growth path so far as the acrylic and modacrylic fibres and fabric is concerned, but even today singular producer groups are roosting the market. Among the categories of imports, the product group of polyesters (550320) has been kept in the exclusion list while other categories can be imported to India in a liberalised duty regime, which could be threats to the Indian industry. India is progressing in man-made staple fibre, yarns and woven fabrics, besides in non-woven (Table 13.9). Besides, both the partners are not significantly positioned in their international markets in these categories. In view of our competing position with them in these product groups, we consider these sectors as sensitive.

In sub-sector 57, India enjoys BC and also GC but ASEAN do not figure anywhere and hence considered safer. As regards to

Table 13.9: Products of Member Countries Contributing to ASEAN Competitiveness (HS 6 Digit)

HS Line	Product	Total ASEAN Exports (2002 to 2008)	Countries in ASEAN	BC RCA$_1$	RCA$_2$	GC RXA	RTA
54	Man-made filaments						
540210	High tenacity yarn of nylon/other polyamids	5781.30	Singapore (68.85), Thailand (31.03)	✓	✓	✗	✗
540220	High tenacity yarn of polyesters	14768.88	Thailand (99.72)	✓	✓	✗	✗
540233	Textured yarn of polyesters	17334.36	Malaysia (16.17), Thailand (82.33)	✓	✓	✓	✓
540241	Othr yarn of nylon/other polymds, untwisted a twist <=50 turns per metre single	41651.40	Malaysia (79.76), Thailand (19.96)	✓	✓	✓	✓
540242	Yarn of polyester, partly orntd, untwisted or wth a twist <= 50 turns per metre, single	39857.53	Malaysia (64.57), Thailand (31.12)	✓	✓	✓	✓
540243	Yarn of other polyster , single untwisted/a twist<=50 turns per metre	237627.05	Malaysia (84.26), Thailand (13.72)	✓	✓	✓	✓
540249	Other yarn, single, untwisted or with a twist not exceeding 50 turns per metre	60056.32	Singapore (88.35), Thailand (10.18)	✓	✓	✓	✓
540252	Othr yarn of polyesters,single,with a twist exceeding 50 turns/per metre	7596.22	Malaysia (88.21), Thailand (11.72)	✓	✓	✓	✓
540410	Monofilament	9067.30	Singapore (76.60), Thailand (23.03)	✓	✓	✗	✗

(Table 13.9 Continued)

(Table 13.9 Continued)

HS Line	Product	Total ASEAN Exports (2002 to 2008)	Countries in ASEAN	BC		GC	
				RCA_1	RCA_2	RXA	RTA
540610	Synthetic filament yarn	23716.96	Thailand (99.74)	✓	✓	✓	✓
540752	Woven fabrics, dyed, cntng by wt>=85% textured polyester filaments	11717.87	Singapore (11.09), Thailand (77.19), Vietnam (8.71)	✗	✓	✗	✗
	Sub Total	**469175.19 (96.05)**	**Malaysia (57.53), Singapore (14.38), Thailand (26.84)**				
	54 Total	**488448.43**	**Malaysia (55.61), Singapore (14.20), Thailand (28.80)**				
55	Man-made staple fibres						
550130	Synthtc filament tow, acrylic/modacrylic	7565.44	Thailand (99.97)	✓	✓	✗	✓
550310	Staple fibres of nylon/other polyamides not carded or combed	3929.53	Singapore (82.07), Thailand (17.93)	✓	✓	✗	✗
550320*	Staple fibres of polyester not carded/combed	110469.98	Malaysia (42.68), Thailand (57.16)	✓	✓	✓	✓
550330	Staple fibrs of acrylic/modacrlylic not carded/combed	45635.96	Thailand (100.00)	✓	✓	✓	✓
550510	Waste, etc., of synthetic fibres	17839.01	Malaysia (5.94), Thailand (93.55)	✓	✓	✗	✗
550932	Multiple(folded)/cabled yarn cntng>=85% of acrylic/modacrylic staple fibres	7800.88	Thailand (95.69)	✓	✓	✓	✓
551219	Other woven fabrics, cntng 85% or more by weight of polyestr staple fibres	9175.65	Singapore (23.50), Thailand (74.13)	✗	✓	✓	✗

Code	Description	Value	Country (share)				
551321*	Woven fabrics of polyester staple fibres, plain weave, dyed	4093.29	Malaysia (72.98), Thailand (25.81)	✓	✓	✓	✓
551513	Fabrics of polyestr stapled fibres mixed mainly/solely with wool/fine animal hair	2427.48	Singapore (99.75)	✗	✗	✗	✗
	Sub Total	**208937.22 (90.79)**	**Malaysia (24.68), Thailand (71.35)**				
	55 Total	**230142.63**	**Malaysia (24.08), Singapore (6.31), Thailand (68.64)**				
56	Wadding, felt and non-wovens; special yarns; twine, cordage, ropes and cables and articles thereof						
560110	Sntry towls and tampons napkins and napkin liners for babies and similar sanitary articles of wadding	575.34	Singapore (9.35), Thailand (86.62)	✓	✓	✓	✓
560122	Wadding; other articles of wadding of man-made fibre	1264.70	Thailand (97.81)	✓	✓	✗	✗
560210	Needleloom felt and stitchbonded fibre	606.64	Malaysia (97.11)	✓	✓	✗	✗
560229	Felt of other textile materials	587.71	Singapore (45.54), Thailand (54.46)	✗	✓	✓	✓
560311	Man-made filament weighing not more than 25 g/m²	2766.30	Malaysia (22.63), Thailand (76.03)	✓	✓	✓	✓
560312	Man-made filament weighing more than 25 g/m² but not	3215.72	Malaysia (30.39), Singapore (19.28), Thailand (50.29)	✓	✓	✗	✗
560313	Man-made filament weighing more than 70 g/m² but not	1471.04	Malaysia (89.73), Thailand (7.32)	✓	✓	✗	✗
560314	Man-made filament weighing more than 150 g/m²	6053.98	Malaysia (91.15), Thailand (6.67)	✓	✓	✗	✓

(Table 13.9 Continued)

(Table 13.9 Continued)

HS Line	Product	Total ASEAN Exports (2002 to 2008)	Countries in ASEAN	BC		GC	
				RCA_1	RCA_2	RXA	RTA
560391	Weighing not more than 25 g/m^2	2768.53	Thailand (98.26)	✓	✓	✗	✗
560394	Other filament weighing more than 150 g/m^2	1464.13	Malaysia (38.69), Thailand (55.31)	✓	✓	✗	✗
560490	Other filament weighing	901.88	Malaysia (61.60), Thailand (33.64)	✓	✓	✓	✗
560750	Twine, cordage, cables, etc, of other synthetic fibres	16277.01	Thailand (98.38)	✓	✓	✓	✓
560790	Other twine, cordage, rope and cables	723.37	Malaysia (10.40), Singapore (38.91), Thailand (47.15)	✗	✓	✓	✗
560811	Made-up fshng nets of man-made textile materials	10703.99	Thailand (99.97)	✓	✓	✓	✓
560890	Knotted netting of twine cordage/rope, etc., of other textile materials	3851.96	Malaysia (97.08)	✓	✓	✓	✓
	Sub Total	**53232.29 (95.60)**	**Malaysia (26.30), Thailand (70.02)**				
	56 Total	**55682.82**	**Malaysia (25.59), Thailand (68.51)**				
61	Articles of apparel and clothing accessories, knitted or crocheted						
610322	Ensembles of cotton	3810.40	Thailand (100.00)	✓	✓	✓	✓
610510*	Men's/boys' shirts of cotton	1402.59	Malaysia (55.09), Singapore (12.60), Thailand (21.03), Vietnam (9.73)	✗	✓	✓	✓

Code	Description	Value	Main suppliers (%)				
610520*	Men's/boys' shirts of man-made fibres	953.99	Thailand (91.71), Vietnam (5.08)	✗	✓	✓	✓
610690	Blouses, etc., of other textile materials	2248.43	Singapore (96.78)	✗	✓	✓	✗
610711*	Underpants and briefs of cotton	574.18	Malaysia (85.09), Thailand (10.63)	✗	✓	✓	✓
610910*	T-shirts, etc., of cotton	8858.34	Malaysia (6.77), Singapore (47.18), Thailand (45.38)	✗	✗	✓	✗
610990*	T-shirt, etc., of other textile materials	9804.50	Malaysia (5.34), Singapore (78.71), Thailand (15.04)	✗	✓	✓	✗
611120	Babies'garments, etc., of cotton	7289.63	Singapore (15.88), Thailand (84.08)	✗	✓	✓	✓
611420	Other garments of cotton	1122.11	Singapore (36.86), Thailand (61.03)	✓	✓	✓	
611520	Women's full-length/knee-length hosiery measuring per single yarn less than 67 decitex	1309.58	Singapore (97.93)	✓	✗	✓	✗
611592	Other hosiery goods of cotton	1002.75	Malaysia (92.42), Singapore (6.14)	✓	✗	✓	✓
611599	Other hosiery of other textile materials	863.32	Malaysia (24.34), Thailand (75.32)	✓	✓	✓	✗
611610	Gloves mittens and mitts impregnated coated/covered wth plastic/rubber, knitted/crocheted	883.12	Malaysia (94.40), Singapore (5.60)	✓	✓	✓	✓

(*Table 13.9 Continued*)

(Table 13.9 Continued)

HS Line	Product	Total ASEAN Exports (2002 to 2008)	Countries in ASEAN	BC		GC	
				RCA_1	RCA_2	RXA	RTA
611780	Other clothing accessories, knitted/crocheted	5453.07	Singapore (96.58)	✓	✓	✓	✗
611790	Parts of garments, knitted/crocheted	585.79	Singapore (94.07)	✗	✓	✗	✗
	Sub Total	**46161.81 (86.90)**	**Malaysia (9.88), Singapore (49.97), Thailand (39.20)**				
	61 Total	**53123.18**	**Malaysia (10.31), Singapore (47.26), Thailand (39.85)**				
62	Articles of apparel and clothing accessories not knitted or crocheted						
620342*	Trousers bib and brace overalls breeches and shorts of cotton for men's and boys'	1210.14	Singapore (9.61), Thailand (84.41)	✗	✓	✗	✗
620343	Trousers, bib and brace, overalls, breeches and shorts of synthetic fibrs, men's or boys'	1467.69	Singapore (55.81), Thailand (35.97), Vietnam (6.57)	✗	✓	✓	✓
620349*	Trousers bib and brace overalls, breeches and shorts of other textile materials-men's/boys'	614.61	Thailand (21.91), Vietnam (73.84)	✗	✓	✓	✗
620422	Ensembles of cotton	1451.81	Singapore (7.03), Thailand (92.97)	✓	✓	✗	✓
620449	Dresses of other textile materials	1247.11	Singapore (93.99), Thailand (5.58)	✗	✓	✗	✗

Code	Description	Value	Country (share)			
620462*	Trousers, bib and brace overalls, breeches and shorts of cotton	609.76	Malaysia (5.65), Singapore (23.80), Thailand (66.94)	✗	✓	✓
620520*	Men's or boys' shirts of cotton	6215.59	Malaysia (6.71), Thailand (91.10)	✗	✓	✓
620590*	Shirts of other textile materials	1130.85	Malaysia (78.90), Singapore (6.82), Thailand (11.86)	✗	✓	✗
620630*	Blouses, shirts and shirts-blouses of cotton	980.19	Singapore (15.87), Thailand (84.13)	✗	✓	✗
620920	Babies' garments and clothing accessories of cotton	976.61	Singapore (44.27), Thailand (53.55)	✗	✓	✓
620990	Babies garments and clothing accessories of other textile materials	443.21	Singapore (9.51), Thailand (87.50)	✗	✓	✗
621010	Garments, made up of fabrics of heading no. 5602 or 5603	336.62	Philippines (42.41), Singapore (52.28)	✗	✓	✓
621142	Othr garments of cotton fibre women's or girls'	660.52	Singapore (23.04), Thailand (76.96)	✗	✓	✗
621149	Other garments of other textile materials	376.31	Singapore (55.09), Thailand (40.80)	✗	✓	✗
621210*	Brassieres	975.16	Malaysia (20.01), Singapore (23.72), Thailand (55.56)	✓	✓	✓
621290	Other articles and parts of hd6212 woven/knitted/crocheted	1936.80	Malaysia (95.72)	✓	✓	✗

(Table 13.9 Continued)

(Table 13.9 Continued)

HS Line	Product	Total ASEAN Exports (2002 to 2008)	Countries in ASEAN	BC RCA₁	RCA₂	GC RXA	RTA
				RCA_1	RCA_2	RXA	RTA
621600	Gloves, mittens and mitts	1050.79	Vietnam (94.27)	✗	✓	✗	✗
621710	Accessories for articles of apparel	786.47	Singapore (80.38), Thailand (16.04)	✗	✓	✗	✗
621790	Parts of garments/of clothing accessories	1453.56	Malaysia (7.35), Singapore (29.34), Thailand (63.20)	✗	✓	✗	✗
	Sub Total	**23923.79 (82.68)**	**Malaysia (15.38), Singapore (21.15), Thailand (55.70), Vietnam (6.73)**				
	62 Total	**28933.67**	**Malaysia (15.58), Singapore (21.51), Thailand (54.13), Vietnam (7.88)**				
63	Other made up textile articles; sets; worn clothing and worn textile articles; rags						
630221*	Other bed linen of cotton, printed	493.77	Malaysia (24.53), Singapore (5.39), Thailand (68.47)	✗	✓	✗	✗
630260*	Toilet linen and kitchen linen, of terry towelling/similar terry fabrics of cotton	1469.68	Thailand (98.64)	✗	✓	✓	✓
630312	Curtain, etc., hand knitted/crocheted of synthetic fibre	1329.22	Vietnam (99.57)	✓	✓	✓	✓
630399	Other curtains of other textile materials	809.63	Malaysia (61.96), Singapore (9.61), Thailand (11.71), Vietnam (16.72)	✗	✓	✓	✓

Code	Description				Value	Country (%)
630532	Flexible intermediate bulk containers of man-made textile materials	✓	✓	✓	1331.97	Malaysia (73.44), Singapore (5.23), Vietnam (21.27)
630533	Sacks and bags of polyethylene or polypropylene strip or the like	✓	✓	✓	1248.38	Singapore (11.21), Thailand (73.85), Vietnam (12.06
630590	Sacks and bags of other textile materials	✓	✓	✗	404.75	Singapore (90.67), Thailand (6.11)
630720	Life jackets and lifebelts	✗	✓	✓	843.79	Singapore (95.17)
630790	Other made up articles	✗	✗	✗	2132.65	Malaysia (20.53), Singapore (35.04), Thailand (43.04)
630800	Sets consisting of woven fabrics and yarn, worn with accessories, for making rugs, tapestry, embroidered table cloth and like in packaging for retail sale	✗	✓	✓	714.16	Malaysia (64.33), Singapore (11.36), Thailand (24.30)
630900	Worn clothing and other worn articles	✓	✓	✗	13281.25	Malaysia (90.36)
631090	Othr rags, scraps twine, cordge, rope, etc	✓	✓	✓	6798.19	Malaysia (90.39)
	Sub Total				**30857.43 (85.28)**	**Malaysia (67.06), Singapore (10.07), Thailand (15.22), Vietnam (6.22)**
	63 Total				**36185.09**	**Malaysia (60.01), Singapore (12.54), Thailand (19.58), Vietnam (6.42)**

Source: Calculations based on data from World Integrated Trade Solution (WITS) database, Reported ASEAN Secretariat, http://wits.worldbank.org/WITS (accessed 15 May 2009) and Export Import Data Bank, Director General of Foreign Trade, Ministry of Commerce and Industry, Government of India, http://dgft.delhi.nic.in (accessed 15 May 2009).

Note: (i) The figures in brackets indicate percentage of exports of the products in the total exports at 6 digit emanating from the country in ASEAN.

(ii) *indicates the inclusion of the product in the exclusion list of India.

(iii) '✓' indicates the revealed comparative advantage, '✗' indicates comparative advantage not revealed.

Chapters 58, 59 and 60, India does not have competitiveness either in BC or GC. The ASEAN's export to India has been significant in case of Chapter 59 (27.47 per cent) and also good amount of export is made in 58 and 60. These exports relate to special woven fabrics, tufted textile fabrics, lace, tapestry, trimmings and embroideries, etc., impregnated, coated, or covered laminated fabrics, textiles articles for industrial use; and knitted and crocheted fabrics. India has been sourcing these kinds of products as the industry of India is not well developed and requires these for the purpose of own consumption or for processing for export. Hence all these product groups of India from 57 to 59 are considered not sensitive, rather complementary in nature.

Though ASEAN bilaterally fails to compete with India in important sub-sectors of 61, 62 and 63, they have clear global presence like India as well. As mentioned earlier, these product groups have been selected as very sensitive sectors for their importance in the value chain and other implications for their importance in employment generation in India. The Indian imports of apparels articles and accessories of cotton (16.68 per cent); and other textiles materials (18.46 per cent); apparels of cotton (13.72 per cent); and apparels and accessories with impregnated, coated or covered (10.26 per cent) are figuring prominently in Chapter 61. While the first two items have been kept in the exclusion list, the latter two products have been put in the liberalised tariff schedules. These products could be possible threats to the Indian apparel industry, particularly the cotton textiles.

As regards to the products in Chapter 62 of apparel articles not knitted and crocheted, the cotton products from the ASEAN exports (21.48 per cent) has been placed under the exclusion list and other items (6.68 per cent) are in the liberalised framework. There are few other products which are also outside the ambit of the exclusion list. The product flow of those items to the country in the FTA period may be monitored so as to avoid possible injury to Indian industry.

Chapter 63 which includes other textiles articles, needle craft sets, worn clothing and worn textiles articles and rags has been a good performer in international markets. The exports of ASEAN shows a huge concentration around worn clothing and other worn articles. Probably India cannot afford to allow liberalised entry into the country on account of its impact on the Indian industry.

From the above analysis, it is established that the product group 54, 55, 56, 61, 62 and 63 are considered sensitive to imports from

ASEAN and there is a possibility that significant threat may emanate from the ASEAN member countries exports. (see Box 13.1 for product descriptions).

Box 13.1: Reference Chapter Headings (HS 2 Digit Level)

Chapter	Description
54	Man-made filaments
55	Man-made staple fibres
56	Wadding, felt and non-wovens; special yarns; twine, cordage, ropes and cables and articles thereof
61	Articles of apparel and clothing accessories, knitted or crocheted
62	Articles of apparel and clothing accessories not knitted or crocheted
63	Other made up textile articles; sets; worn clothing and worn textiles articles; rags

Note

1. ASEAN has a membership of 10 countries, namely Brunei Darussalam, Cambodia, Indonesia, Lao PDR, Malaysia, Myanmar, Philippines, Singapore, Thailand and Vietnam.

References

Balassa, B. 1977. '"Revealed" Comparative Advantage Revisited', *The Manchester School*, 45: 327–44.

Greenaway, D. and C. Milner. 1993. *Trade and Industrial Policy in Developing Countries: A Manual of Policy Analysis*. London: Macmillan. See esp. Part IV, 'Evaluating Comparative Advantage', pp. 181–208.

Joseph, K. J. 2009. 'ASEAN–India Pact and Plantations: Realities of the Myths', *Economic & Political Weekly* 44 (44): 14–18.

Pal, P. and Mitali Dasgupta. 2009. 'The ASEAN–India Free Trade Agreement: An Assessment', *Economic and Political Weekly*, 44 (38): 11–15.

Sen, R, M. G. Asher and R. S. Rajan. 2004. 'ASEAN–India Economic Relations: Current Status and Future Prospects', Discussion Paper No.73. New Delhi: Research and Information System for Non-Aligned and Other Developing Countries (RIS).

Vollrath, T. L. 1991. 'A Theoretical Evaluation of Alternative Trade Intensity Measures of Revealed Comparative Advantage', *Weltwirtschaftliches Archive*, 127 (2): 265–80.

14

Impacts of Foreign Investment on Indian Auto Industry

Badri Narayanan G. and Pankaj Vashisht

The main benefits of foreign investment are higher wages, technology transfer (Porterie and Lichtenberg 2001), employment generation (Miller and Weigel 1972), improved firm-level performance (Doukas and Lang 2003), scale-linked productivity improvement (Patibandla and Sanyal 2000) and impetus to skill improvements, while its costs are social, political and economic tensions arising from some groups that might lose from these Foreign Direct Investments (FDIs) (Safarian 1973; Kathuria 1996). In India, foreign investment flows have been growing in the recent years. While the Multinational Corporations (MNCs) invest in developing countries for various reasons such as 'protection-escalating' investment (Gopinath et. al. 1999) and low cost, there is a lot of debate in FDI recipient countries on its costs and benefits. For example, Sasidharan (2006) shows a lack of spillover effects, which is claimed as the main benefit of FDI. Particularly in this era of trade liberalisation, World Trade Organisation (WTO) and Free Trade Agreements (FTAs)/Preferential Trade Agreements (PTAs), it is essential to know the impact of FDI on overall performance and competitiveness of an economy.

Auto Industry in India provides a good case to assess this impact. First, FDI was almost prohibited in this sector till 1993 and hence the effects of FDI are very conspicuous by now, making it easier to analyse the impacts of FDI flows. Second, impact on domestic firms that have flourished for decades under protective regimes and on domestic market is worth examining. Third, there are many developmental implications for FDIs, such as employment, for which auto industry is crucial in India (NMCC 2006).

In 2005–2006, India manufactured 7.9 million automobiles including 1.3 million passenger cars, comprising 7 per cent of total vehicles and 2.4 per cent of the passenger cars produced globally. India is a global major in the two-wheeler industry, producing 7.6 million motorcycles, scooters and mopeds of engine capacities below 200 cc (OICA 2006). It is the second largest producer of two-wheelers and 13th largest producer of passenger cars in the world. Exports from India in this sector rose from US $1.0 billion in 2003–2004 to US $1.8 billion in 2005–2006, contributing 1 per cent to the world trade in auto components. In India, automotive industry employs 0.5 million. It contributes 4.7 per cent to India's GDP and 19 per cent to India's indirect tax revenue.

Growing middle class, rising per capita income and easier availability of finance[1] have been driving the fast-growing[2] vehicle demand in India, which in turn, has prompted the government to invest at unprecedented levels in roads infrastructure, including projects such as Golden Quadrilateral and North-East-South-West Corridor with feeder roads. Given that passenger car penetration rate is just about 8.5 vehicles per thousand, among the lowest in the world, there is huge potential demand in the future for automobiles.

Government drew an action plan to take the turnover of the automotive industry in India to US $145 billion by 2016, accounting for more than 10 per cent of the GDP and employing 25 million more people, by 2016, specially emphasising small cars, MUVs, two-wheelers and auto-components. Measures implemented include setting up of a National Auto Institute, streamlining institutions, upgrading infrastructure, changes in duty structure and fiscal incentives for R&D (Ministry of Heavy Industries and Public Enterprises 2006a, b; NMCC 2006). India's joining the Working Party or WP 29: 1998 Agreement for global harmonisation of automotive standards, coupled with the funding of National Automotive Testing and Research Infrastructure Project (NATRIP) by the Government of India, has increased prospects of the Indian auto industry rising up to global standards in the near future, in all aspects (ACMA 2006). So, auto industry plays a key role in Indian economy and its future prospects are even brighter.

Pingle (2000) puts the evolution of Indian auto policy framework into 3 phases: protection resulting from socialist ideologies and vested interests in 1940s and 1950s; rules, regulations and politics affecting the auto industry in the 1960s and 1970s; and delicensing, liberalisation and opening up of FDI in the auto sector in 1980s and 1990s. Piplai (2001) argues that vehicle industry has been thrusted upon a high degree of unsustainable competition due to price wars causing job losses and over capacity, due to reforms and FDI.

FDI has impacts on the supply chain of auto industry. Vertical integration, which would have grown otherwise due to in-house component production by foreign firms as predicted by Narayanan (1998), was gradually replaced by subcontracting, because Indian auto-component sector could emerge as a competitive field after the entry of foreign firms (Narayanan 2004). When the global auto assemblers entered India, 'follow-source'[3] was also happening. Now, even Indian component suppliers have entered the global auto supply chains, but the space for domestic industry is diminishing (Humphrey 1999). Capacity development of auto-component firms by foreign automobile firms have even benefited the domestic firms (Sutton 2000), including the smaller ones (Tewari 2000). Many auto-component firms have become world-class in the recent years, with joint ventures and even foreign acquisitions (ACMA 2006). Technology in the auto sector could be improved by foreign collaboration and intra-firm technology transfer (Narayanan 2004).

Few studies have exclusively focused on impact of foreign investment in Indian auto industry in the recent years. Attempting to fill this gap, we analyse the impact of foreign investment on various dimensions of Indian auto industry that include both its performance as well as developmental implications. We not only look at the aggregate performance trends, but also the firm-level aspects.

This chapter is organised as follows: section 2 discusses some aggregate trends in the auto industry. Section 3 summarises the recent trends in firm-level performance in automobile sector, with an attempt to draw contrasts between the domestic firms and those with some foreign equity/FDI. Section 4 analyses the recent trends in prices and links these with the recent FDI trends. Relationship between foreign equity participation and various performance and development indicators is examined in section 5. Conclusions are summarised in section 6.

2. FDI and Performance of Indian Auto Industry

The association between Indian auto players and their global counterparts goes back to 1940s when Hindustan Motors and Premier Auto imported the technical know-how from General Motors and Fiat, respectively. However, this interaction was limited to the import of technology and the foreign players were not involved in decision making. The foreign auto makers started playing an active role in earlier 1980s, when government partially liberalised its rules that ensured the entry of Suzuki Motors (Table 14.1).

Table 14.1: Detail of Foreign Entries in Indian Auto Industry

Company	Year of Entry	Current Installed Capacity
Suzuki	1982	600,000
General Motors	1994	85,000
Daimler Chrysler	1994	2,000
Honda	1995	50,000
Ford	1996	100,000
Toyota	1997	60,000
Hyundai	1998	300,000
Skoda	1999	30,000
Nissan	2004	N.A.
BMW	2005	1,700
Renault	2006	N.A.
Audi	2006	N.A.
Volkaswagen	2006	N.A.
Naza	2006	N.A.

Source: SIAM (2006).

Suzuki, under the banner of Maruti, started assembling small cars and soon become the market leader by outperforming Hindustan Motors which failed to upgrade its fleet over the last three decades. Maruti enjoyed the status of market leader with virtually no competition till mid-1990s before government effectively liberalised its foreign investment related norms in 1993. With the relaxation in FDI-related rules, FDI started flowing into India. The huge market potential induced the global auto majors to establish their manufacturing units in India, which raised the amount of FDI in auto sector from almost scratch to ₹ 180 billion (Figure 14.1). Till 2003, auto sector had around 12 per cent share in total FDI inflow to India, which, however, has declined thereafter to around 6 per cent in 2008, due to the more rapid FDI inflows in other sectors. At present, 14 foreign auto manufacturers are operating in India. The foreign firms have mainly targeted passenger car segment, while the commercial vehicle and two-wheeler segment are still dominated by the Indian firms.

Figure 14.1: Cumulative FDI Stock in Indian Auto Industry

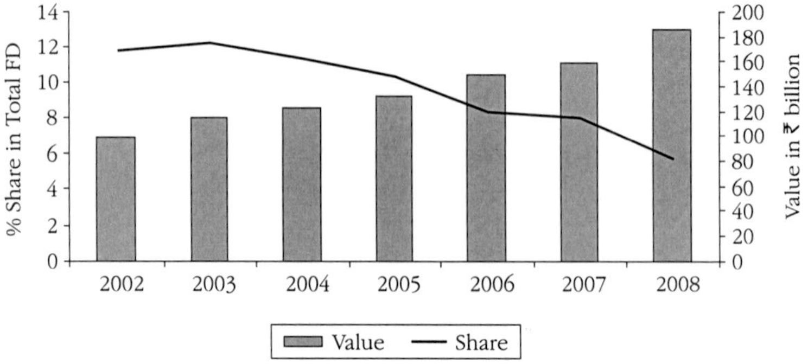

Source: Ministry of Commerce (2005–2009).

This influx of FDI seems to have restructured the Indian auto sector. A simple trend analysis of Indian automobile sector suggests that the growth in the number of factories has been much lower since 1991–1992 than from 1973–1974 to 1980–1981, while the growth rates of output and employment have been much higher from 2003–2004 to 2007–2008, which corresponds to the period when FDI inflows were increasing immensely as seen from Figure 14.1. This indicates that the factories are increasing their scales of operation to reap the economies of scale (Table 14.2). Capital has been growing at a relatively lower pace, since 2003–2004, than that from 1973–1974 to 1980–1981 for the aggregate auto industry, but it has been growing more rapidly than that in the 1990s.

While real emoluments per worker have been increasing very gradually, labour productivity has been rising rather more rapidly in the auto industry, from 1981–1982 to 2007–2008 (Table 14.3). Growth in labour productivity may be because of the FDI from MNCs, especially the Japanese and Korean ones, which focus a lot on training the manpower to be more productive. Rate of growth of capital intensity has been high, but contrary to the general expectation, the recent growth rates are clearly lower than those in the 1970s, in capital intensity.

Capital productivity has grown only from 1991–1992 to 2007–2008 in the case of manufacture of two-/three-wheelers and their accessories, while it has declined in the previous periods. For the manufacture of four-wheelers and their accessories, capital productivity has declined in all the periods shown. Decline in capital

Table 14.2: Automobiles, Parts and Accessories — Average
Annual Growth Rate

Variables	1973–1974 to 1980–1981	1981–1982 to 1990–1991	1991–1992 to 2003–2004	2003–2004 to 2007–2008
Automobiles and parts (excluding 2/3 wheelers — 2/3W)				
No. of Factories (in number)	13.6	1.18	5.89	4.2
Output (in value terms)	6.31	8.49	12.31	22.7
Employment (in number)	4.59	0.71	3.27	13.2
Capital (in value terms)	15.27	9.13	13.51	16.7
2/3 Wheelers and parts				
No. of Factories (in number)	13.23	8.59	3.1	1.3
Output (in value terms)	12.07	21.31	14.28	23.3
Employment (in number)	11.59	10.56	3.78	13.6
Capital (in value terms)	24.98	22.69	9.77	17.1
Aggregate auto industry				
No. of factories (in number)	13.42	4.89	4.50	2.8
Output (in value terms)	9.19	14.90	13.30	23.0
Employment (in number)	8.09	5.64	3.53	13.4
Capital (in value terms)	20.13	15.91	11.64	16.9

Source: Calculations from CSO (1974–2004), SIAM (2009) and ACMA (2009) statistics.
Note: Output and Capital are in ₹ crore at Constant 1993–1994 Prices.

productivity in this sector since 1991–1992 could be partly explained
by the high growth rate of capital intensity, mainly fuelled by change
in technologies and FDI inflows. Total factor productivity has been
growing, albeit at a low rate, over the past two and a half decades,
also attributable to FDI inflows to some extent.

Like other variables, the profitability of auto sector has also been
affected by the foreign entries. It is evident from Figure 14.2 that
each wave of liberalisation has pulled down the profitability for
some time and made the process of structural adjustment inevitable.
The first phase of adjustment coincided with the entry of Suzuki
Motors in mid-1980s and lasted for about four years. During this
period, Maruti made a serious dent into the market share of other
auto players and rendered them bleeding with massive losses. The
second phase of adjustment started in mid-1990s when few prominent global players like Hyundai, Honda and General Motors, etc.,
started their operations.

In order to examine the impact of foreign entry on the level of
market concentration the Indian auto industry, we calculated the

299

Table 14.3: Annual Average Growth Rates of Productivity Measures

Variable	1973–1974 to 1980–1981			1981–1982 to 1990–1991			1991–1992 to 20		
Industry –>	4W	2/3W	Total	4W	2/3W	Total	4W	2/3W	Total
Emoluments per worker	2.4	2.66	2.53	3.13	3.28	3.21	2.4	4.1	3.2
Capital intensity	10.22	11.99	11.11	8.31	10.97	9.64	10.3	6.2	8.2
Capital productivity	–7.77	–1.33	–4.55	–0.59	–1.13	–0.86	–1.3	3.9	1.4
Labour productivity	1.65	0.43	1.04	7.74	9.72	8.73	9.3	10.8	9.7
Total factor productivity	–1.91	–1.42	–1.67	1.05	1.13	1.09	0.57	2.1	1.3

Source: Calculations from CSO (1974–2004), SIAM (2009) and ACMA (2009) statistics.

Notes: 1. All growth rates are in percentage. Emoluments are at constant 1993–1994 prices.
2. Labour productivity is the ratio of output in ₹ crore at constant 1993–1994 prices to employment.
3. Capital intensity is the ratio of capital ₹ crore at constant 1993–1994 prices to employment.
4. Capital productivity is the ratio of output to capital, both in ₹ crore at constant 1993–1994 prices.
5. Total Factor Productivity is measured by translog index, explained in Appendix 1 of Narayanan and Vashisht (2008).
6. '2/3W' stands for 'Manufacture of Two-/Three-Wheelers and Their Accessories' and '4W' stands for 'Manufacture of Four-Wheelers and Their Accessories'.

Figure 14.2: Profit Rates in Indian Auto Industry

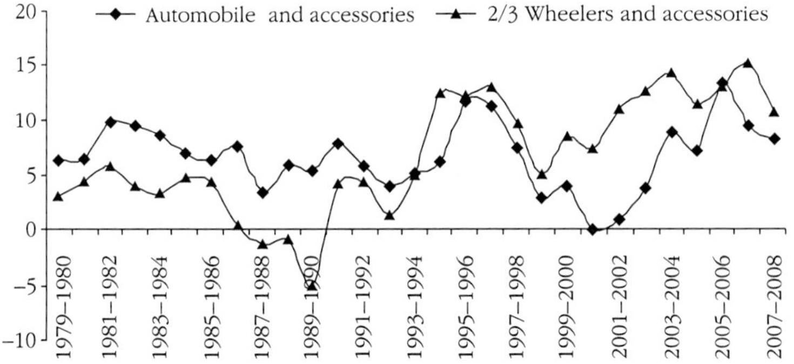

Source: Calculations from CSO (1979–1980 to 2003–2004),
Annual Reports of Auto Companies and our Field Survey.
Note: Ratio of profits to value of output, in constant 1993–1994 prices.

Herschman-Herfindahl's Index (HHI)[4] for all the sub-segment of Indian auto sector. Figure 14.3 shows that market concentration has been lower in the two-/three-wheelers sector than in the other automobile sectors. Interestingly, coinciding with the foreign entries, the other automobile segment, which includes car and commercial vehicle, has seen a major decline in the level of market concentration. However, since 2000–2001 it has once again started showing an increasing trend. Even in the Indian auto-component sector, market concentration has been rising since 2003–2004 showing that companies are scaling up.[5]

Auto-component sector is much more labour-intensive than the automobile sector (Figure 14.4). However, labour intensity, defined as number of employees per ₹ crore of output, has fallen even in the auto-component sector from around 24 in 1999–2000 to 11 in 2005–2006. For the automobile sector, it is very low (less than 1) and has been decreasing over the years. This shows the significance of the auto-component sector from the viewpoint of employment generation. There is a concern in the industry that wages are growing without proportionate improvements in labour productivity. This claim requires empirical investigation. Table 14.4 illustrates that the growth rate of real emoluments per employee has been lower than that of real labour productivity, except in the automobile sector from 2001–2002 to 2002–2003.

Figure 14.3: Market Concentration (HHI) in Indian Auto Industry

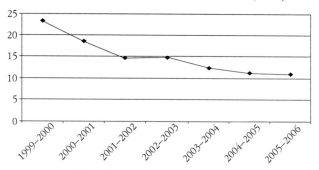

Source: Calculations from CMIE (2009).

Figure 14.4: Labour Intensity in Indian Auto Industry (Number of Employees per ₹ Crore of Output at Constant 1993–1994 prices)

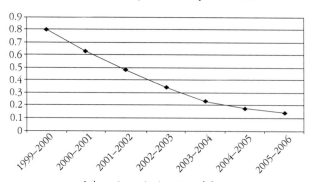

Labour-intensity in auto-component sector

Labour-intensity in automobile sector

Source: Calculations from SIAM (2009), ACMA (2009), CSO (2001–2004 and CMIE (2009).

Table 14.4: Comparison of Growth Rates in Emoluments and Labour Productivity

Industry	Period	Growth in Emoluments per Employee	Growth in Labour Productivity	Differential in Wage-Productivity Growth Rates
Automobile Manufacture	2000–2001 to 2001–2002	5.6%	30%	−24.40%
	2001–2002 to 2002–2003	18.35%	8.33%	10.02%
	2002–2003 to 2003–2004	7.92%	14.29%	−6.37%
	2005–2006 to 2007–2008	4.61%	3.63%	−0.98%
Manufacture of parts, bodies and accessories	2000–2001 to 2001–2002	−3.09%	2%	−5.09%
	2001–2002 to 2002–2003	6.11%	29.41%	−23.30%
	2002–2003 to 2003–2004	4.68%	16.67%	−11.99%
	2005–2006 to 2007–2008	4.13%	4.65%	−0.52%

Source: Calculations from CSO (2001–2004).
Note: Emoluments is in ₹ crore at constant 1993–1994 prices; Labour productivity is the ratio of output in ₹ crore at constant 1993–1994 prices to employment in number.

Figure 14.5 shows that the capacity utilisation has been rising in the recent years in the Indian automobile manufacturing sector. The increase has been more conspicuous in commercial and passenger vehicles (CV/PV) other than two-/three-wheelers. From 65 per cent in 1997–1998, it has increased to over 85 per cent in 2005–2006 in CV/PV sector. It has increased from about 65 per cent in 1997–1998 to more than 70 per cent in two-/three-wheeler sector in 2005–2006, but fell subsequently to about 50 per cent in 2006–2007.[6] Since 2003–2004, capacity utilisation has been higher in CV/PV than two-/three-wheelers, mainly because of higher growth of domestic and export demand for CV/PV and also perhaps due to the FDIs that resulted in MNCs, especially the Asian ones, that follow efficient techniques like lean manufacturing and Just-in-Time.

With recent reduction in auto-component tariffs and ongoing FTA negotiations, Indian auto-component manufacturers are concerned about the threat from imports. Table 14.5 shows that the ratio of imports to total production of auto components in India declined till 2002–2003, but it rose steeply in 2003–2004, when the Indo-Thailand FTA was implemented. This is partly due to the growing imports of auto components, on account of cost, by many Indian subsidiaries of global Original Equipment Manufacturers (OEMs) and even Indian OEMs. The ratio fell until 2007–2008, but rose again

Figure 14.5: Capacity Utilisation in Indian Automobile Industry

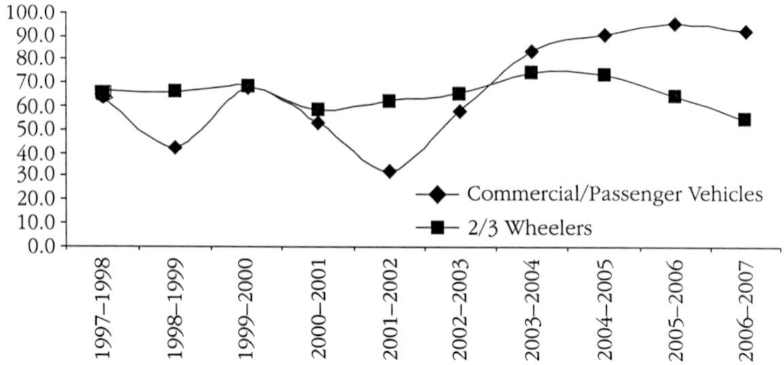

Source: SIAM (2009).

Note: Ratio of actual production to installed capacity, in number of vehicles.

Table 14.5: Import Content of Indian Auto Industry

Year	Domestic Production of Auto Components (US$ Million, Current Prices)	Imports of Auto Components (US$ Million, Current Prices)	Import/Total Auto Components (%)
1996–1997	3278	356.15	10.86
1997–1998	3008	258.49	8.59
1998–1999	3249	225.22	6.93
1999–2000	3894	315.57	8.1
2000–2001	3965	257.4	6.49
2001–2002	4470	258.93	5.79
2002–2003	5430	255.71	4.71
2003–2004	6730	616.28	9.16
2004–2005	8700	777.29	8.93
2005–2006	10000	820.39	8.2
2006–2007	15000	942.09	6.2
2007–2008	18000	1044.15	5.8
2008–2009	19100	1146.20	6.0

Source: Calculations from ACMA (2009) and DGFT (2009).

in 2008–2009. Hence, auto-component imports may partly substitute the domestic production.

Though India has the advantage of low labour costs, policy frameworks in other countries should be studied to ensure that our goods are not subject to unfair competition as a result of FTAs. However, this may not lead us to a conclusion that entry of MNCs to India is affecting the prospects of Indian auto-component industries, because of the fact that most of these MNCs play a vital role in upgrading the skills and technologies of the Indian auto-component manufacturers.

Figure 14.6 shows that export intensity (percentage of exports in output, both in ₹ crore at constant 1993–1994 prices) has been higher in the auto-component sector than in the automobile sector.[7] From about 12 per cent in 1999–2000, it has increased to 28 per cent in 2006–2007 in auto-component sector, but declined to about 20 per cent by 2008–2009, possibly due to the global economic crisis. It has increased from about 2.5 per cent in 1999–2000 to over 10 per cent in 2008–2009, in the automobile sector, exhibiting more sustained but slower growth. Even in terms of absolute value of exports (see Narayanan and Vashisht 2008) auto-component exports are almost as high as those of assembled units. Hence, even in terms of export-orientation, the auto-component sector is much more important than the automobile manufacturing sector.

Table 14.6 shows that the passenger car and two-wheeler segments are not only the most profitable segments of the Indian auto industry but their profitability is also higher than the profitability of many other industrial sectors of India. In contrast, the profitability of commercial vehicles segment is much lower.[8] Interestingly, despite the tariff reforms, the auto ancillaries segment has maintained

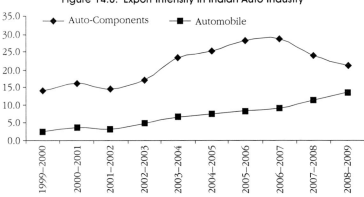

Figure 14.6: Export Intensity in Indian Auto Industry

Source: Calculations from SIAM (2009) ACMA (2009) CSO (1980–2004) DGFT (2010) and CMIE (2010).

Note: This is the percentage of exports in ₹ crore, in output in ₹ crore, at constant 1993–1994 prices.

Table 14.6: Profitability* of Selected Indian Industries

Industry	2004–2005	2005–2006	2006–2007
Machine tools	4.73	14.09	9.28
Generators, transformers and switchgears	7.14	8.84	9.07
Passenger cars and multiutility vehicles$	**6.07**	**7.26**	**8.95**
Material handling equipments	7.26	8.14	8.86
Industrial machinery	5.44	8.29	8.80
Electronics	–1.52	–0.35	8.35
Two-wheelers@	**9.05**	**9.92**	**8.10**
Food and beverages	5.61	5.42	7.94
Automobile ancillaries	**7.40**	**6.60**	**7.19**
Air-conditioners and refrigerators	–5.48	2.44	7.11
Textiles	0.14	3.77	5.62
Industrial furnaces	6.02	3.37	5.54
Chemicals	4.65	4.36	5.46
Commercial vehicles#	**5.48**	**6.34**	**5.30**
Wires and cables	–6.96	5.04	5.15
Dry cells and storage batteries	4.66	6.61	4.32
Miscellaneous. electrical machinery	–7.93	0.34	3.09
Domestic electrical appliances	–0.29	3.10	2.67

Source: CMIE, (2009).

Note: The industries are ranked according to their profitability in 2006–2007.
*Profitability is defined as profit after tax as ratio of sales.
#Tata motors is included in commercial vehicle manufacturers and not in passenger vehicle manufacturers.
@Combined profitability of top four two-wheelers, which account for more than 90 per cent market share.
$Combined profitability of five major passenger cars and utility manufacturers, which accounts for more than 85 per cent of market share.

a healthy profit rate, which indicates the growing competitiveness of this sector. Figures 14.7 and 14.8 show that both exports and imports have been rising sharply since around 2003–2004, despite the global economic crisis of 2008–2009.

3. Firm-level Performance Trends in Indian Auto Industry

Table 14.7 shows that growth rates of production and sales have been impressive for most of the two-/three-wheeler manufacturers in the recent years. However, it also suggests that despite the significant increase in size of domestic market, manufacturers such as Maharashtra Scooters, Kinetic Group and LML are bowing out to

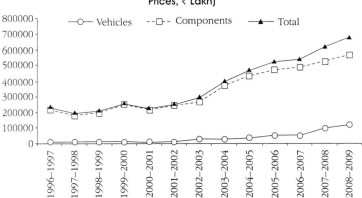

Figure 14.7: Exports of Indian Auto Industry (in Constant 1993–1994 Prices, in ₹ Lakh)

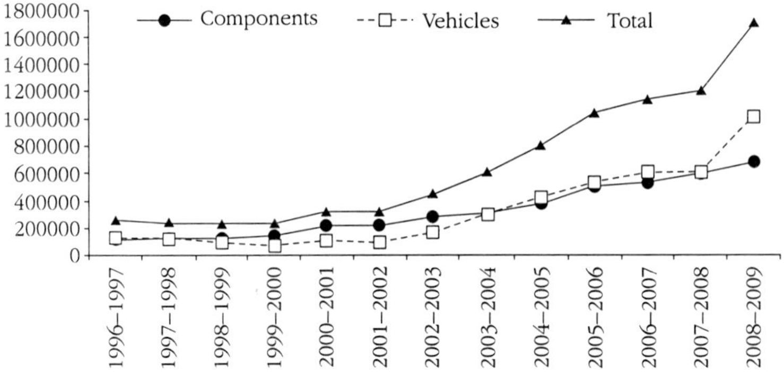

Source: Calculations from DGFT (2009).

Figure 14.8: Imports of Indian Auto Industry (in Constant 1993–1994 Prices, ₹ Lakh)

Source: Calculations from DGFT (2009).

firms such as Hero Honda and Bajaj Auto which source technology from Japanese firms.[9]

Inventories have been growing with sales and production for most players. Growth in emoluments has been mostly modest (negative for few) in comparison with the growth rates of sales, indicating the stringency of labour regulations. High growth of R&D expenses and investment can be seen in 1990s for some Indian companies partly due to the competitive environment. Though the growth trends in R&D expenses show a lot of dynamics, the actual share of R&D

Table 14.7: Percentage of Average Annual Growth Rates in Major Two-/Three-Wheeler Companies

Name of the Company	Period	Sales Growth	Output Growth	Inventory Growth	Emolument Growth	R&D Growth	Capital Growth	R&D as a % of Sales	Export as a % of Sales	Profit as a % of Sales
Atul Auto	1988–1995	N.A.	N.A.	N.A.	N.A.	N.A.	N.A.	0.00	0.00	9.45
	1996–2005	48.40	46.12	38.38	–66.67	25.56	33.86	0.01	0.19	5.13
Bajaj Auto	1988–1995	25.82	26.17	23.42	19.98	8.11	15.30	0.60	4.45	7.79
	1996–2005	12.57	13.08	5.19	14.83	4.32	9.31	1.02	7.38	12.79
Hero Honda Motors	1988–1995	29.23	28.11	35.92	19.30	20.48	14.70	0.08	2.25	4.08
	1996–2005	32.43	31.11	28.60	28.89	15.38	24.44	0.28	2.74	8.90
Kinetic Engineering	1988–1995	14.09	14.19	19.97	–50.25	8.44	16.25	1.00	4.66	4.27
	1996–2005	1.08	–1.02	5.26	15.35	11.33	9.32	1.46	6.76	–2.15
Kinetic Motor	1988–1995	21.98	21.88	26.46	348.00	28.67	14.20	0.10	4.85	2.14
	1996–2005	–1.67	–3.05	9.94	18.19	0.22	11.16	1.07	5.52	–1.63
LML	1988–1995	20.84	20.67	17.46	28.36	18.20	7.88	0.05	3.95	–0.69
	1996–2005	–8.61	–5.14	17.31	39.43	3.44	15.19	1.05	4.75	–2.82
Maharashtra Scooters	1988–1995	14.70	14.94	19.16	N.A.	13.05	8.06	0.00	0.00	7.72
	1996–2005	–16.65	–15.00	3.60	N.A.	27.99	8.78	0.00	0.00	7.30

Majestic Auto	1988–1995	35.34	32.84	25.97	−100.00	33.31	20.71	0.11	14.82	−1.35
	1996–2005	25.33	21.61	20.76	75.93	−5.00	9.75	0.53	13.86	−2.85
Scooters India	1988–1995	39.89	41.33	10.50	N.A.	13.86	1.50	0.00	4.78	−111.88
	1996–2005	8.01	8.66	8.82	12.22	6.23	6.22	0.14	0.77	8.74
TVS Motor Co.	1988–1995	22.63	22.39	17.42	38.93	10.35	15.48	0.39	3.00	2.39
	1996–2005	20.25	19.04	21.45	42.99	23.79	26.46	1.59	1.95	4.68
VCCL	1988–1995	−31.84	−34.79	−20.65	N.A.	−1.54	−0.17	0.00	6.04	−302.72
	1996–2005	95.79	133.65	−10.11	N.A.	−10.86	−0.44	0.00	0.00	652.26
Average	**1988–1995**	**19.09**	**18.56**	**17.57**	**45.99**	**14.97**	**11.78**	**0.23**	**4.49**	**−37.81**
	1996–2005	**19.81**	**22.48**	**13.89**	**20.95**	**10.05**	**13.49**	**0.60**	**3.99**	**57.47**

Source: Calculations from CMIE (2009) and Annual Reports of Companies.

Notes: 1. All values are in ₹ crore in current prices.

2. R&D Share, export share and profit share are the shares of R&D, export and profit expenses in total sales, respectively, in ₹ crore in current prices.

in the turnovers of different companies has not been rising very dramatically, with exceptions.

TVS and Hero Honda, firms with foreign collaboration, had high export shares of 2–7 per cent in this period. Hero Honda, Bajaj and Maharashtra Scooters have profit rates of 10–15 per cent in most of the period between 1988–1989 and 2005–2006. LML, Majestic Auto and Kinetic group faced losses for many years in this period, while TVS has been earning 0–5 per cent profits since the early 1990s, after suffering losses for two years before this. Other than Hyundai, most of the CV/PV manufacturers are less export-oriented than two-/three-wheeler manufacturers.

Table 14.8 shows the trends for major automobile companies, other than two-/three-wheeler manufacturers. The trends for the companies manufacturing merely Commercial Vehicles or CV (i.e., excluding Mahindra and Mahindra, M&M, and Tata Motors) are almost correlated and quite cyclical in nature. Production and capital grew with sales in most companies. However, inventories growth has always been quite high, though it has declined in a few years. Growth in R&D expenses is too low or negative compared to that in other indicators, but their share in sales has grown. Export shares of CV majors have been relatively lower and declining, indicating lack of interest or competitiveness in global arena or focus on domestic market conditions. Ashok Leyland is the only company which has been profitable during the entire period, while Eicher is the most profitable CV firm.

Most passenger vehicle companies have been performing well for the past few years. All foreign firms — Maruti, Honda Siel and Hyundai — have never seen a decline in sales in the period considered. Production growth trends are quite similar to these trends, but higher than those in sales, as confirmed by the higher growth rates of inventories for most companies. They have seen higher growth rates in emoluments. While few firms have seen huge decline in R&D expenditure in a few years, all companies have witnessed high growth rates for some years, which however, do not get translated much into dramatic increases in R&D expenditure as a share of turnover. There is a secular trend of growing capital for the past two decades in other auto manufacturers. Hyundai, a foreign firm, had an export share of 40 per cent in 2005–2006, while all other auto majors are far behind, with 0–10 per cent shares.

Table 14.8: Average Annual Growth Rates in Major Automobile Companies

Name of the Company	Period	Sales Growth	Output Growth	Inventory Growth	Emolument Growth	R&D Growth	Capital Growth	R&D as a % of Sales	Export as a % of Sales	Profit as a % of Sales
Ashok Leyland	1988–1995	22.80	24.30	20.88	22.34	-0.18	23.94	0.33	8.05	3.04
	1995–2005	12.71	13.32	11.53	10.04	8.57	7.97	0.90	7.92	3.60
Daewoo Motors	1988–1995	72.46	68.23	190.97	50.26	23.04	36.76	0.06	9.47	-3.27
	1995–2005	25.79	31.12	-16.28	25.57	139.75	158.27	2.58	18.26	-27.00
Eicher Motors	1988–1995	17.26	17.10	14.16	27.03	N.A.	17.65	0.00	4.19	1.02
	1995–2005	26.60	26.32	10.88	26.97	35.85	20.66	1.46	6.49	4.23
Force Motors	1988–1995	16.22	16.19	23.17	13.45	30.61	18.19	0.99	1.41	2.86
	1995–2005	6.01	6.27	4.23	10.15	-1.58	10.22	1.93	1.38	0.26
Hindustan Motors	1988–1995	13.01	13.28	8.60	12.89	-1.04	8.25	0.36	1.90	0.19
	1995–2005	-2.90	-3.19	0.27	-1.44	-1.43	4.96	0.47	3.61	-2.50
Honda Siel	1995–2005	22.23	26.40	11.62	18.21	48.26	8.53	0.18	0.57	-1.36
Hyundai	1995–2005	27.40	32.54	29.89	34.13	95.85	23.27	0.10	15.79	3.20
Mahindra	1988–1995	16.87	17.14	13.01	12.44	-21.24	17.54	0.05	3.95	2.80
	1995–2005	13.54	14.06	9.87	6.76	2.77	14.57	1.08	3.81	5.41

(Table 14.8 Continued)

(Table 14.8 Continued)

Name of the Company	Period	Sales Growth	Output Growth	Inventory Growth	Emolument Growth	R&D Growth	Capital Growth	R&D as a % of Sales	Export as a % of Sales	Profit as a % of Sales
Maruti Udyog	1988–1995	32.51	31.52	31.34	28.33	-1.68	30.95	0.05	8.77	3.54
	1995–2005	9.20	10.33	6.26	10.98	21.71	13.07	0.38	6.63	4.34
Pal–Peugeot	1988–1995	N.A.	N.A.	N.A.	N.A.	N.A.	N.A.	0.00	0.13	9.41
	1995–2005	36.63	37.08	156.04	131.21	N.A.	19.50	0.00	0.12	-29.30
Swaraj Mazda	1988–1995	12.00	12.61	17.08	16.49	N.A.	2.87	0.00	3.01	-1.02
	1995–2005	15.75	15.09	9.54	16.35	-2.76	8.31	0.30	4.96	2.63
Tata Motors	1988–1995	25.84	27.34	21.19	16.69	46.99	19.85	0.36	8.89	4.41
	1995–2005	14.07	13.79	8.55	7.71	7.72	12.07	1.47	8.62	2.79
Average	**1988–1995**	**25.44**	**25.30**	**37.82**	**22.21**	**10.93**	**19.56**	**0.24**	**5.52**	**1.51**
	1996–2005	**17.25**	**18.59**	**20.20**	**24.72**	**32.25**	**25.12**	**0.90**	**6.51**	**-2.81**

Source: Calculations from CMIE (2009) and Annual Reports of Companies.

Notes: 1. All values are in ₹ crore in current prices.

2. R&D Share, export share and profit share are the shares of R&D, export and profit expenses in total sales, respectively, in ₹ crore in current prices.

4. Price Indices of Automobiles

Figures 14.9 and 14.10 show that the Wholesale Price Index (WPI)[10] of automobiles was almost identical to the WPI of all commodities, till 1991–1992. Since 1992–1993, WPI of automobiles has risen at a lower rate than that of all commodities, and the gap between these two WPIs has become conspicuously wide by 2008–2009. Prices have fallen for cars in 2002–2003 and motorcycles in 2001–2003, thanks to the cuts in excise duties. All WPIs have moved together from 1993–1994 to 2000–2001, but the WPIs of all the automobile segments have been consistently lower than those of all commodities. After 2001–2002, WPIs of trucks and buses have been rising faster than that of cars and motorcycles but at a lower rate than the index for all commodities.

Comparing the growth of auto prices with growth in real per capita GDP, we find that auto prices had been growing at much higher rate than per capita income in the 1970s (Figure 14.11). However, the differential has been falling drastically since the early 1990s, and this has been negative persistently since 2001–2002. This means that compared to the rate at which India's real per capita income has been growing faster than real auto prices, due to tariff cuts in 1990s and huge volumes accumulated by many auto majors, as reflected in the analysis of growth trends in inventories. Increased competition, thanks to the massive FDIs taking place since mid-1990s, could also have driven this.

5. Role of Foreign Equity Participation

Foreign Equity (FE) participation may affect the structural features and performance of the Indian auto companies. Equity participation of foreign promoters could have enhanced efficiency and technologies, but they could also have made the Indian industry more dependent on their countries of origin, in terms of imports from supplier-base in their country. They could also have come to India, viewing it as more of a market base, rather than a production base to cater to their global requirements. Since these companies are more capital-intensive and automation-oriented, their workers may lose jobs.

Figure 14.12 shows that while both exports and imports are more prominent among automobile firms that have higher equity participation, import content is much higher than export share in sales

Figure 14.9: WPIs of Automobiles and All Commodities (Base Year: 1981–1982)

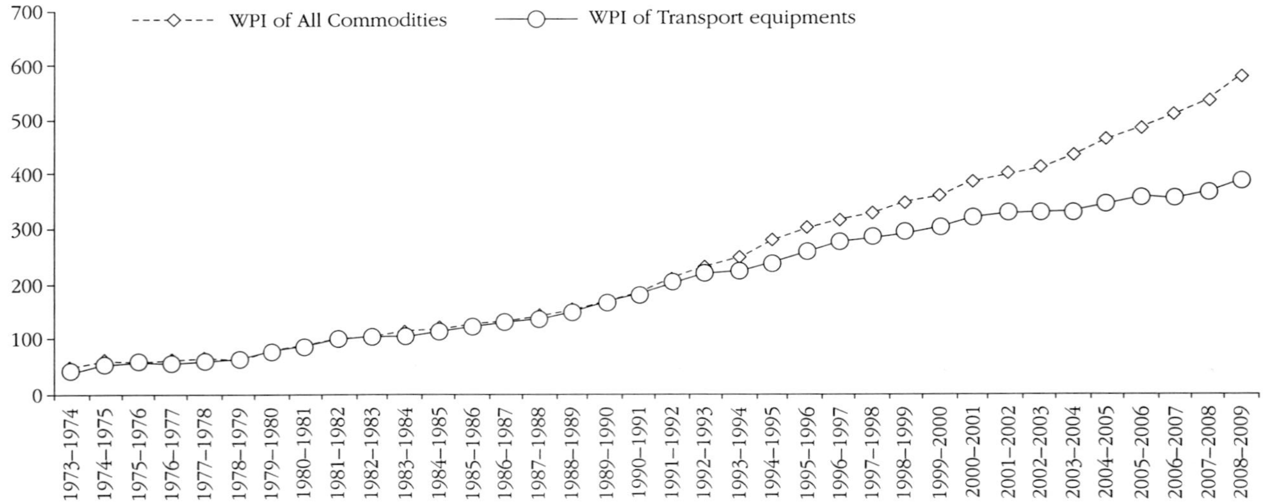

- - - ◇ - - - WPI of All Commodities   —○— WPI of Transport equipments

Source: Office of Economic Advisor (2009).

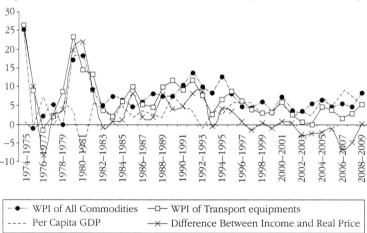

Figure 14.10: WPIs of Different Segments in Automobiles (Base Year: 1993–1994)

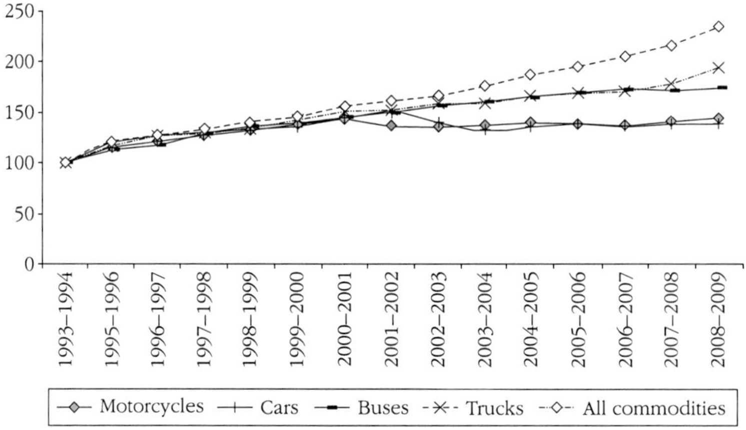

◆— Motorcycles ─┼─ Cars ─■─ Buses -✳- Trucks -◇- All commodities

Source: Office of Economic Advisor (2009)

Figure 14.11: Growth Rates of WPIs of Automobiles (Base Year: 1981–1982)

-●- WPI of All Commodities ─□─ WPI of Transport equipments
---- Per Capita GDP ─✕─ Difference Between Income and Real Price

Source: Calculations from Office of Economic Advisor (2009) and RBI (2009).

for firms that have 75–100 per cent FE. R&D expenditure share in total sales appears to be declining in the automobile industry, with a rise in foreign equity participation. This is probably because of the fact that most of the foreign firms have R&D facility in their parent country. R&D cost share remains almost invariant with respect to FE

316 + Badri Narayanan G. and Pankaj Vashisht

Figure 14.12: Role of Foreign Equity Participation in Indian Auto Industry (2000–2001 to 2005–2006)

1a) Exports and Imports in Automobile Assembly

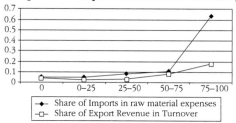

X-Axis: % Equity Share of Foreign Promoters

1b) Exports and Imports in Auto-components

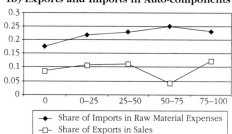

X-Axis: % Equity Share of Foreign Promoters

2a) R&D and Fuel Costs in Automobile Assembly

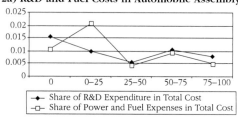

X-Axis: % Equity Share of Foreign Promoters

2b) R&D and Fuel Costs in Auto-components

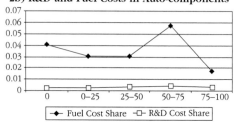

X-Axis: % Equity Share of Foreign Promoters

(Figure 14.12 Continued)

(*Figure 14.12 Continued*)

3a) Emolument Cost Share in Automobile Assembly

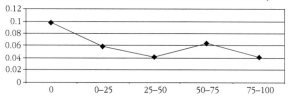

X-Axis: % Equity Share of Foreign Promoters
Y-Axis: Share of emolument costs in total costs

3b) Emolument Cost Share in Auto-components

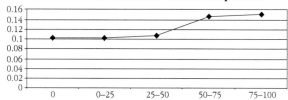

X-Axis: % Equity Share of Foreign Promoters
Y-Axis: Share of emolument costs in total costs

4a) Inventories Cost Share in Automobile Assembly

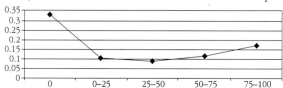

X-Axis: % Equity Share of Foreign Promoters
Y-Axis: Share of inventory costs in total costs

4b) Inventories Cost Share in Auto-components

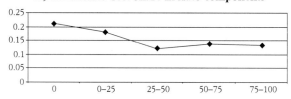

X-Axis: % Equity Share of Foreign Promoters
Y-Axis: Share of inventory costs in total costs

Source: Calculations from CMIE (2009).
Note:　All shares were calculated from values in ₹ crore at current prices, averaged across the firms in the corresponding segment for the period from 2000–2001 to 2005–2006

participation in auto-component firms. Fuel cost share does fall with a higher FE in both automobile and auto-component sectors.

Emoluments' share in total costs falls in automobile firms with higher FE, perhaps because of the fact that most of the foreign OEMs in India have high levels of automation. However, it increases with FE for auto-component firms, indicating that foreign auto-component firms probably want to exploit the low-cost advantage of Indian labour. Higher FE participation corresponds to lower inventory share, which is attributable to better market research, production planning and efficiency of the foreign auto firms in India.

6. Conclusion

FDI has had mostly positive impacts on various aspects of Indian auto industry, mainly through increased competition and improved technologies. All the productivity measures and international trade have been growing for all sub-sectors in the entire auto industry in India, ever since FDI was allowed in this sector. Profitability and market concentration are falling after FDI inflows started pouring in due to increased competition. The ratio of the import of the auto-components to the auto components produced in India has risen, indicating that this sector may face threats from cheaper imports. This could also be because of the higher quality and technology requirements of some foreign firms in India.

There seems to exist a link between equity shares of foreign promoters and performance/nature of an auto firm. Foreign firms in vehicle manufacturing export and import more, as a share of sales, while there is no such clear trend for component firms. The share of R&D in total cost is lower for foreign firms, hinting at lack/absence of their R&D activities in India. Still, their better technical performance could be inferred from lower fuel cost share for foreign vehicle manufacturers. While foreign vehicle manufacturers have lower shares of emoluments in their total costs than Indian firms, foreign component manufacturers have emolument shares comparable to Indian ones. Foreign firms have lower inventories.

In real terms, the growth in prices of automobiles has been lower than the per capita GDP growth in India over the past three decades, while the rise in auto prices has been lower than rise in the aggregate price of all commodities since the 1990s, possibly because of high growth rates of inventories of auto companies,[11] lower tariffs and higher domestic competition that followed the reforms since 1991 and intense competition from foreign firms thanks to the increased FDI limit since 1993. All these conclusions indicate that FDIs have been playing a positive role in Indian auto industry.

The main policy implication of this study is that FDIs should be promoted further in all sub-sectors of Indian auto industry in order to improve productivity and technologies. However, the exact promotional measures are beyond the scope of this study. While some of the investment in the automobiles sector has been tariff-escalating due to the high tariffs in those sectors, most of the investment in the auto-component sector has been due to the expanded market arising from foreign automobile firms and global sourcing of auto components from India. Currently, the tariffs are lower for auto component than for automobiles sector (Narayanan and Vashisht 2008). Further lowering of tariffs in automobiles sector would be a step towards attracting genuine FDI and not merely the tariff-escalating ones. In other words, the tariff reduction in automobiles sector should follow the suit of that in auto-component sector in the recent past, in order to ensure that FDIs benefit the auto industry directly.

Notes

1. RBI's Annual Policy Statement documents an annual growth of 37.9 per cent in credit flow to vehicles industry in 2006. But the subsequent monetary tightening and hike in interest rates would have adversely affected the vehicle demand more recently. Total outstanding consumer durable loans declined by around 11.8 per cent year on year in November 2009.
2. Two-wheeler segment has been growing at 10 per cent per annum. Passenger car segment has been growing at a rapid pace — from over 650,000 vehicles sold during 2001 to over a million vehicles sold during 2004–2005. Diversity in preferences has also risen (Veloso and Kumar 2002).
3. When global auto majors invest in India, their preferred suppliers elsewhere in the world are also encouraged entering India as the wholly-owned subsidiaries of these suppliers. This phenomenon is called 'follow-source'.

4. HHI of a segment is the sum of squares of market shares of the companies in the segment. We calculated this based on the firm sample available in CMIE Prowess database, taking imports as an independent entity, based on CMIE Indiatrades database. For auto-component firms, our sample consists of 228 firms comprising 70 per cent of the total sales in the auto-component segment. The sample consists of 14 and 12 firms, respectively, in the two-/three-wheelers and other automobiles segment, comprising over 90 per cent of total sales in each of these segments.

5. However, it should be noted here that the firms covered in this analysis do not comprise their respective segments in totality, and to that extent these estimates are expected to have an upward bias, implying that market concentration is slightly lower than what is illustrated here. Nevertheless, this analysis shows the trends in market concentration using a time-consistent sample.

6. RBI'S 2008–2009 Annual Report shows that capacity utilisation of Indian automobile industry as a whole had been 81.4 and 78.5 per cent in 2007–2008 and 2008–2009, respectively, indicating further decline most recently.

7. Since labour cost is lower in India and the auto-component sector is labour-intensive, it is probably advantageous to export them from India.

8. It is worth to mention that the profitability of Tata Motors is significantly higher than the other commercial vehicle manufacturers. It may be because of its presence in passenger car segment, which is more profitable as compared to commercial vehicle segment.

9. Hero Honda is sourcing the up-to-date technology from Honda Motors, while Bajaj has acquired technology from Kawasaki from time to time.

10. WPI is calculated with the base year of 1981–1982, which means that all prices considered herein are in real terms, as they have been deflated by the price level of the year 1981–1982.

11. On an average, inventories have grown at the average annual rates of 14 and 20 per cent for two-/three-wheelers manufacturers and other vehicle manufacturers, respectively, during 1996–2005.

References

Automotive Components Manufacturers Association (ACMA). (2006). 'Indian Automotive Component Industry: Engine of Growth Driving the Indian Manufacturing Sector'. http://acmainfo.com/docmgr/Statusof Auto Industry/Status_Indian_Auto_Industry.pdf (accessed 10 December 10 2006).
———. 2009. 'Industry Statistics'. New Delhi. http://www.acmainfo.com/ industry_stat.htm (accessed 8 January 2010).

Central Statistical Office (CSO). 1974–2004. 'Annual Survey of Industry'. Delhi: Ministry of Statistics and Programme Implementation.

Central Statistical Office (CSO). 1980–2004. 'Annual Surveys of Industries (1979–1980 to 2003–2004)'. Delhi: Ministry of Statistics and Programme Implementation.

———. (2001–2004). 'Annual Survey of Industry'. Delhi: Ministry of Statistics and Programme Implementation.

Center for Monitoring Indian Economy (CMIE). 2009. 'Prowess Database'. http://www.cmie.com/database/?service=database-products/firm-level-data-services/prowess (accessed 10 December 2009).

———. 2010. 'IndiaTrades database'. http://www.cmie.com/database/?service=database-products/sectoral-services/india-trades.htm (accessed 10 December 2009).

Director General of Foreign Trade (DGFT). 2009. 'Import Export Data Bank', Ministry of Commerce, New Delhi. http://dgftcom.nic.in/ (accessed on 8 January 2010).

Doukas, J. A. and L. H. P. Lang. 2003. 'Foreign Direct Investment, Diversification and Firm Performance', *Journal of International Business Studies* 34 (2): 153–72.

Gopinath, M., D. Pick and U. Vasavada. 1999. 'The Economics of Foreign Direct Investment and Trade with an Application to the US Food Processing Industry', *American Journal of Agricultural Economics*, 81 (2): 442–52.

Humphrey, J. 1999. 'Globalisation and Supply Chain Networks: The Auto Industry in Brazil and India', in G. Gereffi, F. Palpacuer and A. Parisotto (eds), *Global Production and Local Jobs*. Geneva: International Institute for Labour Studies.

Kathuria, S. 1996. *Competing through Technology and Manufacturing: A Study of the Indian Commercial Vehicles Industry*. New Delhi: Oxford University Press,

Miller, R. R. and D. R. Weigel. 1972. 'The Motivation for Foreign Direct Investment', *Journal of International Business Studies*, 3 (2): 67–79.

Ministry of Commerce. (2005–2009). 'India FDI Fact Sheet', Department of Industrial Policy and Promotion (DIPP). http://www.dipp.nic.in/fdi_statistics/india_fdi_index.htm (accessed on 8 January 2010).

Ministry of Heavy Industries and Public Enterprises. 2006a. *Automotive Mission Plan 2006-2016: A Mission for Development of Indian Automotive Industry*. New Delhi: Ministry of Heavy Industries and Public Enterprises.

———. 2006b. *Report of Working Group on Automotive Industry for the Eleventh Five-Year Plan*. New Delhi: Ministry of Heavy Industries and Public Enterprises.

Narayanan, K. 1998. 'Technology Acquisition, De-regulation and Competitiveness: A Study of Indian Automobile Industry', *Research Policy*, 27 (2): 215–28.

Narayanan, K. 2004. 'Technology Acquisition and Growth of Firms: Indian Automobile Sector under Changing Policy Regimes', *Economic and Political Weekly*, 39 (6): 461–70.

Narayanan, Badri G. and Pankaj Vashisht. 2008. 'Determinants of Competitiveness of Indian Auto industry', Working Paper No. 201. New Delhi: Indian Council for Research on International Economic Relations.

National Manufacturing Competitiveness Council (NMCC). 2006. 'The National Strategy for Manufacturing', National Manufacturing Competitiveness Council, Government of India, New Delhi.

Office of Economic Advisor. 2009. 'Wholesale Price Index', Ministry of Commerce and Industry. http://eaindustry.nic.in/ (accessed 8 January 2010).

Organisation Internationale des Constructeurs d'Automobiles (OICA). 2006. 'World's Automotive Industry: Some Key Figures', Organisation Internationale des Constructeurs d'Automobiles. http://www.oica.net/htdocs/ Main.htm (accessed 10 December 2006).

Patibandla, M. and A. Sanyal. 2000. 'Foreign Investment and Productivity: A Study of Post-reform Indian Industry', Working Paper, Department of International Economics and Management Copenhagen Business School, Frederiksberg, Denmark.

Pingle, V. 2000. *Rethinking the Developmental State: India's Industry in Comparative Perspective*. New Delhi: Oxford University Press.

Piplai, T. 2001. 'Automobile Industry: Shifting Strategic Focus', *Economic and Political Weekly*, 36 (30): 2892–97.

Porterie, B. P. and F. Lichtenberg 2001. 'Does Foreign Direct Investment Transfer Technology across Borders?', *The Review of Economics and Statistics*, 83 (3): 490–97.

Reserve Bank of India (RBI). 2009. *Handbook of Statistics on Indian Economy*. http://www.rbi.org.in/scripts/AnnualPublications.aspx?head=Handbook+of+Statistics+on+Indian+Economy (accessed 8 January 2010).

Safarian, A. E. 1973. 'Perspectives on FDI from the Viewpoint of a Capital Receiving Country', *The Journal of Finance*, 28 (2): 419–38.

Sasidharan 2006. 'Foreign Direct Investment and Technology Spillovers: Evidence from the Indian Manufacturing Sector', UNU-MERIT Working Paper No. 2006-010, Maastricht, The Netherlands.

Society of Indian Automobile Manufacturers (SIAM). 2006. *The Indian Automobile Industry: Statistical Profile 2005–06*. New Delhi: Society of Indian Automobile Manufacturers.

———. 2009. 'Profile of Indian Auto Industry'. New Delhi: Society of Indian Automobile Manufacturers.

Sutton, J. 2000. 'The Globalisation Process: Auto-Component Supply Chains in China and India', World Bank Report. http://personal.lse.ac.uk/sutton/auto_component_printroom_version3.pdf (accessed 10 December 2006).

Tewari, M. 2000. 'Engaging the New Global Interlocutors: Foreign Direct Investment and the Re-shaping of Local Productive Capabilities in Tamil Nadu's Automotive Supply Sector'. http://www.ids.ac.uk/ids/global/pdfs/ tewari.pdf (accessed 10 December 2006).

Veloso, F. and R. Kumar. 2002. 'The Automotive Supply Chain: Global Trends and Asian Perspectives', Economics and Research Department Working Paper Series No. 3. Manila: Asian Development Bank.

Part 5

Some Legal and Other Economic Issues of the WTO Process

15

Escape Clauses under WTO: Complementary or Contradictory to the Liberalisation of International Trade in Goods

Mohammad Alhihi

Exceptions to the General Agreement on Trade and Tariff (GATT) allow members to intervene in the working mechanism of international trade rules by limiting full adherence to such rules under certain circumstances and conditions. For the most part, the exceptions are incorporated to create a logical balance between national social aims and international trade commitments to protect countries from sudden or illegitimate trade practices of other members (Barber et al. 2004). This is because international trade in goods has direct and indirect impacts on all aspects of life in all countries including social, legal, cultural, economic development, diplomatic affairs and security. At the same time, international trade competition is not always in harmony with these aspects, and they sometimes need to be protected by the national governments through national measures (Bossche 2005).

Based on their aims, the GATT exceptions could be categorised into three groups. They include, first, injury protection exceptions designed to limit economic damage to national industries related to the unusual flow of imported goods or unfair trade practices of exporting countries. Second, financial support exceptions intended to improve national productivity through national programmes of subsidies. And third, preferential trade exceptions to restrict the globalised application of international trade rules by enabling the development of small trading blocs between countries with shared economic interests.

Practically, the GATT exceptions have become real threats to the aims of globalising international trade in goods and sources of international trade disputes over Non-tariff Trade Barriers (NTBs).[1]

Mostly the problems with the exceptions are related to their unreasonable application; the justification of massive agricultural subsidies in developed countries; and the formulation of many Preferential Trade Agreements (PTAs) as limitations to the global application of international trade rules. Generally, the exceptions under the GATT have become ways for WTO members to escape the fulfilment of their obligations under international trade rules. Developing countries in particular suffer most from the negative impacts of the GATT exceptions because their weak economies and low level of development do not help them to use the exceptions productively.

The following discussion deals with selected examples of the GATT exceptions, which are the general exceptional restrictions, preferential trade agreements, quantitative restrictions, safeguard measures, subsidy measures and security measures. The discussion highlights the advantages and disadvantages of the exceptions, but the focus is to explain how the measures have become sources of unreasonable kinds of NTBs to international trade in goods.

General Exceptions under Article XX

Article XX of the GATT permits countries to restrict international trade in goods in different cases, such as to protect public morals, human, animal or plant life and health, and the environment. The key condition to apply the exceptions is that the measures do not constitute a means of arbitrary or unjustifiable discrimination between countries, where the same conditions prevail. However, the exceptions under Article XX could lead to the violation of the fundamental objects of the GATT, which could create an imbalance between the obligations and the rights under WTO. This is because exceptions are general and broad which can justify reasonable as well as unreasonable national restriction measures in forms of NTBs (Oxley and Osborne 2002). For example, Article XX(a) allows countries to restrict imports of goods on the ground of protecting public morals. However, the agreement does not provide an explanation to define 'morality' as a condition in international trade. For instance, public morals in Islamic states which forbid alcohol and pork differ from public morals on those issues in western countries or India. The problem with providing elastic exceptions like 'protecting public morals' is that they might lead to a variety of interpretations and, as a result, to countless ways of restricting the importation of different goods (Bhala 2004).

The exceptions under Article XX have caused various trade disputes when countries attempted to use them to legitimise their NTBs. Usually, countries apply Article XX on the grounds of protection to human, animal and plant health and safety, and the environment. However, many of these disputes claim scientific evidence of threats to safety or health, as in the *EU-hormone dispute*.[2] Some of the disputes might have legitimate justifications, such as scientific data, but the same measures are not applied in the same way on national products, and countries use this GATT exception to legitimise their protection to national products. An example is the *US –Gasoline dispute*.[3] There is no doubt that low quality gasoline is a health hazard, but the US did not apply the same measures on similar national products; rather, its aim was to limit the importation of gasoline from other countries (WTO 2007).

Another problem with Article XX is the phrase 'necessary to balance the adoption of its exceptions'. The Article does not include any explanation or definition of the level of necessity that justifies the adoption of any of its exceptions. Moreover, the lack of sufficient explanation will lead each member to interpret the necessity according to its interest as it was highlighted during the *Thailand-cigarettes dispute*.[4] Thailand applied restrictions on imported cigarettes and justified the restrictions on the basis that the imported cigarettes were more harmful to human health than national cigarettes.[5] However, Thailand's action was regarded by the dispute panel as protection to the national cigarette industry, which breached Article XX(b) of the GATT. The protection was achieved by making nationally produced cigarettes cheaper for consumers than imported ones.

In conclusion, Article XX of the GATT is an area of concern because it has many general exceptions which can be used to justify many unreasonable kinds of NTBs. Consequently, countries could use the general exceptions to achieve illegitimate trade benefits from waiving their obligations for short-term benefits. The other negative outcome of the general exceptions under Article XX is that they are a rich source of the increasing load of the Dispute Settlement Body (DSB) and it extends the time of solving trade disputes, which would in turn reduce the efficiency of the dispute settlement process as whole. It is highly recommended that these exceptions be defined clearly and surrounded with clear limitations to prevent their exaggerated use as unfair trade restriction tools, and to limit their application to the minimum level backed by comprehensive and concrete evidence.

Preferential Trade Agreements under Article XXIV

Article XXIV of the GATT allows two or more members of the WTO to arrange different forms of regional and bilateral PTAs. The formation of PTAs could take the shape of customs unions, as in the case of the EU; free trade agreements as in the case of the North American Free Trade Agreement (NAFTA); or bilateral closer partnership arrangements such as that between Australia and New Zealand (AANZFTA). According to the WTO database, between 1948 and 1994 the GATT received 124 notifications of PTAs, but notifications increased sharply after the establishment of the WTO (WTO 2009). Up to December 2008, the number of notifications reached 421. Additionally, about 400 established and proposed PTAs have not been notified to the WTO (ibid.).

The arranged agreements could cover many economic and trade activities, and they grant favoured market access conditions to the parties to the agreements, including special conditions for importing each product, the level of tariff reduction, and the trade position of non-parties (WTO 2007). According to the preamble of understanding of Article XXIV under the WTO, the endorsement of such arrangements would increase the liberalisation of international trade between countries that are geographically adjoined, have close economic ties and share similar cultures and traditions. Some literature also favoured PTAs as an ideal method to benefit trade liberalisation between certain groups in the short term and better than the normal applications for the multilateral working of international trade as a whole (Glania 2006).

The main theoretical conditions for balancing the relationship between the adoption of PTAs and adherence to the obligations under WTO agreements are: (a) the trade barriers against non-members of the PTAs should not be increased or worsen compared with its status prior to the creation of the new PTAs; and (b) the WTO must be informed of all arrangements and conditions under the new PTAs and such agreements must be transparent and available to all members of the WTO as stated in Article XXIV of the GATT (WTO 2005).

Literatures criticised the exceptions of PTAs because they regard such exceptions as departure from the aim of unity of the international marketplace, and contradiction of the Most Favoured Nation (MFN) rules of the GATT and other WTO agreements (Islam 2006). In other words, Article XXIV allows countries to limit their compliance with the non-discrimination rules of the GATT (Lockhart and Mitchell 2005). This is because these arrangements aim to limit the application of the principles of MFN and other favoured conditions within mini-trade regimes between the signatories of the PTAs, and exclude all other members of the WTO who are not partners of the same PTAs (Islam 2006). For example, the geographic justification to form PTAs is no longer an important condition after the massive developments in technology, communication and transportation. Consequently, countries from different regions are arranging many PTAs, such as that between Jordan and the US where the traditional incentives for PTAs do not apply between these countries.

It is true that some PTAs would in certain cases improve the economic relationship between their partners. The benefit is related to the development of favoured trade conditions in the short term, compared with the international application of the MFN, which works on a long-term basis (ibid.: 2006). Nevertheless, the real benefits of PTAs for the parties depend on their tariff level, export capacities and the prices between the members (Asafu-Adjaye and Mahadevan 2009). In the case of PTAs between developed and developing countries, developing countries would not achieve real trade benefits. This is because economically weak countries lack the capacity to limit their trade balance problems (ibid.). In the case of traditional goods, developing countries face many NTBs related to the technical requirements of the developed countries. Developing countries also cannot use this exception to develop strong and sustainable PTAs among themselves to gain more trade benefits. This is because developing countries have inefficient economic policies, weak industries and regard the markets of developed countries as targets for their goods.

Most PTAs promote adherence to international rules and principles relating to technical requirements, conformity assessments and standards, but at the same time these arrangements include the condition of excluding international rules when they are ineffective or inappropriate to achieve the objects of given arrangements (Lesser 2007). This condition creates a doubt about the efficiency of international standards to deal with international trade in goods. The question here is how will a group of countries be able through PTAs to develop effective technical rules, while major international standards organisations cannot? Another example of marginalising technical rules of international trade is when the members of a PTA exclude the Technical Barriers to Trade Agreement from the application of dispute settlement procedures between the PTA's members. This has happened in PTAs between Chile and Korea, Singapore and Panama, and Mexico and Singapore (Lesser 2007).

In practice, countries in different instances have used the PTA exceptions to justify their trade impediments against non-members. For example, Turkey has a customs union with the EU (ATC) and claimed that it had the right to adopt quantitative measures against countries that are not part of that union (Bossche 2005). During *Turkey-Textiles* dispute,[6] Turkey did not deny that its quantitative restriction measures against imported textiles and clothing from India were inconsistent with Articles XI and XIII of the GATT and Article 2.4 of the *Agreement on Textiles and Clothing.* However, Turkey claimed that its measures were justified under Article XXIV (WTO 2007). In the end, the Panel decided and the Appellate Body (AB) confirmed the decision in favour of India because the restrictions were new measures and did not exist during the establishment of the ATC (ibid.). Additionally, the AB in this dispute expressed the view that Article XXIV:5 could be used to justify inconsistent measures necessary to the formation of a customs union, but it did not explain the extent of that necessity (Lockhart and Mitchell 2005). The report of the dispute included some alternative measures such as the rule of origin, which can be implemented by Turkey under Article XXIV 8(a)(i) of the GATT to restrict textile and clothing imports from India (AB report, para 62). Therefore, rules of origin can be used as discriminatory trade tools to restrict goods from non-members of PTAs.

Overall, PTAs are unreasonable exceptions to the rules and principles of the GATT and reflect a decreasing interest in the real liberalisation of international trade in goods by allowing countries to develop mini-trade regimes with their own set of trade rules and conditions. These rules and conditions may be different from and inconsistent with international trade rules. This is because inter-national trade rules are designed to benefit all countries, while the rules of mini-trade regimes are designed to suit and benefit certain countries (Lesser 2007). Consequently, the differences could lead to new kinds of NTBs where each PTA aims to limit trade restrictions between its members and prevent other countries from using its favoured conditions, which is against the WTO aim of creating one global market. Each PTA has its own rules and requirements and when one country is a member of more than one PTA, it has to meet different requirements, which could constitute new NTBs or increase the cost of imported goods (Watson, and Do 2006). Another negative impact of spreading PTAs is the reduction of the legal value of the WTO and the weakening of the responses of some members to decisions of the Dispute Settlement System (DSS) of the WTO. This is because a member which is party to a PTA would depend on the trade benefits that would be gained from their Regional Trade Agreement (RTA) definition partners without giving much concern to the trade benefits which may be gained from trade with all other members of the WTO.

Quantitative Restrictions under Article XI

Article XI of the GATT opens its first paragraph with a general state-ment that members are not allowed to use quantitative restrictions against imports or exports through any type of measure. However, the second paragraph of Article XI has many exceptions that allow members to impose Quantitative Restrictions (QRs) on imported goods. Examples of that are temporary restrictions to prevent critical shortages of foodstuffs and restrictions necessary to apply standards for commodities or agricultural or fisheries products. The theoretical condition of applying those restrictions is that their application has to be on a non-discriminatory basis between all members of the WTO. However, countries have used the exceptions under Article XI to justify their quantitative restrictions, causing various trade disputes, such as *India-Autos*[7] and *India-Quantitative restrictions*.[8]

In the *India-Autos* dispute, India tried to base part of its arguments on Article XI to defend quantitative restrictions on the import of automotive components through licensing measures to achieve a trade balance. The Panel finding was that the Indian measures violated GATT Article XI, and were not justified for balance-of-payment reasons.[9] In the *India-Quantitative restrictions dispute*, India again used the argument of dealing with balance of trade problems. The Panel found that the general condition in Article XI of the GATT was not met by India. This is because India breached Article XI:1 when it applied quantitative restrictions through a licensing system designed to deal with balance of trade problems (WTO 2007).

In order to minimise the negative impacts of exceptions under Article XI on the international trade in goods, the DSB stated in different disputes that the exceptions must be interpreted narrowly.[10] However, the objection to Article XI remains that its exception operates on agricultural trade and is used to justify the majority of trade restrictions in this sector (Islam 2006). For example, Article XI:2(b) justifies imposing QRs by the application of standards, regulations classification, grading or marketing commodities in the international market. Such exceptions are a complete violation of the obligations under section one of the Article.

Safeguard Measures under Article XIX

Article XIX authorises WTO members to safeguard their national industries from the flow of certain imported goods in special circumstances. The justification for applying safeguard measures is the sharp increase in the flow of imported goods above normal quantities associated with unforeseen developments in the international market, which cause or may cause serious injury or threat of injury to the national industries in importing countries. Article 6 of the 'Agreement on Safeguards' defines safeguard measures as emergency and temporary actions. They include measures such as imposing quantitative import restrictions, quotas for each exporting country and tariff-rate quotas, as well as increases to tariff rate, and they may be imposed for a maximum duration of four years. Importing countries are also allowed in critical situations of undoubted injury to national industries to apply safeguard measures rapidly and provisionally before concluding safeguard investigations.

Article XIX of the GATT has a significant problem, namely, the justification for the adoption of extraordinary action by way of trade restrictions when the flow of imported goods increases without artificial interference or unfair trade practices by exporting countries. The stringency of safeguard measures was confirmed in *US-Line Pipe dispute*.[11] The AB stated that safeguard actions are in fact extraordinary actions and do not depend on unfair trade practices by exporting countries to trigger their application.[12] In practice, the exceptions under Article XIX contradict the WTO's main aim of liberalising international trade in goods by creating unrestricted market access for various imported products. In other words, Article XIX is not in harmony with the general fabric of the rules of international trade liberalisation, because the exceptions under this Article produce justifications for many kinds of NTBs, which could lead to substantial reductions to the flow of imported goods. Significantly, safeguard measures disturb the benefit of international trade for members which do fulfill their obligations toward the WTO by adhering to international trade rules (Bossche 2005).

Some literature has tried to relate the existence of Article XIX to economic and political factors (Wilson 1998). The economic ground relies on the idea that when the individual members of the WTO fulfill their obligations according to the rules of the WTO and open their markets for imports, they should not be punished by exporting countries when the importation reaches a stage that could damage national industries of the importing partners. According to the economic justifications, the GATT gives the countries that are being injured the right to restrict the flow of imported goods and provides importing countries with the time to readjust to the new development in the international market within a specific period of time, which may extend to eight years (Article 7:3 of the 'Agreement on Safeguards'). However, under the rules of the GATT and the 'Agreement on Safeguards' there is no working mechanism to observe the way that importing countries use the time during the adoption of safeguard measures. Moreover, it is highly possible that the eight-year period will be used as a trade protection tool and not for the adjustment to the new unforeseen development in the international market and to new productivity trends in global economies (Islam 2006).

The political ground behind Article XIX, which would be more relevant, is related to the interests and concerns of powerful countries as the main players in international trade and politics. Those countries would not have accepted the current rules of trade liberalisation without having loopholes to evade their obligations when it is necessary to protect their national industries and to satisfy the desire of their national economic lobbies (Wilson 1998). These countries often apply safeguard exceptions against imported goods, especially agricultural and textile products from developing countries. Theoretically, Article 9 of the 'Agreement on Safeguards' excludes developing countries exports from the application of safeguard measures if the share of a certain country's export of relevant product to a certain market is less than 3 per cent. However, agricultural products from major developing countries could easily exceed that percentage, which will trigger the application of safeguard measures if injury in importing markets takes place.

Safeguard rules have another problem related to the unrestricted choice of the appropriate action to restrict the flow of imported goods, which could lead to their unfair use as safeguard exceptions. Safeguard rules do not have sufficient restraints to guarantee that importing countries would choose measures with the least trade restriction. This is a problem because both investigations and assessment procedures are controlled by the national authorities of the importing countries without interference from independent authorities. The national authorities are in a position to choose the actions that may give the maximum level of protection, with the possibility of extending the time for applying them for up to eight years.

In practice, many countries have applied safeguard measures without real compliance with non-discrimination and illegitimate trade protection obligations. For example, during *Argentina-Footwear* dispute[13] it was highlighted that Argentina breached the rules of MFN, and Article 2:3 of the 'Agreement on Safeguards' in particular, during its application of the safeguard exception (WTO 2007). The Panel found and AB confirmed that Argentina excluded Brazil, Paraguay and Uruguay as members of the Southern Common Market (MERCOSUR)[14] from the application of safeguard measures on the import of footwear (ibid.).

The illegitimate application of safeguard measures as a trade protection tool is usually related to the unreasonable way importing countries use the condition of unforeseen trade development to justify their import restrictions. For example, in the *US-Lamb* dispute,[15] it was found that the US had violated Article XIX of the GATT and Article 4 of the 'Agreement on Safeguards'. The US authorities could not confirm that actual serious injury had occurred in respect of lamb meat in its national market. However, the US used the unforeseen development condition to limit the increase of imported meat from Australia and New Zealand through tariff rate quotas (ibid.: 2008). In the *US-Steel Safeguard* dispute,[16] the US safeguard measures on different kinds of steel products from many countries were held to be inconsistent with Article XIX of the GATT 2.1, 3.1 of the 'Agreement on Safeguards'. This was because the US authorities could not prove the occurrence of an unforeseen development that had caused an unexpected increase in some of steel products (ibid.: 2007).

Overall, the current forms of safeguard exceptions are not in agreement with the notions of international free trade, because those exceptions justify many kinds of NTBs even when the quantities of imported goods increased naturally. Therefore, importing countries use the exceptions to go beyond the legitimate trade protection. Some countries may strategically abuse them as instruments of trade policy, a disguised form of protectionism to create favoured conditions for national industries. Consequently, safeguard measures have become very restrictive kinds of NTBs to international trade in a wide range of goods, especially steel products, poultry products, cotton yarn, sugar and agricultural produce (Wilson 2005).

Subsidies and Countervailing Measures

The rules subsidies and countervailing measures are laid down in Articles VI and XVI of the GATT and the 'Agreement on Subsidies and Countervailing Measures' (ASCMs). Subsidy is defined in the ASCMs as direct or indirect financial contribution by government or public bodies to national industries to improve their performance. Subsidy includes measures that lower the price to below normal for consumers, make it high for producers, or reduce the production cost for producers and subsequently the cost to consumers (Legg 2003). In the 'Agreement on Agriculture' (AoA), subsidies measures are divided into two types, namely, domestic subsidy and export subsidy. The key difference between the kinds of subsidies is that domestic subsidy improves the competitiveness of national products against like imported ones within the national market. Export subsidy, on the other hand, improves the competitiveness of national products against similar ones in international market.

Countervailing measures are duties imposed by importing countries which suffer the impact of illegal subsidies made by exporting countries, and are intended to offset the harmful damage caused by subsidised imported goods (Islam 2006). Article VI of the GATT and the ASCM deal with countervailing measures as trade remedies to unfair subsidies by exporting countries. The major restriction on imposing countervailing measures in Article VI of the GATT and the ASCM is that the duties must be limited to offset the subsidy granted in an exporting country and must not go beyond that limit.

Subsidisation and countervailing measures represent rich sources of NTBs. The problem of subsidies has arisen since the establishment of the GATT 1947. This is because Article XVI of that agreement does not contain clear definitions and guidelines to limit the misapplication of subsidies. The actual subsidy itself is a direct prejudice to and restriction on international trade because the support limits the real exercise of international trade rules and principles (Bossche 2005). Consequently, subsidised industries obtain unfair benefit from international trade liberalisation, while industries from weak countries are not able to do so because they do not receive a similar level of support. Subsidies also limit international trade competition, especially when exporting countries use allowable subsidies to hide illegitimate financial support to their national industries, or go beyond the legitimate level of subsidies.

Subsidy in general has two stages: stage one includes all processes before the actual contribution is received; and stage two is when that benefit reaches the recipient industry. However, the ASCMs does not explain the stage where countervailing measures can be taken as legitimate action to balance the impact of illegitimate subsidy to national industries. A clear explanation is important to judge the legality or illegality of subsidy and related countervailing measures. The ambiguity and lack of clear explanations give importing countries the option to impose countervailing measures from the first moment that the exporting countries take preparatory steps of subsidies. Therefore, it is important also to restrict the application of countervailing measures to the actual delivery of subsidy to the recipients, because it is possible for any country at any given time, and for any reason, to cancel its plan to subsidise before the contribution reaches the recipients. In the case where countervailing measures take place before the beneficiary receives the subsidies, it would extend the time for imposing countervailing measures as restrictions to international trade in goods, or for taking countervailing measures against unexpected subsidy. Consequently, it was emphasised by the AB during *Canada —Aircraft* dispute,[17] that the benefit must be received and enjoyed by the beneficiary to be considered as a benefit.[18]

The ASCM allows general subsidies, and provides that the actionable subsidies must be specific to certain industries. The definition of specific and non-specific is not clear enough to distinguish between the two types of subsidies, making it difficult to separate the general subsidies from specific ones (Islam 2006). In addition, it is highly likely that countries would use the general subsidies indirectly to support certain industries, but at the same time, it is not an easy task for importing countries to find the proper proof that the exporting countries have conducted illegal subsidies. As a result, the vagueness of these definitions could create disagreements between exporting and importing countries, thereby creating more trade disputes and increasing retaliatory trade measures and trade restrictions.

Another problem with the ASCM is in Article XVI:3 which allows subsidies on the export of primary products, as long as certain countries are still within their equitable share of world export trade in concerned product. However, the Article does not clarify the calculation of the countries' equitable shares (Smeets 1983). In such situations, subsidisation would represent a direct interference by national governments to limit the real application to international trade rules of unrestricted competition. Overall, subsidies must be surrounded with direct rules to limit the trade distortion impact of financial interference by national governments and their agents. The limitations on subsidies are necessary to limit the support that countries, especially those with strong financial and economic positions, provide to their industries in breach of international trade liberalisation principles.

Security Exceptions and NTBs

Article XXI of the GATT allows countries to impose trade restrictions, or sanctions against other trade partners as security exceptions, without treating these restrictions as breaches of international trade. Article XXI has two types of security exceptions relating to national and international security. The national security exceptions are presented in Article XXI(a) and (b) which authorise any country to apply national security restrictions in a number of situations based on its own decision. Such restrictions include withholding information necessary for national security reasons, measures related to fissionable material, measures related to the arms trade and emergency measures during a time of war. International peace and security exceptions are presented in Article XXI(c). It allows members to use the security exceptions and apply economic sanctions against countries which threaten international peace and security. This is in accordance with Article 41 of the UN Charter and after the authorisation of the Security Council. The aims of applying the national security exceptions under Article XXI are to protect national industries, to support foreign policy, or to restrict exports of military arms and materials to other countries which are considered as enemies (Bossche 2005).

Article XXI has been invoked in several cases such as those between the EU and the US over the Helms–Burton Act; Colombia and Nicaragua; the EC, Canada and Australia over trade restrictions against Argentina; and between the US and Nicaragua over the US-imposed trade embargo (Lindsay 2003). However, security exceptions create different trade problems and could become very restrictive kinds of NTBs in the international trade in goods. The main problems with Article XXI are its wide scope, the way that Article is applied and the inability of the affected parties to use the DSS of the WTO.

The scope of Article XXI is unlimited because it uses broad terms to impose security restrictions. Terms like 'necessary', 'essential to security interests', 'time of war', and 'emergency in international relations' have a very broad range of meanings, which can be open to multiple interpretations because they lack clear and precise definitions (ibid.). The vaguest term is 'essential security interests'. The lack of definition and limitations to that term could open the way for justifying unlimited examples of NTBs based on essential security interests. Another problem is that Article XXI does not require any special procedure for its application to national security matters. For example, it does not stipulate that investigations must be carried out or that the WTO, as the competent authority to deal with international trade matters, must be informed before any action is taken. Article XXI has left it up to individual countries to decide the timing of and the measures to be taken as essential national security measures (Bossche 2005). The last problem with the security exceptions is the disagreement about the jurisdiction of the DSS to review disputes over the adoption of security exceptions under Article XXI.

Some argue that the unrestricted scope of Article XXI aims to prevent the DSS of the WTO from having control over the security exceptions disputes. They justify their point of view by arguing that security matters are special issues and do not represent trade-related problems, and that the DSS does not have the proper experience to solve non-economic trade disputes (Lindsay 2003). The contracting parties in 1982 tried to expand the jurisdiction of the panel over the dispute which arose about the application of Article XXI, when the EC, Canada and Australia applied trade restrictions against Argentina because of the armed clash between Argentina and the UK over the Falkland Islands, or Malvinas (Bossche 2005). In 1985, the US imposed trade embargoes on Nicaragua, which caused *United States — Trade Measures Affecting Nicaragua* dispute.[19] The GATT Panel could not judge and make obligatory decision. The Panel did, however, state that the US might not have fulfilled its obligation under the rules of the GATT.[20]

Literally, the rules of DSS in the GATT, particularly Articles XXII, XXIII, and the rules of the DSU, do not exempt disputes related to security from being settled according to normal methods of dispute settlement. For example, Article XXIII of the DSU provides that 'when Members seek the redress of a violation of obligations or other nullification or impairment of benefits under the covered agreements ... they shall have recourse to, and abide by, the rules and procedures of this Understanding'. However, the origin of the security exception in Article XXII of the GATT does not distinguish consultations about security disputes from other disputes. Additionally, Article XXIII does not provide any special ways of handling trade disputes over security exceptions. In principle, it can be said that the DSS of the WTO has jurisdiction over anything related to the application of WTO rules, which should include security exception related matters.

It is true that the application of security exceptions is a critical matter and involves sensitive issues, but they can be used to justify many unreasonable kinds of NTBs in the international trade in goods. Therefore, it is essential to surround the security exceptions with clear limitations and boundaries. The main limitations have to be the adoption of procedural requirements for the application of Article XXI, such as requiring consultation with the WTO before the application of any security measure. Furthermore, the WTO should have full responsibility and authority over dealing with and solving any dispute related to any application of its rules through the DSS. If the DSB of the WTO lacks the experience to solve disputes related to security exceptions, then such problems need to be addressed and solved by the WTO. The incentive for giving the DSS the authority to review all disputes over trade-related measures is to limit all measures which may restrict the principle of international trade and would protect weak countries from being under the mercy of informal diplomatic procedures to solve their disputes with powerful countries.

Conclusion

The importance of the GATT in dealing with NTBs is found under the rules of national treatment, most favoured nation and the prohibition of quantitative restrictions. These are general rules, but they have the advantage of devolving legal obligations to limit NTBs which may restrict the international trade in goods. However, the Agreement contains many shortcomings, currently set out as exceptions, which can be misused and lead to countless kinds of NTBs against the international trade in goods. The exceptions are adopted, in theory, to achieve reasonable aims.

Nevertheless, the exception rules of GATT have become sources of illegitimate NTBs to the international trade in goods, and have also become the major causes of international trade disputes. In the vast majority of disputes, the decisions were made in favour of the exporting countries as complainants because they suffer illegitimate restrictive impacts of NTBs based on the GATT exceptions. From many trade disputes, it is clear that the importing countries which apply the GATT exceptions could not successfully provide the legitimate evidence that they sought the protection of GATT exceptions in trade in goods according to the rules of the WTO.

The problems of the exception rules manifest in many different ways. Some of those exceptions work contrary to the objectives of the WTO. For example, the rules of regional trade agreements legalise and support the idea of creating mini-trade agreements between countries with shared political or economic interests. The idea of PTAs stands against the golden goal of the WTO, which is the unity of the global market and its governance by a single organisation. Another problem with the exception rules of the GATT is that they help countries find loopholes to restrict imports when international competition does not work in favour of their national economic interest. Some countries may impose justified safeguards, or countervailing measures to defer their adherence to the rules of the WTO and to create favoured conditions for their national industries during the time needed to solve international trade disputes.

For developing countries in particular, the GATT exceptions are sites of trade concerns. This is because these countries face the restrictive impacts of these measures when they attempt to export their goods, particularly their export to the markets of developed countries. For example, developing countries face unbeatable trade restrictions in the markets related to exceptional measures of subsidies and safeguard measures. In addition, developing countries are not able to develop applicable PTAs between them or participate in such agreements with developed countries due to weak and unwise economic policies. Developed countries on the other hand regard many of the GATT exceptions, especially subsidy measures, as beneficial tools to help developing countries and gradually integrate them into the international trading system (Qureshi 2006). However, the economic problems that developing countries have do not help them to use the GATT exceptions in their favour. For example, many developing countries have comparative advantages in producing agricultural goods, but the application of subsidy and safeguard exceptions by developed countries diminish most trade benefits developing countries could achieve through agricultural trade.

Finally, to avoid trade problems in the future, all questionable rules of the GATT need to be reconsidered in light of WTO aims, its other agreements and current developments in international trade, and take into account the economic deficiency between countries, which would help to create real discipline in the liberalisation of international trade on a global scale.

Notes

1. NTBs could be defined as any rules, regulations and practices adopted by members of the WTO related to economic, social, administrative or political purposes and negatively affecting international trade in goods.
2. *European Communities — Measures Concerning Meat and Meat Products* Dispute DS26 (*EU-hormone*); the decision was appealed on 13 February 1999.
3. *United States — Standards for Reformulated and Conventional Gasoline* WT/DS2, (US–Gasoline) dispute, adopted on 29 April 1996.

4. *Thailand — Restrictions on Importation of and Internal Taxes on Cigarettes*, GATT disputes, BISD/37S/200, (Thailand-cigarettes) adopted on 7 November 1990.
5. *Thailand — Restrictions on Importation of and Internal Taxes on Cigarettes* DS10/R-375/200 adopted on 7 November 1990.
6. *Turkey — Restrictions on Imports of Textiles and Clothing product,* DS34, (*Turkey-Textile*) adopted on 19 November 1999.
7. India — Measures Affecting the Automotive Sector WT/DS146 (India-Autos) Adopted on 5 April 2002.
8. India — Quantitative Restrictions on Imports of Agricultural, Textile and Industrial Products WT/DS90/AB/R (India – Quantitative Restrictions), adopted on 22 September 1999.
9. Panel Report *India — Autos dispute*, para 5.238–242.
10. *Canada Import Restrictions on Ice Cream and Yoghurt, BISD 36S/68,* adopted 4 December 1989, Panel report, para 59. Also in *Norwegian Procurement of Toll Collection Equipment for the City of Trondheim,* GPR DS2/R, adopted 13 May 1992, BISD 40S/319, panel report para 4.5.
11. *United States — Definitive Safeguard Measures on Imports of Circular Welded Carbon Quality Line Pipe from Korea* WT/DS220 (US-Line pipe dispute), adopted on 8 March 2002.
12. AB report of *US-Line pipe* dispute.
13. *Argentina — Measures Affecting Imports of Footwear,* WT/DS121/AB/R, (*Argentina-Footwear*), adopted on 12 January 2000.
14. *Mercado Commun del Sure* is a treaty which establishes common market between Argentina, Brazil, Paraguay and Uruguay.
15. *United States — Safeguard Measures on Imports of Fresh, Chilled or Frozen Lamb Meat from New Zealand and Australia, WT/DS DS177, 178,* (*US-Lamb* dispute) adopted on 16 May 2001.
16. *United States — Definitive Safeguard Measures on Imports of Certain Steel Products, WT/DS DS248, 249, 251, 252, 253, 254, 258, 259,* (*US-Steel Safeguard* dispute), adopted on 10 December 2003.
17. *Canada — Measures Affecting the Export of Civilian Aircraft WT/DS70/AB/R (Canada –Aircraft)*, adopted on 20 August 199.
18. *Appellate Body Report Canada –Aircraft*, paragraph 154.
19. United States — Trade Measures Affecting Nicaragua, BISD/L6053, dated 13 October 1986.
20. GATT Panel report United States — Trade Measures Affecting Nicaragua, paragraph 5.3.

References

Asafu-Adjaye, J. and R. Mahadevan. 2009. 'Regional Trade Agreements Versus Global Trade Liberalisation: Implications for a Small Island Developing State', *The World Economy* 32 (3): 509–29.

Barber, C., G. Balachandiran and J. Rose. 2004. 'How Rich Country Protectionism in Textiles and Clothing Trade Prevents Poverty Alleviation', OXFAM Organization. http://www.oxfam.org.uk/what_we_do/issues/trade/downloads/bp60_textiles.pdf (accessed 20 May 2007).

Bhala, R. 2004. 'The Intersection of Islam and the WTO: Three Sharî'a Issues in the WTO Accession of Saudi Arabia', *Law in Context*, 21: 152–75.

Bossche, P. V. d. 2005. *The Law and Policy of the World Trade Organisation*. New York: Cambridge University Press.

Glania, G. and Kluttig, B. 2006. 'Rtas Threat or Opportunity for the WTO, Organized by the Federation of German Industries (Bdi)'. Paper presented at the WTO Public Forum 2006 'What WTO for the XXIst Century WTO' on 15 June 2006. http://www.wto.org/english/forums _e/public_forum_e/forum06_e.htm (accessed 15 Jun 2007).

Islam, M. R. 2006. *International Trade Law of the WTO*. Oxford: Oxford University Press.

Legg, W. 2003. 'Agricultural Subsidies: Measurement and Use in Policy Evaluation', *Journal of Agricultural Economics*, 54 (2):175–201.

Lesser, C. 2007. 'Do Bilateral and Regional Approaches for Reducing Technical Barriers to Trade Converge Towards the Multilateral Trading System', OECD. http://www.oecd.org/dataoecd/20/20/39711550.pdf (accessed 10 January 2008).

Lindsay, P. 2003. 'The Ambiguity of GATT Article Xxi: Subtle Success or Rampant Failure?', *Duke Law Journal* 52. http://www.law.duke.edu/journals/dlj/articles/dlj52p1277.htm#H1NTOP> (accessed 10 May 2006).

Lockhart, N. J. and A. Mitchell. 2005. 'Regional Trade Agreements under GATT 1994: An Exception and Its Limits', in A. Mitchell (ed.), *Challenges and Prospects for the WTO*, pp. 217–52. London: Cameron May. http://www.worldtradelaw.net/articles/lockhartmitchellrta.pdf (accessed 15 June 2006).

Oxley, A. and K. Osborne. 2002. 'A Study of the Trade and Environment Issue, 2002', Australian APEC Study Centre, Monash University. http://www.apec.org.au/docs/oxley 2002c.pdf (accessed 25 January 2006).

Qureshi, A. H. 2003. 'Participation of Developing Countries in the WTO Dispute Settlement System', *Journal of African Law* 47 (2): 174–198.

———. *Interpreting WTO Agreements: Problems and Perspective*. Cambridge: Cambride University Press.

Smeets, M. 1983. 'Non-Tariff Barriers in the Tokyo Round with Special Reference to Subsidies and Countervailing Duties'. Unpublished Ph.D. thesis, Graduate Institute of International Studies.

Watson, W. and V. D. Do. 2006. 'Economic Analysis of Regional Trade Agreements', McGill University. http://www.mcgill.ca/files/economics/economicanalysisof.pdf (accessed 20 July 2008).

Wilson, G. 1998. 'The Safeguards Clause: The Rational, Operations and Prospects of GATT Article XIX', University of London. http://www.garretwilson.com/essays/economics/gattarticlexix.html (accessed 18 June 2005).

Wilson, N. 2005. 'Analysis of Non-Tariff Barriers of Concern to Developing Countries'. Paper presented at the Regional Meeting on Agriculture Trade and Development in Southeast Asian Countries, Manila, 24–26 October http://puck.sourceoecd.org/vl=4552714/cl=22/nw=1/rpsv/cgibin/wppdf?file=5lgmv2mff48q.pdf (accessed 5 November 2006).

World Trade Organisation (WTO). 2005. *The Legal Text: The Result of the Uruguay Round Of Multilateral Trade Negotiation.* Cambridge: Cambridge University Press, 2005.

———. 2007. 'WTO Dispute Settlement: One-Page Case Summaries 1995–December 2007', WTO. http://www.wto.org/english/res_e/booksp_e/dispu_sum-mary06_e.pdf (accessed 2 February 2007).

———. 2008. 'World Trade Report 2007', WTO. http://www.wto.org/english/res_e/booksp_e/anrep_e/world_trade_report07_e.pdf (accessed 8 January 2008).

———. 2009. 'Regional Trade Agreements, 2009', WTO. http://www.wto.org/english/tratop_e/region_ e/regfac_e.htm (accessed 29 September 2009).

16

National Treatment Violations: Lessons from Competition Law

Anton P. Petrov

In recent years, the topic of the impact of the WTO[1] disciplines on trade and economic development has spurred many discussions. Of particular attention is the question whether there is any room for national autonomy in determining what adequate actions should be undertaken in order to promote economic development and raise living standards. Contending that the current system is marked by 'democratic insufficiency', many NGOs oppose further liberalisation negotiations, in particular those that will bring new areas under the WTO regime, such as investment, competition policy and government procurement. These representatives of the civil society instead want a comprehensive review and assessment of the existing agreements so that they may address the WTO's impact on marginalised communities, development, democracy, environment, health, human rights, etc.

It is thus necessary to emphasise once more the importance of the question of 'policy space' for the WTO member countries. Many suggest that the 'single undertaking' model of trade negotiations adopted since the Uruguay Round, under which all nations, regardless of their respective levels of development and needs, sign on the same text, to be all but dead.[2] Presently, the purpose of international rules should not be to impose common restraints on countries with different regulatory systems, but to accept these differences and regulate the interface, so as to reduce adverse spillovers between them. Decisions of national governments should be given a margin of difference, since there is no single 'correct' rule.[3]

This chapter attempts to contribute to this debate by arguing that the WTO dispute settlement mechanism should not be envisaged as an instrument for imposition of uniform solutions by attempting to forcefully harmonise the regulatory systems of the Member states. It is argued hereinafter that the national treatment provisions of the General Agreement on Tariffs and Trade (GATT)[4] and General Agreement on Trade in Services (GATS),[5] and in particular the concepts of 'likeness' and 'no less favourable treatment' enshrined therein, may provide sufficient flexibility in reviewing national measures and their impact on international trade. It is suggested that an efficient way to achieve this flexibility is by interpreting these key concepts in the context of a dispute regarding the application of a covered agreement, by relying on the algorithm for definition of the relevant market as developed under competition law — i.e., by adopting the tests for *interchangeability of use and cross-price elasticity of demand and supply*. It is argued that increased reliance on consumer preferences is not only warranted by the principles of economic analysis, but also since it re-establishes the link with the principal bearer of sovereignty — the populus, such reliance will provide an escape way from the current situation of alleged democratic deficiency in the WTO system.

The Current Theoretical Background

Although this is obviously not a clear-sided dispute, two principal approaches to the analysis of alleged violations of the national treatment obligation under WTO law can be distinguished in contemporary academic writings. On the first side, one can group the proponents of the teleological analysis, who favour the so called 'aims-and-effects' test and argue[6], inter alia, that the national treatment obligation should not be violated if a particular Member state enforces legislation, which produces adverse effects on foreign products/services, so far as there is a legitimate regulatory objective and the domestic regulation is the sufficient minimum for the achievement of that objective.

Another group of scholars dismiss the reliance on the aims-and-effects test due to its lack of textual basis and the existing risk of circumvention of the narrow list of policy exceptions which are permitted under Article XX GATT. They consider the concept of 'likeness' to be the fulcrum of the discrimination screening under the national treatment provisions, and stress on physical features and objective properties.[7] Yet another group of scholars (or more correctly, a sub-group within the second camp) focus on end-use and consumer preferences, and suggest that the likeness assessment should be reinforced by the instrumentarium of economic analysis.[8]

The following expose shall continue with a brief presentation of the two leading theoretical lines of reasoning in order to single out the elements of these approaches which are most useful for the analysis of national treatment violations. While the stated purpose of this chapter is clearly more in line with the second theoretical approach, there are certain elements in the aims-and-effect analysis which provide better insights into the question why should WTO panels refrain from application of the 'smell test' — i.e., why the level of thoroughness of the analysis for violation of the national treatment obligation should not be dependent on the importance of the aim, pursued by the measure under review.

Teleological Analysis (Aims-and-Effect Test)

The proponents of the aims-and-effect test state that whether a measure discriminates between two products (services), and whether two products (services) are like or substitutes, depends on the perspective from which their relationship is examined. Accordingly, since the perspective cannot be examined without looking at the context, which is composed of both the aim and the effect of the measure in question, these two factors (aim and effect) should be considered as central in determining national treatment violations. It is even argued that the 'likeness' assessment should be reduced to a mere mechanical test, leaving the three variables (adverse effect, legitimate aim and necessary means) to form the only real playground for judges.[9]

The most often cited example from the practice of the GATT panels, where the aims-and-effect theory has found application, is the panel report in *US — Malt Beverages*.[10] The panel reasoned that the determination of likeness under Article III:2 should be made with regard to the purpose of the whole Article III — i.e., to ensure that 'internal taxes and other internal charges, and laws, regulations, and requirements affecting internal sale ... should not be applied to imported or domestic products so as to afford protection to domestic production'.[11] On the basis of this phrase, the panel concluded that the purpose of Article III is not to prevent contracting parties from using their fiscal and regulatory powers, by differentiating between different product categories, for policy purposes 'other' than to afford protection to domestic production.[12]

350 + Anton P. Petrov

Applying this analytical pattern to the interpretation of Article III of GATT, for example, one reaches the conclusion that if a measure, which discriminates between certain products, is not being applied so as to afford protection to domestic production, the distinction should be deemed prima facie valid.

The success of the aims-and-effect test was rather short lived, and the very first panel established under the new WTO system, convened to rule on the *Japan — Alcoholic Beverages*[13] case, rejected it resolutely. In those proceedings, the application of the aims-and-effect test was suggested by US and Japan[14] but it was rejected by the panellists who made a number of objections, including in particular the lack of textual basis in Article III:2, the important evidentiary repercussions due to the shifting the burden of proof, the practical difficulty of determining the actual aim of the measure under review, and the danger of circumventing the closed list of exceptions under Article XX.[15]

Verhoosel attempts to revive the teleological analysis into a slightly restricted version, which he names an 'integrated necessity test'.[16] While using the same three-prong analytical pattern (adverse effect, legitimate objective and necessary means), Verhoosel limits the expansive penetration of the original test to all kinds of regulatory barriers by concluding that a domestic measure will only be found to have an adverse effect on competitive opportunities if a certain production capacity is inherently confined to domestic producers, i.e., if foreign producers could not change their production plan, possibly away from where their comparative advantage lies, in order to accede to a less burdensome regulatory category, which benefits domestic producers.[17]

From another point of view, what Verhoosel defines as 'adverse effect' is in fact a case of low supply substitutability, where foreign competitors are not able to easily switch into the product, which is favoured by the domestic measure. However, it should be noted that whether and to what extent foreign producers (importers) were to suffer losses in each case would depend primarily on the respective demand elasticity of their products. Furthermore, favouritism of domestic producers on account of foreign competitors is possible only in the hypothesis of simultaneous existence of (i) low supply substitutability and (ii) significant cross-price elasticity between domestic and imported products. If sufficient demand side substitutability exists, domestic consumers would switch to the lower priced (imported) product. Consequently, in a situation marked by existing low supply substitutability, domestic producers may be able to benefit from a protectionist measure and exploit the higher profits from increased consumption in the lower taxed product (assuming such lower price is due to the lower taxes) *only* in the situation of significant demand substitutability. On the other hand, where demand substitutability is also low, or completely absent, the result will be lack of switching and any loss of profit for foreign producers (importers) shall be a result of the sole effect of the receptiveness of domestic consumers to changes in the price — measured by price and income elasticity.

Different Methods for Defining Likeness

It is generally acknowledged that the report of the Working Party in the *Border Tax Adjustments*[18] case sets out the basic list of elements to be considered in determining likeness: (i) the products end-users in a given market, (ii) the consumers' tastes and habits, which change from country to country and (iii) the products properties, nature and quality.[19] In other words, the product classification under the above criteria encompasses both objective (physical properties) and subjective (pertaining to the relevant market) criteria. The first group covers the properties of the product — size, nature, quality, end-use in general — typical use of goods with that particular set of properties and tariff classification. The second set of elements includes consumer perception of the product and its properties — i.e., consumer tastes and habits and end-use in the relevant market.

Probably the most thorough investigation into the concept of likeness so far can be attributed to Choi Won Mog, who states that depending on the context and the purpose of the relevant provision of a covered agreement, the 'like product' concept should be endowed with a different range of likeness, from the narrowest to the broadest meaning of the term.[20] Choi suggests a 'scale of likeness' which has five degrees: (i) identical, (ii) closely similar, (iii) remotely similar, (iv) directly competitive or substitutable and (v) indirectly competitive or substitutable. While in each particular provision of a covered agreement, as per the words of the Appellate Body itself, the accordion of likeness would stretch differently, according to Choi, the analysis, which should be applied in order to determine whether that particular stretch has been reached, follows a common algorithm.

Choi distinguishes four stages in the assessment of likeness, signifying four sets of 'characteristics' that have to be analysed: (i) examination of objective characters, (ii) demand substitutability analysis, (iii) supply substitutability analysis and (iv) examination of future substitution or competition. In the second and third stages, the examination may (or may not) include potential substitution/competition.[21]

It is clear that the algorithm prescribed by Choi rests heavily on economic analysis and borrows many elements from the procedures for definition of the relevant market under competition law.[22] Nevertheless, and as it shall be discussed in greater detail herein below, although the substitutability analysis is modelled according to the leading international trends in competition law, the changes, inserted in order to make it 'compatible' for assessment of likeness, lead to a significant departure from the original. Choi separates the examination of demand substitution and supply substitution in two different stages, and the second one is only facultative in nature. Moreover, he considers supply substitution as a counterbalance of demand substitution — a 'mitigating factor', which is used to determine the effect of demand substitution. But from the point of view of economic analysis, demand and supply substitutability are not so much opposing phenomena, but rather two forces that exercise competitive constraint upon a group of products.[23] In order to create a correct picture of the relevant market, one has to consider 'both' demand and supply-side substitutability and *in the same time*.

Furthermore, Choi separates the examination of potential substitution effects as facultative sub-stages of demand and supply substitution analysis, while future substitution effects are moulded in a separate stage of the examination. While in economic analysis competition is, indeed, usually classified into current and potential, the distinction is based on price responses — i.e., current competitors are those firms, who are content to play on the relevant market with the current prices, while potential are all those competitors, who might be tempted to enter the market (in the future) should the price increase.[24] Consequently, both these categories are important when one is to examine supply substitution.

But what is this market definition analysis of competition law from which so many are eager to borrow?

Relevant Market and Competition Law

While competition law has always been interested with market power, the traditional approach has been of measuring market shares. Thus focus in antitrust analyses is placed on defining the so-called 'relevant market'. This term denotes the market in which one ,or more goods compete and aims to answer the question whether two or more products can be considered substitute goods and whether they constitute a particular and separate market for competition analysis.

The relevant market has two dimensions, combining a product market and a geographic market, defined as follows:

(i) a relevant product market — comprises all those products and/or services which are regarded as interchangeable or substitutable by the consumer by reason of the products' characteristics, their prices and their intended use;

(ii) relevant geographic market — comprises the area in which the firms concerned are involved in the supply of products or services and in which the conditions of competition are sufficiently homogeneous.[25]

Development of the Concept

The notion of a relevant market has its roots in the case law of the US Supreme Court, which in turn was based on the economic theory common at the time of the first major antitrust proceedings in the US.[26] The US Supreme Court first accepted cross-price elasticity of demand in defining the relevant market in *Times-Picayune.*[27] This approach was confirmed in 1956, when in their *Cellophane*[28] ruling the US justices stressed the importance of assessing whether buyers could switch to substitute products, by indicating cross-price elasticity as the standard of measurement to be determined econometrically.

The EU Court of Justice (ECJ) first considered the question of market definition in *Continental Can*[29] where it stressed the role of supply substitutability. Almost two decades after the US, in its *United Brands (Chiquita)*[30] judgement, the ECJ similarly applied the concept of cross-price elasticity and defined the relevant product market as comprising 'the totality of products which, with respect to their characteristics, are particularly suitable for satisfying constant needs, and are only to a limited extent interchangeable[31] with other products in terms of price, usage, and consumer preference'.[32]

The economic theories continued to develop and with the new models provided by econometrics in the 1980s, the US Department of Justice officially adopted the so-called the small but significant and non-transitory increase in price (SSNIP) test for determination of the effects of mergers.[33] The SSNIP test defines a relevant market as 'something worth monopolising'. The relevant market consists of a set of goods and/or services which are considered substitutes by the customer. Such a 'complete' set is worth monopolising because if only one single supplier were to provide it, that supplier could profitably increase its price without its customers turning away and choosing other goods and services from other suppliers, because none of the goods/services offered by other suppliers are adequate substitutes.

SSNIP Summary

The SSNIP test is designed to avoid ad hoc debates about what products compete with each other, based inter alia on presence or lack of common physical characteristics. It seeks to identify the smallest relevant market within which a hypothetical monopolist (or cartel) could impose a profitable significant increase in price. In essence, the test asks whether a hypothetical monopolist of a product (region) would impose a small but significant and non-transitory increase in price (normally of about 5–10 per cent of the price, lasting for at least one year). If the answer is affirmative, that product (region) is the relevant market; if not, that must be because other products (regions) exert competitive pressure on the monopoly attempt, and hence should also be included in the relevant market.

The SSNIP test is an interactive process. If in the first round it is found that the hypothetical monopolist of product A would not increase the price by 5–10 per cent, then product B — the closest substitute — should be included in the relevant market. The test should then be applied again, but *only the price increase for the original product A is relevant*.[34]

Applying the Market Definition Rules to Situations under the Covered Agreements

The principal aim of the rules and principles, enshrined in the GATT and the other covered agreements, is to enhance the development potential of the WTO member states by removing the obstacles to international trade, thus allowing them to exploit in the greatest degree possible the benefits of their comparative advantages. In essence, a great number of the rules in the covered agreements have anti-discriminatory nature and attempt to 'level the ground', in order to ensure that all suppliers (of like and/or directly competitive products/services) shall have equal opportunity to compete on the market. Therefore, the greatest evil in the WTO system are cases of unequal treatment between products/services of different origin and protectionist vacillations by Member states.

The principal aim of competition law, on the other hand, is to safeguard the competitive relations from abusive attempts from firms to influence the market in order to obtain excessive profits. The gravest illicit act in the eyes of an anti-trust judge would be an attempt to influence the market for the purpose to artificially (against the principles and trends of fare competition) raising prices: whether by direct fixing of prices, sharing of resources and markets, or otherwise influencing conditions of production and/or trade.

Lessons from the Contemporary Theory

Going back to the discussion about the principles of WTO, one may say that from a certain point of view, an attempt to provide exceptional privileges to national suppliers may be equated to establishment or strengthening of a monopoly position in favour of national suppliers to the detriment of all other present and potential competitors on the relevant market — foreign suppliers. In other words, a case of violation of the WTO national treatment standard may just as well classify as an illegal practice, contributing to the creation of a cartel, if it was not for the fact that in the WTO context one inevitably has to review acts of sovereign states. But then again, does the specific status of the alleged perpetrator — a national state — require that we should develop a whole new algorithm in order to determine the economical effect of its actions? After all, in economical analysis a monopoly is a monopoly, and its existence and potential negative effects can be established with a more or less fixed set of analytical instruments.

As was shown hereinabove, many researchers have already borrowed a great deal from the market analysis mechanisms of competition law in order to describe phenomena, which are deemed peculiar for international trade. However, there seems to be one common failure in all theoretical attempts to implement the analytical framework of cross-price elasticity in GATT/WTO cases — significant alteration of the original model leads to inaccurate and even distorted results.

For example, Choi's adherence to the 'price-substitution equivalence standard' does indeed simplify the examination of demand substitutability, but unfortunately does not enhance the objectivity and validity of the result. While simplicity of numbers may seem desirable, in a case of 8 per cent raise of prices an 8 per cent substitution rate with another product is not always tantamount to substitutability from a market perspective. The reason being that the switching rate (the number of clients, who have switched to a substitute product) only endangers the position of a prospective monopolist, who is implementing the price rise, but the actual loss of profit will ultimately result from the actual loss of customers. Thus the question how many clients will stop purchasing at the higher price is more important than the question how many will switch to substitutes, the latter being a sub-group of the former. In other words, the market definition test is a dynamic equation, involving several variables, among which prominent place assume the own price elasticity of the product, object of monopolisation.[35]

Revised Test for Discrimination

Is there another way to look at the competitive relations in a dispute under a covered agreement? I believe there is. And it does not require much meddling with the original competition law approach to market definition in order to get to it: Actually all one needs to do to find an almost perfect fit is to rethink the correct way to attach the existing terminology from competition law to the elements of a non-discrimination case under a covered agreement.

The aim of competition law is to combat monopolistic exploits of the market since these are perceived to be economically inefficient, as a price fixing in a monopoly usually results in increased profits for the monopolist but in conjunction with decreased consumer surplus and an overall diminution of the general welfare. Similarly, WTO rules aim to clear protectionist vacillations in international trade, because the latter create economically inefficient trade diversion. In fact, the implementation of a protectionist measure by a specific state has the effect of creating a privilege for domestic producers, which in economic terms is similar to establishing or strengthening a monopoly.[36]

The proposed algorithm for determining the presence or absence of discriminating treatment between products, introduced by an origin neutral measure, is composed of two SSNIP tests applied to the contexts, respectively, prior to and after implementation of the measure under review.

For explanatory purposes, we may use the following simplified case regarding a national measure that distinguishes between two types of tuna fish. Let's assume that the government of country X passes a measure, which distinguishes between two products: tuna type 'A' — fished according to dolphin-friendly procedures, and tuna type 'B' — fished without observance of any procedures ensuring dolphin safety. Furthermore, let's assume that according to that measure a specific consumption tax of 10 per cent ad valorem is levied over each unit of tuna type 'B' sold on the market in X, but no such tax applies to sales of tuna type 'A'.

Applying the suggested two-tier test, in the first stage the arbiters should attempt to determine whether the domestic producers in X of tuna type 'A' are able to implement a small but significant non-transitive increase in the price of tuna type 'A', without facing significant competitive pressure from sales of tuna type 'B' and/or importers of tuna type 'A' (caught outside the territory of X). Within the first stage, arbiters are working with historical data reflecting prices prior to implementation of the measure under review. There are two possible outcomes from the analysis: a price rise (i) would be profitable, or (ii) would not be profitable.[37]

Thereafter, the arbiters should turn to the situation following implementation of the measure under review, and examine whether with the altered price and market conditions, a price increase by domestic producers of tuna type 'A' would be profitable. Again the assessment can render two results: a positive or a negative answer.

The third stage of the analysis — the synthesis — combines the information obtained through the two testing stages. The fulcrum of the analysis rests on whether a change in the market power of domestic producers of tune type 'A' is observable following implementation of the measure under review. Such change in market power should be attributed to the measure, with the effect that where the overall change in competitive conditions reflects an increase in the market power of domestic suppliers of tuna type 'A', then the measure has negative effect and should be quashed. On the other hand, where no significant change in market power is observable following implementation of the measure, then the latter is presumed not to have negative effect and the complaint should be dismissed.

From the point of view of the examination for a violation of the principle of national treatment, the analysis is the following: the first conclusion is that *where dominance over* the market for tuna type 'A' *was not possible prior to implementation of the measure,* then clearly the marker power of domestic producers of tuna type 'A' does not allow them to exercise control over the sale of tuna type 'A' in X. But this does not automatically equate the reason for the lack of dominance to the assumption that type 'A' and type 'B' tuna are like or substitutable products — the case may be that significant competition from foreign suppliers, especially potential competition, curbs any attempt for excessive profit on the side of domestic suppliers of tuna type 'A'. Notwithstanding whether the price rise attempt might fail due to strong demand substitutability or due to supply side constraints, *so long as the second stage test returns a negative result the overall effect of the measure should not be deemed negative* and the measure itself should not be condemned. Table 16.1 presents a simplified version of the possible results and their analysis.

A special attention deserves the situation where both the first and the second test return positive results. This situation signals existing market power in domestic suppliers of tuna type 'A' both prior and after implementation of the measure. Therefore, the question whether the measure itself has an overall negative effect on the competitive relationship between domestic and imported tuna requires additional investigation. Certain guidance as to the direction in which the panel should proceed may be found in the demand substitutability analysis, which was part of the testing process.

Table 16.1: Cross-reference of Results

	Negative Result in Test I	*Positive Result in Test I*
Negative Result in Test II	no significant change in market power = > no potential for negative effect on the competitive relations = > **the measure provides 'no less favourable treatment'**	decrease of market power of domestic suppliers has been established = > potential for negative effect on the competitive relations decreased or negated = > **the measure provides 'no less favourable treatment'**
Positive Result in Test II	significant change in the market power = > potential to strengthen the market position of domestic suppliers = > **the measure has discriminatory effect**	no significant change in the market power, but a potential for negative effect on the competitive relations exists = > panel discretion to be applied in order to determine the effect on competitive relations = > **presumption for lack of discrimination,** if strong demand substitutability is demonstrated by the available market data

Where the consumer preference data demonstrates high demand substitutability, which has not diminished following implementation of the measure, this would indicate that a potential attempt on the part of domestic suppliers to corner the market will most probably fail. On the other hand, where demand substitutability is low, or has diminished following enforcement of the measure, the overall market power of domestic suppliers has most probably increased. Consequently, the measure should be deemed to have negative effect on the competitive relationship and does not accord 'no less favourable treatment'.

Conclusion

Introducing elements of the market power analysis in cases of alleged violation of the national treatment principle under a covered agreement can help to avoid excessive reliance on the 'unavoidable discretionary judgement' of WTO panels. Moreover, the proposed algorithm will enhance the connection between the reasoning and determinations of arbitral decisions and the specific preferences of consumers on the national markets under review. Thus it will override the 'democratic insufficiency' which is alleged to exist in current dispute settlement practice.

The proposal for a new test for analysis of disputes regarding alleged violations of national treatment rests mainly on the SSNIP market definition analysis, developed under competition law. The hypothetical model has three stages: (i) examination of the market power (monopoly potential) of domestic producers prior to implementation of the measure under review; (ii) examination of the market power (monopoly potential) of domestic producers following implementation of the measure under review; and (iii) *assessment of the change in market power due to implementation of the measure*. As the core of the analysis is related to assessment of the change in the market power of domestic producers, the test may be aptly named *dynamic market power analysis*.

The purpose is to establish whether under the changed conditions, following implementation of the measure, the competitive relations between products/services/suppliers, etc., as distinguished under the reviewed measure, have worsened. The test shall return a positive result where the measure has no negative effect on the competitive relations and does not overall contribute to an increase of the market power of domestic suppliers. In such case it should be deemed that the measure does not accord less favourable treatment to imported products/services, and the product classification, proposed by the measure, should be upheld as admissible.

Conversely, the test shall return a negative result where the measure has negative effect on the competitive relations between the distinguished products/services, and will most probably enhance the market power of domestic suppliers (by according a less favourable treatment to imports). In that case, the implemented distinction should not be upheld.

On its face, it may seem that the proposed dynamic market power analysis has a lot in common with the teleological (aims-and-effect) test. Indeed, in the proposed analytical algorithm a measure (or a distinction between products under a measure) would be quashed only where the measure has negative effect on the competitive relations on the market. However, while in the aims-and-effect test the fulcrum of the analysis rests on the legitimacy of the pursued aim and the proportionality of the means through which it is attained, *under the dynamic market power analysis the arbiters are only required to review the economic efficiency of the measure*. Consequently, the second test avoids the discretionary review of the intentions of the national legislature (or executive office), which is inherent in the aims-and-effect analysis.

Moreover, when applying dynamic market power assessment the forum will only examine the economic context and effect of the measure under review. Thus the proper place for discussion of legitimate intentions and the necessity of the aims will remain a separate stage — i.e., a defence under Article XX, should the measure fail the initial screening under, inter alia, Article III. The division of the analysis in separate stages will clearly improve the standing of panel recommendations by removing from them (or at the very least — diminish) the cover of exceptional discretionary power, especially since the analysis will be kept close to the specific of the market under review and the respective preferences of consumers thereon. In this way, the Appellate Body and the panels shall respect domestic preferences and priorities.[38]

The analytical model, advocated herein, would contribute to the strengthening of the 'voice' of consumers worldwide, because the decisive factor for the admissibility of a product classification in national measures would be its consistency with the consumer preferences on the relevant market. In the today's global market, where suppliers based in any point of the world have at least the technological ability to deliver goods and/or services to any other point worldwide, the diversity in consumer interests and preferences should not be exchanged for higher revenues from economy of scale, at least on account of avoiding the danger of sameness and monotony — the principal antagonists of technological innovation and economic development. Varieties in the way of thinking should not be easily discarded as 'obstacles to harmonisation', as they may serve as safety valves in the long run. Without diversity, we may easily fall prey to the inertia of one single 'uniform' way of thinking. After all, the solutions prescribed by trade and competition laws have great impact not only on the economy, but also (whether directly or indirectly) on the society of each country.

Notes

1. World Trade Organisation, as established pursuant to the Agreement Establishing the World Trade Organization done in Marrakesh on 15 April 1995.
2. See Rodrik (2007: 149).
3. See Guzman (2009: 49).

4. General Agreement on Tariffs and Trade, as amended and in force since 1 January 1994.
5. General Agreement on Trade in Services, in force since 1 January 1995.
6. Mattoo and Subramanian (1998: 305).
7. Ehring (2002: 946).
8. See Choi (2003: 21).
9. Verhoosel (2002: 78).
10. *US — Measures Affecting Alcoholic and Malt Beverages*, Panel Report adopted 19 June 1992 (DS23/39S/206).
11. See Article III: 1 GATT.
12. Verhoosel, n. 9 *supra* at 24.
13. *Japan — Taxes on Alcoholic Beverages*, Panel Report adopted on 1st November 1996 (WT/DS8/R).
14. *Id.* at 4.24 *et seq.*
15. *Id.* at 6.16 *et seq.*
16. Verhoosel, n. 9 *supra* at 2.
17. *Id.* at 53.
18. *Border Tax Adjustment*, Report of the Working Party adopted on 2nd December 1970 (BISD 18S/97).
19. See *Choi*, n..9 *supra* at 18.
20. *Id.* at 19.
21. *Id.* at 89.
22. Choi cites primarily sources of EU competition law, but his analysis is not related to a particular system of law.
23. See Motta (2004: 103).
24. See Bush and Massa (2004: 1035–1160).
25. See *Commission notice on the definition of the Relevant Market for the purposes of Community competition law*, OJ C 372, 09.12.1997, p. 5 at para. 7 *et seq.*
26. Van den Bergh and Camesasca (2001: 96).
27. *Times-Picayune Publishing Compeny v. US*, 345 US 594 (1952).
28. *US v. E.I.DuPont de Nemours & Co. (Cellophane)*, 351 US 377 (1956).
29. Case C-6/72, *Europemballage Corporation and Continental Can Inc. v. Commission*, ECR 215/1973.
30. Case C-27/76 *United Brands v Commission*, ECR 207/1978.
31. However, the ECJ decided not to rely on cross-elasticity of demand data, opting for a more subjective test based on what the Court regarded as the banana's 'special features'.
32. *United Brands*, n. 42 *supra* at para. 12 and 31.
33. *US Department of Justice and Federal Trade Commission Horizontal Merger Guidelines*, adopted 2 April 1992, as revised in 1997 ('US Merger Guidelines').
34. A simple example can illustrate why the increase in the price of B is irrelevant. Suppose that the first round of the SSNIP test shows that a

hypothetical monopolist would only increase the price by 3 per cent. Next, the closest substitute product — B, is brought under the control of the to-be monopolist. Consequently, the firm may now increase the price more than before, since it is no longer concerned by sales being diverted to B (so far as the price of B is not significantly lower so that a diversion could result in aggregate losses). Suppose in the new situation the effective price increase of A is 10 per cent. This shows that the sales of A are constrained by B to an extent that satisfies the SSNIP test. This conclusion does not depend on the price of B after monopolisation. It may be that its price also rises by 5–10 per cent. But it is also possible that the price of B only increases by less — say 2 per cent, indicating that product B faces strong competition from another product — C. Should product C be also included in the relevant market? The answer is: no. If the relevant market was to be broadened with the inclusion of C, the analysis would fail to note that there is sufficient market power in the firm that controls A and B to exercise monopolistic influence in the smaller AB market. This illustrates an important point that the relevant market should not be bigger than necessary to satisfy the SSNIP test — i.e., the smallest market in which a monopolist can increase the price (*see* Section 10, US Merger Guidelines).

35. It is easy to forget that cross-price elasticity comes into play only after own-price elasticity; consequently a monopolistic attempt may be ineffective irrespective of the absence of substitutes.

36. Of course, in most cases the national government will be acting for the benefit of more than one firm, but this fact has no effect on the analysis. Moreover, several firms acting in tandem can collectively exercise the same market power and have similar control over output and prices as a single monopolist.

37. Since we are only interested in defining likeness between A and B tuna, there is no need to continue with the SSNIP test in a case of a negative result and further the analysis by examining whether monopolization of a broader market of combined A and B tuna sales would be profitable.

38. *Cf.* Guzman, n. 3 *supra* at 50.

References

Baumann, Michael and Paul Godek. 1995. 'Could and Would Understood: Critical Elasticities and the Merger Guidelines', *Antitrust Bulletin*, 40 (4): 885–99.

Bush, Darren and Salvatore Massa. 2004. 'Rethinking the Potential Competition Doctrine', *Wisconsin Law Review*, 4: 1035–1160.

Choi, Won-Mog. 2003. *'Like Products' in International Trade Law: Towards a Consistent GATT/WTO Jurisprudence*. Oxford: Oxford University Press.

Ehring, Lothar. 2002. 'De Facto Discrimination in WTO Law: National and Most-Favoured-Nation Treatment — or Equal Treatment?', *Journal of World Trade*, 36 (5): 921–77.

Guzman, Andrew. 2009. 'Determining the Appropriate Standard of Review in WTO Disputes', *Cornell Journal of International Law*, 42 (1): 45–76.

Massey, Patrick. 2000. 'Market Definition and Market Power in Competition Analysis: Some Practical Issues', *Economic and Social Review*, 31 (4): 309–28.

Mattoo, Aaditya and Arvind Subramanian. 1998. 'Regulatory Autonomy and Multilateral Disciplines: The Dilemma and a Possible Resolution', *Journal of International Economic Law*, 1 (2): 303–22.

Motta, Massimo. 2004. *Competition Policy: Theory and Practice.* Cambridge: Cambridge University Press.

Rodrik, Dani. 2007. *One Economics, Many Recipes: Globalization, Institutions and Economics of Growth.* Princeton: Princeton University Press.

Van den Bergh, Roger and Peter Camesasca. 2001. *European Competition Law and Economics: A Comparative Perspective.* New York: Intersentia.

Verhoosel, Gaëtan. 2002. *National Treatment and WTO Dispute Settlement: Adjudicating the Boundaries of Regulatory Autonomy.* Oxford: Hart Publishing Limited.

17

Multilateralism under GATT–WTO Regime: A Conceptual and Methodological Investigation

Naushad Ali Azad

In the context of General Agreement on Tariffs and Trade–World Trade Organisation (GATT–WTO) regime, an important subject of current debate is its multilateral orientation. In GATT–WTO framework, the spirit of multilateralism is reflected in the form of 'non-discrimination' that, in turn, is enshrined as 'most-favoured-nation' (MFN) and 'national treatment' clauses. Theoretical justification of multilateralism as a policy instrument lies in the presumption that it tends to promote 'free trade' and therefore, the latter can be made to work as an 'engine of growth' as well as an 'effective instrument of development'. It is, however, not very clear how far the GATT–WTO regime has been successful in maintaining this often-cited and largely-desired objective. There is a growing suspicion that multilateralism in GATT–WTO regime may be on the decline. Also, attempts to quantify the multilateral aspect of trade policy are scanty and there is perhaps a need of developing efficient measures for capturing the degree of multilateral orientation.

Keeping this in view, it may be pertinent to assess some of the conceptual, theoretical and methodological dimensions of multi-lateralism in trade of contemporary times. This chapter is an attempt in this direction that begins with exploring the roots of the concept of multilateralism in international relations in section 2. In section 3, we briefly present a historical background of the GATT–WTO regime and focus on its role with respect to the regional trading arrangements. Section 4 attempts to explain how the concept of multilateralism has been incorporated in various models of trade theory. In section 5, we discuss some methods of quantifying the multilateral orientation of countries, regions and the world trading

system as a whole. In particular, this chapter points out that an
entropy measure earlier suggested in literature for measuring
symmetry in international trade can fill this gap. The chapter ends
with concluding remarks in section 6.

2. Concept of Multilateralism in International Relations

Multilateralism refers to a system of multiple countries working in
tandem on a given economic, political or social issue. For better
understanding, it needs to be contrasted with notions of unilateralism
and bilateralism. Particularly applicable in situations of market
failures and conflicts of high intensity, the doctrine of multilateralism
asserts that collective interest is served better by larger participation.
Proponents of multilateralism argue that multilateral policies by a
group of countries provide access to greater economic and political resources and, at the same time, also strengthen the bonds
between nations and peoples. On the other hand, the opponents
of multilateralism would argue that divided responsibility inevitably
results in divided authority and, therefore, multilateral negotiations
may slow down the process of decision making.

3. GATT–WTO Regime

The functional history of WTO–GATT regime can be divided into four
phases: the first, from 1947 until the Geneva Round in 1956, largely
concerned with selection of commodities for tariff reduction. A
second phase, encompassing three rounds from 1959 to 1979 (Dillon,
1959–1962; Kennedy, 1963–1967; Tokyo, 1973–1979), focused on
reducing tariffs. The third phase, consisting of the Uruguay Round
from 1986 to 1994, focused on extending the agreement to new
areas such as intellectual property, services, capital and agriculture.
This phase culminated in the birth of WTO in 1995. The fourth and
final phase of WTO–GATT regime belongs to the aftermath of 'Doha
Development Round' in 2001 and is yet to conclude.

It is easy to see that the transformation of GATT into WTO has
accompanied various quantitative and qualitative changes in international trade. The decades of 1950s and 1960s are considered as
its 'golden era' in terms of high aggregate growth and expansion.
During this phase, the nature of trade was mostly 'inter-industry'
with strong tendencies of 'complimentarity' between goods exported

from the North and South blocks of countries. In the second phase beginning in early 1970s, the 'golden era' was disrupted by a sudden display of oil-power by the Organisation of Petroleum Exporting Countries (OPEC). At the same time, emergence of a group of newly industrialised countries (NICs) changed the notion of 'North-South relationship' to the so-called 'new economic order'. Another striking feature of this period was a perceptible change in trade structure from 'inter-industry' to 'intra-industry' accompanied by a transformation of comparative advantage from 'natural and static' to 'strategic and dynamic'. The final phase can be considered to have begun in 1980s when most countries focused attention on economic reforms. During this phase, the 'reformed policy agenda' of China in early 1980s, the 1989 disintegration of erstwhile USSR in favour of market orientation and the subsequent period of world wide market reforms became the basis of a process called 'global economic integration' or simply 'globalisation'.

Role of GATT–WTO as a Trade Regime

Various questions can be asked about the role of GATT–WTO regime during its existence of more than six decades. Of these, the questions related to its role in promoting the cause of multilateralism in global trading system and that in bridging the gap between countries of North and South, remain largely unanswered. However, we focus on the multilateral aspect only.

Krasner (1983) defines international regimes as 'implicit or explicit principles, norms, rules and decision-making procedures around which actors' expectations converge in a given area'. He also mentions that the most widely accepted explanation of an international regime is its ability to resolve market failure problems and that its members must agree on policies represented by a certain set of Pareto-efficient equilibria. These remarks clearly point out to free-trade policies based on market competition implying that an explicit role of the GATT–WTO regime is to promote efficiency and equity in international trade. We argue that this is possible, if at all, by means of multilateral policies only.

The RTAs

In the context of multilateral orientation, a major challenge of the GATT–WTO regime is proliferation of regional trading arrangements

(RTAs) that have become a dominant feature of the world trading system in contemporary times. RTAs are preferential trading blocs formed to enhance level of economic cooperation and integration in a region for maximising gains from international trade. Depending on the level of economic integration, they can take the shape of free trade area, custom union, common market or economic union. The European Economic Community (EEC) was the first RTA to be born under the Treaty of Rome in 1957. Later, European Free Trade Association (EFTA) came into being in 1960 out of the Stockholm Convention. The erstwhile centrally planned economies of Eastern Europe formed the Council of Mutual Economic Assistance (CMEA) as early as 1949. The North American Free Trade Agreement (NAFTA), a trilateral regional trading bloc of North America comprising United States, Canada and Mexico, came into effect in January 1994. In Africa, about a dozen of regional groupings came into existence. In Latin America, the Latin American Free Trade Association (LAFTA) formed in 1960 was replaced by the Association for Latin American Development and Integration (ALADI) in 1980. Asia, having three giant economies of China, India and Japan, does not have an RTA of its own. However, the Association of South East Asian Nations (ASEAN), founded in 1967 by the then fast growing economies of East Asia, turned out to be a successful RTA while the South Asian Association for Regional Cooperation (SAARC), established in 1985, is still trying hard to find a place as a regional political and economic outfit of South Asia. But with centre of gravity of world economy gradually shifting towards Asia, new regional equations are expected to emerge in future. China and India, the two fastest growing giant economies, have formed free trade areas with ASEAN with effect from January 2010. Above all, the Asia Pacific Economic Cooperation (APEC), a forum of 21 Pacific Rim countries that came into existence immediately after disintegration of the erstwhile USSR in 1989, may be slated to be the biggest RTA of contemporary times.

Article XXIV of the GATT–WTO regime allows the formation of regional and sectoral groupings of countries with rider conditions that they do not violate its basic principles of non-discrimination and reciprocity and such groupings have strong impulse of trade liberalisation. The basic argument justifying RTAs is that they tend to promote international economic integration (IEI). Before the theory of second-best was developed by Meade, Lipsey, Lancaster etc., formation of RTA was justified by theory of custom unions (CU). It was argued that since free trade maximised world welfare and since CU formation was a move towards free trade, CUs increased welfare even though they did not maximise it.

Do RTAs Promote Multilateralism?

It is well known that Viner (1950) challenged the argument that CU formation was equivalent to a move towards free trade. He argued that it amounted to free trade between the members (M) but protection vis-a-vis the rest of the world (R). As a result, a CU could result in trade creation (TC) and/or trade diversion (TD). Viner stressed that since TC is beneficial while TD is harmful, the relative strength of these two effects should determine the rationale for CUs and FTAs. Later, Tinbergen (1954) explained that the role of RTAs in promoting the cause of IEI depends on their relative contributions to 'positive' and 'negative' aspects of integration of world economy.

The positive contributions of RTAs, similar to those of multi-national corporations (MNCs), are seen in furthering the process of globalisation through expanding the scope of trade cooperation among countries as well as facilitating economic integration in areas of production, consumption, distribution, technology transfer, capital markets, etc. However, the trade diverting effects of RTAs may contribute negatively to the process of international economic integration. Bhagwati (1992) has also expressed concern about the negative effects of growing regionalism on the rules-based multilateral trading system and at the same time emphasised the importance of multilateralism for undistorted freer trade. Similarly, Patrick and Forman (2002) claimed that rich countries had been deeply ambivalent about multilateral engagements and, therefore, GATT–WTO regime with ever increasing tendencies of regional cooperation in world trade has not been able to maintain, leave alone to promote, its stance of multilateralism in global trade practices.

In a recent work, Gowa and Kim (2005) point out that trans-formation of 'GATT of 1947' to 'WTO of 1995' reflects a dilution of the principle of non-discrimination as embodied in the rules on MFN and national treatment. The new policy architecture pro-vides incentives, they claim, to regime leaders for developing new methods of international cooperation that are less multilateral in nature. This is why the US brought in the issue of free riders[1] under

GATS as a pretext for not making full commitments on 'non-discrimination' (MFN and national treatment) without getting liberalising commitments from a 'critical mass' of countries. Such trends of trade diplomacy do not support the hypothesis of increasing trade cooperation and definitely contribute negatively to multilateral orientation of countries. In the mist of diverging views, a pertinent question is whether there is something inherently wrong in the framework of the GATT–WTO regime that may be undermining multilateral orientation.

Bargaining Protocol (BP) and Principal Supplier Rule (PSR) — The Archaic Rules of the Game

Curiously, one of the main reasons for a slack in multilateral orientation in international trade is an unwritten rule of 'BP' that was in operation in the US even before the GATT came into existence and is now inherently built in the GATT–WTO negotiations. Following the tradition, GATT started operating with the protocol that, in turn, is based on 'principal-supplier-rule'[2] (PSR). Over time, BP and PSR became the main instruments of negotiations on tariff reduction. Now inherent to the GATT–WTO regime, they make trade negotiations look like multilateral that are in essence bilateral. It follows that BP and PSR are responsible for accentuating 'product-by-product' method of selecting items for tariff negotiations and thus encouraging bilateral mode of negotiations in GATT–WTO regime. A multilateral approach would mean evolving a suitable formula for application across the board. And given a choice between linear formula and Swiss non-linear formula, it can be seen that the latter is more multilateral in spirit than the former because it suggests proportionately greater reduction on high tariffs.

4. Analysis of Multilateralism in Trade Theory

As argued earlier, the concept of multilateral orientation hinges on policies of 'free and fair trade'. It is based on the twin objectives of efficiency and equity and remains a desirable policy trait of the world trading system. These aspects are central to any course on trade theory and policy.

Heckscher-Ohlin theory based on neoclassical assumptions provides the simplest form of the long-run general equilibrium model dealing with multilateral aspect in the form of 'free trade policy'.

The medium-term version of this model was given by Ronald Jones (1971) and is known as the 'specific-factors' model. Besides the 'gains from trade' arising from efficient allocation of factor resources, these models also explain the medium and long term effects of 'free trade' on the distribution of income — a subject area known as 'political economy of free trade'.

On the other hand, 'political economy of protection' explaining the effects of 'restrictive' and 'protective' trade policies is incorporated in theories given by Stolper, Samuelson and others. 'Perfectly competitive markets' and 'free and unhindered' flow of goods and services are the basic assumptions of these different versions of neoclassical models (see Krugman and Obstfeld 2008). In this way, free trade policy comes very close to the spirit of multilateralism. But for reasons explained by these very models, 'free trade policy' is likely to have asymmetric impacts on the internal distribution of income of the trading countries leading to the formation of lobbies that exert political pressure to protect the interest of their respective groups. Further, quite often trade between countries is governed by non-economic considerations. In practice, therefore, global trade is likely to be less multilateral than desired by collective interest.

There are a number of political economy models that touch upon the multilateral, regional, bilateral and unilateral aspects of trade policy. The analysis of these aspects is based on the methodology of 'welfare ranking of trade policy instruments'. In a pioneering paper, Bhagwati (1980) modelled the operation of interest groups in international trade to analyse their effects on country's welfare. He argued that one could not rule out the possibility that the use of resources in lobbying to influence trade policy might actually be socially beneficial. This proposition, which on first reflection appeared somewhat counter-intuitive, followed directly from another theory associated with Bhagwati, that of immiserizing growth. Since it is possible for a small trading economy in a protected equilibrium to lose in aggregate from increased availability of a factor of production, an economy can conversely gain if the same factor is withdrawn from domestic production and is used instead in an unproductive activity such as lobbying. Bhagwati (1982) therefore characterises lobbying activities as 'directly' wasteful but 'potentially and indirectly' productive. Since then, the literature on lobbying in international trade has evolved from the 'tariff-formation function' approach (see Findlay-Wellisz 1982; Feenstra and Bhagwati 1982) to the 'political contributions' model (see Grossman and Helpman 1994). The Grossman-Helpman model is multisectoral and provides micro foundations to the behavior of organised lobbies and politicians. While Findlay and Wellisz (1982) use a specific-factors framework, the set up in Feenstra and Bhagwati (1982) is based on Heckscher-Ohlin model. Mayer (1984) has applied 'median voter approach' to model political economy of protection and Rodrik (1995) has done a general equilibrium analysis of endogenous protection using 'tariff-formation' function approach.

A policy issue relevant in the present context is that of the alternative ways of getting to free trade. Bhagwati (2002) has dealt with this issue by breaking it into two sub-issues — one being the issue of unilateralism versus reciprocity, and second, if reciprocity is the mode of liberalisation, should it be bilateral (regional) or should it be multilateral. He summarises the issue of unilateralism versus reciprocity and the link between the two in three propositions: (1) Go alone (that is, cut trade barriers unilaterally) if others will not go with you; (2) If others go simultaneously with you (i.e., there is reciprocity in reducing trade barriers), that is still better; and (3) If you must go alone, others may follow suit later: unilateralism then leads to sequential reciprocity.

Standard trade theory easily defends proposition (1) on welfare grounds (i.e., the optimal trade policy for a country, in the absence of any distortions, is free trade). But Krishna and Mitra (2005) focus on the additional gain to the unilaterally liberalising country coming from the induced reciprocity from its partner countries and thereby provide an additional channel for the said proposition to hold. While reciprocal reduction in trade barriers can reasonably be expected to occur in trade negotiations between countries, Krishna and Mitra examine instead the question of whether unilateral trade liberalisation by one country can induce reciprocal liberalisation by its partner in the absence of any communication or negotiations between the two countries. In this context, they show that unilateral liberalisation by one country can impact the political economy equilibrium in the partner country through the formation of an export lobby in a manner that induces it to liberalise trade. Bagwell and Staiger (2002) have analysed the issues related with propositions (2) and (3) of reciprocal trade liberalisation both in bilateral and multilateral settings. In their models, reciprocity is a way of eliminating terms-of-trade externalities. They develop a rationale for the GATT/WTO and its different rules and show that even when political economy considerations are taken into account, the only rationale for (reciprocal) trade agreements is the elimination of terms-of-trade externalities. In brief, these studies are suggestive of a rationale for 'trade-talks' as opposed to 'trade wars'.

Finally, we come to the issue of regionalism and bilateralism versus multilateralism where a great deal of political economy research has been done on the question of whether regionalism is a 'stumbling block' or a 'stepping stone' to multilateralism. Bhagwati (1993, 1994) provides several reasons why regionalism might not lead to global free trade. These arguments have been formally modeled by Levy (1997) and Krishna (1998). Levy (1997) uses a Heckscher-Ohlin set-up with monopolistic competition and uses median-voter approach to address this issue. He finds that bilateral agreements between countries similar in factor endowments result in the subsequent blocking of multilateral trade agreements. He also finds that bilateral agreements can never increase the political support for multilateralism. Krishna (1998) addresses the same issue in a political economy set-up and finds greater political support for trade-diverting bilateral agreements (regionalism) than for trade-creating ones. Such agreements can also make previously feasible multilateral agreements politically infeasible. The gist of these arguments is that tendencies of bilateralism or regionalism do not support the policies of multilateralism.

5. Quantifying the Multilateral Orientation

The performance of GATT–WTO regime has to be judged on the basis of its contribution to: (1) multilateral orientation in trade negotiations, and (2) the degree of economic integration so attained. A number of studies are available that have focused on the integration effect but attempts to quantify and analyse the aspect of multilateral orientation are rare. In most cases, the integration effect has been analysed in terms of the relative strengths of trade-creation and trade-diversion caused by a particular custom union or a free trade area. For example, Williamson and Bottrill (1971) have estimated integration impact of European Community (EC) on manufacturing sector and concluded that 'intra-EC trade in 1969 was something like 50 per cent greater than it would have been if the EC has not been created' (ibid.: 342) that 'this was due to trade creation rather than trade diversion' (ibid.); and that 'the harm done to other countries' exports by diversion was largely offset by positive external trade creation' (ibid.). The study by Gowa and Kim (2005) point out that the integration effects of RTAs have been parochial in nature. Taking example of EC in Europe and ASEAN in Asia, they maintain that though the effects are significant but they remain confined to a small group of countries and therefore, have harmed the multilateral orientation of the global trading system. In what follows, we propose a simple 'entropy measure of symmetry' and discuss that it can be used to monitor both the aspects of trade policy mentioned above.

The Concept of Symmetry and its Applications

Symmetry is a mathematical concept which deals with correspondence or equivalence in the elements of a matrix. In the context of international trade, it deals with 'regularity or uniformity' in the behavior of the aggregate trade flows among the countries participating in trade. Hirschman (1945), Michaely (1958, 84) and MacBean and Nguyen (1987) have used them to demonstrate the contrasting trends in terms of commodity concentration and geographical dispersion of the developed and the developing countries. It was argued that trends of these features calculated from the aggregate trade matrix belonging to a group of countries reflect on the various important aspects such as power of nations, elasticity differences, nature of specialisation, export earnings instability, etc. Theil (1979) was the first to use the well known 'entropy measure' for the purpose of analysing the symmetry behavior of the trade flows pertaining to a group of countries. But his objective was confined to establish the relevance of symmetry with the gravity models and the probability models of trade. Azad (1992, 1998) suggested that symmetry behavior of aggregate trade flows itself reflects on some broad features of international trade such as integration and multilateral orientation. We argue that Theil's symmetry measure reflects simultaneously on these two important aspects of trade policy of GATT–WTO regime and that it is much simpler than the tedious methodology used by Williamson-Bottril and others.

Concept of Symmetry in Trade Flows

In order to explain some relevant concepts of symmetry and their applications, we begin with the definition of a 'share matrix'. Suppose that X_{ij} denotes aggregate exports from country i to country j and that $[X_{ij}]_{nxn}$ represents the 'aggregate trade matrix' for a group of n countries (e.g., an RTA).

Now, let $T = \sum_{i=1}^{n} \sum_{j=1}^{n} X_{ij}$ represent the total world trade, so that $x_{ij} = X_{ij}/T$ is nothing but the share of exports from country i to country j in the total world trade. Then $[X_{ij}]_{nxn}$ is known as the 'share matrix'. And since:

$$\sum_{i=1}^{n} \sum_{j=1}^{n} x_{ij} = 1$$ it follows that $[X_{ij}]_{nxn}$ is a stochastic matrix.

Bilateral Symmetry and its Application

Theil (1979) deals with information-based approach to symmetry. However, Azad (1992, 1998) explain a simpler way of dealing with concept of symmetry that relates to pair-wise equivalence in corresponding elements of a trade matrix. Since it deals with bilateral trade flows among partner countries of a group, it is called 'bilateral symmetry' and is defined as follows:

Definition: If the corresponding elements of the trade matrix are equal i.e., if $x_{ij} = x_{ji}$ for all i, j, then the trade flows will be called as bilaterally symmetric; otherwise they will be known as bilaterally asymmetric.

Applications of Bilateral Symmetry to Multilateralism

The above concept of symmetry is both simple as well as novel. It is simple, because it represents nothing more than a situation of bilateral or pair-wise balance, i.e., the trade of each country is balanced with each of its trading partners. The concept is novel because it leads us to very useful implications for two important issues related with international trade — namely, the extent of multilateralism and the existence of intra-industry trade. The two are explained in the following paragraphs.

Multilateralism and Bilateral Symmetry

A slightly deep thought on trade relationship tells us that the concept of bilateral symmetry as defined in (1) above can relate to following hypothetical but theoretically possible situations: (a) the world economy consisting of two countries only, (b) a world trading system where the goods are only barter-exchanged, and (c) a trading system where, for some reason or the other, the partner countries strictly follow the policy of the bilateral balancing of their trade. Clearly, the first two cases are incompatible with reality but the situation of deliberate bilateral balancing as implied in (c) is of particular consequence.

For the sake of analytical simplicity, we further assume that multilateralism in international trade means absence of the mutually-balancing trade flows. The practical importance of this assumption, which is not quite restrictive, is that multilateralism implies bilateral asymmetry and that the extent of multilateralism in international trade is now directly related to the degree of bilateral asymmetry of the trade flows. Other things remaining constant, stronger the tendency of multilateralism larger will be the pair-wise trade gaps and, hence, greater will be the bilateral asymmetry. It follows, therefore, that the concept of bilateral asymmetry can be employed as an aggregate technique to examine whether or not the trade among a group of countries in an RTA or any other group of countries is taking place on the basis of multilateralism as the main objective of their trade policy.

Main Reasons of Tendencies of Bilateral Balancing

Despite tall claims for more and more multilateralism in their trade, many countries including the US are known to have preferences for bilateral arrangements in order to mitigate their domestic and external problems. In general, preference for bilateral arrangements may arise due to various reasons, e.g., (1) continued deficits in the balance of payments, (2) non-convertibility of national currencies and uncertainties of the exchange rate mechanism, (3) shortage of international liquidity, (4) formation of RTAs followed by an agreement on policy of bilateral balancing in the name of mutual economic cooperation, (5) prevalence of counter-trade amongst the less developed countries (LDCs), and finally, (6) for some countries, bilateral trade may be a political necessity or a compulsion, for example, the countries of the erstwhile East European block including USSR. Whatever be the reason, any deliberate attempt on part of countries to bilaterally balance their trade with their trade partners is likely to be a trade-restricting activity and thus contributes negatively to the process of multilateralism.

Intra-Industry Trade and Bilateral Symmetry

The association of bilateral symmetry with the tendencies of bilateral balancing as discussed in the preceding paragraphs depends, very crucially, on the assumption of other things remaining constant.

In the long run, the symmetry behavior of the trade flows may be influenced by factors other than the policies of mutual balancing. We find that existence of intra-industry trade (IIT) among more developed countries (MDCs), known as an important cause of their economic integration, may also be influencing the trade flows of these countries. As a result, their trade flows tend to be more bilaterally symmetric than those of the LDCs.

It may be claimed that IIT, which crucially depends on how the industry is defined, may have nothing to do with the symmetry in the aggregate trade flows among the partner countries. But in the case of MDCs, which are characterised by modern industrial structure of large size and the levels of income high enough to have preference similarities for these goods, it is quite possible that the existence of IIT provides these countries an easy opportunity for mutual balancing of the trade flows in order to overcome the problems of balance of payments. In other words, IIT may not be directly related with the symmetry behavior but it can certainly strengthen the already existing tendencies of bilateral balancing. Also, since specialisation cannot change in the short run, the IIT and the tendency of bilateral symmetry resulting there from, are long-term phenomena and, therefore, they may not clash with the short-run analysis of bilateral balancing or counter-trade tendencies.

The Mutual Information Formula

Initially, Theil (1979) suggested a simple 'mutual information formula' for the extent of bilateral symmetry between pairs of countries. It is given by:

$$S_{ij} = x_{ij} \log_2 x_{ij} - x_{ji} \log_2 x_{ji} \qquad\qquad 1$$

where x_{ij} is the amount of exports from country i to country j, measured as a fraction of the total trade between the two countries, so that $x_{ij} + x_{ji} = 1$. Also known as the entropy of the mutual trade flows, S_{ij} takes the maximum value of 1 ('one bit') when $x_{ij} = x_{ji}$ for all i, j and a minimum of value 0 (zero) when x_{ij} and $x_{ji} =$ or $x_{ij} = 0$ and $x_{ji} = 1$. It follows that S_{ij} is a direct proportional measure of symmetry and its range is (0, 1).

In order to apply (1) for a group of n countries, we will have to compute mutual symmetry for the $^nC_2$ pairs. Such computations, particularly for a large sample, are obviously clumsy. For example, for a sample of 30 countries, one has to compute S_{ij} for 435 pairs of countries and then aggregate the behaviour of the group by computing median or some other suitable statistical measure for different homogenous groups of countries.[3]

Thus it is preferable to use another measure, again suggested by Theil (1979) and based on information theory, which may be called the index of 'bilateral group asymmetry'. It will be seen that the computation of this index is straightforward and can be applied to all countries as well as to a group of countries simultaneously.

Index of Bilateral Group Asymmetry

The asymmetry of the trade flows can be defined as the deviation from the state of perfect symmetry. For a given share matrix $[x_{ij}]_{nxn}$, and following Theil (ibid.), a simple direct measure for the extent to which the trade flows deviate from symmetry is given by[4]:

$$A = \sum_{i=1}^{n} \sum_{j=1}^{n} x_{ij} \log \frac{x_{ij}}{(x_{ij} + x_{ji})/2} \qquad 2$$

Now, if $x_{ij} = x_{ji}$ for all (i, j), then clearly A equals zero. Also, A is necessarily positive when the total exports of at least one country differ from its total imports. The maximum value of A is not explicitly determined. However, it can be shown that for a completely asymmetric triangular trade matrix, A assumes a value of log 2. Thus assuming that a triangular trade matrix conforms to the extreme case of asymmetric trade flows, the range of the index A can be stated as $(0, \log_2)$.

It may be noted that the indices (1) and (2) are the direct and indirect measures of symmetry respectively. Both of them can be applied for analysing the symmetry behaviour of the trade flows of any specific group of countries (an RTA) or the world economy as a whole.[5] In addition to the property of easier computability, (2) is superior to (1) in that the former can be extended for the purpose of analysing the symmetry behaviour of individual countries. Such an extension, however, remains beyond the scope of this chapter whose main objective was to focus on the multilateral orientation in GATT–WTO regime.[6]

6. Conclusion

In the context of GATT–WTO regime, an important subject of current debate is its multilateral orientation. Initially, the concept of multilateralism was applied in the area of international relations for the prevention of big wars. The same spirit was attempted in international trade for minimising trade rivalries across the globe. It is reflected in GATT–WTO framework in the form of 'non-discrimination' that, in turn, is enshrined as 'most-favoured-nation' and 'national treatment' clauses. Theoretical justification of multilateralism as an optimal policy instrument lies in the presumption that it will promote 'free trade' so that international trade under GATT–WTO regime works not only as an 'engine of growth' but also an 'effective instrument of development'. It is, however, not very clear how far the GATT–WTO regime has been successful in maintaining this often-cited and largely-desired objective. There is a growing suspicion that multilateralism may actually be on the decline.

In this context, this chapter highlights the continuation of discriminatory practices in trade negotiations. It reveals that the GATT–WTO regime has not changed archaic rules of negotiating strategy. As a result, developing countries have not been able to realise the potential benefits of multilateral trading system. The study further emphasises the need of quantification for the degree of multilateral orientation. Finally, the chapter also suggests that a symmetry measure of the trade flows based on the concept of entropy can be used for this purpose.

Notes

1. 'Free-riders' are those who consume more than their fair share of a public good (common resource), or shoulder less than a fair share of the costs of its production. 'Free-riding' is usually considered to be an economic 'problem' only when it leads to either non-production (or under-production) of the public resources (due to Pareto inefficiency), or to their excessive use.
2. It may be noted that PSR and 'most-favored-nation (MFN) were the two main but contrasting provisions of the 'Reciprocal Trade Agreements Act' (RTAA) of 1934 passed by Roosevelt administration. As already mentioned, MFN and 'national treatment' are main pillars of multilateralism under GATT–WTO regime. The contrast between PSR and MFN arises because the spirit of the former is anti-multilateral as it ruled out liberalisation of trade between large and small countries. According to PSR, trade barriers were reduced on the basis of concessions on particular

goods exchanged between their principal suppliers — namely Britain and the United States. It is considered to be an outcome of the divergent trade policy goals of Roosevelt government that sought to destroy the interwar trade blocs and promote European and transatlantic trade in a bid to stabilise Europe and contribute to the creation of a Western bloc strong enough to deter Soviet expansion. On the other hand, the Congress was wary of import competition and wanted to continue with the provisions of RTAA.

3. Theil, using a sample of 13 countries, had to compute mutual symmetry for 78 pairs of countries and then aggregate the behaviour of the group by computing the median for six different categories of countries depending on their share in total trade concluding that the symmetry was greater in the trade flows of major trading partners than those of the minor ones.

4. According to Theil, $(X_{ij} + X_{ji})/2$ is taken as a symmetric approximation of xij. He showed that this is the best symmetric approximation in the informational sense.

5. For extending the application of (2) to analyse the symmetry behavior of individual countries, see Azad (1998).

6. Theil did not carry out any extensive exercise about symmetry. However, he applied (1) and (2) to a small set of data and concluded that during the period 1971–1975 the world's trading patterns had moved a bit away from symmetry.

References

Azad, N. A. 1992. 'Trade Performance and Trade Distribution — A Study of North v/s South'. Ph.D. dissertation, Jawaharlal Nehru University, New Delhi.

———. 1998. 'Multilateralism in the World Economy, in M. Agarwal, A. Barua, S. K. Das and M. Pant (eds), *Indian Economy in Transition — Environmental and Development Issues*, pp. 325–44. Delhi: Har Anand Publications.

Bagwell, K. and R. Staiger. 2002. *The Economics of the World Trading System*. Cambridge: MIT Press.

Bhagwati, Jagdish N. 1980. 'Lobbying and Welfare', *Journal of Public Economics* 14 (3): 355–64.

———. 1982. 'Directly-Unproductive Profit-Seeking (DUP) Activities', *Journal of Political Economy*, 90 (5): 988–1002.

———. 1992. 'Regionalism versus Multilateralism', *The World Economy*, 15 (5): 535–55.

———. 1993. 'Regionalism and Multilateralism: An Overview', in A. Panagariya and J. De Melo (eds), *New Dimensions in Regional Integration*, pp. 22–51. Washington, DC: World Bank.

Bhagwati, Jagdish N. 1994. 'Threats to the World Trading System: Income Distribution and the Selfish Hegemon', Working Paper No. 696. New York: Columbia University, Department of Economics.

———. 2002. *Free Trade Today*. Princeton: Princeton University Press.

Culpin, Christopher and Ruth Henig 2004. *Modern Europe 1870–1945*. London: Longman.

Feenstra, R. and J. Bhagwati 1982. 'Tariff Seeking and the Efficient Tariff', in J. Bhagwati (ed.), *Import Competition and Response*, pp. 245–58. Chicago: University of Chicago Press.

Findlay, R. and S. Wellisz. 1982. 'Endogenous Tariffs, the Political Economy of Trade Restrictions and Welfare', in J. Bhagwati (ed.), *Import Competition and Response*, pp. 223–34.Chicago: University of Chicago Press.

Gowa, J. and S. Y. Kim. 2005. 'An Exclusive Country Club: The Effects of GATT on Trade, 1950–94', *World Politics*, 57 (4): 453–78.

Grossman, G. and E. Helpman. 1994. 'Protection for Sale', *American Economic Review*, 84 (4): 833–50.

Hirschman, A. O. 1945. *National Power and the Structure of Foreign Trade*, Berkeley: University of California Press.

Jones, Ronald W. 1971. 'A Three-Factor Model in Theory, Trade, and History', in Jagdish Bhagwati, Ronald W. Jones, Robert Mundell and Jaroslav Vanek (eds), *Trade, Balance of Payments, and Growth*, pp. 3–21. Amsterdam: North-Holland.

Krasner, Stephen D. 1983. (ed.). *International Regimes*. Ithaca: Cornell University Press.

Krishna, P. 1998. 'Regionalism and Multilateralism: A Political Economy Approach', *Quarterly Journal of Economics*, 113 (1): 227–51.

Krishna, Pravin and Devashish Mitra. 2005. 'Reciprocated Unilateralism in Trade Policy', *Journal of International Economics*, 65 (2): 461–87.

Krugman, Paul R. and M. Obstfeld. 2008. *International Economics: Theory and Policy*. London: Addison-Wesley.

Levy, P. 1997. 'A Political–Economic Analysis of Free Trade Agreements', *American Economic Review*, 87 (4): 506–19.

MacBean, Alasdair I. and D. T. Nguyen. 1987. *Commodity Policies — Problems and Prospects*. New York: Croom Helm.

Mayer, W. 1984. 'Endogenous Tariff Formation', *American Economic Review*, 74 (5): 970–85.

Michaely, Michael. 1958. 'Concentration of Exports and Imports: An International Comparison', *Economic Journal*, 68 (272): 722–36.

———. 1984. *Trade, Income Levels and Dependence: Studies in International Economics*, vol. 8. Amsterdam: North Holland.

Mitra, Devashish. 2005. 'Political Economy of Trade Policy'. Paper presented at the conference on the occasion of Professor Jagdish Bhagwati's 70th birthday held at Columbia University on 5 and 6 August, 2005. www.columbia.edu/~ap2231/jbconference/JB_Program.doc (accessed 14 September 2009).

Patrick, Stewart and Shepherd Forman. (eds). 2002. *Multilateralism and U. S. Foreign Policy: Ambivalent Engagement.* Boulder: Lynn Reinner.

Rodrik, Dani. 1995. 'Political Economy of Trade Policy', in G. Grossman and K. Rogoff (eds), *Handbook of International Economics*, vol. 3, pp. 1457–94. Amsterdam: North-Holland.

Theil, H. 1979. 'How Symmetric is International Trade?', *Empirical Economics*, 4 (1): 53–62.

Tinbergen, Jan. 1954. *International Economic Integration.* Amsterdam: Elsevier.

Viner, I. 1950. The Customs Union Issue. New York: Carnegie Endowment for International Peace.

Williamson, J. and A. Bottril. 1971. 'The Impact of Customs Unions on Trade in Manufactures', *Oxford Economic Papers*, 23 (3): 323–51.

18

India's Position in Doha Development Round of WTO: An Assessment

Nilanjan Banik

Notwithstanding the recent global financial crisis, countries in South Asia are still one of the fastest growing regions in the world. Among South Asian economies, India is the largest and the fastest growing economy — growing at a rate of around 7.3 per cent (in real term) since 2001. Much of the reason for this fast growth process is attributed to full-fledged economic reforms programme that India has embarked upon since early 1990s. These reforms essentially brought down interest rates, and government liberal attitude to allow private participation in manufacturing and services sectors did the rest. The effect of reforms on India's external sector has been positive. Its exports have crossed the $159 billion mark in 2007–2008. There has been an increase in both the volume and the value of exports. During 2007–2008, the export unit value has increased by 25.8 per cent over the previous year. There was a marked improvement in overall trade figures with India's two-way trade (merchandise exports plus imports), as a proportion of GDP increasing from 21.2 per cent in 1997–1998 (the year of the Asian crisis) to 34.7 per cent in 2007–2008 (Reserve Bank of India, various years).

This feel good factor about India's trade figure is presently under scanner with global financial crisis adversely affecting most parts of the world. Three of India's largest trading partners — USA, Japan and the European Union (EU) — are worst hit. In early January 2009, the International Monetary Fund (IMF) revised its forecast for global growth downwards — from 3.9 to 3.7 per cent for 2008, and from 3.0 to 0.5 per cent for 2009 (IMF 2009). Faced with a slump demand condition, policymakers in emerging developing economies, like China and India, are focusing on increasing trade among them, and with other countries in Asia, Africa and Latin America. On August 2009,

Table 18.1: India's Merchandise Trade

Year	Exports	Imports	Total	Trade in GDP (%)
	(US$ billion)			
1990–1991	18.15	24.07	42.22	15.48
1995–1996	31.80	36.68	68.48	23.13
2000–2001	44.56	50.54	95.10	27.38
2001–2002	43.83	51.41	95.24	26.38
2002–2003	52.72	61.41	114.13	29.92
2003–2004	63.84	78.15	141.99	30.78
2004–2005	83.54	111.52	195.06	38.22
2005–2006	103.09	149.17	252.26	43.61
2006–2007	126.26	185.60	311.86	48.78
2007–2008	163.13	251.65	414.78	49.38
2008–2009 (P)	168.70	287.76	456.46	

Source: 'Economic Survey 2007–2008', Ministry of Finance, Government of India.

India signed a Free Trade Agreement (FTA) with South Korea and ASEAN. India is also contemplating about signing FTAs with the developed countries as well.

However, this effort to increase trade by aligning with various regional trade blocks is yielding limited results. Slump in world demand condition has made countries more cautious about giving additional market access. Protectionism is becoming evident in terms of higher tariffs; Non-tariff Barriers (NTBs) mainly in the form of antidumping measures, and sanitary and phytosanitary sanctions; or even through provisions of subsidies to the domestic producers. However, it should be noted that most part of this protectionism does not break any World Trade Organisation (WTO) rules. So although there might not be any direct evidences about protectionism, countries are subtly using them. For example, countries are increasing tariffs above their applied rate while keeping them below the bound rates. The recent increase in import tariffs for steel items by India is a case in point (The Economic Times 2009). Similarly, countries are using NTBs in the pretext of safeguarding health of their consumer, and to stop predatory pricing strategy — again perfectly permissible under WTO rules. India has recently banned imports of a number of live animal products including processed meat, eggs, pigs, etc., from rest of the world because of avian influenza (swine flu) virus.[1] India has also emerged as the largest user of anti-dumping measures, having initiated 68 anti-dumping investigations between January 2008 and June 2009.[2]

India's case should not be looked in isolation. In Asia, China banned imports of Irish pork, Belgian chocolate, Italian brandy, British sauce, Dutch eggs and Spanish diary products. Indonesia has restricted imports by allowing entry points only through five designated ports and airports. Japan and South Korea have restricted foreigners from bidding for any government projects worth less than $ 22 million. Elsewhere, in the US, 'Buy American' provisions in their $ 787 billion economic stimulus package, and generous provisions of subsidies in France, Germany and UK, are nothing but reflection of protectionism.

It seems that to have greater market access, more fruitful negotiations are needed at WTO. At present, negotiation to further reduce tariff barriers and to remove NTBs are not yielding much result. This is because within developing countries as a group, individual bargaining interests vary. Regarding agriculture, for example, India is rather passive when it comes to negotiating for greater market access. In contrast, countries such as Brazil, Mexico, Chile and South Africa — which are net agricultural exporters — want to reduce tariffs on agricultural items. India's justification for maintaining high tariffs is to protect interests of its marginal farmers. The average land holdings size for Indian farmer is around 1.3 hectare.

A reduction in agricultural tariffs would help the domestic consumers but not benefit the marginal farmers. Cheaper agricultural imports may jeopardise income of the majority of 58 per cent of India's 1.14 billion population earning their livelihood from agriculture and the agriculture-related informal sector (like, cooperatives, fishing, dairies, etc.). Although the overall average applied tariffs fell from over 32 per cent in 2001–2002 to almost 10 per cent in 2009–2010, in case for agricultural products the median applied agricultural duty remained at 35.2 per cent.[3] India, however, did not provide any direct subsidies for its agricultural exports.

Compared with its policy towards agriculture and manufactured items, India has been more aggressive in negotiating market access in services. Trade in services accounts for 30 per cent of India's exports; its BPO sector is a $7.7 billion industry, which is seven times the figure of China's BPO sector (Hummels and Klenow 2005). In addition, the movement of natural persons, mostly in the IT sector (that is, Mode 4 type services) and BPO-type activities (that is, Mode 1 type services) contribute significantly to the export earnings of India. Hence in case of India, promoting the growth of the services sector and improving market access for services have priority over improving market access for agriculture.

When developing countries as a group has diversified trade interests, it is no surprise why multilateral talks, such as the one under WTO umbrella, are yielding limited results. Countries around the world in an effort to increase their trade shares are increasingly entering into Regional Trading Agreement (RTA) with other countries. India, in fact, is a member of South Asian Association of Regional Cooperation (SAARC), which comprises Afghanistan, Bangladesh, Bhutan, India, Maldives, Nepal, Pakistan and Sri Lanka, as other member countries. During 1995, the SAARC Preferential Trading Arrangement (SAPTA) was formed. Beginning 1 January 2006, the South Asian Free Trade Area (SAFTA) came into effect. Unfortunately, SAFTA has not emerged as a success story, mainly because of India's strained relation with Pakistan.

Moreover, although RTAs are preferable to autarky and high tariff walls, they are suboptimal in terms of global growth and welfare. The recent decision of Hyundai Motor — a South Korean automobile manufacturer — to move production of one of its hatchback cars from India to Turkey because India does not have an FTA with Europe is a classic example where a FTA can cause trade diversion, and can actually make any firm settle for the second-best option.[4] Trade diversion happens as Turkey is a high-cost country compared to India, leading to loss in global welfare.

Against this backdrop, this chapter tries to understand the following: (a) North–South negotiations under WTO umbrella from the perspective of compatibility issues; (b) policy recommendations on the basis of what can be doable; and (c) conclusion.

North-South Negotiation under WTO with Special Reference to India

A RTA becomes successful when like-minded countries with similar economic interests and characteristics are able to address issues such as harmonisation of custom procedures and removals of NTBs at a smaller period of time. However, SAFTA is still not mature to reap benefits in terms of trade creation. Under present circumstances, an attempt by India to forge economic co-operation with other countries and regional grouping like ASEAN is nothing but a reflection of 'spaghetti bowl' effect. Bhagwati et al. (1998)

introduce the concept of 'spaghetti bowl' phenomenon to explain the harmful effect caused by multiple and complicated rules of origin in RTAs, particularly from overlapping RTAs among member of different RTAs. Hence from the perspective of economies in South Asia, at least in the short to medium run, successful completion of the Doha Development Round seems to be more beneficial.

The Doha Development Round (Geneva, July 2008) which was on its seventh year of negotiations since its inception in November 2001, failed to reach any conclusion. This was mainly because of arguments centering around agriculture and safeguards, although Non-Agricultural Market Access (NAMA), services, Trade Related Aspects of Intellectual Property Rights (TRIPS), Trade Related Investment Measurements (TRIMS), and trade in services, were the other important areas where there was lack of compliance between developed and the developing economies. Let us look at these issues by turns.

Agriculture

Broadly, the association of developing nations — the G-20 group of countries — want subsidies given by the developed countries to their farmers and processed food producers, (items like beef, poultry, etc.) to be reduced. On the other side, the US and the EU wanted big developing economies like China and India to open up their markets in industrial goods as well as farm products in return for reducing subsides on agriculture items. The argument of G-20 group was that farm subsidies are against livelihood security and subsistence of poor farmer living in developing and less developed countries.[5] Therefore, without further reduction in subsidies and without a proper modification on the safeguard clause any further negotiation has to be stalled. Although the US was willing to reduce their farm subsidies from the present $15 billion level to $14.5 billion, they had problem with a key demand of India, which is holding out for a lower threshold level of imports than the 40 per cent proposed in a compromise text by WTO.[6] This brings us to the issues relating to safeguards.

Safeguards

Over the years, incidence of safeguard measures has fallen and has been instead replaced by other measures like anti-dumping and countervailing measures (Banik 2005). This is because imposing safeguards measures require compensating trading partners whereas imposing anti-dumping and countervailing measures do not requires any such compensation. Keeping in mind the vulnerability of marginal farmers because of cheap foreign farm imports, developing nations spearheaded by India wanted that they be allowed to use the safeguard clause when imports exceed 20 per cent of the average of previous three years' imports.

NAMA

On NAMA, developing countries submitted a number of proposals to modify the Swiss formula. According to this formula, the tariffs should be reduced on a pro rata basis — higher tariffs subject to a greater cut as compared to lower tariffs. Since bound tariffs level for most developing countries are higher compared to high income countries, the former group of countries including Argentina, India and Brazil are opposing the Swiss formula. Instead, they are willing to negotiate tariffs cut on the basis of average applied tariffs level as opposed to bound tariffs level which means a lesser amount tariffs cut compared to the Swiss formula. Interestingly, developing countries are less vocal about other types of NTBs, specifically anti-dumping measures, which has emerged as the most predominant type of NTB starting late 1990s (Banik 2005). This is because some of the developing nations like India and South Africa are themselves using anti-dumping measures to protect their own market.

TRIPS

Developing countries have problem with inclusion of TRIPS on the ground that it doesn't seem to be non-discriminatory and welfare improving. About discrimination, TRIPS agreement provides higher degree of protection for wines and spirit, with lesser degree of protection for items like Basmati rice and Darjeeling tea from India; Tequila from Mexico; and Szatmar plums from Hungary. Also, royalty accruing to firms from patent protection are seldom welfare improving. Examining 177 patent policy changes across 60 countries over a period of 150 years, Lerner (2001) found that patent protection does not necessarily lead to innovation. Similarly, Sakakibara and Bransetter (2001) examined patent data on 307 Japanese firms, and found no evidence of increase in research and development expenditure resulting from patent protection. On the contrary, monopoly rights accrued because patent protection raises price of life saving drugs, and this has serious implication on health of poor.

TRIMS

It applies to investment related measures pertaining to trade in goods only. Developing countries have for long opposed inclusion of TRIMS. Their argument is that the provisions laid under TRIMS impede the process of industrialisation and balance of payment stability for the developing and less developed nations. Moreover, there is a belief that firms with considerable lobbying power in the developed countries are using this agreement for their own benefit. Hence developing countries want removal of private sector induced distortion before implementation of TRIMS. To remove this distortion, what is essential is to lay down an effective competition policy.

Services

Since January 2000, WTO member countries have started submitting requests for greater market access in the area they perceive to have comparative advantage. Typically, developing countries have advantages in Mode 1 and Mode 4 types of services. Developed countries have advantages in Mode 3 type services. In Mode 4 or temporary movement of natural persons, developing countries want issuing of short-term visas at very short notice; greater transparency, simplicity and certainty in the visa regime; exemption from social security contributions; de-linking movement of natural persons from the requirement to set up an office or firm in a foreign country; removal of quantitative restrictions on issuance of visa; and removing Economic Needs Tests (ENTs).[7] In Mode 1 or cross-border trade in business services, the demands are for removal of any form of government ban on outsourcing; removal of federal and state level protectionist legislation and caller identification requirements. In addition as tourism industry could play a significant role in the trade basket of developing countries, India has raised objection against the present structure of the global tourism industry characterised by vertically integrated market structures and consolidated distribution channels controlled by limited number of large international players. In Mode 2 (tourism) type services, some of the developing countries like the ones in the Caribbean regions are pushing for forming a tourism regulatory framework that will prevent anti-competitive practices followed by some big tourist firms in the EU region.

Policy Recommendations

Given repeated failures at various ministerial meets of WTO to successfully conclude Doha Development Round, it makes sense to understand the causes behind these failures, and the plausible way out. This is particularly relevant, especially when implementing free trade within RTA is becoming increasingly difficult. SAFTA is a case in point. For SAFTA to emerge as a successful RTA, it is essential that the member countries work on political differences and remove trade costs (Banik and Gilbert 2010). An easier way out is to make an attempt where concerns raised by both developed and developing countries will be addressed. Based on the aforementioned discussion, here are some suggestions:

Agriculture

While protecting the interests of the marginal farmers are justified, developing countries like India should also make conscious effort to remove domestic distortion. For the marginal farmers, much of the producer surplus is lost because of market imperfection wherein the middlemen between the farmer and retailer of farm products gets to keep most part of the agricultural income, leaving little for the farmers. Likewise, as subsidy generates large economic inefficiencies and distort the world market price for agricultural produce, policy-makers in the developed countries should make an attempt to reduce subsidy. It is known that redistributive policy in terms of subsidy provisions always yield less favourable results than pursuing allocative policies of diverting fund for public agricultural research investment. The latter can be an important source of productivity growth. Public investment on the corn hybrid seed technology in the US is a classic example. Despite the overwhelming evidence of high social rates of return to public agricultural research investments, significant under-investment persists in both developing countries and industrial countries (Huffman and Evenson 1992). So from the perspective of normative economics, countries should work towards removing domestic distortion.

TRIMS

One of the issues here is about the need to have an effective com-petition policy. The idea is to reduce market imperfection. There is a need to address private sector induced distortion before market access is granted to firms from richer nations. While competition policy deals with micro level issues, it is essential to have property rights from the macro perspectives. The problem is that most of the least developed nations lack property rights. Since some of the developing economies and other less develop economies lack adequate resources and/or willingness to put an effective com-petition policy and property right regimes in place, the developed countries might gain by putting conditionality, such as linking government assistance programmes with proper enforcement of property rights. Lack of property rights and an effective competition policy in many less developed nations have direct implication on distribution of resources. For instance, although endowed with abundant natural resources, Sierra Leone was ranked as the poorest country in the world by 1998. While Revolutionary United Front in Sierra Leone controlled the diamond trade and openly indulged in arms and drugs trafficking, the people remained among the poorest on earth.

NAMA

There is a need for conducting joint exercises, by the relevant ministries among the partner countries in order to understand whether the reasons for restricting market access are genuine. For instance, in the era of globalisation, predatory pricing policy is very difficult to practice. So using anti-dumping measures on the presumption for stopping predatory pricing strategy would be meaningless. There is a need to scrap agreements, like anti-dumping measures which are mostly used as NTB (Banik 2005). By the same logic, there should be some uniformity in product standards. For instance, if some items are considered safe going by World Health Organisation (WHO) regulations, then there is a little justification to restrict market access for these products using sanitary and phytosanitary sanctions.

Services

There will be lot of resistance if services like basic provision of health, education, water and sanitation are privatised, especially in the context of developing and less develop economies. Privatisation means one has to pay a price for using these services. Citizens from less developed nations are averse towards paying price for these basic services — something they consider as part of their democratic right. So asking for market access for these types of services will not be meaningful, and also not desirable from the welfare perspective. Instead, developed countries can argue for market access in services like finance, telecommunication, etc. However, there are allegations about developing countries not giving required market access. For instance, the US and the EU allege about India not providing enough market access to Mode 3 type services. India can use this argument to negotiate a better market access for its principal export interest falling under Mode 1 and Mode 4 type services.

Conclusion

There are enough evidences that suggest countries across the world have become protectionist in the wake of global economic slowdown. India is not an exception. Protectionist measures, high trade costs and political animosity with neighbouring Pakistan have restricted SAFTA from emerging as a successful FTA. While it is recognised that negotiation under WTO umbrella takes time, and sometime progress remains limited because of diversity of its membership, this chapter argues that India stands to gain from successful conclusion of the Doha Development Round. In fact, the effort has been clearly there on the part of India to see to a successful conclusion of the Doha Development Round. For instance, just before the Hong Kong Ministerial Meet, Kamal Nath — the then India's trade minister — proclaimed that India would not settle for anything less but for a decline in support provided by the US treasury. The minister was referring to a US offer of reducing domestic support by 53 per cent and the European Union following it up with another offer of 70 per cent. Interestingly, post-Hong Kong the minister has agreed to the same commitment.

India's official stance has changed from 'removal' to 'reduction' of subsidies provided by the US and the EU. India's flexible approach merely reflects its hope about realising greater market share under the WTO umbrella, and at the same time, when required restrict market access under the garb of NTBs like anti-dumping measures. It is to be noted that India has now emerged as the largest user of anti-dumping measures. Quite on the contrary, the SAFTA story suffers more because of political reason. India has flourishing bilateral trading relations with Nepal, Bhutan and Sri Lanka. Its relation with Bangladesh (trade and otherwise) is also picking up, especially after the pro-India Awami League party under the leadership of Sheikh Hasina took over during early part this year. So India has little at stake whether Pakistan agrees or conforms to smooth functioning of SAFTA.

Notes

1. 'Prohibition of import of Specified Livestock', Notification number S.O. 2208 (E) dated 28 August 2009, and issued by Department of Animal Husbandry, Dairying and Fisheries, Government of India.
2. Chad Bown, Global Antidumping Database (July 2009). http://people.brandeis.edu/~cbown/global_ad/ad/ (accessed 9 September 2009).
3. 'India — Agricultural Economy and Policy Report', January 2009, USDA Report. http://www.fas.usda.gov/country/India/Indian%20Agricultural%20Economy%20and%20Policy%20Paper.pdf (accessed 9 September 2009).
4. *The Hindu* (2009).
5. The group known by G20 — comprising 21 developing countries from Africa, Asia and Latin America — was formed during Cancun ministerial meet (September 2003). This group was formed with the objective 'to defend an outcome in the agricultural negotiations which would reflect the level of ambitions of the Doha mandate and the interests of the developing countries'. www.g-20.mre.gov.br/history.asp (accessed 19 August 2009).
6. 'Farm Tariffs Sink World Trade Talks', *Washington Times.* http://www.washingtontimes.com/news/2008/jul/30/farm-tariffs-sink-world-trade-talks/ (accessed 19 August 2009).
7. An ENT is a way to check if one's income or assets in his/her home country qualifies him/her to avail financial grants and other welfare benefits in the foreign country.

References

Banik, N. 2005. 'Reviewing Contigency Measures', in D. Sengupta, D. Chakraborty and P. Banerjee (ed.), *Beyond the Transition Phase of WTO*, pp. 213–37. New Delhi: Center de Sciences Humaines, French Ministry of Foreign Affairs.

Banik, N. and J. Gilbert. 2010. 'Trade Cost and Regional Integration in South Asia', in D. Brooks (ed.), *Trade Facilitation and Regional Cooperation in Asia*, pp. 123–55. Northampton: Edward Elgar.

Bhagwati, J., D. Greenaway and A. Panagariya. 1998. 'Trading Preferentially: Theory and Policy', *The Economic Journal*, 108 (449): 1128–48.

Hummels, D. L. and P. J. Klenow. 2005. 'The Variety and Quality of a Nation's Exports', *American Economic Review*, 95 (3): 704–23.

Huffman, W. E. and R. E. Evenson. 1992. 'Contributions of Public and Private Science and Technology to US Agricultural Productivity", *American Journal of Agricultural Economics*, 74 (3): 751–56.

International Monetary Fund. 2008. 'Direction of Trade Statistics (DOTS) Database'. http://www.imfstatistics.org/DOT/ (accessed 1 October 2009).

———. 2009. *World Economic Outlook*, 28 January 2009, Washington, DC.

Lerner, J. 2001. '150 years of patent protection'. Mimeograph, Harvard University.

Reserve Bank of India. 1998–2008. *Bulletin*, Mumbai, India.

Sakakibara, M. and L. Branstetter. 2001. 'Do Stronger Patents Induce More Innovation? Evidence from the 1988 Japanese Patent Law Reforms', *Rand Journal of Economics*, 32 (1): 77–100.

The Hindu. 2009. 'Turkey to be Production Base for Hyundai's i20 Cars for European Markets', 2 September. http://beta.thehindu.com/news/cities/Chennai/article13672.ece (accessed 12 October 2009).

About the Editors

Shahid Ahmed is Associate Professor in the Department of Economics, Jamia Millia Islamia, Delhi. Earlier, he has served as Consultant, Economist and Senior Economist in United Nations Conference on Trade and Development (UNCTAD-India). He has worked extensively on policy-related issues and has provided technical advice to the Department of Commerce, Government of India and has published several research papers in national and international journals.

Shahid Ashraf is Professor of Finance and Industry in the Department of Economics, Jamia Millia Islamia, Delhi. He has earlier taught at Aligarh Muslim University and had been associated with different international funding agencies regarding project work in development economics.

Notes on Contributors

Abd El-Wakil Mohammed Abo-Taleb is Senior Researcher, Agricultural Economic Research Institute, Ministry of Agriculture and Land Reclamation, Egypt.

Shakeel Ahamed is Junior Investigator, Textiles Committee, Government of India, Mumbai, India.

Shahid Ahmed is Associate Professor, Department of Economics, Jamia Millia Islamia, New Delhi, India.

Mohammad Alhihi is Ph.D. in Law from Macquarie University, Australia.

Asif Anwar is Senior Research Associate, Centre for Policy Dialogue (CPD), Dhaka, Bangladesh.

Naushad Ali Azad is Professor, Department of Economics, Jamia Millia Islamia, New Delhi, India.

Mirza Allim Baig is Assistant Professor, Department of Economics, Jamia Millia Islamia, New Delhi, India.

Nilanjan Banik is Associate Professor, Institute for Financial Management and Research, Chennai, India.

B. P. Sarath Chandran is Assistant Professor, VVM's Shree Damodar College of Commerce and Economics, Goa, India.

Syed Saifuddin Hossain is Senior Research Associate, Centre for Policy Dialogue (CPD), Dhaka, Bangladesh.

Prahalathan S. Iyer is General Manager, Research and Planning Group, Export-Import Bank of India, Mumbai, India.

K. J. Joseph is Ministry of Commerce Chair Professor, Centre for Development Studies, Thiruvananthapuram, India.

Olayinka Idowu Kareem is a Consultant at the World Bank, Nigeria Country Office, Nigeria.

Anthony Kimotho Macharia is Principal Consultant, Consortium Services (Pty) Ltd., Gaborone, Botswana.

Imogen Bonolo Mogotsi is Senior Lecturer and Head, Department of Economics, University of Botswana, Gaborone, Botswana.

K. N. Murty is Professor, Department of Economics, School of Social Sciences, University of Hyderabad, Hyderabad, India.

Badri Narayanan G. is Research Economist, Center for Global Trade Analysis, Purdue University, USA.

P. Nayak is Director, Textiles Committee, Government of India, Mumbai, India.

Anton P. Petrov is a S. J. D. candidate in Public International Law and International Relations, Institute for Legal Studies, Bulgarian Academy of Sciences, Bulgaria.

Kazi Mahmudur Rahman is Senior Research Associate, Centre for Policy Dialogue (CPD), Dhaka, Bangladesh.

Md. Tariqur Rahman is Research Associate, Centre for Policy Dialogue (CPD), Dhaka, Bangladesh.

Rajan Sudesh Ratna is Professor, Centre for WTO Studies, Indian Institute of Foreign Trade (IIFT), New Delhi, India.

Rizwana Siddiqui is Senior Research Economist, Pakistan Institute of Development Economics, Islamabad, Pakistan.

Narain Sinha is Professor, Department of Economics, University of Botswana, Gaborone, Botswana.

P. K. Sudarsan is Associate Professor and Head, Department of Economics, Goa University, Goa, India.

Pankaj Vashisht is Research Associate, Indian Council for Research on International Economic Relations (ICRIER), India.

Hossam Younes is a Research and Trade Facilitation Manager, Egyptian International Trade Point, Ministry of Trade and Industry, Egypt.

Index

relevant market: concept of 353–54; definition of 353; geographic 353; product 353; SSNIP test 354

reserve bank foreign assets (RBFA) 26

Reserve Bank of Asia 147

resource-based economies, sustainability of 156

resource rich economies, role of institutions in 158–59

Revealed Comparative Advantage (RCA), between India and ASEAN: concept of 216, 217; under HS-4 digits classification 231–32; India's comparative advantage with ASEAN countries 225–28; in major commodity groups 221; at product groups level 220–25; revealed comparative advantage for HS-2 digits classification 228–31

Revealed Competitiveness (RC) 217, 279–80

revenue loss, mechanism for compensation of 98

Revolutionary United Front, Sierra Leone 391

Ricardo goods 217

Rome, Treaty of (1957) 368

rural poverty 26; relation with urban poverty 28

SAARCFINANCE 147

SAARC Member Countries (SMC) 96, 103

SAARC Preferential Trading Arrangement (SAPTA): intra-regional trade 102; non-tariff barriers (NTBs) 96; Special and Differential Treatment (S&DT) provision 95

safeguard measures, North–South negotiation under WTO 387–88

SAFTA countries, percentage of weighted tariff rate imposed by 5

Sanitary and Physio Sanitary Measures (SPS) 102, 117

'scale of likeness', degrees of 351

services sector: North–South negotiation under WTO 389–90; policy recommendations by WTO 391–92

share matrix, definition of 374

simulation methodology, for estimating crowding-in effect between private and public sector investment 21–22

small economy effect, definition of 162

SMART model 69; estimation of revenue effects using 73, 75–76, 87

Social Accounting Matrix (SAM) 45, 48; gender features 50–51; for textile industry in Pakistan 49–51

South Africa Customs Union (SACU) 163, 166–67, 169, 181, 255, 263

South Asia: bilateral FTAs within the region vs. SAFTA 119–20; challenges for promoting trade 116–20; correlation of growth rate of real GDP in 139; correlation of inflation in 141; countries in different trade arrangements 111; degree of openness 143; export to different regions 109; extra-regional Free Trade Agreements (FTAs) 119; feasibility of OCA in 137–45; fiscal balance 143; infrastructure constraints and impact on international trade 118–19; intra and extra-regional trade (2008) 108; intra-industry and inter-industry trade in 114–16; intra-regional export (% share) 110;